Trends in Parsing Technology

Text, Speech and Language Technology

VOLUME 43

For further volumes:
http://www.springer.com/series/6636

Trends in Parsing Technology

Dependency Parsing, Domain Adaptation, and Deep Parsing

Edited by

Harry Bunt
Tilburg University, The Netherlands

Paola Merlo
University of Geneva, Switzerland

and

Joakim Nivre
Växjö University and Uppsala University, Sweden

Springer

Editors
Harry Bunt
Tilburg University
Tilburg Center for Cognition and Communication (TiCC) and Dept. of Communication and Information Sciences
Warandelaan 2
5000 LE Tilburg
Netherlands
Harry.Bunt@uvt.nl

Paola Merlo
Université de Genève
Dépt. Linguistique
rue de Candolle 2
1211 Genève
Switzerland
paola.merlo@unige.ch

Joakim Nivre
Växjö University
Uppsala University
Pimpstensvägen 16
752 67 Uppsala
Sweden
joakim.nivre@lingfil.uu.se

ISSN 1386-291X
ISBN 978-90-481-9351-6 e-ISBN 978-90-481-9352-3
DOI 10.1007/978-90-481-9352-3
Springer Dordrecht Heidelberg London New York

Library of Congress Control Number: 2010936679

Printed on acid-free paper

Springer is part of Springer Science+Business Media (www.springer.com)

Contents

Contributors

Giuseppe Attardi Università di Pisa, I-56127, Pisa, Italy, attardi@di.unipi.it

Pierre Boullier INRIA-Rocquencourt, Domaine de Voluceau, 78153 Le Chesnay Cedex, France, pierre.boullier@inria.fr

Ted Briscoe Computer Laboratory, University of Cambridge, Cambridge, UK, Ted.Briscoe@cl.cam.ac.uk

Harry Bunt Tilburg University, Tilburg Center for Cognition and Communication (TiCC) and Department of Communication and Information Sciences, Tilburg, The Netherlands, harry.bunt@uvt.nl

John Carroll Department of Informatics, University of Sussex, UK, J.A.Carroll@sussex.ac.uk

Massimiliano Ciaramita Yahoo! Research, S-08018, Barcelona, Catalonia, Spain, massi@alumni.brown.edu

Jason Eisner Johns Hopkins University, Baltimore, MD, USA, jason@cs.jhu.edu

Johan Hall Växjö University, Växjö, Sweden, johan.hall@vxu.se

Keith Hall Google Research, Zurich, Switzerland, kbhall@google.com

Tadayoshi Hara Department of Computer Science, Faculty of Information Science and Technology, University of Tokyo, Tokyo 113-0033, Japan, harasan@is.s.u-tokyo.ac.jp

James Henderson Department of Computer Science, University of Geneva, Geneva, Switzerland, james.henderson@unige.ch

Dekang Lin Google Inc., Mountain View, CA 94043, USA, lindek@google.com

Takuya Matsuzaki Graduate School of Information Science and Technology, The University of Tokyo, 7-3-1 Hongo, Bunkyo-ku, Tokyo, Japan, matuzaki@is.s.u-tokyo.ac.jp

Paola Merlo University of Geneva, Geneva, Switzerland, Paola.Merlo@unige.ch

Yusuke Miyao Department of Computer Science, Faculty of Information Science and Technology, University of Tokyo, Tokyo, 113-0033, Japan, yusuke@nii.ac.jp

Tetsuji Nakagawa Knowledge Creating Communication Research Center, National Institute of Information and Communications Technology, Kyoto 619-0289, Japan, tnaka@nict.go.jp

Jens Nilsson Växjö University, Växjö, Sweden, jens.nilsson@vxu.se

Takashi Ninomiya Graduate School of Science and Engineering, Ehime University, 3 Bunkyo-cho, Matsuyama, Ehime, Japan, ninomiya@cs.ehime-u.ac.jp

Joakim Nivre Uppsala University, Uppsala, Sweden, joakim.nivre@lingfil.uu.se

Václav Novák Charles University, Prague, Czech Republic, novak@ufal.mff.cuni.cz

Stephan Oepen Department of Informatics, University of Oslo, Oslo, Norway, oe@ifi.uio.no

Detlef Prescher 76307 Karlsbad, Czech Republic, prescher@snlp.de

Kenji Sagae Institute for Creative Technologies, University of Southern California, Marina del Rey, CA 90292, USA, sagae@ict.usc.edu

Benoît Sagot INRIA-Rocquencourt, Domaine de Voluceau, 78153 Le Chesnay Cedex, France, benoit.sagot@inria.fr

Dale Schuurmans Department of Computing Science, University of Alberta, Edmonton, AB, Canada T6G 2E8, dale@cs.ualberta.ca

Noah A. Smith Carnegie Mellon University, Pittsburgh, PA, USA, nasmith@cs.cmu.edu

Ivan Titov Cluster of Excellence, MMC, Saarland University, Saarbrücken, Germany, titov@mmci.uni-saarland.de

Jun-ichi Tsujii Department of Computer Science, Faculty of Information Science and Technology, University of Tokyo, Tokyo, 113-0033, Japan; School of Computer Science, University of Manchester, Manchester, UK; National Center for Text Mining (NaCTeM), tsujii@is.s.u-tokyo.ac.jp

Yoshimasa Tsuruoka School of Information Science, Japan Advanced Institute of Science and Technology (JAIST), 1-1 Asahidai, Nomi, Ishikawa, Japan, tsuruoka@jaist.ac.jp

Gertjan van Noord Faculty of Arts, University of Groningen, 9700 AS Groningen, The Netherlands, G.J.M.van.Noord@rug.nl

Qin Iris Wang Yahoo! Inc., Santa Clara, CA 95054, USA, wangqin@gmail.com

Rebecca Watson Computer Laboratory, University of Cambridge, Cambridge, UK, Rebecca.Watson@cl.cam.ac.uk

Yi Zhang Language Technology Laboratory, Department of Computational Linguistics, Saarland University, DFKI GmbH, Saarbrücken, Germany, yzhang@coli.uni-sb.de

Chapter 1
Current Trends in Parsing Technology

Paola Merlo, Harry Bunt, and Joakim Nivre

1.1 Introduction

Significant advances in natural language processing require the development of adaptive sytems both for spoken and written language: systems that can interact naturally with human users, extend easily to new domains, produce readily usable translations of several languages, search the web rapidly and accurately, summarise news coherently, and detect shifts in moods and emotions. Recent statistical data-driven techniques in natural language processing aim at acquiring the needed adaptivity by modelling the syntactic and lexical properties of large quantities of naturally occurring text. By data-driven, it is meant that these methods employ automatic techniques to extract and learn linguistic information implicitly encoded in texts (corpora), which can be raw or appropriately annotated, instead of using an explicit grammar. The shift in the field from grammar-based techniques anchored in formal language theory and compilers to data-driven techniques formalised by learning theory and probability theory is apparent in all publications in computational linguistics today. Research on data-driven methods for parsing has seen great success and lies at the heart of many data-driven applications. The current volume is no exception and it continues the trend already detectable in the previous volume of the same series (Bunt et al., 2004). Most of the chapters in the current volume describe a statistical model for parsing trained on large amounts of text.

Statistical, shallow linguistic methods are not the only ones to have benefitted from the shift in attention to data development and data exploitation. The organisers of the deep linguistic processing workshop (Baldwin et al., 2007) indicate that grammar-based techniques are starting to take great advantage of annotated linguistic resources.

> Recent advances in using the same treebanks that have advanced shallow techniques to extract more expressive grammars or to train statistical disambiguators for them, and in developing framework-specific treebanks, have made it possible to obtain similar coverage, robustness, and disambiguation accuracy for parsers that use richer structural representations (Baldwin et al., 2007, 37).

P. Merlo (✉)
University of Geneva, Geneva, Switzerland
e-mail: Paola.Merlo@unige.ch

H. Bunt et al. (eds.), *Trends in Parsing Technology*, Text, Speech and Language Technology 43, DOI 10.1007/978-90-481-9352-3_1,

Moreover, there is increasing convergence in methods and objectives between "deep", grammar-based methods and "shallow", statistical approaches. On the one hand, as data-driven, statistical methods become more sophisticated, they become capable of learning structured representations and multiple layers of annotations more accurately. For example, many statistical approaches use rich linguistic features, and are tackling problems that were traditionally thought to require deep systems, such as the recovery of semantic roles and logical levels of semantic interpretation (Wong and Mooney, 2007; Zettlemoyer and Collins, 2007; Surdeanu et al., 2008). On the other hand, as witnessed by many of the papers in the deep linguistic processing workshop, many of the current deep systems have statistical components: either as pre- or post-processing to control ambiguity, or as means of acquiring and extending lexical resources, or they even use machine learning techniques to acquire deep grammars automatically. The current volume reflects this trend.

1.2 Current Trends in Parsing Research

Beside the evolution of data-driven systems and the increasing convergence with the goals and problems traditionally tackled by grammar-based methods, we can identify three main trends more specifically related to parsing and parsing technologies in the last few years. The first trend indicates a sustained interest in dependency parsing, both in its aspects related to representation and to technology. The development of data for recent shared tasks in this formalism has fostered research on multi-lingual aspects and on semantic representation. Growing interest in new methods to reduce supervision in learning constitutes another major trend in parsing at the moment, such as semi-supervised and self-training techniques. Finally, the most recent and novel development is the creation of models with latent variables to eschew complex annotation. We discuss these topics in more detail, as they are represented in our collection of articles.

1.2.1 Parsing with Dependencies

The goal to predict structure accurately and to process large amounts of text efficiently has led to renewed interest in grammatical representations that firmly anchor the syntactic structures in observable lexical information. Unlike traditional context-free grammars, which make large use of nonterminal symbols, these representations do not posit many levels of unobserved structure, thus enabling the words to constrain the learning and parsing process successfully. Dependency grammars are such representations (Tesnière, 1959). (For an introduction to the formalism and an overview of different approaches to dependency grammar—see Nivre, 2006; Kübler et al., 2009.)

After playing a rather marginal role in natural language processing for many years, parsing methods based on dependency grammar have recently attracted considerable interest from researchers and developers in the field. One reason for this increasing popularity is the fact that dependency-based syntactic representations seem to be useful in many applications of language technology, such as machine translation and information extraction, thanks to their transparent encoding of predicate-argument structure (Ding and Palmer, 2004; Quirk et al., 2005; Culotta and Sorensen, 2004). Another reason is the perception that dependency grammar is better suited than phrase-structure grammar for languages with free or flexible word order, making it possible to analyze typologically diverse languages within a common framework (Buchholz and Marsi, 2006; Nivre et al., 2007a). Furthermore, because of the constrained nature of the representation—essentially defining a single head word and dependency type for each word of the sentence—dependency parsers tend to be very efficient (McDonald et al., 2005; Nivre, 2006). But perhaps the most important reason is that this approach has led to the development of accurate syntactic parsers for a number of languages, particularly in combination with machine learning from syntactically annotated corpora, or treebanks (Buchholz and Marsi, 2006; Nivre et al., 2007a, b; Nivre and McDonald, 2008). The present volume contains several chapters describing such parsers.

1.2.2 Reducing Supervision

While data-driven techniques for parsing have exhibited great success, they rely very much on the existence of large amounts of annotated text. Large-scale annotated corpora are extremely valuable to bootstrap research in new directions, clarify representational issues through the development of annotation guidelines, and provide indispensable evaluation benchmarks. However, they are very time-consuming to develop, and therefore very expensive, and the resulting corpora risk being limited to a particular domain or application. This shortcoming undermines the very philosophy of data-driven techniques. From a methodological point of view, there is increasing consensus that long-term progress in natural language processing will depend on the use of techniques that do not require complete and complex annotation of the data. The problem has been tackled in several ways, mostly by exploring ways to reduce the needed annotation, in unsupervised and semi-supervised learning techniques, for parsing (Klein and Manning, 2004; Klein, 2005; Smith, 2006; Bod, 2007; Seginer, 2007; Kate and Mooney, 2007; Wang et al., 2008; Koo et al., 2008), for part of speech tagging Snyder et al. (2008), for semantic role labelling Swier and Stevenson (2005), and in the automatic development of new annotated corpora by transfer from existing corpora and other resources Padó and Lapata (2005), Padó (2007), Hwa et al. (2005), Nivre and Megyesi (2007).

Domain portability is another aspect of reduction of supervision in which current data-driven techniques still fall short of expectation and that is being actively studied. The main problem consists in adapting parsers from domains with plentiful resources, such as financial text, to domains with less plentiful annotated resources but with great need and utility for parsing, such as biomedical abstracts. Previous domain adaptation studies have shown that large gains can be made when a small amount of annotated resources exist in the new domain (Roark and Bacchiani, 2003;

Daumée III and Marcu, 2006; Titov and Henderson, 2006). However, in many cases no resources are available for the new domain, making the extension more difficult. Recent work has shown that a large unlabeled corpus in the new domain can be useful in this kind of adaptation (McClosky et al., 2006, 2008; Blitzer et al., 2006).

1.2.3 Latent Variables

More recent techniques of grammar induction rely on developing models with latent variables. Much has been said on the role of lexicalisation in parsing. When lexicalised statistical parsing was first presented, much of the improvement in the results was ascribed to the lexicalisation of the grammar (Collins, 1999). Further detailed studies of the influence of lexicalisation showed that the importance of words had been overstimated, both for English and other languages (Gildea, 2001; Bikel, 2004; Dubey and Keller, 2004). Careful investigations of the factors that underlie parsing performance has shown that carefully annotated class information on the nonterminal labels of a syntactic tree could capture very predictive syntactic distributions (Klein and Manning, 2003) without lexicalisation.

Great savings in annotation and a better fit to properties of the observed data can be achieved if at least part of this class-level annotation is done only implicitly in the probabilistic model, as a hidden or latent variable of the model, for which distributions can be inferred. These methods hold promise for the accuracy of the results. Since some events are hidden, we can construct models where the hidden variables are only probabilistically related to the observed data, and hence we can infer the underlying structure that is most appropriate for the problem at hand. These methods also hold promise for the coverage and portability of the results. The fact that some of the annotation is only inferred, but does not have to be explicitly annotated, eschews the need for time-consuming, and complete annotation of the data and makes the approach more data-driven and hence more portable across domains (Henderson, 2003; Titov and Henderson, 2007; Petrov and Klein, 2008; Musillo and Merlo, 2008).

1.3 Tour of the Volume

The volume comprises fifteen chapters, loosely organised in three thematic groups. The first group of chapters clearly illustrates the focussing effect of shared tasks on research topics, as these chapters describe systems that participated in the CoNLL 2007 shared task on dependency parsing. Some of them were also presented as a longer research paper in the IWPT 2007 conference. Because they responded to the shared task call, these systems are all implementations of dependency parsers for multi-lingual processing and in some cases for domain adaptation. The chapters present the three best systems in the shared task (Hall et al., Nagakawa, and Titov and Henderson). Other chapters illustrate interesting combinations of classic parsing techniques, frequently discussed in previous IWPT meetings, such as GLR parsing, with ensemble learning and history-based statistical approaches (Sagae and Tsujii) or they illustrate an interesting investigation of the reciprocal interaction of semantic information, here represented by named entities, and parsing accuracy (Ciaramita and Attardi).

Four chapters on more varied parsing issues follow. They were presented initially either at IWPT 2005 or IWPT 2007. They illustrate the many challenging open problems that still exist in the area of parsing: some of these chapters have opened the way to extremely frutiful areas of resarch, like the chapter on latent variables by Prescher; while others address crucial parsing issues from an original point of view, such as the interaction between structure and lexicalisation (Wang et al.), the properties of dependencies, especially length, as approximations of structural properties (Eisner and Smith), and a novel technique to correct parser output (Hall and Novak).

Efficiency is an ever-present problem for parsing, and it concerns both data-driven and grammar-based approaches. The third group of chapters reports on parsers mostly addressing issues of efficiency from several points of view. While data-driven mehods usually adopt measures of performance focussed on accuracy of results, without much discussion of computational efficiency, Watson et al. investigate how to reduce annotation needs. They are therefore concerned with one of the forms of efficiency one has to consider in the development of corpus-based parsers. This chapter also addresses the issue of domain adaptation. Zhang et al. address the efficiency of computing the n-best analyses from a parse forest produced by a unification grammar, taking non-local features into account. Three other chapters are concerned with how to introduce or re-train lexical probabilities in symbolic parsers, to make the parser more efficient and more portable to a new domain (Van Noord, Hara et al., Ninomiya et al.). In grammar-based parsing the issue of efficiency often takes one of two forms: either it concerns algorithm complexity, or it concerns methods to reduce the large grammar size constants that are involved in theoretically efficient context-free parsing algorithms. Boullier and Sagot address the latter long-standing open problem—already stated by Berwick and colleagues in the early 1980s (Berwick and Weinberg, 1984)—and propose several interesting filtering techniques that reduce the size of otherwise overlarge grammars, making them usable in practice.

1.3.1 Cross-Cutting Threads

Many of the chapters in this volume describe parsers for languages other than English (Arabic, Basque, Catalan, Chinese, Czech, Dutch, French, Greek, Hungarian, Italian, Japanese, and Turkish), and also many were tested multi-lingually. As well as showing practical interest in providing support for linguistic applications beyond the English-speaking world, this interest for cross-linguistic validity is indicative of a growing concern for linguistic issues. Multi-lingual work provides important lessons: for example, it was the attempt at extending bilexical statistical parsers to German that led to new conclusions of the value of lexicalisation (Dubey and Keller, 2004). In this volume, many of the parsers in the first group are valid cross-linguistically, some with specific adaptations for each language (Hall et al.), some without (Titov and Henderson). This result is expected under current linguistic theories, which describe languages as expressions of abstract universals.

From the point of view of parsing methods, many of the chapters in this volume explore pre- or post-processing methods to improve parsing performance, ranging from the pre-processing filtering techniques to reduce grammar size proposed by Boullier and Sagot, to several chapters using ensemble learning techniques, to corrective parsing (Hall and Novak), and to the in-depth study of reranking methods in Watson et al.

The interaction between the structural syntactic component and the lexicon continues to be a crucial topic of investigation for parsing. Several aspects are important. First of all the simple question of how much specific lexical information is needed for accurate and efficient parsing. The usefulness of rich lexicalisation is clearly shown in the chapters by Hara and by van Noord, where lexical information improves performance and enables porting to new domains. While work on lexicalised grammars confirms the fundamental role of the lexicon in determining and disambiguating structure, the work by Wang et al. and Prescher points to the usefulness of a different level of granularity of lexical information. In these chapters, we are dealing with word classes and their predictive role in building syntactic structure: classes are either defined implicitly, as in latent variable models, or explicitly, by word-clustering techniques. The chapter by Ciaramita and Attardi brings forth another level of interaction between the lexicon and syntax: words are bearers of semantic information and they provide grounding in the world. Finally, words, and specifically head words, project their relational properties in the structure and are bearers of information on the syntactic domains of locality that are so crucial to correctly building structure and correctly defining domains of probabilistic independence, as witnessed by the many chapters that incorporate the notion of head or that adopt the formalism of Head-driven Phrase Structure Grammar (HPSG), a formalism that posits very richly structured lexical entries. (For an introduction to HPSG see (Pollard and Sag, 1987, 1994; Sag et al., 2003). Several of the research teams working on parsing with HPSG, some of which are included in this volume, have created the DELPH-IN consortium http://www.delph-in.net/).

1.3.2 The Chapters in Short

1.3.2.1 Single Malt or Blended? A Study in Multilingual Parser Optimization

Johan Hall, Jens Nilsson, and Joakim Nivre

This chapter addresses the problem of feature optimisation for a given language and system combination. The system is a two-stage optimisation of the MaltParser system, where the first stage is optimised for the ten languages of the CoNLL 2007 shared task, while the second stage consists in an ensemble system that combines six different parsing strategies, extrapolating from the optimal parameter settings for each language. The ensemble system significantly outperforms the single-parser system. It is interesting to note that this combined system performs best overall in the shared task. This result confirms once more the now widely-established result that system combination is often quite useful, and it provides an interesting novel view on the cross-lingual influences showing that optimisation in each language can further improve results.

1.3.2.2 A Latent Variable Model for Generative Dependency Parsing

Ivan Titov and James Henderson

This chapter presents a new version of one of the first latent variable models introduced to the parsing community (Henderson, 2003). The generative dependency parsing model uses binary latent variables to induce conditioning features. The induced conditioning features are assumed to be local in the dependency structure, but because induced features are conditioned on other induced features, information can propagate arbitrarily far. The model is formally defined as a recently proposed class of Bayesian Networks for structured prediction, Incremental Sigmoid Belief Networks, and approximated by two methods. The error analysis in this chapter shows that the features induced by the ISBN's latent variables are crucial to this success, and shows that the induced features result in the proposed model being particularly good on long dependencies.

1.3.2.3 Dependency Parsing and Domain Adaptation with LR Models and Parser Ensembles

Kenji Sagae and Jun'ichi Tsujii

This chapter presents a stepwise or "transition-based" approach to dependency parsing, where sequences of shift-reduce derivations are learned to produce dependency graphs. Each of the derivation steps is learned individually, using a rich set of local features based on the current state of the parser and the parsing history. A data-driven variant of the well-known LR parsing algorithm is used, that is equivalent to the arc-standard shift-reduce algorithm for dependency parsing proposed by Yamada and Matsumoto (2003) and Nivre (2004), extended with a best-first search for probabilistic generalized LR dependency parsing. This provides a connection between current research on data-driven dependency parsing and previous research in parsing using LR and GLR models. The approach was successfully applied to both tracks of the CoNLL 2007 shared task on dependency parsing, in each case taking advantage of the use of multiple models trained with different learners.

1.3.2.4 Multilingual Dependency Parsing Using Global Features

Tetsuji Nakagawa

Recent methods for dependency parsing have largely relied on the very effective determinism of transition-based methods or on the local features of search-based approaches to curbe the complexity of finding the most probable parse. Nakagawa addresses the complex problem of how to integrate global features in learning in an efficient and scalable way. The proposed method allows for the use of arbitrary features in a dependency tree, including relationships between sibling nodes and between a child and its grandparent nodes. Experimental results on multiple multilingual corpora show that the global features are useful and that the proposed method is highly accurate.

1.3.2.5 Dependency Parsing with Second-Order Feature Maps and Annotated Semantic Information

Massimiliano Ciaramita and Giuseppe Attardi

This chapter explores the efficiency and performance trade-offs involved in adopting rich feature spaces that can encode second-order features—defined here as pairs of atomic features—and semantic information provided by named entities for dependency parsing. A simple, deterministic parsing algorithm with a simple perceptron classifier with rich features exhibits competitive performance with the best published results. Morover, named entity tagging, a form of semantic grounding of the sentence, yields improvement in parsing, probably because named entities correspond to basic nouns. This result confirms and extends other results in using semantic information to improve parsing (Merlo and Musillo, 2005), a topic that has been brought to the attention of a greater audience by the CoNLL 2008 shared task.

1.3.2.6 Strictly Lexical Dependency Parsing

Qin Iris Wang, Dale Schuurmans, and Dekang Lin

This chapter tries to do away with part-of-speech categories, using only lexical information in parsing. Klein and Manning (2003) illustrate that a linguistically-informed careful splitting of part of speech tags can achieve very good performance, approximating lexical classes without the need to know the words, and approaching lexicalised parsers in performance. In this context, this chapter asks the converse question: if tag splitting achieves so much, then clearly what matters are word classes and their syntactic behaviour to guide parsing. Can we then build an entirely lexical parser, without part of speech tags or nonterminals, but using word clustering? The evaluation on Chinese confirms that word clustering works better than simple gold part-of-speech tags. This model uses distributional word similarity to generalize the observed frequency counts in the training corpus.

1.3.2.7 Parsing with Soft and Hard Constraints on Dependency Length

Jason Eisner and Noah A. Smith

This chapter illustrates a different use of bilexical dependencies than the standard one. Bilexical dependencies are recovered to augment the features of a phrase-structure tree with the length of the dependency. The intuition that the length of the dependency can be predictive of structure is based on the observation that a word's lexical modifiers are usually close to it in the string, and that languages often exhibit mechanisms, such as English heavy-NP shift, for example, to keep dependencies short. But this locality is lost in the tree topology. Experiments with both soft and hard versions of this constraint are performed. In the first case, it is shown that parsing accuracy benefits from length constraints for languages with predictable word order, but results are more mixed with languages like German, where heads and modifiers can be far apart. Length used as a hard constraint severely limits the expressive power of the grammar and gives rise to a linear time parsing algorithm without much loss in performance.

1.3.2.8 Corrective Modeling for Non-projective Dependency Parsing

Keith Hall and Václav Novák

This chapter reports on a technique for correcting errors in automatically generated dependency trees. The technique concentrates on "structurally local" errors, based on the observation that often the correct governor for a dependency is in a local context of the proposed governor. This method enables searching over a large set of alternate dependency trees simply by making small perturbations to individual dependency edges, and handles non-projective dependencies well. Experimental results on a Czech corpus are presented using four different parsers, both projective and non-projective, showing the robustness of the technique.

1.3.2.9 Head-Driven PCFGs with Latent-Head Statistics

Detlef Prescher

This chapter is one of the first papers in parsing to use latent variables. As indicated by previous studies, lexicalisation is not as useful as initially thought, and careful linguistic mark-up can lead to very good results. However, such mark-up is language-specific and knowledge-rich. Latent variables, that split the categories according to the data and not according to some predefined set of categories, promise to be more accurate and to be more portable. Prescher demonstrates how to induce head-driven probabilistic parsers with latent heads from a treebank. The results are very promising, showing that learning with latent heads is better than having best head annotation and almost as good as full lexicalisation.

1.3.2.10 Using Self-Trained Bilexical Preferences to Improve Disambiguation Accuracy

Gertjan van Noord

This chapter addresses directly whether incorporating bilexical preferences between phrase heads is helpful to parsing. In particular, it approximates selectional restrictions by calculating bilexical dependencies between heads of phrases. The estimations are performed on a very large corpus (about 500 million words). The preferences are incorporated in the Maximum-Entropy framework as auxiliary distributions, using a previously proposed technique (Johnson and Riezler, 2000). These preferences are self-trained, since they are estimated based on the output of the parser to which they are integrated. They improve the parser accuracy significantly.

1.3.2.11 Are Very Large Context-Free Grammars Tractable?

Pierre Boullier and Benoît Sagot

The vast majority of parsers, both grammar-based and corpus-based, use parsing techniques based on a context-free backbone, for reasons of efficiency. However, these algorithms still exhibit large grammar constants, which can become the predominant factor for the complexity in practice. This chapter illustrates a method to harness the practical complexity introduced by very large grammars. Parsing is performed in two steps. A first step computes a sub-grammar which is a specialized part of the large grammar selected by the input text and various filtering strategies. The second step is a traditional parser which works with the sub-grammar and the input text. This approach is validated by practical experiments performed on an Earley-like parser running on a test set with two large context-free grammars.

1.3.2.12 Efficiency in Unification-Based n-Best Parsing

Yi Zhang, Stephan Oepen, and John Carroll

This chapter explores a range of techniques for integrating broad-coverage grammars with sophisticated statistical parse selection models. A new algorithm is presented for efficiently computing the n-best analyses from a parse forest produced by a unification grammar, based on the selective unpacking technique developed by Carroll and Oepen (2005), but with a Maximum Entropy model containing larger-context features. The algorithm is shown to exhibit a linear relationship between processing time and the number of analyses unpacked, and to show better speed, coverage, and accuracy than other approaches to parsing with Maximum Entropy models.

1.3.2.13 HPSG Parsing with a Supertagger

Takashi Ninomiya, Takuya Matsuzaki, Yusuke Miyao, and Jun'ichi Tsujii

This chapter investigates alternative ways to achieve fast and accurate wide-scale probabilistic HPSG parsing making use of a supertagger. The best performance both in speed and accuracy is achieved by a model in which the supertagger is trained first, and the log-linear model for probabilistic HPSG is then trained so as to maximize its likelihood, given the supertagger probabilities as a reference distribution. This is the first model which properly incorporates supertagger probabilities into a probabilistic parse tree model, and can be seen as an extension of a unigram reference distribution to an n-gram distribution with features that are used in HPSG supertagging.

1.3.2.14 Evaluating the Impact of Re-training a Lexical Disambiguation Model on Domain Adaptation of an HPSG Parser

Tadayoshi Hara, Yusuke Miyao, and Jun'ichi Tsujii

In this chapter, the authors address several issues in domain adaptation, focussing on adapting an HPSG parser trained on the Penn Treebank to a biomedical domain. The main insight of this work lies in porting only lexical probabilities: probabilities of lexical entry assignments to words in a target domain are estimated and then incorporated into the original parser. Experimental results show that this method can obtain higher parsing accuracy than previous work on domain adaptation for parsing the same data. Moreover, the results show that the combination of the proposed method with existing methods achieves parsing accuracies that are as high as those of a parser retrained on a new biomedical dataset, but with much lower training cost. The results also extend to the balanced domain mixture of the Brown corpus.

1.3.2.15 Semi-supervised Training of a Statistical Parser from Unlabeled Partially Bracketed Data

Rebecca Watson, Ted Briscoe, and John Carroll

This chapter discusses confidence-based methods that reduce the need for fully annotated treebanks and that are more efficient than iterative training methods for unsupervised learning such as Expectation-Maximisation. Confidence-based semi-supervised techniques similar to self-training outperform Expectation-Maximisation when both are constrained by partial bracketing. Tuning the model to a different domain and the effect of in-domain data in the semi-supervised training processes are also explored. As well as being portable, the methods investigated in this chapter are efficient, as they are not iterative and require less annotation than similar self-training techniques.

1.4 The Future of Parsing and Parsing Technologies

Traditionally, research on parsing and parsing technologies have been reliable trendsetters of conceptual shifts and of new methodologies in natural language processing. One clear shift that is occurring in parsing is its relation to multi-lingual applications and the study of techniques to deal with multiple levels of representation.

After at least a decade of skepticism on the practical usefulness of parsing and syntactic information for NLP applications, a new trend of research concerns the use of synchronous parsing techniques (Wu, 1997; Wu and Chiang, 2007; Chiang and Wu, 2008). Interest in these formalisms and methods has been spurred by recent successes in syntax-aware machine translation and also by the availability of treebanks of parallel syntactic and semantic representations. Besides the specific interest in synchronous parsing techniques and synchronous grammars as the core of a machine translation system, we can expect better integration of syntactic representations for parsing with other components of a syntax-based SMT system. In a clear trend towards more abstract transfer representations, models in statistical machine translation, which started as word-based models, have mastered the use of phrases and word sequences and are now successfully integrating hierarchical information, either as treelets (Chiang, 2005) or as tree spines (Shen et al., 2008) or as even more complex objects (Cowan et al., 2006). Coupled with the interest for synchronous parsing, which can be equally applied to parallel representations within a language as well as two (or more) languages, statistical machine translation will provide a very interesting and challenging testbed for theories and technologies of parsing, both grammar-based and statistical. As well as parsing being useful for cross-lingual applications, we are starting to see researchers who use multiple languages to improve parsing and related tasks (Snyder and Barzilay, 2008; Burkett and Klein, 2008).

Another area where techniques developed for syntactic parsing are being successfully extended is semantic representations. Successes in syntactic tasks, such as statistical parsing and tagging, have recently paved the way to statistical learning techniques for levels of semantic representation, such as recovering the logical form of a sentence for information extraction and question-answering applications (Miller et al., 2000; Ge and Mooney, 2005; Zettlemoyer and Collins, 2007; Wong and Mooney, 2007) or jointly learning the syntactic structure of the sentence and the propositional argument-structure of its main predicates (Merlo and Musillo, 2008; Surdeanu et al., 2008). We can expect the development of synchronous or parallel algorithms for several levels of representation for syntax and semantics.

Most current approaches to language analysis assume that the structure of a sentence depends on the lexical semantics of the verb and of other predicates in the sentence. It is also assumed that only certain aspects of the meaning of a sentence are grammaticalised. Semantic role labels are the grammatical representation of the linguistically relevant aspects of this meaning. Previous and recent editions of IWPT have hosted papers describing systems that use semantic information for parsing with good results (Musillo and Merlo, 2005; Ciaramita and Attardi, 2007; Prescher, 2005). The development of PropBank (Palmer et al., 2005) especially has enabled the parsing community to study the relationship between syntax and the lexical semantic and argumental properties of verbs. In this vein, the CoNLL 2008 shared task set the challenge of learning jointly both syntactic dependencies (extracted from the Penn Treebank (Marcus et al., 1993)) and semantic dependencies (extracted both from PropBank and NomBank (Meyers et al., 2004) under a unified representation (Surdeanu et al., 2008)). Some of the systems presented in this volume have been extended at the time of writing to capture levels of semantic representation (Ciaramita et al., 2008; Henderson et al., 2008) either as ensembles or as joint learning systems. For 2009 the shared task has been extended to multiple languages, underlining another prominent trend in the field.

The renewed interest in developing models of syntax and some simple semantic representations will probably direct research in parsing in two directions: on the one hand, a deeper relationship between grammars and probabilistic modelling will have to be developed, to process richer representations. Richer representations for English as well as properties of other languages will bring about new classes of parsing problems: for example the parsing of disconnected graphs and graphs that do not form a tree, expressed as traces or non-projective dependency graphs. Some recent developments in these directions can already be seen (Attardi, 2006; Nivre, 2008; Sagae and Tsujii, 2008; Titov et al., 2009).

References

Attardi, G. (2006). Experiments with a multilanguage non-projective dependency parser. In *Proceedings of the 10th Conference on Computational Natural Language Learning (CoNLL-X)*, New York, NY, pp. 166–170.

Baldwin, T., M. Dras, J. Hockenmaier, T. Holloway King, and G. van Noord (2007). The impact of deep linguistic processing on parsing technology. In *Proceedings of the 10th International Conference on Parsing Technologies*, Prague, pp. 36–38.

Baldwin, T., M. Dras, J. Hockenmaier, T. H. King, and G. van Noord (Eds.) (2007). *ACL 2007 Workshop on Deep Linguistic Processing*, Prague.

Berwick, R. C. and A. S. Weinberg (1984). *The Grammatical Basis of Linguistic Performance*. Cambridge, MA: MIT Press.

Bikel, D. (2004). Intricacies of Collins' parsing model. *Computational Linguistics 40*(4), 479–511.

Blitzer, J., R. McDonald, and F. Pereira (2006). Domain adaptation with structural correspondence learning. In *Proceedings of the 2006 Conference on Empirical Methods in Natural Language Processing*, Sydney, pp. 120–128.

Bod, R. (2007). Is the end of supervised parsing in sight? In *Proceedings of the 45th Annual Meeting of the Association of Computational Linguistics*, Prague, pp. 400–407.

Buchholz, S. and E. Marsi (2006). CoNLL-X shared task on multilingual dependency parsing. In *Proceedings of the 10th Conference on Computational Natural Language Learning (CoNLL'06)*, New York, NY, pp. 149–164.

Bunt, H., J. Carroll, and G. Satta (Eds.) (2004). *New Developments in Parsing Technology*. Dordrecht: Kluwer Academic Publishers.

Burkett, D. and D. Klein (2008). Two languages are better than one (for syntactic parsing). In *Proceedings of the 2008 Conference on Empirical Methods in Natural Language Processing*, Honolulu, HI, pp. 877–886.

Carroll, J. and S. Oepen (2005). High efficiency realization for a wide-coverage unification grammar. In *Proceedings of the 2nd International Joint Conference on Natural Language Processing (IJCNLP05)*, Jeju Island, pp. 165–176.

Chiang, D. (2005). A hierarchical phrase-based model for statistical machine translation. In *Proceedings of the 43rd Annual Meeting of the Association for Computational Linguistics (ACL'05)*, Ann Arbor, MI, pp. 263–270.

Chiang, D. and D. Wu (Eds.) (2008). *Proceedings of the ACL-08: HLT 2nd Workshop on Syntax and Structure in Statistical Translation (SSST-2)*. Columbus, OH: Association for Computational Linguistics.

Ciaramita, M. and G. Attardi (2007). Dependency parsing with second-order feature maps and annotated semantic information. In *Proceedings of the 10th International Conference on Parsing Technologies*, Prague, pp. 133–143.

Ciaramita, M., G. Attardi, F. Dell'Orletta, and M. Surdeanu (2008). DeSRL: a linear-time semantic role labeling system. In *CoNLL 2008: Proceedings of the 12th Conference on Computational Natural Language Learning*, Manchester, pp. 258–262.

Collins, M. J. (1999). *Head-Driven Statistical Models for Natural Language Parsing*. Ph. D. thesis, Department of Computer Science, University of Pennsylvania.

Cowan, B., I. Kučerová, and M. Collins (2006). A discriminative model for tree-to-tree translation. In *Proceedings of the 2006 Conference on Empirical Methods in Natural Language Processing*, Sydney, pp. 232–241.

Culotta, A. and J. Sorensen (2004). Dependency tree kernels for relation extraction. In *Proceedings of the 42nd Annual Meeting of the Association for Computational Linguistics (ACL'04)*, Barcelona, pp. 423–429.

Daumée III, H. and D. Marcu (2006). Domain adaptation for statistical classifiers. *Journal of Artificial Intelligence Research 26*, 101–126.

Ding, Y. and M. Palmer (2004). Synchronous dependency insertion grammars: a grammar formalism for syntax based statistical MT. In *Proceedings of the Workshop on Recent Advances in Dependency Grammar*, Geneva, pp. 90–97.

Dubey, A. and F. Keller (2004). Probabilistic parsing for German using sister-head dependencies. In *Proceedings of the 41st Annual Meeting of the Association for Computational Linguistics (ACL'03)*, Sapporo, pp. 96–103.

Ge, R. and R. J. Mooney (2005). A statistical semantic parser that integrates syntax and semantics. In *Proceedings of the 9th Conference on Computational Natural Language Learning (CONLL-05)*, Ann Arbor, MI, pp. 9–16.

Gildea, D. (2001). Corpus variation and parser performance. In *2001 Conference on Empirical Methods in Natural Language Processing (EMNLP-2001)*, Pittsburgh, PA, pp. 167–202.

Henderson, J. (2003). Inducing history representations for broad-coverage statistical parsing. In *Proceedings of the Joint Meeting of the North American Chapter of the Association for Computational Linguistics and the Human Language Technology Conference (NAACL-HLT'03)*, Edmonton, pp. 103–110.

Henderson, J., P. Merlo, G. Musillo, and I. Titov (2008). A latent variable model of synchronous parsing for syntactic and semantic dependencies. In *Proceedings of CONLL 2008*, Manchester, pp. 178–182.

Hwa, R., P. Resnik, A. Weinberg, C. Cabezas, and O. Kolak (2005). Bootstrapping parsers via syntactic projection across parallel text. *Natural Language Engineering 11*(3), 311–325.

Johnson, M. and S. Riezler (2000). Exploiting auxiliary distributions in stochastic unification-based grammars. In *Proceedings of the 1st meeting of the North American Chapter of the Association for Computational Linguistics (NAACL 2000)*, Seattle, WA pp. 154–161.

Kate, R. and R. Mooney (2007). Semi-supervised learning for semantic parsing using support vector machines. In *Human Language Technologies 2007: the Conference of the North American Chapter of the Association for Computational Linguistics; Companion Volume, Short Papers*, Rochester, NY, pp. 81–84.

Klein, D. (2005). *The Unsupervised Learning of Natural Language Structure*. Ph. D. thesis, Department of Computer Science, Stanford University.

Klein, D. and C. Manning (2004). Corpus-based induction of syntactic structure: models of dependency and constituency. In *Proceedings of the 42nd Meeting of the Association for Computational Linguistics (ACL'04)*, Barcelona, pp. 478–485.

Klein, D. and C. D. Manning (2003). Accurate unlexicalized parsing. In *Proceedings of the 41st Annual Meeting of the ACL (ACL'03)*, Sapporo, pp. 423–430.

Koo, T., X. Carreras, and M. Collins (2008, June). Simple semi-supervised dependency parsing. In *Proceedings of ACL-08: HLT*, Columbus, OH, pp. 595–603.

Kübler, S., R. McDonald, and J. Nivre (2009). *Dependency Parsing*. San Francisco, CA: Morgan & Claypool.

Marcus, M., B. Santorini, and M. Marcinkiewicz (1993). Building a large annotated corpus of English: the Penn Treebank. *Computational Linguistics 19*, 313–330.

McClosky, D., E. Charniak, and M. Johnson (2006). Reranking and self-training for parser adaptation. In *Proceedings of the 21st International Conference on Computational Linguistics and 44th Annual Meeting of the Association for Computational Linguistics*, Sydney, pp. 337–344.

McClosky, D., E. Charniak, and M. Johnson (2008). When is self-training effective for parsing? In *Proceedings of the 22nd International Conference on Computational Linguistics (Coling 2008)*, Manchester, pp. 561–568.

McDonald, R., K. Crammer, and F. Pereira (2005). Online large-margin training of dependency parsers. In *Proceedings of the 43rd Annual Meeting of the Association for Computational Linguistics (ACL'05)*, Ann Arbor, MI, pp. 91–98.

Merlo, P. and G. Musillo (2005). Accurate function parsing. In *Proceedings of the Human Language Technology Conference and Conference on Empirical Methods in Natural Language Processing (HLT/EMNLP 2005)*, Vancouver, BC, pp. 620–627.

Merlo, P. and G. Musillo (2008). Semantic parsing for high-precision semantic role labelling. In *Proceedings of the 12th Conference on Computational Natural Language Learning (CONLL-08)*, Manchester, pp. 1–8.

Meyers, A., R. Reeves, C. Macleod, R. Szekely, V. Zielinska, B. Young, and R. Grishman (2004, May). The NomBank project: an interim report. In A. Meyers (Ed.), *HLT-NAACL 2004 Workshop: Frontiers in Corpus Annotation*, Boston, MA, pp. 24–31.

Miller, S., H. Fox, L. Ramshaw, and R. Weischedel (2000). A novel use of statistical parsing to extract information from text. In *Proceedings of the First Meeting of the North American Chapter of the Association for Computational Linguistics (NAACL 2000)*, Seattle, WA pp. 226–233.

Musillo, G. and P. Merlo (2005). Lexical and structural biases for function parsing. In *Proceedings of the 9th International Workshop on Parsing Technology (IWPT'05)*, Vancouver, BC, pp. 83–92.

Musillo, G. and P. Merlo (2008). Unlexicalised hidden variable models of split dependency grammars. In *Proceedings of the Annual Conference for Computational Linguistics (ACL'08)*, Columbus, OH, pp. 213–216.

Nivre, J. (2004). Incrementality in deterministic dependency parsing. In *Proceedings of the Workshop on Incremental Parsing: Bringing Engineering and Cognition Together (ACL)*, Barcelona, pp. 50–57.

Nivre, J. (2006). *Inductive Dependency Parsing*. Dordrecht: Springer.

Nivre, J. (2008). Sorting out dependency parsing. In *Proceedings of GoTAL 2008*, Gothenburg, pp. 16–27.

Nivre, J., J. Hall, S. Kübler, R. McDonald, J. Nilsson, S. Riedel, and D. Yuret (2007). The CoNLL 2007 shared task on dependency parsing. In *Proceedings of the CoNLL Shared Task of EMNLP-CoNLL 2007*, Prague, pp. 915–932.

Nivre, J., J. Hall, J. Nilsson, A. Chanev, G. Eryiğit, S. Kübler, S. Marinov, and E. Marsi (2007). Maltparser: a language-independent system for data-driven dependency parsing. *Journal of Natural Language Engineering 13*, 95–135.

Nivre, J. and R. McDonald (2008). Integrating graph-based and transition-based dependency parsers. In *Proceedings of the 46th Annual Meeting of the Association for Computational Linguistics (ACL'08)*, Columbus, OH, pp. 950–958.

Nivre, J. and B. Megyesi (2007). Bootstrapping a Swedish treeebank using cross-corpus harmonization and annotation projection. In *Proceedings of the 6th International Workshop on Treebanks and Linguistic Theories*, Bergen, pp. 97–10.

Padó, S. (2007). *Cross-lingual Annotation Projection Models for Role-Semantic Information*. Ph. D. thesis, Saarland University.

Padó, S. and M. Lapata (2005). Cross-linguistic projection of role-semantic information. In *Proceedings of Human Language Technology Conference and Conference on Empirical Methods in Natural Language Processing*, Vancouver, BC, pp. 859–866.

Palmer, M., D. Gildea, and P. Kingsbury (2005). The Proposition Bank: An annotated corpus of semantic roles. *Computational Linguistics 31*, 71–105.

Petrov, S. and D. Klein (2008). Discriminative log-linear grammars with latent variables. In J. Platt, D. Koller, Y. Singer, and S. Roweis (Eds.), *Advances in Neural Information Processing Systems 20 (NIPS)*, pp. 1153–1160.

Pollard, C. and I. A. Sag (1987). *Information-Based Syntax and Semantics. Volume 1: Fundamentals*. Stanford, CA: CSLI Publications.

Pollard, C. and I. A. Sag (1994). *Head-Driven Phrase Structure Grammar*. Chicago, IL: University of Chicago Press.

Prescher, D. (2005, October). Head-driven PCFGs with latent-head statistics. In *Proceedings of the 9th International Workshop on Parsing Technology (IWPT)*, Vancouver, BC, pp. 115–124.

Quirk, C., A. Menezes, and C. Cherry (2005). Dependency treelet translation: syntactically informed phrasal SMT. In *Proceedings of the 43rd Annual Meeting of the Association for Computational Linguistics (ACL'05)*, Ann Arbor, MI, pp. 271–279.

Roark, B. and M. Bacchiani (2003). Supervised and unsupervised PCFG adaptation to novel domains. In *Proceedings of the 2003 Human Language Technology Conference of the North American Chapter of the Association for Computational Linguistics (HLT-NAACL 2003)*, Edmonton, AB, pp. 126–133.

Sag, I. A., T. Wasow, and E. Bender (2003). *Syntactic Theory: a Formal Introduction* (2nd ed.). Chicago, IL: University of Chicago Press.

Sagae, K. and J. Tsujii (2008). Shift-reduce dependency DAG parsing. In *Proceedings of the 22nd International Conference on Computational Linguistics (Coling 2008)*, Manchester, pp. 753–760.

Seginer, Y. (2007). Fast unsupervised incremental parsing. In *Proceedings of the 45th Annual Meeting of the Association of Computational Linguistics*, Prague, pp. 384–391.

Shen, L., J. Xu, and R. Weischedel (2008). A new string-to-dependency machine translation algorithm with a target dependency language model. In *Proceedings of the 46th Annual Meeting of the Association for Computational Linguistics: Human Language Technologies (ACL-08: HLT)*, Columbus, OH, pp. 577–585.

Smith, N. A. (2006). *Novel Estimation Methods for Unsupervised Discovery of Latent Structure in Natural Language Text*. Ph. D. thesis, Johns Hopkins University.

Snyder, B. and R. Barzilay (2008). Unsupervised multilingual learning for morphological segmentation. In *Proceedings of the 46th Annual Meeting of the Association for Computational Linguistics: Human Language Technologies (ACL-08: HLT)*, Columbus, OH, pp. 737–745.

Snyder, B., T. Naseem, J. Eisenstein, and R. Barzilay (2008). Unsupervised multilingual learning for POS tagging. In *Proceedings of the 2008 Conference on Empirical Methods in Natural Language Processing (EMNLP'08)*, Honolulu, HI, pp. 1041–1050.

Surdeanu, M., R. Johansson, A. Meyers, L. Màrquez, and J. Nivre (2008). The CoNLL-2008 shared task on joint parsing of syntactic and semantic dependencies. In *Proceedings of the 12th Conference on Computational Natural Language Learning (CoNLL-2008)*, Manchester pp. 159–177.

Swier, R. and S. Stevenson (2005). Exploiting a verb lexicon in automatic semantic role labelling. In *Proceedings of the Conference on Empirical Methods in Natural Language Processing (EMNLP-05)*, Vancouver, BC, pp. 883–890.

Tesnière, L. (1959). *Elments de syntaxe structurale*. Paris: Klincksieck.

Titov, I. and J. Henderson (2006). Loss minimization in parse reranking. In *Proceedings of the Conference on Empirical Methods in Natural Language processing (EMNLP'05)*, Sydney.

Titov, I. and J. Henderson (2007). Constituent parsing with Incremental Sigmoid Belief Networks. In *Proceedings of the 45th Annual Meeting of the Association of Computational Linguistics (ACL'07)*, Prague, pp. 632–639.

Titov, I., J. Henderson, P. Merlo, and G. Musillo (2009, July). Online projectivisation for synchronous parsing of semantic and syntactic dependencies. *Proceedings of the 21st International Conference on Artificial Intelligence (IJCAI'09)*, Pasadena, CA.

Wang, Q. I., D. Schuurmans, and D. Lin (2008). Semi-supervised convex training for dependency parsing. In *Proceedings of the 46th Annual Meeting of the Association for Computational Linguistics: Human Language Technologies (ACL-08: HLT)*, Columbus, OH, pp. 532–540.

Wong, Y. W. and R. Mooney (2007). Learning synchronous grammars for semantic parsing with lambda calculus. In *Proceedings of the 45th Annual Meeting of the Association of Computational Linguistics (ACL'07)*, Prague, pp. 960–967.

Wu, D. (1997). Stochastic inversion transduction grammars and bilingual parsing of parallel corpora. *Computational Linguistics 23*(3), 377–403.

Wu, D. and D. Chiang (Eds.) (2007, April). *Proceedings of SSST, NAACL-HLT 2007/AMTA Workshop on Syntax and Structure in Statistical Translation.* Rochester, NY: Association for Computational Linguistics.

Yamada, H. and Y. Matsumoto (2003). Statistical dependency analysis with support vector machines. In *Proceedings of the 8th International Workshop on Parsing Technologies (IWPT'03)*, Nancy, pp. 195–206.

Zettlemoyer, L. and M. Collins (2007). Online learning of relaxed CCG grammars for parsing to logical form. In *Proceedings of the 2007 Joint Conference on Empirical Methods in Natural Language Processing and Computational Natural Language Learning (EMNLP-CoNLL)*, Prague, pp. 678–687.

Chapter 2
Single Malt or Blended? A Study in Multilingual Parser Optimization

Johan Hall, Jens Nilsson, and Joakim Nivre

2.1 Introduction

In recent years, data-driven dependency parsing has become a popular method for parsing natural language text, and the shared tasks on multilingual dependency parsing at CoNLL 2006 (Buchholz and Marsi, 2006) and CoNLL 2007 (Nivre et al., 2007) have contributed greatly to the increase in interest. One of the advantages of data-driven parsing models is that they can be ported to new languages, given that there is a treebank available for the language.

This chapter is a study in multilingual parser optimization, based on work done for the CoNLL shared task 2007, using a transition-based dependency parser and an implementation of the theoretical framework of inductive dependency parsing presented by Nivre (2006).[1]

In order to maximize parsing accuracy, optimization has been carried out in two stages, leading to two different, but related parsers. The first of these is a single-parser system, similar to the one described in Nivre et al. (2006), which parses a sentence deterministically in a single left-to-right pass over the input, with post-processing to recover non-projective dependencies, and which has been tuned for each language by optimizing parameters of the parsing algorithm, the feature model, and (to some degree) the learning algorithm. We call this system Single Malt, to emphasize the fact that it consists of a single instance of MaltParser. The second parser is an ensemble system, which combines the output of six deterministic parsers, each of which is a variation of the Single Malt parser with parameter settings extrapolated from the first stage of optimization. It seems natural to call this system Blended.

The chapter is structured as follows. Section 2.2 gives the necessary background and Section 2.3 briefly presents the CoNLL shared task 2007. Section 2.4

J. Hall (✉)
Växjö University, Växjö, Sweden
e-mail: johan.hall@vxu.se

[1] We have used MaltParser 0.4, which can be downloaded free of charge from the following page: http://w3.msi.vxu.se/users/nivre/research/MaltParser.html

H. Bunt et al. (eds.), *Trends in Parsing Technology*, Text, Speech and Language Technology 43, DOI 10.1007/978-90-481-9352-3_2,

summarizes the work done to optimize the Single Malt parser, while Section 2.5 explains how the Blended parser was constructed from the Single Malt parser. Section 2.6 gives a brief analysis of the experimental results, and Section 2.5 concludes.

2.2 Data-Driven Dependency Parsing

The goal of parsing a sentence with dependency structure representations is to create a dependency graph consisting of lexical nodes linked by binary relations. A dependency relation connects words with one word acting as *head* and the other as *dependent*. Moreover, data-driven dependency parsing induces a parser model from a treebank of syntactically annotated sentences of a given language. There are several methods for data-driven dependency parsing and McDonald and Nivre (2007) define two dominating methods: graph-based dependency parsing and transition-based dependency parsing. MaltParser is a typical example of a transition-based dependency parser and is based on three essential components:

- Deterministic algorithms for building labeled dependency graphs (Nivre, 2003; Covington, 2001)
- History-based feature models for predicting the next parser action at nondeterministic choice points (Black et al., 1992; Magerman, 1995; Ratnaparkhi, 1997)
- Support vector machines for mapping histories to parser actions (Kudo and Matsumoto, 2002; Hall et al., 2006)

In this section, we begin by defining dependency graphs in Section 2.2.1 and continue with an overview of MaltParser in Section 2.2.2. The Single Malt system uses a projective parsing algorithm and therefore we use graph transformations for recovering non-projective structures, a technique called pseudo-projective parsing (Nivre and Nilsson, 2005). This is explained in Section 2.2.3. Finally, in Section 2.2.4, we give the necessary background on parser combination for the Blended system.

2.2.1 Dependency Graph

In dependency parsing, the syntactic representation of a sentence is a dependency graph, which is built from binary relations between tokens (or words) labeled with syntactic functions or dependency types. We define a dependency graph as follows:

Definition 2.1 *Given a set* $R = \{r_0, r_1, \ldots, r_m\}$ *of dependency types, a* dependency graph G *for a sentence* $x = (w_1, \ldots, w_n)$ *is a quadruple* $G = (V, E, <, L)$*, where*

1. $V = \{v_0, v_1, \ldots, v_n\}$ *is a non-empty finite set of nodes, one for each* $w_i \in x$*, plus an extra root node* v_0*,*
2. E *is a set of directed arcs* (v_i, v_j) $(v_i, v_j \in V)$*,*

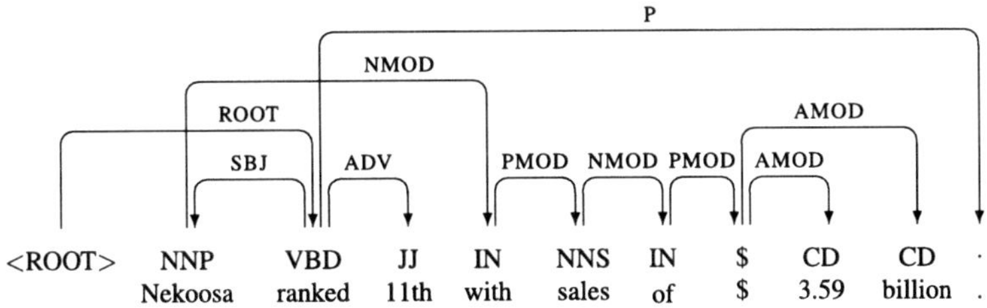

Fig. 2.1 Dependency graph for an English sentence from the WSJ section of the Penn Treebank. Conversion into dependency graphs by Johansson and Nugues (2007)

3. *$<$ is a linear order on V (defined by the order of words in x),*
4. *L is a function $L : E \to R$ that labels every arc (v_i, v_j) with a dependency type $r \in R$.*

A dependency graph G is well-formed if it is a directed tree rooted at v_0.

The token nodes $\{v_1, \ldots, v_n\}$ in the set V have a direct connection to the words in x and we assume that token nodes are labeled with additional information like part-of-speech tags and lemmas. In addition, there is a special root node v_0, which is the root of the dependency graph and has no corresponding token in the sentence x.

The set E of arcs is a set of ordered pairs (v_i, v_j), where v_i and v_j are nodes. Since arcs are used to represent dependency relations, we will say that v_i is the *head* and v_j is the *dependent* of the arc (v_i, v_j). The function L assigns a dependency type or arc label $r \in R$ to every arc $e \in E$.

A dependency graph G is said to be projective if, for every arc $(v_i, v_j) \in E$ and every node $v_k \in V$ such that v_k occurs between v_i and v_j in the linear order (i.e., $v_i < v_k < v_j$ or $v_j < v_k < v_i$), v_i dominates v_k (where dominance is the transitive closure of the arc relation E). Figure 2.1 shows a non-projective dependency graph for an English sentence, where each word of the sentence is tagged with its part-of-speech and each arc labeled with a dependency type. The graph is non-projective because the arc connecting *Nehoosa* and *with* spans two words (*ranked*, *11th*) that are not dominated by *Nehoosa*.

2.2.2 MaltParser

The MaltParser system has two deterministic parsing algorithms that derive dependency graphs as described by Nivre (2003) and Covington (2001), respectively. Both algorithms can be executed in two modes: learning mode and parsing mode. During learning the dependency graphs are reconstructed by an oracle function using syntactically annotated sentences. The oracle function derives the correct sequences of transitions by reconstructing the dependency graphs. These transitions are used as training data to approximate the oracle function by history-based feature models and inductive learning. During parsing the dependency graphs are created by predicting sequences of transitions using the induced model.

2.2.2.1 Parsing Algorithms

The Nivre parsing algorithm performs labeled projective dependency parsing in linear time, using a stack S to store partially processed tokens and an input queue I of remaining tokens. The algorithm comes with two transition systems. The *arc-eager* transition system attaches the right dependents to their head as soon as possible, and the *arc-standard* transition system postpones the attachment of right dependents until they have found all their own dependents.

For example, the arc-eager transition-system has four parser actions (Next denotes the next token node and Top is the node on top of the stack):

1. SHIFT: Pushes Next onto the stack.
2. REDUCE: Pops Top from the stack.
3. RIGHT-ARC(r): Adds an arc (Top, Next) labeled r and pushes Next onto the stack.
4. LEFT-ARC(r): Adds an arc (Next, Top) labeled r and pops Top from the stack.

Another parameter of the Nivre algorithm is the stack initialization. It can be initialized with the artificial root node (v_0) on the stack, so that arcs originating from the root can be added explicitly during parsing. The other option is to initialize the parser with an empty stack, in which case arcs from the root are only added implicitly (to any token that remains a root after parsing is completed). *Root node* initialization allows more than one label for dependencies from the artificial root, but with *empty stack* initialization, all such dependencies are assigned a default label. On the other hand, empty stack initialization reduces the amount of nondeterminism.

After completing the left-to-right pass over the input, there can be unattached tokens (which by default will be attached to the artificial root node v_0). The final parameter of the Nivre algorithm specifies whether the parser should allow a second post-processing pass or not, where only unattached tokens are processed. This technique is similar to the one used by Yamada and Matsumoto (2003), but with only a single post-processing pass parsing complexity remains linear (in string length).

In addition to the Nivre algorithm, the Blended parser uses the Covington algorithm that implements an incremental parsing strategy for dependency representations that can recover non-projective graphs in quadratic time (Covington, 2001), which has been used for deterministic classifier-based parsing by Nivre (2007).

2.2.2.2 Feature Models

Both parsing algorithms build the dependency graphs by a sequence of transitions, and the choice between different transitions is nondeterministic in the general case. MaltParser uses history-based feature models for predicting the next parser action at nondeterministic choice points. The task is to predict the next transition given the current parser configuration, where the configuration is represented by a feature vector. Each feature in the feature vector is an attribute of a token defined relative to the current stack S, input queue I, or the partially built dependency graph G. An attribute can be the word form, the lemma or another attribute available in the input data and the dependency type of the partially built dependency graph G.

2.2.2.3 Learning Algorithm

MaltParser supports several learning algorithms but the best results have so far been obtained with support vector machines, using the LIBSVM package (Chang and Lin, 2001) with a quadratic kernel $K(x_i, x_j) = (\gamma x_i^T x_j + r)^2$ and the one-versus-one strategy for multi-class classification. Symbolic features are converted to numerical ones using the standard technique of binarization, and the set of training instances can be split into smaller sets for training separate classifiers in order to reduce training times.

2.2.3 Pseudo-Projective Parsing

Nivre and Nilsson (2005) apply a technique for recovering non-projectivity in the parser output that complements post-processing with pre-processing, known as pseudo-projective parsing. The pre-processor starts by identifying all non-projective arcs in the training data. These arcs are then lifted upward in the tree, one step at a time, until the entire dependency graph is projective. This lifting strategy is guaranteed to produce a projective dependency structure, which in practice seldom requires more than three lifts for a non-projective arc. The dependency labels of a lifted arc or surrounding arcs are augmented with additional information that partially encodes the original position of the arc in the tree. This information is used to guide a heuristic top-down breadth-first search for non-projective heads in the parser output, which approximates the inverse of the pseudo-projective transformation.

The overall methodology for pseudo-projective parsing looks like this:

1. Apply the pseudo-projective transformation to the training data and augment the dependency labels.
2. Train a parser on the transformed data.
3. Parse new sentences.
4. Apply the approximate inverse transformation to the output of the parser.

2.2.4 Parser Combination

Parser combination for dependency parsers has gained interest in recent years. It is a natural next step in order to increase accuracy further for existing dependency parsers. Zeman and Žabokrtský (2005) proposed a language independent ensemble approach, which for each token greedily chooses a head token based on the head tokens of all single parsers. They present improved results in comparison to the best single parser for Czech, but—unless explicitly forbidden—their approach can cause cycles in the combined dependency graph even though all single parses are acyclic.

By contrast, the ensemble approach proposed by Sagae and Lavie (2006), who also report significantly increased accuracies, is based on finding the maximum directed spanning tree given a dense weighted graph. The output is guaranteed to be acyclic even if some single parses contain cycles. The arc weights of the dense graph are determined based on the m output dependency graphs according to the following description.

Given the output dependency graphs G_i $(1 \leq i \leq m)$ of m different parsers for an input sentence x, they construct a new graph containing all the labeled dependency arcs proposed by some parser and weight each arc a by a score $s(a)$ reflecting its popularity among the m parsers. The output of the ensemble system for x is the maximum spanning tree of this graph (rooted at the node v_0), which can be extracted using the Chu-Liu-Edmonds algorithm, as shown by McDonald et al. (2005). Sagae and Lavie (2006) let $s(a) = \sum_{i=1}^{m} w_i^c a_i$, where w_i^c is the average labeled attachment score of parser i for the word class c of the dependent of a, and a_i is 1 if $a \in G_i$ and 0 otherwise.

2.3 The CoNLL Shared Task 2007

The CoNLL shared tasks in both 2006 and 2007 were devoted to dependency parsing, where the shared task 2007 was divided into two tracks: a multilingual track and a domain adaptation track. The focus in this chapter is on how we optimized parsers for the ten languages in the multilingual track. The characteristics of the data sets for the ten languages are shown in Table 2.1.

The task is to derive labeled dependency graphs for input sentences from a wide range of languages. The parser system used in the shared task must be able to

Table 2.1 Information about the data sets, taken from Nivre et al. (2007)

		Training data									Test data		
Language		AS	#T(k)	#S(k)	T/S	LF	#C	#P	#D	%N	#T	#S	T/S
Arabic	Hajič et al. (2004)	d	112	2.9	38.3	Y	15	21	29	10.1	5,124	131	39.1
Basque	Aduriz et al. (2003)	d	51	3.2	15.8	Y	25	64	35	26.2	5,390	334	16.1
Catalan	Martí et al. (2007)	c+f	431	15.0	28.8	Y	17	54	42	2.9	5,016	167	30.0
Chinese	Chen et al. (2003)	c+f	337	57.0	5.9	N	13	294	69	0.0	5,161	690	7.5
Czech	Böhmová et al. (2003)	d	432	25.4	17.0	Y	12	59	46	23.2	4,724	286	16.5
English	Marcus et al. (1993)	c+f	447	18.6	24.0	N	31	45	20	6.7	5,003	214	23.4
Greek	Prokopidis et al. (2005)	d	65	2.7	24.2	Y	18	38	46	20.3	4,804	197	24.4
Hungarian	Csendes et al. (2005)	c+f	132	6.0	21.8	Y	16	43	49	26.4	7,344	390	18.8
Italian	Montemagni et al. (2003)	c+f	71	3.1	22.9	Y	14	28	22	7.4	5,096	249	20.5
Turkish	Oflazer et al. (2003)	d	65	5.6	11.6	Y	14	31	25	33.3	4,513	300	15.0

AS, annotation scheme (c, constituency, d, dependency, f, grammatical functions); #T, number of tokens; #S, number of sentences; T/S, mean sentence length; LF, lemma and syntactic and/or morphological features is available; #C, number of coarse-grained part-of-speech tags; #P, number of fine-grained part-of-speech tags; #D, number of dependency types; %N, percentage of non-projective sentences.

learn, by only adjusting a number of hyper-parameters, from the annotated training data and to parse unseen test data. Both data sets were provided for ten different languages by the shared task organizers. The data sets were formatted according to the CoNLL dependency data format (Buchholz and Marsi, 2006), which is a column-based format with six input columns: token counter (ID), word form (FORM), lemma or stem of word form (LEMMA), coarse-grained part-of-speech tag (CPOSTAG), fine-grained part-of-speech tag (POSTAG) and unordered set of syntactic and/or morphological features (FEATS), and four output columns: head of the current token (HEAD), dependency relation to the head (DEPREL), and two unused output columns PHEAD and PDEPREL.

2.4 The Single Malt Parser

The parameters available in the MaltParser system can be divided into three groups: parsing algorithm parameters, feature model parameters, and learning algorithm parameters, which were briefly described in Section 2.2.2. It is essential to optimize these parameters for each language to get a good overall result. There are an infinite number of combinations of these parameters and it is intractable to try out all combinations. Our overall optimization strategy for the Single Malt parser can be described as follows:

1. Define a good baseline system with the same parameter settings for all languages. This baseline system uses parameters that have performed well for other languages and data sets in previous experiments. For example, the experience of optimizing the 13 languages in the CoNLL shared task 2006 came in handy when defining this baseline system.
2. Tune the parsing algorithm and the pseudo-projective parsing parameters once and for all for each language (with baseline settings for the feature model and learning algorithm parameters).
3. Optimize the feature model and the learning algorithm parameters in an interleaved fashion for each language.

We used nine-fold cross-validation on 90% of the training data for all languages with a training set size smaller than 300,000 tokens and an 80–10% train-devtest split for the remaining languages (Catalan, Chinese, Czech, English). The remaining 10% of the data was in both cases saved for a final dry run, where the parser was trained on 90% of the data for each language and tested on the remaining (fresh) 10%.[2] We consistently used the labeled attachment score (LAS) as the single optimization criterion.

Below we describe the most important parameters in each group, define baseline settings, and report notable improvements for differentlanguages during

[2] Note that this was an internally defined test set, taken out of the training data and distinct from the official test set distributed by the organizers for the final evaluation.

Table 2.2 Development results for Single Malt (Base, baseline; PA, parsing algorithm; F+L, feature model and learning algorithm); dry run and test results for Single Malt (SM) and Blended (B) (with corrected test scores for Blended on Chinese). All scores are labeled attachment scores (LAS) except the last two columns, which report unlabeled attachment scores (UAS) on the test sets

	Development			Dry run		Test		Test: UAS	
Language	Base	PA	F+L	SM	B	SM	B	SM	B
Arabic	70.31	70.31	71.67	70.93	73.09	74.75	76.52	84.21	85.81
Basque	73.86	74.44	76.99	77.18	80.12	74.97	76.92	80.61	82.84
Catalan	85.43	85.51	86.88	86.65	88.00	87.74	88.70	92.20	93.12
Chinese	83.85	84.39	87.64	87.61	88.61	83.51	84.67	87.60	88.70
Czech	75.00	75.83	77.74	77.91	82.17	77.22	77.98	82.35	83.59
English	85.44	85.44	86.35	86.35	88.74	85.81	88.11	86.77	88.93
Greek	72.67	73.04	74.42	74.89	78.17	74.21	74.65	80.66	81.22
Hungarian	74.62	74.64	77.40	77.81	80.04	78.09	80.27	81.71	83.55
Italian	81.42	81.64	82.50	83.37	85.16	82.48	84.40	86.26	87.77
Turkish	75.12	75.80	76.49	75.87	77.09	79.24	79.79	85.04	85.77
Average	77.78	78.10	79.81	79.86	82.12	79.80	81.20	84.74	86.13

development. The improvements for each language from step 1 (baseline) to step 2 (parsing algorithm) and step 3 (feature model and learning algorithm) can be tracked in Table 2.2.[3]

2.4.1 Parsing Algorithm

We decided to only explore the different parameters of the Nivre parsing algorithm for the Single Malt parser. The baseline algorithm uses the arc-eager transition-system, initializes the stack with an artificial root node and performs only a single left-to-right pass over the input without a second pass where only unattached tokens are processed.

Since the parsing algorithm only produces projective dependency graphs, we may use pseudo-projective parsing to recover non-projective dependencies. The different settings of the pseudo-projective parsing software were also varied in this optimization round, except for the Chinese data set, which does not contain any non-projective dependencies.

The settings after the first optimization phase are shown in column 2–5 of Table 2.3 for each language. The arc-standard order was found to improve parsing accuracy for Chinese, while the arc-eager order was maintained for all other languages. Empty stack initialization (which reduces the amount of nondeterminism in parsing) led to improved accuracy for Catalan, Chinese, Hungarian, Italian and Turkish. For Arabic, Basque, Czech, and Greek, the lack of improvement can be explained by the fact that these data sets allow more than one label for dependencies

[3] Complete specifications of all parameter settings for all languages, for both Single Malt and Blended, are available at http://w3.msi.vxu.se/users/jha/conll07/

Table 2.3 Parameter settings

Language	AO	SI	Post	PP	#F	SA	ST	γ	r	C	ε
Arabic	E	R	N	N	21	POSTAG	I:Next	0.2	0.0	0.5	1.0
Basque	E	R	Y	Y	21	POSTAG	I:Next	0.2	0.0	0.5	1.0
Catalan	E	E	Y	N	27	POSTAG	I:Next	0.2	0.0	0.5	1.0
Chinese	S	E	N	N	21	none	none	0.2	0.3	0.25	0.1
Czech	E	R	Y	Y	27	CPOSTAG	I:Next	0.2	0.3	0.25	1.0
English	E	R	N	N	19	CPOSTAG	I:Next	0.18	0.4	0.4	1.0
Greek	E	R	Y	Y	50	none	none	0.2	0.0	0.5	1.0
Hungarian	E	E	Y	Y	56	none	none	0.2	0.0	0.5	1.0
Italian	E	E	N	N	25	CPOSTAG	I:Next	0.1	0.6	0.5	1.0
Turkish	E	E	N	Y	18	CPOSTAG	S:Top	0.12	0.3	0.7	0.5

AO, arc order (E, arc-eager; S, arc-standard); SI, stack initialization (R, root node; E, empty stack); Post, post-processing; PP, pseudo projective parsing; #F, number of features; SA, split attribute; ST, split token. LIBSVM parameters: γ and r, kernel parameters; C, penalty parameter; ε, termination criterion.

from the artificial root. With empty stack initialization all such dependencies are assigned a default label, which leads to a drop in labeled attachment score. For English, however, empty stack initialization did not improve accuracy despite the fact that dependencies from the artificial root have a unique label. A second pass, where only unattached tokens are processed, improved results for Basque, Catalan, Czech, Greek and Hungarian.

Pseudo-projective parsing was found to have a positive effect on overall parsing accuracy only for Basque, Czech, Greek and Turkish. This result can probably be explained in terms of the frequency of non-projective dependencies in the different languages. For Basque, Czech, Greek and Turkish, more than 20% of the sentences have non-projective dependency graphs; for all the remaining languages the corresponding figure is 10% or less. In fact, for Arabic, having about 10% non-projective sentences, it was later found that, with an optimized feature model, it is beneficial to projectivize the training data without trying to recover non-projective dependencies in the parser output. This was also the setting that was used for Arabic in the dry run and final test.

The cumulative improvement after optimization of parsing algorithm parameters was a modest 0.32 percentage points on average over all ten languages, with a minimum of 0.00 (Arabic, English) and a maximum of 0.83 (Czech) (cf. Table 2.2).

2.4.2 Feature Model

An important factor to increase the accuracy is to optimize the feature model for each language, but doing an exhaustive search for all ten languages is an impossible task. Instead we used two different strategies:

1. Batch testing of new features by forward and backward selection
2. Investigating properties of the languages and using features defined to capture these properties

Tokens	FORM	LEMMA	CPOSTAG	POSTAG	FEATS	DEPREL
	Attributes					
S: top	+	+	+	+	+	+
S: top−1				+		
I: next	+	+	+	+	+	
I: next + 1	+			+		
I: next + 2				+		
I: next + 3				+		
G: head of top	+					
G: leftmost dependent of top						+
G: rightmost dependent of top						+
G: leftmost dependent of next						+

Fig. 2.2 Baseline feature model (S, Stack, I, Input, G, Graph)

As a starting point, we used the baseline feature model depicted in Fig. 2.2, where rows denote tokens, columns denote attributes, and each cell containing a plus sign represents a used model feature. Each feature of this model is an attribute of a token defined relative to the current stack S, input queue I, or partially built dependency graph G. The attribute can be any of the symbolic input attributes in the CoNLL format: FORM, LEMMA, CPOSTAG, POSTAG and FEATS (split into atomic attributes), as well as the DEPREL attribute of tokens in the graph G. The names Top and Next refer to the token on top of the stack S and the first token in the remaining input I, respectively (cf. Section 2.2.2.1). This model is an extrapolation from many previous experiments on different languages (Nivre et al., 2006, 2007).

Column 6 in Table 2.3 presents the total number of features in the tuned models, which varies from 18 (Turkish) to 56 (Hungarian). However, the number is typically between 20 and 30.[4] This feature selection process constituted the major development effort for the Single Malt parser and also gave the greatest improvements in parsing accuracy, but since the feature selection was to some extent interleaved with learning algorithm optimization, we only report the cumulative effect of both together in Table 2.2.

2.4.3 Learning Algorithm

We decided to use the LIBSVM implementation of SVM as the learning method. This library comes with many parameters which are used for optimizing the SVM learner for a specific task, in our case dependency parsing. We consistently used the polynomial kernel $K(x_i, x_j) = (\gamma x_i^T x_j + r)^d$ of degree 2 ($d = 2$).

As our baseline settings, we used $\gamma = 0.2$ and $r = 0$ for the kernel parameters, $C = 0.5$ for the penalty parameter, and $\varepsilon = 1.0$ for the termination criterion. In order to reduce training times during development, we also split the training data for each language into smaller sets using the POSTAG of Next as the defining feature for the split.

[4] These numbers refer to the number of multi-valued categorical features, as defined in Fig. 2.2. The number of binarized features fed to the SVM learner is of course much higher and depends on the number of possible values for each categorical feature.

The time spent on optimizing learning algorithm parameters varies between languages, mainly due to lack of time. For Arabic, Basque, and Catalan, the baseline settings were used also in the dry run and final test. Column 7–8 in Table 2.3 presents the feature for splitting the training data into smaller sets. For Chinese, Greek and Hungarian, slightly better results were obtained by not splitting the training data. For the remaining languages, accuracy improved by using the CPOSTAG of Next or Top as the defining feature for the split (instead of POSTAG). With respect to the SVM parameters (γ, r, C, and ε, shown in column 9–12), Arabic, Basque, Catalan, Greek and Hungarian retain the baseline settings, while the other languages have slightly different values for some parameters.

The cumulative improvement after optimization of feature model and learning algorithm parameters was 1.71% points on average over all ten languages, with a minimum of 0.69 (Turkish) and a maximum of 3.25 (Chinese) (cf. Table 2.2).

2.5 The Blended Parser

The Blended parser is an ensemble system based on the methodology proposed by Sagae and Lavie (2006), where we let c in w_i^c (see Section 2.2.4) be the values of the coarse parts-of-speech (CPOSTAG). It uses six component parsers, with two different parsing algorithms: two variants of the Nivre algorithm (arc-eager and arc standard) and the non-projective version of the Covington algorithm, each of which is used to construct one left-to-right parser and one right-to-left parser. Thus, the six component parsers for each language were instances of the following:

1. Nivre arc-eager pseudo-projective left-to-right
2. Nivre arc-eager pseudo-projective right-to-left
3. Nivre arc-standard pseudo-projective left-to-right
4. Nivre arc-standard pseudo-projective right-to-left
5. Covington non-projective left-to-right
6. Covington non-projective right-to-left

The final Blended parser was constructed by reusing the tuned Single Malt parser for each language (arc-standard left-to-right for Chinese, arc-eager left-to-right for the remaining languages) and training five additional parsers with the same parameter settings except for the following mechanical adjustments:

1. Pseudo-projective parsing was not used for the two non-projective parsers.
2. Feature models were adjusted by adding and removing features defined on the dependency graph according to the constraints of different parsing algorithms.[5]
3. Learning algorithm parameters were adjusted to speed up training (e.g., by always splitting the training data into smaller sets).

[5] For example, the DEPREL of Top row 1 in Fig. 2.2 was removed for the arc-standard version of the Nivre algorithm, because it will always be null.

Having trained all parsers on 90% of the training data for each language, the weights w_i^c for each parser i and coarse part of speech c were determined by the labeled attachment score on the remaining 10% of the data. This means that the results obtained in the dry run were bound to be overly optimistic for the Blended parser, since it was then evaluated on the same data set that was used to tune the weights.

Finally, we want to emphasize that the time for developing the Blended parser was severely limited, which means that several shortcuts had to be taken, such as optimizing learning algorithm parameters for speed rather than accuracy and using extrapolation, rather than proper tuning, for other important parameters. This probably means that the performance of the Blended system can be improved further by optimizing parameters for all six parsers separately.

2.6 Results and Discussion

Table 2.2 shows the labeled attachment score results from our internal dry run (training on 90% of the training data, testing on the remaining 10%) and the official test runs for both of our systems. It should be pointed out that the test score for the Blended parser on Chinese is different from the official one (75.82), which was much lower than expected due to a corrupted specification file required by MaltParser. Restoring this file and rerunning the parser on the Chinese test set, without retraining the parser or changing any parameter settings, resulted in the score reported here. This also improved the average score from 80.32 to 81.20, the former being the highest reported official score.

For the Single Malt parser, the test results are on average very close to the dry run results, indicating that models have not been overfitted (although there is considerable variation between languages). For the Blended parser, there is a drop of almost 1% point, which can be explained by the fact that weights could not be tuned on held-out data for the dry run (as explained in Section 2.5).

Comparing the results for different languages, we see a tendency that languages with rich morphology, usually accompanied by flexible word order, get lower scores. Thus, the labeled attachment score is below 80% for Arabic, Basque, Czech, Greek, Hungarian, and Turkish. By comparison, the more configurational languages (Catalan, Chinese, English, and Italian) all have scores above 80%. Linguistic properties thus seem to be more important than, for example, training set size, which can be seen by comparing the results for Italian, with one of the smallest training sets, and Czech, with one of the largest. The development of parsing methods that are better suited for morphologically rich languages with flexible word order appears as one of the most important goals for future research in this area.

Comparing the results of our two systems, we see that the Blended parser outperforms the Single Malt parser for all languages, with an average improvement of 1.40% points, a minimum of 0.44 (Greek) and a maximum of 2.40 (English). As shown by McDonald and Nivre (2007), the Single Malt parser tends to suffer from two problems: error propagation due to the deterministic parsing strategy, typically affecting long dependencies more than short ones, and low precision on

Table 2.4 Recall (R) and precision (P) of Single Malt and Blended for dependencies of different length, averaged over all languages (Root, dependents of root node, regardless of length)

	Root		1		2		3–6		7+	
Parser	R	P	R	P	R	P	R	P	R	P
Single Malt	87.01	80.36	95.08	94.87	86.28	86.67	77.97	80.23	68.98	71.06
Blended	92.09	74.20	95.71	94.92	87.55	88.12	78.66	83.02	65.29	78.14

dependencies originating in the artificial root node due to fragmented parses. A fragmented parse is a dependency forest, rather than a tree, and is automatically converted to a tree by attaching all (other) roots to the artificial root node. Hence, children of the root node in the final output may not have been predicted as such by the treebank-induced classifier. The question is which of these problems is alleviated by the multiple views given by the component parsers in the Blended system.

Table 2.4 throws some light on this by giving the precision and recall for dependencies of different length, treating dependents of the artificial root node as a special case. As expected, the Single Malt parser has lower precision than recall for root dependents, but the Blended parser has even lower precision (and somewhat better recall), indicating that the fragmentation is even more severe in this case. This conclusion is further supported by the observation that the single most frequent "frame confusion" of the Blended parser, over all languages, is to attach two dependents with the label ROOT to the root node, instead of only one. The frequency of this error is more than twice as high for the Blended parser (180) as for the Single Malt parser (83). By contrast, we see that precision and recall for other dependencies improve across the board, especially for longer dependencies, which probably means that the effect of error propagation is mitigated by the use of an ensemble system, even if each of the component parsers is deterministic in itself.

2.7 Conclusion

We have shown that deterministic, classifier-based dependency parsing, with careful optimization, can give highly accurate dependency parsing for a wide range of languages, as illustrated by the performance of the Single Malt parser. We have also demonstrated that an ensemble of deterministic, classifier-based dependency parsers, built on top of a tuned single-parser system, can give even higher accuracy, as shown by the results of the Blended parser, which has the highest labeled attachment score for five languages (Arabic, Basque, Catalan, Hungarian, and Italian), as well as the highest multilingual average score.

Acknowledgements We want to thank all treebank providers for making the data available for the CoNLL 2007 Shared Task and the (other) organizers for their efforts in organizing it. Special thanks to Ryan McDonald, for fruitful discussions and assistance with the error analysis, and to Kenji Sagae, for showing us how to produce a good blend. Thanks also to Gülşen Eryiğit, Beáta Megyesi, Mattias Nilsson and Markus Saers for helping us with the optimization of the Single Malt parser.

References

Abeillé, A. (Ed.) (2003). *Treebanks: Building and Using Parsed Corpora*. Dordrecht, Netherlands: Kluwer.

Aduriz, I., M. J. Aranzabe, J. M. Arriola, A. Atutxa, A. D. de Ilarraza, A. Garmendia, and M. Oronoz (2003). Construction of a Basque dependency treebank. In *Proceedings of the 2nd Workshop on Treebanks and Linguistic Theories*, Växjö, Sweden, pp. 201–204.

Black, E., F. Jelinek, J. D. Lafferty, D. M. Magerman, R. L. Mercer, and S. Roukos (1992). Towards history-based grammars: using richer models for probabilistic parsing. In *Proceedings of the 5th DARPA Speech and Natural Language Workshop*, Harriman, NY, pp. 31–37.

Böhmová, A., J. Hajič, E. Hajičová, and B. Hladká (2003). The PDT: a 3-level annotation scenario. See Abeillé (2003), Chapter 7, pp. 103–127.

Buchholz, S. and E. Marsi (2006). CoNLL-X shared task on multilingual dependency parsing. In *Proceedings of the 10th Conference on Computational Natural Language Learning*, New York, NY, pp. 149–164.

Chang, C.-C. and C.-J. Lin (2001). *LIBSVM: a Library for Support Vector Machines*. Software available at http://www.csie.ntu.edu.tw/ cjlin/libsvm.

Chen, K., C. Luo, M. Chang, F. Chen, C. Chen, C. Huang, and Z. Gao (2003). Sinica treebank: design criteria, representational issues and implementation. See Abeillé (2003), Chapter 13, pp. 231–248.

Covington, M. A. (2001). A fundamental algorithm for dependency parsing. In *Proceedings of the 39th Annual ACM Southeast Conference*, Athens, GA, pp. 95–102.

Csendes, D., J. Csirik, T. Gyimóthy, and A. Kocsor (2005). *The Szeged Treebank*. Berlin/ Heidelberg, Germany: Springer.

Hajič, J., O. Smrž, P. Zemánek, J. Šnaidauf, and E. Beška (2004). Prague Arabic dependency treebank: development in data and tools. In *Proceedings of the Network for Euro-Mediterranean Language Resources International Conference on Arabic Language Resources and Tools*, Cairo, Egypt, pp. 110–117.

Hall, J., J. Nivre, and J. Nilsson (2006). Discriminative classifiers for deterministic dependency parsing. In *Proceedings of the 21st International Conference on Computational Linguistics and 44th Annual Meeting of the Association for Computational Linguistics Main Conference Poster Sessions*, Sydney, Australia, pp. 316–323.

Johansson, R. and P. Nugues (2007). Extended constituent-to-dependency conversion for English. In *Proceedings of the 16th Nordic Conference on Computational Linguistics*, Tartu, Estonia, pp. 105–112.

Kudo, T. and Y. Matsumoto (2002). Japanese dependency analysis using cascaded chunking. In *Proceedings of the 6th Workshop on Computational Language Learning*, Taipei, Taiwan, pp. 63–69.

Magerman, D. M. (1995). Statistical decision-tree models for parsing. In *Proceedings of the 33rd Annual Meeting of the Association for Computational Linguistics*, Cambridge, MA, pp. 276–283.

Marcus, M., B. Santorini, and M. Marcinkiewicz (1993). Building a large annotated corpus of English: the Penn Treebank. *Computational Linguistics 19*(2), 313–330.

Martí, M. A., M. Taulé, L. Màrquez, and M. Bertran (2007). CESS-ECE: a multilingual and multilevel annotated corpus. Available for download from: http://www.lsi.upc.edu/~mbertran/cess-ece/.

McDonald, R. and J. Nivre (2007). Characterizing the errors of data-driven dependency parsing models. In *Proceedings of the 2007 Joint Conference on Empirical Methods in Natural Language Processing and Computational Natural Language Learning*, Prague, Czech Republic, pp. 122–131.

McDonald, R., F. Pereira, K. Ribarov, and J. Hajič (2005). Non-projective dependency parsing using spanning tree algorithms. In *Proceedings of the Human Language Technology*

Conference and the Conference on Empirical Methods in Natural Language Processing, Vancouver, Canada, pp. 523–530.

Montemagni, S., F. Barsotti, M. Battista, N. Calzolari, O. Corazzari, A. Lenci, A. Zampolli, F. Fanciulli, M. Massetani, R. Raffaelli, R. Basili, M. T. Pazienza, D. Saracino, F. Zanzotto, N. Nana, F. Pianesi, and R. Delmonte (2003). Building the Italian Syntactic-Semantic Treebank. See Abeillé (2003), Chapter 11, pp. 189–210.

Nivre, J. (2003). An efficient algorithm for projective dependency parsing. In *Proceedings of the 8th International Workshop on Parsing Technologies*, Nancy. France, pp. 149–160.

Nivre, J. (2006). *Inductive Dependency Parsing*. Dordrecht, Netherlands: Springer.

Nivre, J. (2007). Incremental non-projective dependency parsing. In *Human Language Technologies: the Annual Conference of the North American Chapter of the Association for Computational Linguistics*, Rochester, NY, pp. 396–403.

Nivre, J., J. Hall, S. Kübler, R. McDonald, J. Nilsson, S. Riedel, and D. Yuret (2007). The CoNLL 2007 shared task on dependency parsing. In *Proceedings of the Joint Conference on Empirical Methods in Natural Language Processing and Computational Natural Language Learning*, Prague, Czech Republic, pp. 915–932.

Nivre, J., J. Hall, J. Nilsson, A. Chanev, G. Eryiğit, S. Kübler, S. Marinov, and E. Marsi (2007). MaltParser: a language-independent system for data-driven dependency parsing. *Natural Language Engineering 13*(2), 95–135.

Nivre, J., J. Hall, J. Nilsson, G. Eryiğit, and S. Marinov (2006). Labeled pseudo-projective dependency parsing with support vector machines. In *Proceedings of the 10th Conference on Computational Natural Language Learning*, New York, NY, pp. 221–225.

Nivre, J. and J. Nilsson (2005). Pseudo-projective dependency. In *Proceedings of the 43rd Annual Meeting of the Association for Computational Linguistics*, Ann Arbor, MI, pp. 99–106.

Oflazer, K., B. Say, D. Z. Hakkani-Tür, and G. Tür (2003). Building a Turkish Treebank. See Abeillé (2003), Chapter 15, pp. 261–277.

Prokopidis, P., E. Desypri, M. Koutsombogera, H. Papageorgiou, and S. Piperidis (2005). Theoretical and practical issues in the construction of a Greek dependency treebank. In *Proceedings of the 4th Workshop on Treebanks and Linguistic Theories*, Barcelona, Spain, pp. 149–160.

Ratnaparkhi, A. (1997). A linear observed time statistical parser based on maximum entropy models. In *Proceedings of the 2nd Conference on Empirical Methods in Natural Language Processing*, Providence, RI, pp. 1–10.

Sagae, K. and A. Lavie (2006). Parser combination by reparsing. In *Proceedings of the Human Language Technology Conference and the Annual Meeting of the North American Chapter of the Association for Computational Linguistics, Companion Volume: Short Papers*, New York, NY, pp. 129–132.

Yamada, H. and Y. Matsumoto (2003). Statistical dependency analysis with support vector machines. In *Proceedings of the 8th International Workshop on Parsing Technologies*, Nancy, France, pp. 195–206.

Zeman, D. and Z. Žabokrtský (2005). Improving parsing accuracy by combining diverse dependency parsers. In *Proceedings of the 9th International Workshop on Parsing Technologies*, Vancouver, Canada, pp. 171–178.

Chapter 3
A Latent Variable Model for Generative Dependency Parsing

Ivan Titov and James Henderson

3.1 Introduction

Dependency parsing has been a topic of active research in natural language processing during the last several years. The CoNLL-2006 shared task (Buchholz and Marsi, 2006) made a wide selection of standardized treebanks for different languages available for the research community and allowed for easy comparison between various statistical methods on a standardized benchmark. One of the surprising things discovered by this evaluation is that the best results are achieved by methods which are quite different from state-of-the-art models for constituent parsing, e.g. the deterministic parsing method of Nivre et al. (2006) and the minimum spanning tree parser of McDonald et al. (2006). All the most accurate dependency parsing models are fully discriminative, unlike constituent parsing where all the state-of-the-art methods have a generative component (Charniak and Johnson, 2005; Henderson, 2004; Collins, 2000). Another surprising thing is the lack of latent variable models among the methods used in the shared task. Latent variable models would allow complex features to be induced automatically, which would be highly desirable in multilingual parsing, where manual feature selection might be very difficult and time consuming, especially for languages unknown to the parser developer.

In this chapter we propose a generative latent variable model for dependency parsing. It is based on Incremental Sigmoid Belief Networks (ISBNs), a class of directed graphical models for structured prediction problems recently proposed in Titov and Henderson (2007), where they were demonstrated to achieve competitive results on the constituent parsing task. As discussed in Titov and Henderson (2007), computing the conditional probabilities which we need for parsing is in general intractable with ISBNs, but they can be approximated efficiently in several ways. In particular, the neural network constituent parsers in Henderson (2003) and Henderson (2004) can be regarded as coarse approximations to their corresponding ISBN model.

I. Titov (✉)
Cluster of Excellence, MMC, Saarland University, Saarbrücken, Germany
e-mail: titov@mmci.uni-saarland.de

H. Bunt et al. (eds.), *Trends in Parsing Technology*, Text, Speech and Language Technology 43, DOI 10.1007/978-90-481-9352-3_3,

ISBNs use history-based probability models. The most common approach to handling the unbounded nature of the parse histories in these models is to choose a pre-defined set of features which can be unambiguously derived from the history (e.g. Charniak, 2000; Collins, 1999; Nivre et al., 2004). Decision probabilities are then assumed to be independent of all information not represented by this finite set of features. ISBNs instead use a vector of binary latent variables to encode the information about the parser history. This history vector is similar to the hidden state of a Hidden Markov Model. But unlike the graphical model for an HMM, which specifies conditional dependency edges only between adjacent states in the sequence, the ISBN graphical model can specify conditional dependency edges between states which are arbitrarily far apart in the parse history. The source state of such an edge is determined by the partial output structure built at the time of the destination state, thereby allowing the conditional dependency edges to be appropriate for the structural nature of the problem being modeled. This structure sensitivity is possible because ISBNs are a constrained form of switching model (Murphy, 2002), where each output decision switches the model structure used for the remaining decisions.

We build an ISBN model of dependency parsing using the parsing order proposed in Nivre et al. (2004). However, instead of performing deterministic parsing as in Nivre et al. (2004), we use this ordering to define a generative history-based model, by integrating word prediction operations into the set of parser actions. Then we propose a simple, language independent set of relations which determine how latent variable vectors are interconnected by conditional dependency edges in the ISBN model. ISBNs also condition the latent variable vectors on a set of explicit features, which we vary in the experiments.

In experiments we evaluate both the performance of the ISBN dependency parser compared to related work, and the ability of the ISBN model to induce complex history features. Our model achieves state-of-the-art performance on the languages we test from the CoNLL-2006 shared task, significantly outperforming the model of Nivre et al. (2006) on two languages out of three and demonstrating about the same results on the third. In order to test the model's feature induction abilities, we train models with two different sets of explicit conditioning features: the feature set individually tuned by Nivre et al. (2006) for each considered language, and a minimal set of local features. These models achieve comparable accuracy, unlike with the discriminative SVM-based approach of Nivre et al. (2006), where careful feature selection appears to be crucial. We also conduct a controlled experiment where we used the tuned features of Nivre et al. (2006) but disable the feature induction abilities of our model by elimination of the edges connecting latent state vectors. This restricted model achieves far worse results, showing that it is exactly the capacity of ISBNs to induce history features which is the key to its success. It also motivates further research into how feature induction techniques can be exploited in discriminative parsing methods.

We analyze how the relation accuracy changes with the length of the head-dependent relation, demonstrating that our model very significantly outperforms the state-of-the-art baseline of Nivre et al. (2006) on long dependencies. Additional experiments suggest that both feature induction abilities and use of the beam search contribute to this improvement.

We participated with this parser in the CoNLL-2007 shared task on dependency parsing. The model achieved the third overall results, which were only 0.4% worse than results of the best participating system. It is also important to note, that it achieved the best result among single model parsers: the parsers which achieved better results (Hall et al., 2007; Nakagawa, 2007) used combinations of models. We also study parser efficiency on the datasets from the CoNLL-2007 shared task.

The fact that our model defines a probability model over parse trees, unlike the previous state-of-the-art methods (Nivre et al., 2006; McDonald et al., 2006), makes it easier to use this model in applications which require probability estimates, e.g. in language processing pipelines. Also, as with any generative model, it may be easy to improve the parser's accuracy by using discriminative retraining techniques (Henderson, 2004) or data-defined kernels (Henderson and Titov, 2005), with or even without introduction of any additional linguistic features. In addition, there are some applications, such as language modeling, which require generative models. Another advantage of generative models is that they do not suffer from the label bias problems (Bottou, 1991), which is a potential problem for conditional or deterministic history-based models, such as Nivre et al. (2004).

In the remainder of this chapter, we will first review general ISBNs and how they can be approximated. Then we will define the generative parsing model, based on the algorithm of Nivre et al. (2004), and propose an ISBN for this model. The empirical part of the chapter then evaluates both the overall accuracy of this method and the importance of the model's capacity to induce features. Additional related work will be discussed in the last section before concluding.

3.2 The Latent Variable Architecture

In this section we will begin by briefly introducing the class of graphical models we will be using, Incremental Sigmoid Belief Networks (Titov and Henderson, 2007). ISBNs are designed specifically for modeling structured data. They are latent variable models which are not tractable to compute exactly, but two approximations exist which have been shown to be effective for constituent parsing (Titov and Henderson, 2007). Finally, we present how these approximations can be trained.

3.2.1 Incremental Sigmoid Belief Networks

An ISBN is a form of Sigmoid Belief Network (SBN) (Neal, 1992). SBNs are Bayesian Networks with binary variables and conditional probability distributions in the form:

$$P(S_i = 1|Par(S_i)) = \sigma\left(\sum_{S_j \in Par(S_i)} J_{ij} S_j\right),$$

where S_i are the variables, $Par(S_i)$ are the variables which S_i depends on (its parents), σ denotes the logistic sigmoid function, and J_{ij} is the weight for the edge from variable S_j to variable S_i in the graphical model. SBNs are similar to feed-forward neural networks, but unlike neural networks, SBNs have a precise probabilistic semantics for their hidden variables. ISBNs are based on a generalized version of SBNs where variables with any range of discrete values are allowed. The normalized exponential function ("soft-max") is used to define the conditional probability distributions at these nodes.

To extend SBNs for processing arbitrarily long sequences, such as a parser's sequence of decisions $D^1, \ldots, D^m$, SBNs are extended to a form of Dynamic Bayesian Network (DBN). In DBNs, a new set of variables is instantiated for each position in the sequence, but the edges and weights are the same for each position in the sequence. The edges which connect variables instantiated for different positions must be directed forward in the sequence, thereby allowing a temporal interpretation of the sequence.

Incremental Sigmoid Belief Networks (Titov and Henderson, 2007) differ from simple dynamic SBNs in that they allow the model structure to depend on the output variable values. Specifically, a decision is allowed to affect the placement of any edge whose destination is after the decision. This results in a form of switching model (Murphy, 2002), where each decision switches the model structure used for the remaining decisions. The incoming edges for a given position are a discrete function of the sequence of decisions which precede that position. This makes the ISBN an "incremental" model, not just a dynamic model. The structure of the model is determined incrementally as the decision sequence proceeds.

ISBNs are designed to allow the model structure to depend on the output values without overly complicating the inference of the desired conditional probabilities $P(D^t|D^1, \ldots, D^{t-1})$, the probability of the next decision given the history of previous decisions. In particular, it is never necessary to sum over all possible model structures, which in general would make inference intractable.

3.2.2 Modeling Structures with ISBNs

ISBNs are designed for modeling structured data where the output structure is not given as part of the input. In dependency parsing, this means they can model the probability of an output dependency structure when the input only specifies the sequence of words (i.e. parsing). The difficulty with such problems is that the statistical dependencies in the dependency structure are local in the structure, and not necessarily local in the word sequence. ISBNs allow us to capture these statistical dependencies in the model structure by having model edges depend on the output variables which specify the dependency structure. For example, if an output specifies that there is a dependency arc from word w_i to word w_j, then any future decision involving w_j can directly depend on its head w_i. This allows the head w_i to be treated as local to the dependent w_j even if they are far apart in the sentence.

This structurally defined notion of locality is particularly important for the model's latent variables. When the structurally-defined model edges connect latent variables, information can be propagated between latent variables, thereby providing an even larger structural domain of locality than that provided by single edges. This provides a potentially powerful form of feature induction, which is nonetheless biased toward a notion of locality which is appropriate for the structure of the problem, as discussed further in Section 3.4.

3.2.3 Approximating ISBNs

In Titov and Henderson (2007) we proposed two approximations for inference in ISBNs, both based on variational methods. The main idea of variational methods (Jordan et al., 1999) is, roughly, to construct a tractable approximate model with a number of free parameters. The values of the free parameters are set so that the resulting approximate model is as close as possible to the original graphical model for a given inference problem.

The simplest example of a variational method is the mean field method, which uses a fully factorized distribution $Q(H|V) = \prod_i Q_i(h_i|V)$ as the approximate model, where V are the visible (i.e. known) variables, $H = h_1, \ldots, h_l$ are the hidden (i.e. latent) variables, and each Q_i is the distribution of an individual latent variable h_i. The free parameters of this approximate model are the means μ_i of the distributions Q_i.

We proposed two approximate models based on the variational approach in Titov and Henderson (2007). First, we showed that the neural network of Henderson (2003) can be viewed as a coarse mean field approximation of ISBNs, which we call the feed-forward approximation. This approximation imposes the constraint that the free parameters μ_i of the approximate model are only allowed to depend on the distributions of their parent variables. This constraint increases the potential for a large approximation error, but it significantly simplifies the computations by allowing all the free parameters to be set in a single pass over the model.

The second approximation proposed in Titov and Henderson (2007) takes into consideration the fact that, after each decision is made, all the preceding latent variables should have their means μ_i updated. This approximation extends the feed-forward approximation to account for the most important components of this update. We call this approximation the mean field approximation, because a mean field approximation is applied to handle the statistical dependencies introduced by the new decisions. This approximation was shown to be a more accurate approximation of ISBNs than the feed-forward approximation, but to remain tractable. It was also shown to achieve significantly better accuracy on constituent parsing.

3.2.4 Learning

Training these approximations of ISBNs is done to maximize the fit of the *approximate* models to the data. We use gradient descent, and a regularized maximum likelihood objective function. Gaussian regularization is applied, which is equivalent to the weight decay standardly used in neural networks. Regularization was reduced through the course of learning.

Gradient descent requires computing the derivatives of the objective function with respect to the model parameters. In the feed-forward approximation, this can be done with the standard Backpropagation learning used with neural networks. For the mean field approximation, propagating the error all the way back through the structure of the graphical model requires a more complicated calculation, but it can still be done efficiently (see Titov and Henderson, 2007, for details).

3.3 The Dependency Parsing Algorithm

The sequences of decisions $D^1, \ldots, D^m$ which we will be modeling with ISBNs are the sequences of decisions made by a dependency parser. For this we use the parsing strategy for projective dependency parsing introduced in Nivre et al. (2004), which is similar to a standard shift-reduce algorithm for context-free grammars (Aho et al., 1986). It can be viewed as a mixture of bottom-up and top-down parsing strategies, where left dependencies are constructed in a bottom-up fashion and right dependencies are constructed top-down. For details we refer the reader to Nivre et al. (2004). In this section we briefly describe the algorithm and explain how we use it to define our history-based probability model.

In this chapter, as in the CoNLL-2006 and CoNLL-2007 shared tasks, we consider labeled dependency parsing. The state of the parser is defined by the current stack S, the queue I of remaining input words and the partial labeled dependency structure constructed by previous parser decisions. The parser starts with an empty stack S and terminates when it reaches a configuration with an empty queue I. The algorithm uses 4 types of decisions:

1. The decision *Left-Arc*$_r$ adds a dependency arc from the next input word w_j to the word w_i on top of the stack and selects the label r for the relation between w_i and w_j. Word w_i is then popped from the stack.
2. The decision *Right-Arc*$_r$ adds an arc from the word w_i on top of the stack to the next input word w_j and selects the label r for the relation between w_i and w_j.
3. The decision *Reduce* pops the word w_i from the stack.
4. The decision *Shift*$_{w_j}$ shifts the word w_j from the queue to the stack.

Unlike the original definition in Nivre et al. (2004) the *Right-Arc*$_r$ decision does not shift w_j to the stack. However, the only thing the parser can do after a *Right-Arc*$_r$ decision is to choose the *Shift*$_{w_j}$ decision. This subtle modification does not change the actual parsing order, but it does simplify the definition of our graphical model, as explained in Section 3.4.

We use a history-based probability model, which decomposes the probability of the parse according to the parser decisions:

$$P(T) = P(D^1, \ldots, D^m) = \prod_t P(D^t | D^1, \ldots, D^{t-1}),$$

where T is the parse tree and $D^1, \ldots, D^m$ is its equivalent sequence of parser decisions. Since we need a generative model, the action $Shift_{w_j}$ also predicts the next word in the queue I, w_{j+1}, thus the $P(Shift_{w_j}|D^1, \ldots, D^{t-1})$ is a probability both of the shift operation and the word w_{j+1} conditioned on current parsing history.[1]

Instead of treating each D^t as an atomic decision, it is convenient to split it into a sequence of elementary decisions $D^t = d_1^t, \ldots, d_n^t$:

$$P(D^t|D^1, \ldots, D^{t-1}) = \prod_k P(d_k^t|h(t,k)),$$

where $h(t,k)$ denotes the parsing history $D^1, \ldots, D^{t-1}, d_1^t, \ldots, d_{k-1}^t$. We split *Left-Arc*$_r$ and *Right-Arc*$_r$ each into two elementary decisions: first, the parser decides to create the corresponding arc, then, it decides to assign a relation r to the arc. Similarly, we decompose the decision $Shift_{w_j}$ into an elementary decision to shift a word and a prediction of the word w_{j+1}. In our experiments we use datasets from the CoNLL-2006 and CoNLL-2007 shared tasks, which provide additional properties for each word token, such as its part-of-speech tag and some fine-grain features. This information implicitly induces word clustering, which we use in our model: first we predict a part-of-speech tag for the word, then a set of word features, treating feature combination as an atomic value, and only then a particular word form. This approach allows us to both decrease the effect of sparsity and to avoid normalization across all the words in the vocabulary, significantly reducing the computational expense of word prediction.

To overcome a minor shortcoming of the parsing algorithm of Nivre et al. (2004) we introduce a simple language independent post-processing step. Nivre's parsing algorithm allows unattached nodes to stay on the stack at the end of parsing, which is reasonable for treebanks with unlabeled attachment to root. However, this sometimes happens with languages where only labeled attachment to root is allowed. In these cases (only 35 tokens in Greek, 17 in Czech, 1 in Arabic, on the final testing set of the CoNLL-2007 shared task) we attached them using a simple rule: if there are no tokens in the sentence attached to root, then the considered token is attached to root with the most frequent root-attachment relation used for its part-of-speech tag. If there are other root-attached tokens in the sentence, it is attached to the next root-attached token with the most frequent relation. Preference is given to the most frequent attachment direction for its part-of-speech tag. This rule guarantees that no loops are introduced by the post-processing.

---

[1] In preliminary experiments, we also considered look-ahead, where the word is predicted earlier than it appears at the head of the queue I, and "anti-look-ahead", where the word is predicted only when it is shifted to the stack S. Early prediction allows conditioning decision probabilities on the words in the look-ahead and, thus, speeds up the search for an optimal decision sequence. However, the loss of accuracy with look-ahead was quite significant. The described method, where a new word is predicted when it appears at the head of the queue, led to the most accurate model and quite efficient search. The anti-look-ahead model was both less accurate and slower.

3.4 An ISBN for Dependency Parsing

In this section we define the ISBN model we use for dependency parsing. An example of this ISBN for estimating $P(d_k^t|h(t,k))$ is illustrated in Fig. 3.1. It is organized into vectors of variables: latent state variable vectors $S^{t'} = s_1^{t'}, \ldots, s_n^{t'}$, representing an intermediate state at position t', and decision variable vectors $D^{t'}$, representing a decision at position t', where $t' \leq t$. Variables whose value are given at the current decision (t,k) are shaded in Fig. 3.1, latent and current decision variables are left unshaded.

As illustrated by the edges in Fig. 3.1, the probability of each state variable $s_i^{t'}$ (the individual circles in $S^{t'}$) depends on all the variables in a finite set of relevant previous state and decision vectors, but there are no direct dependencies between the different variables in a single state vector. We will first discuss the state-to-state statistical dependencies, then the decision-to-state statistical dependencies, and finally the statistical dependencies to decision variables.

The most important design decision in building an ISBN model is choosing the finite set of relevant previous state vectors for the current decision. By connecting to a previous state, we place that state in the local context of the current decision. This specification of the domain of locality determines the inductive bias of learning with ISBNs. When deciding what information to store in its latent variables, an ISBN is more likely to choose information which is immediately local to the current decision. This stored information then becomes local to any following connected decision, where it again has some chance of being chosen as relevant to that decision. In this way, the information available to a given decision can come from arbitrarily far away in the chain of interconnected states, but it is much more likely to come from a state which is relatively local. Thus, we need to choose the set of local (i.e. connected) states in accordance with our prior knowledge about which previous decisions are likely to be particularly relevant to the current decision.

To choose which previous decisions are particularly relevant to the current decision, we make use of the partial dependency structure which has been decided so far in the parse. Specifically, the current latent state vector is connected to a set of 7 previous latent state vectors (if they exist) according to the following relationships:

1. *Input Context*: the last previous state with the same queue I.
2. *Stack Context*: the last previous state with the same stack S.

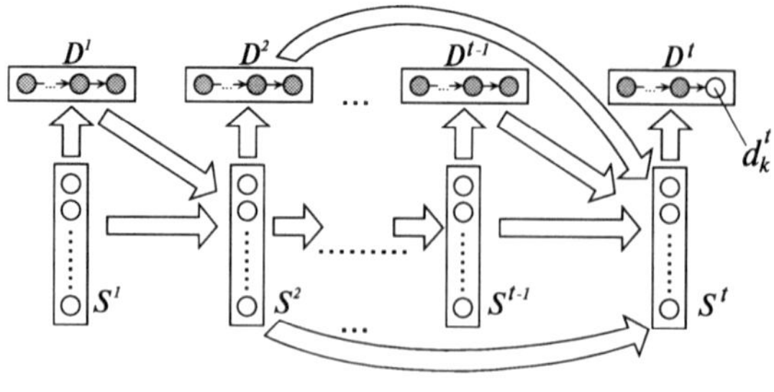

Fig. 3.1 An ISBN for estimating $P(d_k^t|h(t,k))$

3. *Right Child of Top of S*: the last previous state where the rightmost right child of the current stack top was on top of the stack.
4. *Left Child of Top of S*: the last previous state where the leftmost left child of the current stack top was on top of the stack.
5. *Left Child of Front of I*[2]: the last previous state where the leftmost child of the front element of I was on top of the stack.
6. *Head of Top*: the last previous state where the head word of the current stack top was on top of the stack.
7. *Top of S at Front of I*: the last previous state where the current stack top was at the front of the queue.

Each of these 7 relations has its own distinct weight matrix for the resulting edges in the ISBN, but the same weight matrix is used at each position where the relation is relevant.

All these relations but the last one are motivated by linguistic considerations. The current decision is primarily about what to do with the current word on the top of the stack and the current word on the front of the queue. The *Input Context* and *Stack Context* relationships connect to the most recent states used for making decisions about each of these words. The *Right Child of Top of S* relationship connects to a state used for making decisions about the most recently attached dependent of the stack top. Similarly, the *Left Child of Front of I* relationship connects to a state for the most recently attached dependent of the queue front. The *Left Child of Top of S* is the leftmost dependent of the stack top, which is a particularly informative dependent for many languages. Likewise, the *Head of Top* can tell us a lot about the stack top, if it has been chosen already.

A second motivation for including a state in the local context of a decision is that it might contain information which has no other route for reaching the current decision. In particular, it is generally a good idea to ensure that the immediately preceding state is always included somewhere in the set of connected states. This requirement ensures that information, at least theoretically, can pass between any two states in the decision sequence, thereby avoiding any hard independence assumptions. The last relation, *Top of S at Front of I*, is included mainly to fulfill this requirement. Otherwise, after a $Shift_{w_j}$ operation, the preceding state would not be selected by any of the relationships.

Each latent variable in the ISBN parser is also conditionally dependent on a set of explicit features of the parsing history, which are depicted in Fig. 3.1 as connections from decision vectors to state vectors. The precise set of explicit features can be adapted to a particular language. However, as long as these explicit features include all the new information from the last parser decision, the performance of the model is not very sensitive to this design choice. This is because the state-to-state connections give ISBNs the ability to induce their own complex features of the parse history, as discussed above. For the CoNLL-2006 experiments, we tried different

[2] We refer to the *head* of the queue as the *front*, to avoid unnecessary ambiguity of the word *head* in the context of dependency parsing.

feature sets to validate this hypothesis that the feature set is not very important. For most of the languages in the CoNLL-2007 experiments we used the set proposed in Nivre et al. (2006). However, we had to remove from this set all the lookahead features to obtain a valid generative history-based model.

As indicated in Fig. 3.1, the probability of each elementary decision $d_k^{t'}$ depends both on the current state vector $S^{t'}$ and on the previously chosen elementary action $d_{k-1}^{t'}$ from $D^{t'}$. This probability distribution has the form of a normalized exponential:

$$P(d_k^{t'} = d | S^{t'}, d_{k-1}^{t'}) = \frac{\Phi_{h(t',k)}(d)\, e^{\sum_j W_{dj} s_j^{t'}}}{\sum_{d'} \Phi_{h(t',k)}(d')\, e^{\sum_j W_{d'j} s_j^{t'}}},$$

where $\Phi_{h(t',k)}$ is the indicator function of the set of elementary decisions that may possibly follow the last decision in the history $h(t', k)$, and the W_{dj} are the weights. Now it is easy to see why the original decision *Right-Arc*$_r$ (Nivre et al., 2004) had to be decomposed into two distinct decisions: the decision to construct a labeled arc and the decision to shift the word. Use of this composite *Right-Arc*$_r$ would have required the introduction of individual parameters for each pair (w, r), where w is an arbitrary word in the lexicon and r an arbitrary dependency relation.

3.5 Searching for the Best Tree

ISBNs define a probability model which does not make any a-priori assumptions of independence between any decision variables. As we discussed in Section 3.4, the use of relations based on partial output structure makes it possible to take into account statistical interdependencies between decisions closely related in the output structure, but separated by multiple decisions in the input structure. This property leads to exponential complexity for complete search. However, the success of the deterministic parsing strategy using the same parsing order (Nivre et al., 2006), suggests that it should be relatively easy to find an accurate approximation to the best parse with heuristic search methods. Unlike Nivre et al. (2006), we can not use a lookahead in our generative model, as was discussed in Section 3.3, so a greedy method is unlikely to lead to a good approximation. Instead we use a pruning strategy similar to that described in Henderson (2003), where it was applied to a considerably harder search problem: constituent parsing with a left-corner parsing order.

We apply fixed beam pruning after each decision *Shift*$_{w_j}$, because knowledge of the next word in the queue I helps distinguish unlikely decision sequences. We could have used best-first search between *Shift*$_{w_j}$ operations, but this still leads to relatively expensive computations, especially when the set of dependency relations is large. However, most of the word pairs can possibly participate only in a very limited number of distinct relations. Thus, we pursue only a fixed number of relations r after each *Left-Arc*$_r$ and *Right-Arc*$_r$ operation.

Experiments with a variety of post-shift beam widths confirmed that very small validation performance gains are achieved with widths larger than 30, and sometimes even a beam of 5 was sufficient. We found also that allowing 5 different relations after each dependency prediction operation was enough to ensure that it had virtually no effect on the validation accuracy. For some experiments for the CoNLL-2007 shared task we used a larger beam, but as we will discuss in the empirical section, again, gains were not large.

3.6 Empirical Evaluation

In this section we evaluate the ISBN model for dependency parsing on three of the treebanks from the CoNLL-2006 shared task, and on all ten of the languages from the CoNLL-2007 shared task. Most of this section focuses on the experiments using the CoNLL-2006 data, but we also report our performance relative to the other systems which participated in the CoNLL-2007 shared task, and we analyze the efficiency of the model on this data.

We compare our generative models with the best parsers from the CoNLL-2006 task, including the SVM-based parser of Nivre et al. (2006) (the MALT parser), which uses the same parsing algorithm. To test the feature induction abilities of our model we compare results with two feature sets, the feature set tuned individually for each language by Nivre et al. (2006), and another feature set which includes only obvious local features. This simple feature set comprises only features of the word on top of the stack S and the front word of the queue I. We compare the gain from using tuned features with the similar gain obtained by the MALT parser. To obtain these results we train the MALT parser with the same two feature sets.[3]

In order to distinguish the contribution of ISBN's feature induction abilities from the contribution of our estimation method and search, we perform another experiment. We use the tuned feature set and disable the feature induction abilities of the model by removing all the edges between latent variables vectors. Comparison of this restricted model with the full ISBN model shows how important the feature induction is. Also, comparison of this restricted model with the MALT parser, which uses the same set of features, indicates whether our generative estimation method and use of beam search is beneficial.

3.6.1 Experimental Setup for the CoNLL-2006 Data

For the CoNLL-2006 experiments, we used the CoNLL-2006 distributions of Danish DDT treebank (Kromann, 2003), Dutch Alpino treebank (van der Beek et al., 2002) and Slovene SDT treebank (Dzeroski et al., 2006). The choice of these treebanks was motivated by the fact that they all are freely distributed and have very

---

[3] The tuned feature sets were obtained from http://w3.msi.vxu.se/~nivre/research/MaltParser.html. We removed lookahead features for ISBN experiments but preserved them for experiments with the MALT parser. Analogously, we extended simple features with 3 words lookahead for the MALT parser experiments.

different sizes of their training sets: 195,069 tokens for Dutch, 94,386 tokens for Danish and only 28,750 tokens for Slovene. It is generally believed that discriminative models win over generative models with a large amount of training data, so we expected to see a similar trend in our results. Test sets are about equal and contain about 5,000 scoring tokens.

We followed the experimental setup of the shared task and used all the information provided for the languages: gold standard part-of-speech tags and coarse part-of-speech tags, word form, word lemma (lemma information was not available for Danish) and a set of fine-grain word features. As we explained in Section 3.3, we treated these sets of fine-grain features as an atomic value when predicting a word. However, when conditioning on words, we treated each component of this composite feature individually, as it proved to be useful on the development set. We used frequency cutoffs: we ignored any property (e.g., word form, feature or even part-of-speech tag[4]) which occurs in the training set less than 5 times. Following Nivre et al. (2006), we used the pseudo-projective transformation they proposed to cast non-projective parsing tasks as projective.

ISBN models were trained using a small development set taken out from the training set, which was used for tuning learning parameters and for early stopping. The sizes of the development sets were: 4,988 tokens for the larger Dutch corpus, 2,504 tokens for Danish and 2,033 tokens for Slovene. The MALT parser was trained always using the entire training set. We expect that the mean field approximation should demonstrate better results than feed-forward approximation on this task as it is theoretically expected and confirmed on the constituent parsing task (Titov and Henderson, 2007). However, the sizes of testing sets would not allow us to perform any conclusive analysis, so we decided not to perform these comparisons here. Instead we used the mean field approximation for the smaller two corpora and used the feed-forward approximation for the larger one. Training the mean field approximations on the larger Dutch treebank is feasible, but would significantly reduce the possibilities for tuning the learning parameters on the development set and, thus, would increase the randomness of model comparisons.

All model selection was performed on the development set and a single model of each type was applied to the testing set. We used a state variable vector consisting of 80 binary variables, as it proved sufficient on the preliminary experiments. For the MALT parser we replicated the parameters from Nivre et al. (2006) as described in detail on their web site.

The labeled attachment scores for the ISBN with tuned features (TF) and local features (LF) and ISBN with tuned features and no edges connecting latent variable vectors (TF-NA) are presented in Table 3.1, along with results for the MALT parser both with tuned and local features, the MST parser (McDonald et al., 2006), and the average score across all systems in the CoNLL-2006 shared task. The MST parser is included because it demonstrated the best overall result in the task,

[4] Part-of-speech tags for multi-word units in the Dutch treebank were formed as concatenation of tags of the words, which led to quite a sparse set of part-of-speech tags.

Table 3.1 Labeled attachment score on the CoNLL-2006 testing sets of Danish, Dutch and Slovene treebanks

		Danish	Dutch	Slovene
ISBN	TF	85.0	79.6	72.9
	LF	84.5	79.5	72.4
	TF-NA	83.5	76.4	71.7
MALT	TF	85.1	78.2	70.5
	LF	79.8	74.5	66.8
MST		84.8	79.2	73.4
Average score		78.3	70.7	65.2

non-significantly outperforming the MALT parser, which, in turn, achieved the second best overall result. The labeled attachment score is computed using the same method as in the CoNLL-2006 shared task, i.e. ignoring punctuation. Note, that though we tried to completely replicate training of the MALT parser with the tuned features, we obtained slightly different results. The original published results for the MALT parser with tuned features were 84.8% for Danish, 78.6% for Dutch and 70.3% for Slovene. The improvement of the ISBN models (TF and LF) over the MALT parser is statistically significant for Dutch and Slovene. Differences between their results on Danish are not statistically significant.

3.6.2 Discussion of Results on the CoNLL-2006 Data

The ISBN with tuned features (TF) achieved significantly better accuracy than the MALT parser on 2 languages (Dutch and Slovene), and demonstrated essentially the same accuracy on Danish. The results of the ISBN are among the two top published results on all three languages, including the best published results on Dutch. All three models, MST, MALT and ISBN, demonstrate much better results than the average result in the CoNLL-2006 shared task. These results suggest that our generative model is quite competitive with respect to the best models, which are both discriminative.[5] We would expect further improvement of ISBN results if we applied discriminative retraining (Henderson, 2004) or reranking with data-defined kernels (Henderson and Titov, 2005), even without introduction of any additional features.

We can see that the ISBN parser achieves about the same results with local features (LF). Local features by themselves are definitely not sufficient for the construction of accurate models, as seen from the results of the MALT parser with local features (and look-ahead). This result demonstrates that ISBNs are a powerful model for feature induction.

[5] Note that the development set accuracy predicted correctly the testing set ranking of ISBN TF, LF and TF-NA models on each of the datasets, so it is fair to compare the best ISBN result among the three with other parsers.

The results of the ISBN without edges connecting latent state vectors is slightly surprising and suggest that without feature induction the ISBN is significantly worse than the best models. This shows that the improvement is coming mostly from the ability of the ISBN to induce complex features and not from either using beam search or from the estimation procedure. It might also suggest that generative models are probably worse for the dependency parsing task than discriminative approaches (at least for larger datasets). This motivates further research into methods which combine powerful feature induction properties with the advantage of discriminative training. Although discriminative reranking of the generative model is likely to help, the derivation of fully discriminative feature induction methods is certainly more challenging.

In order to better understand differences in performance between ISBN and MALT, we analyzed how relation accuracy changes with the length of the head-dependent relation. The harmonic mean between precision and recall of labeled attachment, F_1 measure, for the ISBN and MALT parsers with tuned features is presented in Table 3.2. F_1 score is computed for four different ranges of lengths and for attachments directly to root. Along with the results for each of the languages, the table includes their mean (Average) and the absolute improvement of the ISBN model over MALT (Improvement). It is easy to see that accuracy of both models is generally similar for small distances (1 and 2), but as the distance grows the ISBN parser starts to significantly outperform MALT, achieving 5.7% average improvement on dependencies longer than 6 word tokens. When the MALT parser does not manage to recover a long dependency, the highest scoring action it can choose is to reduce the dependent from the stack without specifying its head, thereby attaching the dependent to the root by default. This explains the relatively low F_1 scores for attachments to root (evident for Dutch and Slovene): though recall of attachment to root is comparable to that of the ISBN parser (82.4% for MALT against 84.2% for ISBN, on average over 3 languages), precision for the MALT parser is much worse (71.5% for MALT against 83.1% for ISBN, on average).

The considerably worse accuracy of the MALT parser on longer dependencies might be explained both by the use of a non-greedy search method in the ISBN and the ability of ISBNs to induce history features. To capture a long dependency, the

Table 3.2 F_1 score of labeled attachment as a function of dependency length on the CoNLL-2006 testing sets of Danish, Dutch and Slovene

		To root	1	2	3–6	> 6
Danish	ISBN	95.1	95.7	90.1	84.1	74.7
	MALT	95.4	96.0	90.8	84.0	71.6
Dutch	ISBN	79.8	92.4	86.2	81.4	71.1
	MALT	73.1	91.9	85.0	76.2	64.3
Slovene	ISBN	76.1	92.5	85.6	79.6	54.3
	MALT	59.9	92.1	85.0	78.4	47.1
Average	ISBN	83.6	93.5	87.3	81.7	66.7
	MALT	76.2	93.3	87.0	79.5	61.0
	Improvement	**7.5**	**0.2**	**0.4**	**2.2**	**5.7**

MALT parser should keep a word on the stack during a long sequence of decisions. If at any point during the intermediate steps this choice seems not to be locally optimal, then the MALT parser will choose the alternative and lose the possibility of the long dependency.[6] By using a beam search, the ISBN parser can maintain the possibility of the long dependency in its beam even when other alternatives seem locally preferable. Also, long dependencies are often more difficult, and may be systematically different from local dependencies. The designer of a MALT parser needs to discover predictive features for long dependencies by hand, whereas the ISBN model can automatically discover them. Thus we expect that the feature induction abilities of ISBNs have a strong effect on the accuracy of long dependencies. This prediction is confirmed by the differences between the results of the normal ISBN (TF) and the restricted ISBN (TF-NA) model. The TF-NA model, like the MALT parser, is biased toward attachment to root; it attaches to root 12.0% more words on average than the normal ISBN, without any improvement of recall and with a great loss of precision. The F_1 score on long dependencies for the TF-NA model is also negatively effected in the same way as for the MALT parser. This confirms that the ability of the ISBN model to induce features is a major factor in improving accuracy of long dependencies.

3.6.3 The CoNLL-2007 Experiments

We also evaluated the ISBN parser on all ten languages considered in the CoNLL-2007 shared task (Hajič et al., 2004; Aduriz et al., 2003; Martí et al., 2007; Chen et al., 2003; Böhmová et al., 2003; Marcus et al., 1993; Johansson and Nugues, 2007; Prokopidis et al., 2005; Csendes et al., 2005; Montemagni et al., 2003; Oflazer et al., 2003). For these experiments we used only the simplest feed-forward approximation of an ISBN. We would expect better performance with the more accurate approximation based on variational inference proposed and evaluated in Titov and Henderson (2007). We did not try this because, on larger treebanks it would have taken too long to tune the model with this better approximation, and using different approximation methods for different languages would not be compatible with the shared task rules.

ISBN models were trained using a small development set taken out from the training set, which was used for tuning learning and decoding parameters, for early stopping and very coarse feature engineering. The sizes of the development sets were different: starting from less than 2,000 tokens for smaller treebanks to 5,000 tokens for the largest one. The relatively small sizes of the development sets limited our ability to perform careful feature selection, but this should not have significantly affected the model performance, as suggested by the small difference in

[6] The MALT parser is trained to keep the word as long as possible: if both *Shift* and *Reduce* decisions are possible during training, it always prefers to shift. Though this strategy should generally reduce the described problem, it is evident from the low precision score for attachment to root that it can not completely eliminate it.

scores between the model with tuned features (TF) and the model with local features (LF) obtained in the previous set of experiments.[7] We used the base feature model defined in Nivre et al. (2006) for all the languages but Arabic, Chinese, Czech, and Turkish. For Arabic, Chinese, and Czech, we used the same feature models used in the CoNLL-2006 shared task by Nivre et al. (2006), and for Turkish we used again the base feature model but extended it with a single feature: the part-of-speech tag of the token preceding the current top of the stack. We used frequency cutoffs of 20 for Greek and Chinese and a cutoff of 5 for the rest. Because the threshold value affects the model efficiency, we selected the larger threshold when validation results with the smaller threshold were comparable.

Results on the final testing set are presented in Table 3.3. Unlike the 2006 shared task, in the CoNLL-2007 shared task punctuation tokens were included in evaluation. The model achieves relatively high scores on each individual language, significantly better than each average result in the shared task. This leads to the third best overall average results in the shared task, both in average labeled attachment score and in average unlabeled attachment score. The absolute error increase in labeled attachment score over the best system is only 0.4%. We attribute ISBN's success mainly to its ability to automatically induce features, as this significantly reduces the risk of omitting any important highly predictive features. This makes an ISBN parser a particularly good baseline when considering a new treebank or language, because it does not require much effort in feature engineering.

It is also important to note that the model is quite efficient. Figure 3.2 shows the tradeoff between accuracy and parsing time as the width of the search beam is varied, on the development set. This curve plots the average labeled attachment score over Basque, Chinese, English, and Turkish as a function of parsing time per token.[8] Accuracy of only 1% below the maximum can be achieved with average processing time of 17 ms per token, or 60 tokens per second.[9]

Table 3.3 Labeled attachment score (LAS) and unlabeled attachment score (UAS) on the final CoNLL-2007 testing sets

	Arabic	Basque	Catalan	Chinese	Czech	English	Greek	Hungarian	Italian	Turkish	Average
LAS	74.1	75.5	87.4	82.1	77.9	88.4	73.5	77.9	82.3	79.8	**79.90**
UAS	83.2	81.9	93.4	87.9	84.2	89.7	81.2	82.2	86.3	86.2	**85.62**

[7] Use of cross-validation with our model is relatively time-consuming and, thus, not quite feasible for the shared task.

[8] A piecewise-linear approximation for each individual language was used to compute the average. Experiments were run on a standard 2.4 GHz desktop PC.

[9] For Basque, Chinese, and Turkish this time is below 7 ms, but for English it is 38 ms. English, along with Catalan, required the largest beam across all ten languages. Note that accuracy in the lowest part of the curve can probably be improved by varying latent vector size and frequency cut-offs. Also, efficiency was not the main goal during the implementation of the parser, and it is likely that a much faster implementation is possible.

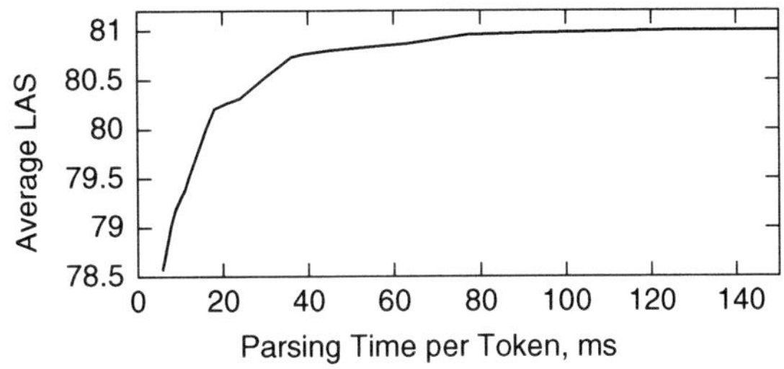

Fig. 3.2 Average labeled attachment score on Basque, Chinese, English, and Turkish CoNLL-2007 development sets as a function of parsing time per token

3.7 Related Work

There has not been much previous work on latent variable models for dependency parsing. Dependency parsing with Dynamic Bayesian Networks was considered in Peshkin and Savova (2005), with limited success. Roughly, the model considered the whole sentence at a time, with the DBN being used to decide which words correspond to leaves of the tree. The chosen words are then removed from the sentence and the model is recursively applied to the reduced sentence. Recently several latent variable models for constituent parsing have been proposed (Koo and Collins, 2005; Matsuzaki et al., 2005; Prescher, 2005; Riezler et al., 2002; Petrov et al., 2006; Liang et al., 2007; Petrov and Klein, 2007). In Matsuzaki et al. (2005), Prescher (2005), Petrov et al. (2006), Liang et al. (2007), and Petrov and Klein (2007), non-terminals in a standard PCFG model are augmented with latent variables. The best model from this class used the split-and-merge approach to discover the appropriate split of non-terminals (Petrov et al., 2006; Petrov and Klein, 2007) and demonstrated state-of-the-art results on constituent parsing. This approach was very recently extended to dependency parsing (Musillo and Merlo, 2008), where the authors proposed transforms of dependency grammars to CFG grammars annotated with latent variables. However, the resulting parser does not achieve state-of-the-art accuracy. In Koo and Collins (2005), an undirected graphical model for constituent parse reranking uses dependency relations to define the edges. Thus, it should be easy to apply a similar method to reranking dependency trees.

Undirected graphical models, in particular Conditional Random Fields, are the standard tools for shallow parsing (Sha and Pereira, 2003). However, shallow parsing is effectively a sequence labeling problem and therefore differs significantly from full parsing. As discussed in Titov and Henderson (2007), undirected graphical models do not seem to be suitable for history-based parsing models.

Sigmoid Belief Networks (SBNs) were used originally for character recognition tasks, but later a dynamic modification of this model was applied to the reinforcement learning task (Sallans, 2002). However, their graphical model, approximation method, and learning method differ significantly from those of this chapter. The extension of dynamic SBNs with incrementally specified model structure (i.e. Incremental Sigmoid Belief Networks, used in this chapter) was proposed and applied to constituent parsing in Titov and Henderson (2007).

Recent work has extended this ISBN model of dependency parsing to joint dependency parsing and semantic role labeling (Henderson et al., 2008). There, ISBNs are used to model synchronous derivations of syntactic and semantic structures. Semantic role label (SRL) structures are specified with a less constrained version of the derivations discussed here. The incremental nature of these derivations is exploited by synchronising the two derivations at each word. An ISBN is designed which induces features which capture statistical dependencies both within each derivation and between derivations. The ISBN is trained as a generative model of these synchronous derivations, thereby providing an estimate of the joint probability of the syntactic and semantic structures. The model achieves competitive results despite minimal feature engineering.

3.8 Conclusions

We proposed a latent variable dependency parsing model based on Incremental Sigmoid Belief Networks. Unlike state-of-the-art dependency parsers, it uses a generative history-based model. We demonstrated that it achieves state-of-the-art results on a selection of languages from the CoNLL-2006 shared task, and achieves competitive accuracy on all ten languages in the CoNLL-2007 shared task. This parser was ranked third best overall in the CoNLL-2007 shared task, and the best single-model system. It uses a vector of latent variables to represent an intermediate state and uses relations defined on the output structure to construct the edges between latent state vectors. These properties make it a powerful feature induction method for dependency parsing, and it achieves competitive results even with very simple explicit features.

The ISBN model is especially accurate at modeling long dependencies, achieving average improvement of 5.7% over the state-of-the-art baseline on dependencies longer than 6 words. Empirical evaluation demonstrates that competitive results are achieved mostly because of the ability of the model to induce complex features and not because of the use of a generative probability model or a specific search method. This automatic feature induction means that the proposed model requires minimal design effort, which is highly desirable when using new treebanks or languages. The parsing time needed to achieve high accuracy is also quite small, making this model a good candidate for use in practical applications. As with other generative models, it can be further improved by the application of discriminative reranking techniques. Discriminative methods are likely to allow it to significantly improve over the current state-of-the-art in dependency parsing.[10]

Acknowledgements This work was funded by Swiss NSF grant 200020-109685, Swiss NSF Fellowship PBGE22-119276, UK EPSRC grant EP/E019501/1, EU FP6 grant 507802 (TALK project), and EU FP7 grant 216594 (CLASSiC project).

---

[10] The ISBN dependency parser is downloadable from http://flake.cs.uiuc.edu/ titov/idp/

References

Abeillé, A. (Ed.) (2003). *Treebanks: Building and Using Parsed Corpora*. Dordrecht: Kluwer.

Aduriz, I., M. J. Aranzabe, J. M. Arriola, A. Atutxa, A. D. de Ilarraza, A. Garmendia, and M. Oronoz (2003). Construction of a Basque dependency treebank. In *Proceedings of the 2nd Workshop on Treebanks and Linguistic Theories (TLT)*, Växjö, pp. 201–204.

Aho, A. V., R. Sethi, and J. D. Ullman (1986). *Compilers: Principles, Techniques and Tools*. Reading, MA: Addison Wesley.

Böhmová, A., J. Hajič, E. Hajičová, and B. Hladká (2003). The PDT: a 3-level annotation scenario. See Abeillé (2003), Chapter 7, pp. 103–127.

Bottou, L. (1991). *Une approche théoretique de l'apprentissage connexionniste: Applications à la reconnaissance de la parole*. Ph. D. thesis, Université de Paris XI, Paris.

Buchholz, S. and E. Marsi (2006). CoNLL-X shared task on multilingual dependency parsing. In *Proceedings of the 10th Conference on Computational Natural Language Learning*, New York, NY, pp. 149–164.

Charniak, E. (2000). A maximum-entropy-inspired parser. In *Proceedings of the 1st Meeting of North American Chapter of Association for Computational Linguistics*, Seattle, WA, pp. 132–139.

Charniak, E. and M. Johnson (2005). Coarse-to-fine n-best parsing and MaxEnt discriminative reranking. In *Proceedings of the 43rd Meeting of Association for Computational Linguistics*, Ann Arbor, MI, pp. 173–180.

Chen, K., C. Luo, M. Chang, F. Chen, C. Chen, C. Huang, and Z. Gao (2003). Sinica treebank: design criteria, representational issues and implementation. See Abeillé (2003), Chapter 13, pp. 231–248.

Collins, M. (1999). *Head-Driven Statistical Models for Natural Language Parsing*. Ph. D. thesis, University of Pennsylvania, Philadelphia, PA.

Collins, M. (2000). Discriminative reranking for natural language parsing. In *Proceedings of the 17th International Conference on Machine Learning*, Stanford, CA, pp. 175–182.

Csendes, D., J. Csirik, T. Gyimóthy, and A. Kocsor (2005). *The Szeged Treebank*. Springer, Berlin/ Heidelberg.

Dzeroski, S., T. Erjavec, N. Ledinek, P. Pajas, Z. Zabokrtsky, and A. Zele (2006). Towards a Slovene dependency treebank. In *Proceedings of the International Conference on Language Resources and Evaluation (LREC)*, Genoa, pp. 1388–1391.

Hajič, J., O. Smrž, P. Zemánek, J. Šnaidauf, and E. Beška (2004). Prague Arabic dependency treebank: development in data and tools. In *Proceedings of the NEMLAR International Conference on Arabic Language Resources and Tools*, Caira, pp. 110–117.

Hall, J., J. Nilsson, J. Nivre, G. Eryigit, B. Megyesi, M. Nilsson, and M. Saers (2007). Single malt or blended? a study in multilingual parser optimization. In *Proceedings of the CoNLL Shared Task Session of EMNLP-CoNLL 2007*, Prague, pp. 933–939.

Henderson, J. (2003). Inducing history representations for broad coverage statistical parsing. In *Proceedings of the Joint Meeting of North American Chapter of the Association for Computational Linguistics and the Human Language Technology Conference*, Edmonton, AB, pp. 103–110.

Henderson, J. (2004). Discriminative training of a neural network statistical parser. In *Proceedings of the 42nd Meeting of Association for Computational Linguistics*, Barcelona, pp. 95–102.

Henderson, J., P. Merlo, G. Musillo, and I. Titov (2008). A latent variable model of synchronous parsing for syntactic and semantic dependencies. In *Proceedings of the CoNLL-2008 Shared Task*, Manchester, pp. 178–182.

Henderson, J. and I. Titov (2005). Data-defined kernels for parse reranking derived from probabilistic models. In *Proceedings of the 43rd Meeting of Association for Computational Linguistics*, Ann Arbor, MI, pp. 181–188.

Johansson, R. and P. Nugues (2007). Extended constituent-to-dependency conversion for English. In *Proceedings of the 16th Nordic Conference on Computational Linguistics (NODALIDA)*, Tartu, pp. 105–112.

Jordan, M. I., Z. Ghahramani, T. S. Jaakkola, and L. K. Saul. (1999). An introduction to variational methods for graphical models. In M. I. Jordan (Ed.), *Learning in Graphical Models*, pp. 183–233. Cambridge, MA: MIT Press.

Koo, T. and M. Collins (2005). Hidden-variable models for discriminative reranking. In *Proceedings of the Conference on Empirical Methods in Natural Language Processing*, Vancouver, BC, pp. 507–514.

Kromann, M. T. (2003). The Danish dependency treebank and the underlying linguistic theory. In *Proceedings of the 2nd Workshop on Treebanks and Linguistic Theories (TLT)*, Vaxjo.

Liang, P., S. Petrov, M. Jordan, and D. Klein (2007). The infinite PCFG using hierarchical dirichlet processes. In *Joint Conference on Empirical Methods in Natural Language Processing and Computational Natural Language Learning (EMNLP-CoNLL)*, Prague, pp. 688–697.

Marcus, M., B. Santorini, and M. Marcinkiewicz (1993). Building a large annotated corpus of English: the Penn Treebank. *Computational Linguistics 19*(2), 313–330.

Martí, M. A., M. Taulé, L. Màrquez, and M. Bertran (2007). CESS-ECE: a multilingual and multilevel annotated corpus. Available for download from: http://www.lsi.upc.edu/ mbertran/cess-ece/

Matsuzaki, T., Y. Miyao, and J. Tsujii (2005). Probabilistic CFG with latent annotations. In *Proceedings of the 43rd Annual Meeting of the ACL*, Ann Arbor, MI, pp. 75–82.

McDonald, R., K. Lerman, and F. Pereira (2006). Multilingual dependency analysis with a two-stage discriminative parser. In *Proceeding of the 10th Conference on Computational Natural Language Learning*, New York, NY, pp. 216–220.

Montemagni, S., F. Barsotti, M. Battista, N. Calzolari, O. Corazzari, A. Lenci, A. Zampolli, F. Fanciulli, M. Massetani, R. Raffaelli, R. Basili, M. T. Pazienza, D. Saracino, F. Zanzotto, N. Nana, F. Pianesi, and R. Delmonte (2003). Building the Italian Syntactic-Semantic Treebank. See Abeillé (2003), Chapter 11, pp. 189–210.

Murphy, K. P. (2002). *Dynamic Belief Networks: Representation, Inference and Learning*. Ph. D. thesis, University of California, Berkeley, CA.

Musillo, G. and P. Merlo (2008). Unlexicalised hidden variable models of split dependency grammars. In *Proceedings of the 46th Annual Meeting of the Association for Computational Linguistics: Human Language Technologies*, Columbus, OH, pp. 213–216.

Nakagawa, T. (2007). Multilingual dependency parsing using global features. In *Proceedings of the CoNLL Shared Task Session of EMNLP-CoNLL 2007*, pp. 952–956.

Neal, R. (1992). Connectionist learning of belief networks. *Artificial Intelligence 56*, 71–113.

Nivre, J., J. Hall, and J. Nilsson (2004). Memory-based dependency parsing. In *Proceedings of the 8th Conference on Computational Natural Language Learning*, Boston, MA, pp. 49–56.

Nivre, J., J. Hall, J. Nilsson, G. Eryigit, and S. Marinov (2006). Pseudo-projective dependency parsing with support vector machines. In *Proceedings of the 10th Conference on Computational Natural Language Learning*, New York, NY, pp. 221–225.

Oflazer, K., B. Say, D. Z. Hakkani-Tür, and G. Tür (2003). Building a Turkish treebank. See Abeillé (2003), Chapter 15, pp. 261–277.

Peshkin, L. and V. Savova (2005). Dependency parsing with dynamic Bayesian network. In *AAAI, 20th National Conference on Artificial Intelligence*, Pittsburgh, PA, pp. 1112–1117.

Petrov, S., L. Barrett, R. Thibaux, and D. Klein (2006). Learning accurate, compact, and interpretable tree annotation. In *Proceedings of the Annual Meeting of the ACL and the International Conference on Computational Linguistics*, Sydney, pp. 433–44.

Petrov, S. and D. Klein (2007). Improved inference for unlexicalized parsing. In *Proceedings of the Conference on Human Language Technology and North American chapter of the Association for Computational Linguistics (HLT-NAACL 2007)*, Rochester, NY, pp. 404–411.

Prescher, D. (2005). Head-driven PCFGs with latent-head statistics. In *Proceedings of the 9th International Workshop on Parsing Technologies*, Vancouver, BC, pp. 115–124.

Prokopidis, P., E. Desypri, M. Koutsombogera, H. Papageorgiou, and S. Piperidis (2005). Theoretical and practical issues in the construction of a Greek dependency treebank. In *Proceedings of the 4th Workshop on Treebanks and Linguistic Theories (TLT)*, Barcelona, pp. 149–160.

Riezler, S., T. H. King, R. M. Kaplan, R. Crouch, J. T. Maxwell, and M. Johnson (2002). Parsing the Wall Street Journal using a Lexical-Functional Grammar and discriminative estimation techniques. In *Proceedings of the 40th Meeting of Association for Computational Linguistics*, Philadelphia, PA, pp. 271–278.

Sallans, B. (2002). *Reinforcement Learning for Factored Markov Decision Processes*. Ph. D. thesis, University of Toronto, Toronto, ON.

Sha, F. and F. Pereira (2003). Shallow parsing with conditional random fields. In *Proceedings of the Joint Meeting of North American Chapter of the Association for Computational Linguistics and the Human Language Technology Conference*, Edmonton, AB, pp. 213–220.

Titov, I. and J. Henderson (2007). Constituent parsing with Incremental Sigmoid Belief Networks. In *Proc. 45th Meeting of Association for Computational Linguistics (ACL)*, Prague, pp. 632–639.

van der Beek, L., G. Bouma, J. Daciuk, T. Gaustad, R. Malouf, G. van Noord, R. Prins, and B. Villada (2002). The Alpino dependency treebank. In *Computational Linguistic in the Netherlands (CLIN)*, Enschede, pp. 8–22.

Chapter 4
Dependency Parsing and Domain Adaptation with Data-Driven LR Models and Parser Ensembles

Kenji Sagae and Jun-ichi Tsujii

4.1 Introduction

Natural language parsing with data-driven dependency-based frameworks has received an increasing amount of attention in recent years, as observed in the shared tasks hosted by the Conference on Computational Natural Language Learning (CoNLL) in 2006 (Buchholz and Marsi, 2006) and 2007 (Nivre et al., 2007). Dependency representations of syntactic structure directly reflect word-to-word relationships in a dependency graph, where words in a sentence are the nodes, and labeled edges correspond to head-dependent syntactic relations. In addition to being inherently lexicalized, dependency analyses can be generated efficiently and have been shown to be useful in a variety of practical tasks, such as question answering (Wang et al., 2007), information extraction in biomedical text (Erkan et al., 2007; Saetre et al., 2007) and machine translation (Quirk and Corston-Oliver, 2006).

There are now several approaches for multilingual dependency parsing, as demonstrated in the recent CoNLL shared tasks, but most can be classified into one of two overall categories that characterize both inference and parsing strategy. In the first category, commonly referred to as *all-pairs* or *graph-based* parsing, the parser performs global inference taking into account all possible edges in the dependency graph (McDonald et al., 2005). The parsing approach presented here falls mostly into the second category, *stepwise* or *transition-based* parsing, where instead of evaluating dependency graphs directly, the parser learns sequences of steps in a shift-reduce derivation to produce dependency graphs. Each of the derivation steps is learned individually, using a rich set of local features based on the current state of the parser and the parsing history (Nivre and Scholz, 2004). Our approach extends the existing body of work mainly in four ways:

1. Although stepwise or transition-based dependency parsing has commonly been performed using parsing algorithms designed specifically for this task, such as those described by Nivre (2003) and Yamada and Matsumoto (2003), we

---

K. Sagae (✉)
Institute for Creative Technologies, University of Southern California, Marina del Rey, CA 90292, USA
e-mail: sagae@ict.usc.edu

H. Bunt et al. (eds.), *Trends in Parsing Technology*, Text, Speech and Language Technology 43, DOI 10.1007/978-90-481-9352-3_4,

show that state-of-the-art results can also be obtained using a data-driven variant of the well known LR parsing algorithm (Knuth, 1965) that is equivalent to the arc-standard shift-reduce algorithm for dependency parsing proposed by Nivre (2004). This provides a connection between current research on data-driven dependency parsing and previous parsing work using LR and GLR models.
2. We generalize the standard deterministic stepwise framework to probabilistic parsing, with the use of a beam search strategy similar to the one employed in constituent parsing by Ratnaparkhi (1997) and later by Sagae and Lavie (2006a).
3. We provide additional evidence that the graph-based parser ensemble approach proposed by Sagae and Lavie (2006b) can be used to improve parsing accuracy, even when only a single parsing algorithm is used. We show that sufficient diversity can be obtained by using different learning techniques or changing parsing direction from *forward*, or left to right, to *backward*, or right to left (of course, even greater gains may be achieved when different algorithms are used, although this is not pursued here).
4. Lastly, we present a straightforward way to perform parser domain adaptation using unlabeled data in the target domain. In our domain adaptation approach we use a semi-supervised scheme, where two parsers trained in a source domain are used to produce training data automatically for the target domain. In contrast to some of the recent successful efforts on semi-supervised learning for parsing (McClosky et al., 2006; Koo et al., 2008), our scheme depends crucially on parser diversity.

We entered a system based on the approach described in this paper in the CoNLL 2007 shared task (Nivre et al., 2007), which differed from the 2006 edition (Buchholz and Marsi, 2006) by featuring two separate tracks: one in multilingual parsing, and a new track on domain adaptation for dependency parsers. In the multilingual parsing track, participants train dependency parsers using treebanks provided for ten languages: Arabic (Hajič et al., 2004), Basque (Aduriz et al., 2003), Catalan (Martí et al., 2007), Chinese (Chen et al., 2003), Czech (Böhmová et al., 2003), English (Marcus et al., 1993; Johansson and Nugues, 2007), Greek (Prokopidis et al., 2005), Hungarian (Csendes et al., 2005), Italian (Montemagni et al., 2003), and Turkish (Oflazer et al., 2003). In the domain adaptation track, participants were provided with English training data from the Wall Street Journal portion of the Penn Treebank (Marcus et al., 1993) converted to dependencies (Johansson and Nugues, 2007) to train parsers to be evaluated on material in the biological (development set) and chemical (test set) domains (Kulick et al., 2004), and optionally on text from the CHILDES database (MacWhinney, 2000; Brown, 1973).

Our system's accuracy was the highest in the domain adaptation track (with labeled attachment score of 81.06), and only 0.43 below the top scoring system in the multilingual parsing track (our average labeled attachment score over the ten languages was 79.89). We first describe our approach to multilingual dependency parsing using a graph-based ensemble of transition-based parsers, and follow with our approach for domain adaptation using semi-supervised learning. We then provide an analysis of the results obtained with our system, and discuss possible improvements.

4.2 A Data-Driven Probabilistic LR Approach for Dependency Parsing

The algorithm at the core of our parsing approach is a best-first probabilistic shift-reduce algorithm inspired by LR parsing (Knuth, 1965). The algorithm follows a bottom-up strategy, or *bottom-up-trees*, as defined by Buchholz and Marsi (2006), in contrast to the widely used shift-reduce dependency parsing algorithm described by Nivre (2003), which is a bottom-up/top-down hybrid, or *bottom-up-spans*. In practice, Nivre's bottom-up-spans dependency parsing algorithm always attaches words to their heads at the first opportunity as the input string is processed from left to right. For that reason, it is referred as *arc-eager* (Nivre, 2004). Our algorithm, instead, adopts a strategy for dependency parsing that follows the bottom-up-trees shift-reduce behavior of the LR algorithm, only attaching a word to its head after all of its own dependents have already been attached. Nivre (2004) refers to this strategy as *arc-standard*. The main difference between our data-driven parser and a traditional LR parser is that we do not use an LR table derived from an explicit grammar to determine shift/reduce actions. Instead, the parser learns when to apply shift/reduce actions from labeled examples consisting of gold-standard parse trees. By running the algorithm on the labeled examples, we can associate parser states with the correct parser actions. Instead of using a simple look-up table for predicting parser actions based on parser states, we use a classifier with features derived from much of the same information contained in an LR table: the top few items on the stack, and a look-ahead of the next few items remaining in the input string. Additionally, following Sagae and Lavie (2006a), we extend the basic deterministic data-driven variant of the LR algorithm with a best-first search, which results in a parsing strategy similar in concept to generalized LR parsing (Tomita, 1987, 1990). However, unlike in Tomita's GLR parsing, once processing is split into different branches due to ambiguities, these branches are never merged.

The resulting algorithm is projective, which limits the trees that can be produced as output. Non-projectivity is handled by pseudo-projective transformations (Nivre and Nilsson, 2005). The general idea is to transform non-projective trees into projective trees by lifting non-projective arcs, so the projective trees can be used to train a parser that uses a projective algorithm. When the parser produces a projective tree as output, the tree can then be detransformed into a non-projective tree. This detransformation process is made possible by annotations added to arcs that were lifted in the projectivization process. We use Nivre and Nilsson's *PATH* scheme, which marks the labels of each arc in the lifting path.

For clarity, we first describe the basic data-driven variant of the LR algorithm for dependency parsing, which is a deterministic stepwise algorithm. We then show how we extend the deterministic parser into a best-first probabilistic parser.

4.2.1 Dependency Parsing with a Data-Driven Variant of the LR Algorithm

The two main data structures in the algorithm are a stack S and a queue Q. S holds subtrees of the final dependency tree for an input sentence, and Q holds the words in the input sentence. S is initialized to be empty, and Q is initialized to hold every word in the input in order, so that the first word in the input is in the front of the queue.[1]

The parser performs two main types of actions: *shift* and *reduce*. When a shift action is taken, a word is shifted from the front of Q, and placed on the top of S (as a tree containing only one node, the word itself). When a reduce action is taken, the two top items in S (s_1 and s_2) are popped, and a new item is pushed onto S. This new item is a tree formed by making the root of s_1 a dependent of the root of s_2, or the root of s_2 a dependent of the root of s_1. Depending on which of these two cases occur, we call the action *reduce-left* or *reduce-right*, according to whether the head of the new tree is to the left or to the right of its new dependent. In addition to the direction of the reduce action, the label of the newly formed dependency arc must also be decided in a reduce action.

Parsing terminates successfully when Q is empty (all words in the input have been processed) and S contains only a single tree (the final dependency tree for the input sentence). If Q is empty, S contains two or more items, and no further reduce actions can be taken, parsing terminates and the input is rejected. In such cases, the remaining items in S contain partial analyses for contiguous segments of the input.

4.2.2 A Probabilistic LR Model for Dependency Parsing

In the traditional LR algorithm, parser states are placed onto the stack, and an LR table is consulted to determine the next parser action. In our case, the parser state is encoded as a set of features derived from the contents of the stack S and queue Q, and the next parser action is determined by a machine learning component according to that set of features. In the deterministic case described above, the procedure used for determining parser actions (a classifier, in our case) returns a single action. If, instead, this procedure returns a list of several possible actions with corresponding probabilities, we can then parse with a model similar to the probabilistic LR models described by Briscoe and Carroll (1993), where the probability of a parse tree is the product of the probabilities of each of the actions taken in its derivation.

To find the most probable parse tree according to the probabilistic LR model, we use a best-first strategy. This involves an extension of the deterministic shift-reduce into a best-first shift-reduce algorithm. To describe this extension, we first introduce a new data structure T_i that represents a parser state, which includes a stack S_i, a queue Q_i, and a probability P_i. The deterministic algorithm is a special case of the

[1] We append a "virtual root" word to the beginning of every sentence, which is used as the head of every word in the dependency structure that does not have a head in the sentence.

probabilistic algorithm where we have a single parser state T_0 that contains S_0 and Q_0, and the probability of the parser state is 1.0. The best-first algorithm, on the other hand, keeps a heap H containing multiple parser states $T_0 \ldots T_m$. These states are ordered in the heap according to their probabilities, which are determined by multiplying the probabilities of each of the parser actions that resulted in that parser state. The heap H is initialized to contain a single parser state T_0, which contains a stack S_0, a queue Q_0 and probability $P_0 = 1.0$. S_0 and Q_0 are initialized in the same way as S and Q in the deterministic algorithm. The best-first algorithm then loops while H is non-empty. At each iteration, first a state $T_{current}$ is popped from the top of H. If $T_{current}$ corresponds to a final state ($Q_{current}$ is empty and $S_{current}$ contains a single item), we return the single item in $S_{current}$ as the dependency structure corresponding to the input sentence. Otherwise, we get a list of parser actions $act_0 \ldots act_n$ (with associated probabilities $Pact_0 \ldots Pact_n$) corresponding to state $T_{current}$. For each of these parser actions act_j, we create a new parser state T_{new} by applying act_j to $T_{current}$, and set the probability T_{new} to be $P_{new} = P_{current} * Pact_j$. Then, T_{new} is inserted into the heap H. Once new states have been inserted onto H for each of the n parser actions, we move on to the next iteration of the algorithm.

4.3 Multilingual Parsing Experiments

For each of the ten languages for which training data was provided in the multilingual track of the CoNLL 2007 shared task, we created a graph-based ensemble using three data-driven LR models, trained as follows. The first LR model for each language uses maximum entropy classification (Berger et al., 1996) to determine possible parser actions and their probabilities. To control overfitting in the maximum entropy (MaxEnt) models, we used box-type inequality constraints (Kazama and Tsujii, 2003). The second LR model for each language also uses MaxEnt classification, but parsing is performed *backwards*, which is accomplished simply by reversing the input string before parsing starts. Sagae and Lavie (2006b) and Zeman and Žabokrtský (2005) have observed that reversing the direction of stepwise parsers can be beneficial in parser combinations. The third model uses support vector machines (Vapnik, 1995) with the polynomial kernel with degree 2. Probabilities were estimated for SVM outputs using the method described in (Platt, 2000), but accuracy improvements were not observed during development when these estimated probabilities were used instead of simply the single best action given by the classifier (with probability 1.0), so in practice the SVM parsing models we used were deterministic.

At test time, the three data-driven LR models are combined in a graph-based ensemble: each input sentence is parsed using each of the three LR models, and the three resulting dependency structures are combined (after deprojectivization) according to the maximum-spanning-tree parser combination scheme proposed by Sagae and Lavie (2006b). The ensemble approach is comprised of three simple steps. The first step is to parse the same input string using each of the three parsing models to produce three dependency trees as output (one for each model). The second step is to construct a graph where each of the words in the input string is a node, and every dependency arc in each of the three dependency trees is a directed edge. In other words, the three dependency trees are merged into a single graph. Each edge is weighted according to how many of the trees contain that edge. Sagae and Lavie report that higher parse accuracy is obtained when edges in the combined graph are weighted according to more sophisticated schemes, but these were not attempted with the shared task data. The final step is to find the maximum spanning tree of this graph, which is the final analysis for the input sentence.

4.3.1 Classifier Features

The features used with the classifiers that determine parser actions reflect the state of the parser in terms of the context of the stack, input look-ahead, and parsing history. Although it is likely that fine-tuning specific feature sets for each of the different languages in the shared task could provide accuracy improvements for each of the models in each language, the same set of meta-parameters and features were used for all of the ten languages, due to time constraints during system development for the shared task. If we let $S(n)$ denote the nth item from the top of the stack (where $S(1)$ is the item on top of the stack), and $Q(n)$ denote the nth item in the queue, the features used were:

- For the subtrees in $S(1)$ and $S(2)$
  - the number of children of the root word;
  - the number of children of the root word that appear in the sentence to the right of the root word;
  - the number of children of the root word that appear in the sentence to the left of the root word;
  - the part-of-speech tag and dependency label of the rightmost and leftmost children;
- The part-of-speech tag of the word immediately to the right of the root word of $S(2)$;
- The part-of-speech tag of the word immediately to the left of the root word of $S(1)$;
- The previous parser action;
- The features listed for the root words of the subtrees in Table 4.1.

In addition, in the MaxEnt models we also used selected combinations of these features. The classes used to represent parser actions were designed to encode all aspects of an action (shift vs. reduce, right vs. left, and dependency label) simultaneously.

Results for each of the ten languages are shown in Table 4.2 as labeled and unlabeled attachment scores (LAS and UAS, respectively), along with the average

Table 4.1 Additional features, where WORD is the surface form of the word, LEMMA is the lemma of the word, POS is the part-of-speech tag of the word, CPOS is a coarse-grained part-of-speech tag, and FEATS is a string that represents morphological features of the word

	$S(1)$	$S(2)$	$S(3)$	$Q(1)$	$Q(2)$	$Q(3)$
WORD	•	•	•	•	•	
LEMMA	•	•		•		
POS	•	•	•	•	•	•
CPOS	•	•		•		
FEATS	•	•		•		

Table 4.2 Our results in the multilingual parsing task

Language	LAS	UAS	Avg LAS	Top LAS
Arabic	74.71	84.04	68.34	76.52
Basque	74.64	**81.19**	68.06	76.94
Catalan	**88.16**	**93.34**	79.85	88.70
Chinese	**84.69**	**88.94**	76.59	84.69
Czech	74.83	81.27	70.12	80.19
English	**89.01**	**89.87**	80.95	89.61
Greek	73.58	80.37	70.22	76.31
Hungarian	**79.53**	**83.51**	71.49	80.27
Italian	**83.91**	**87.68**	78.06	84.40
Turkish	75.91	82.72	70.06	79.81
ALL	79.90	85.29	65.50	80.32

labeled attachment score and highest labeled attachment score for all participants in the shared task. Our results shown in boldface were among the top three scores for those particular languages (five out of the ten languages).

4.4 Domain Adaptation Experiments

In the domain adaptation task, we are provided with training data in a source domain, Wall Street Journal (WSJ) text, and evaluated on accuracy in a target domain: Biomedical text (bio) in the development stage, and Chemistry text (chem) in final testing. Although we are not provided with any labeled data in the target domain, we are provided with a large amount of unlabeled data (text). The unlabeled data is provided in three files for each target domain: one file with roughly 300,000 tokens (including words and punctuation), a larger file with 1.5 million tokens, and an even larger with over 8 million tokens.

Our domain adaptation approach is based on parser diversity. Similarly to how we used the same parsing algorithm with multiple data-driven LR models in the multilingual parsing task, in the domain adaptation track we start with two data-driven LR models, both trained on the source-domain labeled training data (WSJ). The first is a forward (left to right) MaxEnt model, and the second is a backward (right to left) SVM model. We use these two models to perform a procedure similar to a single iteration of co-training, except that selection of the newly (automatically) produced training instances was done by selecting sentences for which the two models produced identical analyses. On the development data we verified that sentences for which there was perfect agreement between the two models had labeled attachment score just above 90 on average, even though each of the models had individual accuracy between 78 and 79 over the entire development set.

Following the assumption that agreement between the two models is an indication of reliability for the analyses of specific sentences, we used the following procedure to train a parser adapted to a target domain, using labeled data in the source domain (WSJ) and only unlabeled data in the target domain (bio or chem):

1. Train the forward MaxEnt and backward SVM models using the source domain (WSJ) labeled training data;
2. Use each of the models to parse the first two of the three sets[2] of unlabeled data that were provided in the target domain (bio or chem);
3. Compare the output for the two models, and select only identical analyses that were produced by each of the two separate models;
4. Add those analyses (about 200k tokens in the target domain) to the original (source domain) labeled training set;
5. Retrain the forward MaxEnt model with the new larger training set;
6. Finally, use this new MaxEnt model to parse the test data in the target domain.

Following this procedure we obtained a labeled attachment score of 81.06, and unlabeled attachment score of 83.42, both the highest scores for this track. This was done without the use of any additional resources (closed track), but these results are also higher than the top score for the open track, where the use of certain additional resources was allowed (Nivre et al., 2007).

4.5 Analysis and Discussion

One of the main assumptions in our use of different models based on the same algorithm is that while the output generated by those models may often differ, agreement between the models is an indication of parse quality. The graph-based ensemble we used for multilingual parsing relies on this assumption, as does the semi-supervised procedure we used for domain adaptation. It is likely that if agreement did not reflect reliability, the final parser trained for the domain adaption task would perform with accuracy below those of the parsers trained only with source-domain training data. Instead, experiments on the development set were encouraging. As stated before, when the parsers agreed, labeled attachment score was over 90, even though the score of each model alone was lower than 79. The domain-adapted parser had a score of 82.1, a statistically significant improvement. Interestingly, the ensemble used in the multilingual track also produced good results on the development set for

[2] The larger third set was not used.

the domain adaptation data, without the use of the unlabeled data at all, with a score of 81.9 (although the ensemble is more expensive to run).

The different models used in each track were distinct in a few ways: (1) direction (forward or backward); (2) learner (MaxEnt or SVM); and (3) search strategy (best-first or deterministic). Of those differences, the first one is particularly interesting in single-pass shift-reduce models, as ours. In these models, the context to each side of a (potential) dependency differs in a fundamental way. To one side, we have tokens that have already been processed and are already in subtrees, and to the other side we simply have a look-ahead of the remaining input sentence. This way, the context of the same dependency in a forward parser may differ significantly from the context of the same dependency in a backward parser. Interestingly, the accuracy scores of the MaxEnt backward models were found to be generally just below the accuracy of their corresponding forward models when tested on development data, with two exceptions: Hungarian and Turkish. In Hungarian, the accuracy scores produced by the forward and backward MaxEnt LR models were not significantly different, with both labeled attachment scores at about 77.3 (the SVM model score was 76.1, and the final combination score on development data was 79.3). In Turkish, however, the backward score was significantly higher than the forward score, 75.0 and 72.3, respectively. The forward SVM score was 73.1, and the combined score was 75.8. In experiments performed after the official submission of results, we evaluated a *backward* SVM model (which was trained after submission) on the same development set, and found it to be significantly more accurate than the forward model, with a score of 75.7. Adding that score to the combination raised the combination score to 77.9 (a large improvement from 75.8). The likely reason for this difference is that over 80% of the dependencies in the Turkish data set have the head to the right of the dependent, while only less than 4% have the head to the left. This means that the backward model builds much more partial structure in the stack as it consumes input tokens, while the forward model must consume most tokens before it starts making attachments. In other words, context in general in the backward model has more structure, and attachments are made while there are still look-ahead tokens, while the opposite is generally true in the forward model.

4.6 Conclusion

Our results demonstrate the effectiveness of even small ensembles of parsers that are relatively similar (using the same features and the same algorithm). There are several possible extensions and improvements to the approach we have described. For example, in Section 4.3 we mention the use of different weighting schemes in dependency voting.

One of the simplest improvements to our approach is to train more models with no other changes to our set-up. As mentioned in Section 4.4, the addition of a backward SVM model did improve accuracy on the Turkish set significantly, and it is likely that improvements would also be obtained in other languages. In addition, other learning approaches, such as memory-based language processing (Daelemans and den Bosch, 2005), could be used. A drawback of adding more models that became obvious in our experiments was the increased cost of both training (for example, the SVM parsers we used required significantly longer to train than the MaxEnt parsers) and run-time (parsing with MBL models can be several times slower than with MaxEnt, or even SVM). A similar idea that may be more effective, but requires more effort, is to add parsers based on different approaches. For example, using MSTParser (McDonald et al., 2005), a large-margin all-pairs parser, in our domain adaptation procedure results in significantly improved accuracy (83.2 LAS). Of course, the use of different approaches used by different groups in the CoNLL 2006 and 2007 shared tasks represents great opportunity for parser ensembles.

Acknowledgements We thank the shared task organizers and treebank providers. We also thank the CoNLL 2007 shared task reviewers for their comments and suggestions, and Yusuke Miyao for insightful discussions. This work was supported in part by Grant-in-Aid for Specially Promoted Research 18002007.

References

Abeillé, A. (Ed.) (2003). *Treebanks: Building and Using Parsed Corpora*. Dordrecht: Kluwer.

Aduriz, I., M.J. Aranzabe, J.M. Arriola, A. Atutxa, A.D. de Ilarraza, A. Garmendia, and M. Oronoz (2003). Construction of a Basque dependency treebank. In *Proceedings of the 2nd Workshop on Treebanks and Linguistic Theories (TLT)*, Växjö, Sweden, pp. 201–204.

Berger, A., S.A.D. Pietra, and V.J.D. Pietra (1996). A maximum entropy approach to natural language processing. *Computational Linguistics 22*(1), 39–71.

Böhmová, A., J. Hajič, E. Hajičová, and B. Hladká (2003). The PDT: a 3-level annotation scenario. In Abeillé (2003), Chapter 7, pp. 103–127.

Briscoe, E. and J. Carroll (1993). Generalized probabilistic lr parsing of natural language (corpora) with unification-based grammars. *Computational Linguistics 19*(1), 25–59.

Brown, R. (1973). *A First Language: The Early Stages*. Cambridge, MA: Harvard University Press.

Buchholz, S. and E. Marsi (2006). CoNLL-X shared task on multilingual dependency parsing. In *Proceedings of the CoNLL-X Shared Task. Tenth Conference on Computational Natural Language Learning (CoNLL-X)*, New York, NY, pp. 149–164.

Chen, K., C. Luo, M. Chang, F. Chen, C. Chen, C. Huang, and Z. Gao (2003). Sinica treebank: design criteria, representational issues and implementation. In Abeillé (2003), Chapter 13, pp. 231–248.

Csendes, D., J. Csirik, T. GyimÓthy, and A. Kocsor (2005). *The Szeged Treebank*. Berlin: Springer.

Daelemans, W. and A.V. den Bosch, (2005). *Memory-Based Language Processing*. Cambridge: Cambridge Press.

Erkan, G., A. Ozgur, and D. Radev (2007). Semisupervised classification for extracting protein interaction sentences using dependency parsing. In *Proceedings of the Joint Conference on Empirical Methods in Natural Language Processing and Computational Natural Language Learning (EMNLP-CoNLL)*, Prague, Czech Republic, pp. 228–237.

Hajič, J., O. Smrž, P. Zemánek, J. Šnaidauf, and E. Beška (2004). Prague Arabic dependency treebank: development in data and tools. In *Proceedings of the NEMLAR International Conference on Arabic Language Resources and Tools*, Cairo, Egypt, pp. 110–117.

Johansson, R. and P. Nugues (2007). Extended constituent-to-dependency conversion for English. In *Proceedings of the 16th Nordic Conference on Computational Linguistics (NODALIDA)*, Tartu, Estonia, pp. 105–112.

Kazama, J. and J. Tsujii (2003). Evaluation and extension of maximum entropy models with inequality constraints. In *Proceedings of the Conference on Empirical Methods in Natural Language Processing*, Sapporo, Japan, pp. 137–144.

Knuth, D. (1965). On the translation of languages from left to right. *Information and Control 8*, 607–639.

Koo, T., X. Carreras, and M. Collins (2008). Simple semi-supervised dependency parsing. In *Proceedings of the 46th Annual Meeting of the Association for Computational Linguistics (ACL)*, Columbus, OH, pp. 595–603.

Kulick, S., A. Bies, M. Liberman, M. Mandel, R. McDonald, M. Palmer, A. Schein, and L. Ungar (2004). Integrated annotation for biomedical information extraction. In *Proceedings of BioLINK 2004: Linking Biological Literature, Ontologies and Databases*, Boston, MA, pp. 61–68.

MacWhinney, B. (2000). *The CHILDES Project: Tools for Analyzing Talk*. Mahwah, NJ: Lawrence Erlbaum.

Marcus, M., B. Santorini, and M. Marcinkiewicz (1993). Building a large annotated corpus of English: the Penn Treebank. *Computational Linguistics 19*(2), 313–330.

Martí, M.A., M. Taulé, L. Màrquez, and M. Bertran (2007). CESS-ECE: A multilingual and multilevel annotated corpus. Available for download from: http://www.lsi.upc.edu/_mbertran/cessece/

McClosky, D., E. Charniak, and M. Johnson (2006). Effective self-training for parsing. In *Proceedings of the 2006 Human Language Technology Conference of the North American Chapter of the Association for Computational Linguistics (HLT-NAACL)*, New York, NY, pp. 152–159.

McDonald, R., F. Pereira, K. Ribarov, and J. Hajič (2005). Non-projective dependency parsing using spanning tree algorithms. In *Proceedings of the Human Language Technology Conference and the Conference on Empirical Methods in Natural Language Processing (HLT/EMNLP)*, Vancouver, BC, pp. 523–530.

Montemagni, S., F. Barsotti, M. Battista, N. Calzolari, O. Corazzari, A. Lenci, A. Zampolli, F. Fanciulli, M. Massetani, R. Raffaelli, R. Basili, M.T. Pazienza, D. Saracino, F. Zanzotto, N. Nana, F. Pianesi, and R. Delmonte (2003). Building the Italian syntactic-semantic treebank. In Abeillé (2003), Chapter 11, pp. 189–210.

Nivre, J. (2003). An efficient algorithm for projective dependency parsing. In *Proceedings of the 8th International Workshop on Parsing Technologies*, Nancy, France, pp. 149–160.

Nivre, J. (2004). Incrementality in deterministic dependency parsing. In *Proceedings of the ACL Workshop on Incremental Parsing: Bringing Engineering and Cognition Together (Workshop at ACL-2004)*, Barcelona, Spain, pp. 50–57.

Nivre, J. and J. Nilsson (2005). Pseudo-projective dependency parsing. In *Proceedings of the 43rd Annual Meeting of the Association for Computational Linguistics (ACL)*, pp. 99–106.

Nivre, J. and M. Scholz (2004). Deterministic dependency parsing of English text. In *Proceedings of the 20th International Conference on Computational Linguistics (COLING)*, Geneva, Switzerland, pp. 64–70.

Nivre, J., J. Hall, S. Kübler, R. McDonald, J. Nilsson, S. Riedel, and D. Yuret (2007). The CoNLL 2007 shared task on dependency parsing. In *Proceedings of the CoNLL 2007 Shared Task. Joint Conference on Empirical Methods in Natural Language Processing and Computational Natural Language Learning (EMNLP-CoNLL)*, Prague, Czech Republic, pp. 915–932.

Oflazer, K., B. Say, D.Z. Hakkani-Tür, and G. Tür (2003). Building a Turkish treebank. In Abeillé (2003), Chapter 15, pp. 261–277.

Platt, J. (2000). Probabilities for SV machines. In A. Smola, P. Bartlett, B. Scholkopf, and D. Schuurmans (Eds.), *Advances in Large Margin Classifiers*. Cambridge, MA: MIT Press, pp. 61–74.

Prokopidis, P., E. Desypri, M. Koutsombogera, H. Papageorgiou, and S. Piperidis (2005). Theoretical and practical issues in the construction of a Greek dependency treebank. In *Proceedings of the 4th Workshop on Treebanks and Linguistic Theories (TLT)*, Barcelona, Spain, pp. 149–160.

Quirk, C. and S. Corston-Oliver (2006). The impact of parse quality on syntactically-informed statistical machine translation. In *Proceedings of the Conference on Empirical Methods in Natural Language Processing*, Sydney, Australia, pp. 62–69.

Ratnaparkhi, A. (1997). A linear observed time statistical parser based on maximum entropy models. In *Proceedings of the 2nd Conference on Empirical Methods in Natural Language Processing*. Brown University, Providence, RI, pp. 1–10.

Saetre, R., K. Sagae, and J. Tsujii (2007). Syntactic features for protein–protein interaction extraction. In *Short Paper Proceedings of the 2nd International Symposium on Languages in Biology and Medicine*, Biopolis, Singapore, pp. 6.1–6.14.

Sagae, K. and A. Lavie (2006a). A best-first probabilistic shift-reduce parser. In *Proceedings of the 44th Annual Meeting of the Association for Computational Linguistics Main Conference Poster Session (COLING-ACL 2006)*, Syndey, Australia, pp. 691–698.

Sagae, K. and A. Lavie (2006b). Parser combination by reparsing. In *Proceedings of the Human Language Technology Conference of the NAACL, Companion Volume: Short Papers*, New York, NY, pp. 129–132.

Tomita, M. (1987). An efficient augmented context-free parsing algorithm. *Compuatational Linguist 31*, 31–46.

Tomita, M. (1990). The generalized lr parser/compiler – version 8.4. In *Proceedings of the International Conference on Computational Linguistics (COLING'90)*, Helsinki, pp. 59–63.

Vapnik, V.N. (1995). *The Mature of Statistical Learning Theory*. New York, NY: Springer.

Wang, M., N.A. Smith, and T. Mitamura (2007). What is the jeopardy model? a quasisynchronous grammar for qa. In *Proceedings of the Joint Conference on Empirical Methods in Natural Language Processing and Computational Natural Language Learning (EMNLPCoNLL)*, Prague, Czech Republic, pp. 22–32.

Yamada, H. and Y. Matsumoto (2003). Statistical dependency analysis with support vector machines. In *Proceedings of the 8th International Workshop on Parsing Technologies (IWPT)*, Nancy, France, pp. 195–206.

Zeman, D. and Žabokrtský, Z. (2005). Improving parsing accuracy by combining diverse dependency parsers. In *Proceedings of the 9th International Workshop on Parsing Technologies (IWPT 2005)*, Vancouver, BC, pp. 171–178.

Chapter 5
Dependency Parsing Using Global Features

Tetsuji Nakagawa

5.1 Introduction

Many methods for statistical dependency parsing have been studied. For example, McDonald et al. (2005a) proposed a method for projective dependency parsing using an online large-margin training algorithm, and later extended it to a non-projective dependency parsing method (McDonald et al., 2005b). However, these studies assumed that the heads of tokens in a sentence were independent from each other, and had limited available features.

Recently, several methods for incorporating non-local features have been investigated, though such features generally make models complex and thus complicate inference. Collins and Koo (2005) proposed a reranking method for phrase structure parsing in which any type of global feature in a parse tree can be used. For dependency parsing, McDonald and Pereira (2006) proposed a method which incorporates some types of global features, and Riedel and Clarke (2006) studied a method using integer linear programming which incorporates global linguistic constraints. In this chapter, a dependency parsing method which uses Gibbs sampling and can incorporate any type of global feature in a sentence is examined.

The rest of this chapter is organized as follows: Section 5.2 describes a method for unlabeled dependency parsing using Gibbs sampling, and explains the features used. Section 5.3 describes a method for dependency relation labeling using Support Vector Machines. Section 5.4 shows experimental results on multiple corpora. Section 5.5 discusses related work, and Section 14.5 presents the conclusions.

5.2 Unlabeled Dependency Parsing Using Global Features

Dependency parsing is the task of identifying the dependency structure (head-modifier relations between tokens) in a given sentence (Covington, 2001; Nivre,

T. Nakagawa (✉)
Knowledge Creating Communication Research Center, National Institute of Information and Communications Technology, Kyoto 619-0289, Japan
e-mail: tnaka@nict.go.jp

H. Bunt et al. (eds.), *Trends in Parsing Technology*, Text, Speech and Language Technology 43, DOI 10.1007/978-90-481-9352-3_5,

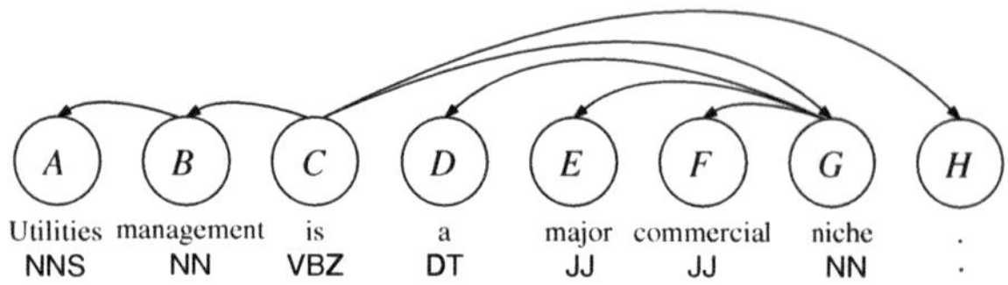

Fig. 5.1 Example of a dependency tree

2003). Dependency structures can be represented as dependency trees, and Fig. 5.1 shows an example. Here, each node represents a token,[1] and dependency relations are represented by arrows pointing from a head to a dependent. Each arrow may have a label indicating the relationship between the head and the dependent, such as a verb and its subject. Each token must have only one head except for the root node of the sentence, which has no head. Dependency trees are usually projective (trees with no crossing edges) in the English language, but non-projective dependency trees appear in some languages with relatively free word order, such as Czech. The rest of this section describes a probabilistic model for dependency parsing, methods for decoding and parameter estimation, and the features used.

5.2.1 Probabilistic Model

The proposed method uses a probabilistic model of a whole dependency tree. Two types of features are considered in the model, token-level local features and sentence-level global features, whose parameters are respectively represented by $\Lambda = \{\lambda_k\}$ and $\mathrm{M} = \{\mu_l\}$. This subsection describes the probabilistic model in detail.

Let $\mathbf{w}$ denote an input sentence consisting of $|\mathbf{w}|$ tokens, and let w_t denote the t-th token in the sentence:

$$\mathbf{w} = w_1 \cdots w_{|\mathbf{w}|}.$$

Let h_t denote the index of the head of the t-th token w_t, and let $\mathbf{h}$ denote the sequence of h_t. The root node of a sentence does not have a head, and the index of the root node's head is regarded as 0:

$$\mathbf{h} = h_1 \cdots h_{|\mathbf{w}|},$$
$$h_t \in \{0, 1, \cdots, |\mathbf{w}|\} \setminus \{t\} \qquad (t = 1, \cdots, |\mathbf{w}|).$$

The dependency parsing task when a sentence $\mathbf{w}$ is given, is to determine the heads of the tokens $\mathbf{h}$.

[1] The term *token* is used here to represent the basic unit of dependency parsing. Words are used as the basic unit in many languages, but other kinds of units are used in some languages (e.g. a chunk called *bunsetsu* is often used in Japanese). A part of speech (POS) tag is assumed to be attached to each token.

Rosenfeld et al. (2001) proposed whole-sentence exponential language models which can incorporate arbitrary features in a sentence; a similar probabilistic model is considered here for dependency parsing with the ability to incorporate any sentence-level feature. The probability distribution of a dependency structure **h** given a sentence **w** using exponential models is defined as follows:

$$P_{\Lambda,\mathrm{M}}(\mathbf{h}|\mathbf{w}) = \frac{1}{Z_{\Lambda,\mathrm{M}}(\mathbf{w})} Q_{\mathrm{M}}(\mathbf{h}|\mathbf{w}) \exp\left\{\sum_{k=1}^{K} \lambda_k f_k(\mathbf{w}, \mathbf{h})\right\}. \tag{1}$$

$$Z_{\Lambda,\mathrm{M}}(\mathbf{w}) = \sum_{\mathbf{h}' \in \mathcal{H}(\mathbf{w})} Q_{\mathrm{M}}(\mathbf{h}'|\mathbf{w}) \exp\left\{\sum_{k=1}^{K} \lambda_k f_k(\mathbf{w}, \mathbf{h}')\right\}. \tag{2}$$

where $Q_{\mathrm{M}}(\mathbf{h}|\mathbf{w})$ is an initial distribution, $f_k(\mathbf{w}, \mathbf{h})$ is the k-th feature function, K is the number of feature functions, and λ_k is the weight of the k-th feature. A feature function $f_k(\mathbf{w}, \mathbf{h})$ returns 1 if **w** and **h** satisfy certain conditions, and otherwise 0; for example:

$$f_{123}(\mathbf{w}, \mathbf{h}) = \begin{cases} 1 & \text{if a word in } \mathbf{w} \text{ has POS tag DT} \wedge \text{its parent is NN} \wedge \text{its grandparent is VBZ} \\ 0 & \text{otherwise.} \end{cases}$$

$\mathcal{H}(\mathbf{w})$ is the set of possible configurations of heads for the given sentence **w**. Although it is appropriate for $\mathcal{H}(\mathbf{w})$ to be defined as the set of projective trees for projective languages and the set of non-projective trees (which is a superset of the set of projective trees) for non-projective languages, in this study it is defined as the set of all the possible graphs which contains $|\mathbf{w}|^{|\mathbf{w}|}$ elements. $P_{\Lambda,\mathrm{M}}(\mathbf{h}|\mathbf{w})$ and $Q_{\mathrm{M}}(\mathbf{h}|\mathbf{w})$ are defined over $\mathcal{H}(\mathbf{w})$.[2] $P_{\Lambda,\mathrm{M}}(\mathbf{h}|\mathbf{w})$ is a joint distribution of all the heads conditioned by the sentence, and any information in the sentence can be modeled with the distribution. Therefore, $P_{\Lambda,\mathrm{M}}(\mathbf{h}|\mathbf{w})$ is called a *sentence-level model*. The feature function $f_k(\mathbf{w}, \mathbf{h})$ is defined on the sentence **w** with heads **h**, and any information in the sentence can be used without assuming independence among the heads of the tokens. Therefore $f_k(\mathbf{w}, \mathbf{h})$ is called a *sentence-level global feature*. The global features are described in detail in Section 5.2.5.

The initial distribution $Q_{\mathrm{M}}(\mathbf{h}|\mathbf{w})$ is defined as the product of $q^t_{\mathrm{M}}(h|\mathbf{w})$; this is the probability distribution of the head h of the t-th token calculated with maximum entropy models:

$$Q_{\mathrm{M}}(\mathbf{h}|\mathbf{w}) = \prod_{t=1}^{|\mathbf{w}|} q^t_{\mathrm{M}}(h_t|\mathbf{w}). \tag{3}$$

[2] $\mathcal{H}(\mathbf{w})$ is a superset of the set of non-projective trees; it is an unnecessarily large set and contains ill-formed dependency structures such as graphs with cycles. This issue may cause a reduction in parsing performance, but this approximation is adopted for computational efficiency.

$$q_{\mathrm{M}}^{t}(h|\mathbf{w}) = \frac{1}{Y_{\mathrm{M}}(\mathbf{w}, t)} \exp\left\{\sum_{l=1}^{L} \mu_l g_l(\mathbf{w}, t, h)\right\}. \tag{4}$$

$$Y_{\mathrm{M}}(\mathbf{w}, t) = \sum_{\substack{h'=0 \\ h' \neq t}}^{|\mathbf{w}|} \exp\left\{\sum_{l=1}^{L} \mu_l g_l(\mathbf{w}, t, h')\right\}. \tag{5}$$

where $g_l(\mathbf{w}, t, h)$ is the l-th feature function, L is the number of feature functions, and μ_l is the weight of the l-th feature. $q_{\mathrm{M}}^{t}(h|\mathbf{w})$ is a model of the head of a single token, calculated independently from other tokens. Therefore, $q_{\mathrm{M}}^{t}(h|\mathbf{w})$ is called a *token-level model*, and $g_l(\mathbf{w}, t, h)$ is a *token-level local feature*. The local features are described in detail in Section 5.2.4.

5.2.2 Decoding with Gibbs Sampling

This subsection describes how to find the optimal dependency tree $\hat{\mathbf{h}}$, given a sentence $\mathbf{w}$, the parameters of the sentence-level model $\Lambda = \{\lambda_1, \cdots, \lambda_K\}$ and the parameters of the token-level model $\mathrm{M} = \{\mu_1, \cdots, \mu_L\}$. Since the probabilistic model contains global features and efficient algorithms such as dynamic programming cannot be used, Gibbs sampling is used to obtain an approximate solution.

The proposed method searches for the following solution $\hat{\mathbf{h}}$, which maximizes the product of the marginal distribution of each token:

$$\hat{\mathbf{h}} = \underset{\mathbf{h} \in \mathcal{T}(\mathbf{w})}{\arg\max} \prod_{t=1}^{|\mathbf{w}|} P_t(h_t|\mathbf{w}). \tag{6}$$

where $P_t(h|\mathbf{w})$ is the marginal distribution of the head of the t-th token given $\mathbf{w}$, and $\mathcal{T}(\mathbf{w})$ is the set of the possible dependency trees for the sentence $\mathbf{w}$. The marginal distribution for the t-th token, $P_t(h|\mathbf{w})$, can be obtained from the joint distribution $P_{\Lambda,\mathrm{M}}(\mathbf{h}|\mathbf{w})$ by summing out all the other variables:

$$P_t(h|\mathbf{w}) = \sum_{\substack{h_1, \cdots, h_{t-1}, h_{t+1}, \cdots, h_{|\mathbf{w}|} \\ h_t = h}} P_{\Lambda,\mathrm{M}}(\mathbf{h}|\mathbf{w}). \tag{7}$$

McDonald et al. (2005a) solved the projective dependency parsing problem as a maximum spanning tree (MST) problem. They defined the scores of edges in dependency graphs, and searched for the MST as the optimal dependency tree, where the summation of the edge scores was maximized. They then used the Eisner algorithm (Eisner, 1996) to find the maximum projective spanning tree. They later extended the method to a non-projective dependency parsing method with the Chu-Liu-Edmonds (CLE) algorithm (McDonald et al., 2005b). The MST framework is used here to obtain the optimal solution of Equation (6). Let $s(h, t)$ denote the score of the edge from a parent node h to a child node t. The score $s(h, t)$ is defined as follows:

$$s(h, t) = \log P_t(h|\mathbf{w}). \tag{8}$$

The logarithm of the marginal distribution is used as the score because the summation of the edge scores is maximized by the MST algorithms but the product of the marginal distributions should be maximized. The best projective parse tree is obtained by using the Eisner algorithm with the scores, and the best non-projective one is obtained using the CLE algorithm.

Next is the explanation on how to efficiently calculate the marginal distribution $P_t(h|\mathbf{w})$. R samples $\{\mathbf{h}^{(1)}, \cdots, \mathbf{h}^{(R)}\}$ are generated from $P_{\Lambda,\mathrm{M}}(\mathbf{h}|\mathbf{w})$ using Gibbs sampling, and the marginal distribution is then calculated approximately as follows:

$$\begin{aligned} P_t(h|\mathbf{w}) &= \sum_{\substack{h_1,\cdots,h_{t-1},h_{t+1},\cdots,h_{|\mathbf{w}|} \\ h_t = h}} P_{\Lambda,\mathrm{M}}(\mathbf{h}|\mathbf{w}), \\ &= \sum_{\mathbf{h}} P_{\Lambda,\mathrm{M}}(\mathbf{h}|\mathbf{w}) \delta(h, h_t), \\ &\simeq \frac{1}{R} \sum_{r=1}^{R} \delta(h, h_t^{(r)}). \end{aligned} \tag{9}$$

where $\delta(i, j)$ is the Kronecker delta. Gibbs sampling is one of the Markov chain Monte Carlo (MCMC) methods; these can efficiently generate samples from high-dimensional probability distributions with complex dependencies among variables (Andrieu et al., 2003). The algorithm is shown in Fig. 5.2. First, the initial state $\mathbf{h}^{(0)}$ is set; then, one new random variable is sampled at a time from the conditional distribution where all other variables are fixed. New samples are created by repeating the process. Gibbs sampling is guaranteed to converge to the true distribution. In this study, the initial state $\mathbf{h}^{(0)}$ is set to the set of heads which maximizes $Q_{\mathrm{M}}(\mathbf{h}|\mathbf{w})$.

The computational cost of Gibbs sampling is relatively large because many samples are repeatedly generated and probabilities for all the candidates of heads are calculated. Therefore, candidates of heads are ignored if their probabilities calculated with the token-level model are less than a threshold value θ because, intuitively, if the probabilities of the candidates calculated with only token-level features are small enough, the probabilities calculated with sentence-level features are thought to be also small enough to be ignored. θ is set to 0.5% in this study.

Initialize $\mathbf{h}^{(0)}$
for $r := 1$ **to** R
  for $t := 1$ **to** $|\mathbf{w}|$
    Sample $h_t^{(r)} \sim P(h_t|\mathbf{w}, h_1^{(r)}, \cdots, h_{t-1}^{(r)}, h_{t+1}^{(r-1)}, \cdots, h_{|\mathbf{w}|}^{(r-1)})$

Fig. 5.2 Gibbs sampling

5.2.3 Parameter Estimation

Here is the explanation for how the parameters of the proposed models are estimated, given training data consisting of N examples $\{\langle \mathbf{w}^1, \mathbf{h}^1 \rangle, \cdots, \langle \mathbf{w}^N, \mathbf{h}^N \rangle\}$.

First, the parameters for the token-level model $\mathrm{M} = \{\mu_1, \cdots, \mu_L\}$ are estimated. A maximum a posteriori (MAP) estimation with Gaussian priors is used. The following objective function $\mathcal{M}$ is defined, and the optimal solution which maximizes $\mathcal{M}$ is found:

$$\begin{aligned} \mathcal{M} &= \log \prod_{n=1}^{N} Q_{\mathrm{M}}(\mathbf{h}^n | \mathbf{w}^n) - \frac{1}{2\sigma^2} \sum_{l=1}^{L} \mu_l^2, \\ &= \sum_{n=1}^{N} \sum_{t=1}^{|\mathbf{w}^n|} \left[-\log Y_{\mathrm{M}}(\mathbf{w}^n, t) + \sum_{l=1}^{L} \mu_l g_l(\mathbf{w}^n, t, h_t^n) \right] - \frac{1}{2\sigma^2} \sum_{l=1}^{L} \mu_l^2. \end{aligned} \tag{10}$$

where σ is a hyper parameter of Gaussian priors. The partial derivatives of the objective function are as follows:

$$\begin{aligned} \frac{\partial \mathcal{M}}{\partial \mu_l} &= \sum_{n=1}^{N} \sum_{t=1}^{|\mathbf{w}^n|} \left[-\frac{\partial}{\partial \mu_l} \log Y_{\mathrm{M}}(\mathbf{w}^n, t) + g_l(\mathbf{w}^n, t, h_t^n) \right] - \frac{1}{\sigma^2} \mu_l, \\ &= \sum_{n=1}^{N} \sum_{t=1}^{|\mathbf{w}^n|} \left[- \sum_{\substack{h'=0 \\ h' \neq t}}^{|\mathbf{w}^n|} q_{\mathrm{M}}^t(h' | \mathbf{w}^n) g_l(\mathbf{w}^n, t, h') + g_l(\mathbf{w}^n, t, h_t^n) \right] - \frac{1}{\sigma^2} \mu_l. \end{aligned} \tag{11}$$

The optimal parameter M that maximizes $\mathcal{M}$ is obtained using the L-BFGS algorithm (Liu and Nocedal, 1989), a quasi-Newton method.

The parameters of the sentence-level model $\Lambda = \{\lambda_1, \cdots, \lambda_K\}$ are similarly estimated with the following objective function $\mathcal{L}$ after the parameter for the token-level model $\mathcal{M}$ is estimated:

$$\begin{aligned} \mathcal{L} &= \log \prod_{n=1}^{N} P_{\Lambda,\mathrm{M}}(\mathbf{h}^n | \mathbf{w}^n) - \frac{1}{2\sigma'^2} \sum_{k=1}^{K} \lambda_k^2, \\ &= \sum_{n=1}^{N} \left[-\log Z_{\Lambda,\mathrm{M}}(\mathbf{w}^n) + \sum_{k=1}^{K} \lambda_k f_k(\mathbf{w}^n, \mathbf{h}^n) \right] \\ &\quad - \frac{1}{2\sigma'^2} \sum_{k=1}^{K} \lambda_k^2 + \sum_{n=1}^{N} \log Q_{\mathrm{M}}(\mathbf{h}^n | \mathbf{w}^n). \end{aligned} \tag{12}$$

where σ' is a hyper parameter of Gaussian priors. The partial derivatives of the objective function are as follows:

$$\frac{\partial \mathcal{L}}{\partial \lambda_k} = \sum_{n=1}^{N} \left[-\frac{\partial}{\partial \lambda_k} \log Z_{\Lambda,\mathrm{M}}(\mathbf{w}^n) + f_k(\mathbf{w}^n, \mathbf{h}^n) \right] - \frac{1}{\sigma'^2}\lambda_k,$$

$$= \sum_{n=1}^{N} \left[- \sum_{\mathbf{h}' \in \mathcal{H}(\mathbf{w}^n)} P_{\Lambda,\mathrm{M}}(\mathbf{h}'|\mathbf{w}^n) f_k(\mathbf{w}^n, \mathbf{h}') + f_k(\mathbf{w}^n, \mathbf{h}^n) \right] - \frac{1}{\sigma'^2}\lambda_k. \quad (13)$$

The optimal parameter Λ is obtained with the L-BFGS algorithm. However, the partial function in Equation (12) and the expected value of a feature function in Equation (13) contain summations over all the possible configurations, which are difficult to calculate. These values are approximately calculated using a static Monte Carlo—not the MCMC—method. S samples $\{\mathbf{h}^{n(1)}, \cdots, \mathbf{h}^{n(S)}\}$ are generated from the probability distribution $Q_{\mathrm{M}}(\mathbf{h}|\mathbf{w})$ for the n-th sentence $\mathbf{w}^n$ in training data. The partial function and the expected value of a feature function are approximately calculated as follows:

$$\log Z_{\Lambda,\mathrm{M}}(\mathbf{w}^n) = \log \sum_{\mathbf{h}' \in \mathcal{H}(\mathbf{w}^n)} Q_{\mathrm{M}}(\mathbf{h}'|\mathbf{w}^n) \exp\left\{ \sum_{k=1}^{K} \lambda_k f_k(\mathbf{w}^n, \mathbf{h}') \right\},$$

$$\simeq \log \frac{1}{S} \sum_{s=1}^{S} \exp\left\{ \sum_{k=1}^{K} \lambda_k f_k(\mathbf{w}^n, \mathbf{h}^{n(s)}) \right\}. \quad (14)$$

$$\sum_{\mathbf{h}' \in \mathcal{H}(\mathbf{w}^n)} P_{\Lambda,\mathrm{M}}(\mathbf{h}'|\mathbf{w}^n) f_k(\mathbf{w}^n, \mathbf{h}')$$

$$= \sum_{\mathbf{h}' \in \mathcal{H}(\mathbf{w}^n)} Q_{\mathrm{M}}(\mathbf{h}'|\mathbf{w}^n) \frac{f_k(\mathbf{w}^n, \mathbf{h}')}{Z_{\Lambda,\mathrm{M}}(\mathbf{w}^n)} \exp\left\{ \sum_{k'=1}^{K} \lambda_{k'} f_{k'}(\mathbf{w}^n, \mathbf{h}') \right\},$$

$$\simeq \frac{1}{S} \sum_{s=1}^{S} \frac{f_k(\mathbf{w}^n, \mathbf{h}^{n(s)})}{Z_{\Lambda,\mathrm{M}}(\mathbf{w}^n)} \exp\left\{ \sum_{k'=1}^{K} \lambda_{k'} f_{k'}(\mathbf{w}^n, \mathbf{h}^{n(s)}) \right\}. \quad (15)$$

Obtaining the samples from $Q_{\mathrm{M}}(\mathbf{h}|\mathbf{w})$ is easy because there are no dependencies among variables in $Q_{\mathrm{M}}(\mathbf{h}|\mathbf{w})$. The same samples are reused in all the iterations of the L-BFGS algorithm.[3]

5.2.4 Local Features

The token-level local features used are the same as those used in MSTParser version 0.4.2.[4] The features include lexical forms and POS tags of parent tokens, child

[3] Although more accurate methods for the parameter estimation may give better performance, the static Monte Carlo method using fixed samples is adopted here in order to approximately estimate the parameters at a reasonable computational cost.

[4] `http://sourceforge.net/projects/mstparser/`

tokens, their surrounding tokens and tokens between the child and the parent. The direction and the distance from a parent to its child are also included. Features that appear less than five times in training data are discarded.

5.2.5 Global Features

Global features can be used to represent any information in dependency trees. Nine types of global features are used, most of which are similar to those used by Collins and Koo (2005), though the features they used were tailored for phrase structure parsing. In the following explanation, *parent node* refers to a head token, and *child node* to a dependent token. The dependency tree in Fig. 5.1 is used here as an example.

5.2.5.1 Child Unigram+Parent+Grandparent

This feature template is a 4-tuple consisting of (1) a child node, (2) its parent node, (3) the direction from the parent node to the child node: left (l) or right (r), and (4) the grandparent node (or the special symbol ϕ if the parent node is a root node).

Each node in the feature template is expanded to its lexical form and POS tag in order to obtain the actual features. Features that appear in four or less sentences are discarded. The same procedure is applied to the following other features.

Example (Fig. 5.1): $\langle A, B, l, C\rangle$, $\langle B, C, l, \phi\rangle$, $\langle D, G, l, C\rangle$, $\langle E, G, l, C\rangle$, $\langle F, G, l, C\rangle$, $\langle G, C, r, \phi\rangle$, $\langle H, C, r, \phi\rangle$.

5.2.5.2 Child Bigram+Parent

This feature template is a 4-tuple consisting of (1) a child node, (2) its parent node, (3) the direction from the parent node to the child node (4) the nearest outer sibling node (the nearest sibling node which lies on the opposite side of the parent node) of the child node (or the special symbol ϕ if the child node is the outermost child node). This feature template is almost the same as the one used by McDonald and Pereira (2006).

Example (Fig. 5.1): $\langle A, B, l, \phi\rangle$, $\langle B, C, l, \phi\rangle$, $\langle D, G, l, \phi\rangle$, $\langle E, G, l, D\rangle$, $\langle F, G, l, E\rangle$, $\langle G, C, r, H\rangle$, $\langle H, C, r, \phi\rangle$.

5.2.5.3 Child Bigram+Parent+Grandparent

This feature template is a 5-tuple. The first four elements (1)–(4) are the same as the *Child Bigram + Parent* feature template, and the additional element (5) is the grandparent node.

Example (Fig. 5.1): $\langle A, B, l, \phi, C\rangle$, $\langle B, C, l, \phi, \phi\rangle$, $\langle D, G, l, \phi, C\rangle$, $\langle E, G, l, D, C\rangle$, $\langle F, G, l, E, C\rangle$, $\langle G, C, r, H, \phi\rangle$, $\langle H, C, r, \phi, \phi\rangle$.

5.2.5.4 Child Trigram+Parent

This feature template is a 5-tuple. The first four elements (1)–(4) are the same as the **ChildBigram + Parent** feature template, and the additional element (5) is the next nearest outer sibling node of the child node.

Example (Fig. 5.1): $\langle A, B, l, \phi, \phi \rangle$, $\langle B, C, l, \phi, \phi \rangle$, $\langle D, G, l, \phi, \phi \rangle$, $\langle E, G, l, D, \phi \rangle$, $\langle F, G, l, E, D \rangle$, $\langle G, C, r, H, \phi \rangle$, $\langle H, C, r, \phi, \phi \rangle$.

5.2.5.5 Parent+All Children

This feature template is a tuple with more than one element. The first element is a parent node, and the other elements are all its child nodes. The child nodes in the left hand side of the parent node should be distinguished from those in the right hand side, and the latter nodes are indicated by primes in the examples below.

Example (Fig. 5.1): $\langle A \rangle$, $\langle B, A \rangle$, $\langle C, B, G', H' \rangle$, $\langle D \rangle$, $\langle E \rangle$, $\langle F \rangle$, $\langle G, D, E, F \rangle$, $\langle H \rangle$.

5.2.5.6 Parent+All Children+Grandparent

This feature template is a tuple with more than two elements. The elements other than the last one are the same as the **Parent + AllChildren** feature template, and the last element is the grandparent node.

Example (Fig. 5.1): $\langle A, B \rangle$, $\langle B, A, C \rangle$, $\langle C, B, G', H', \phi \rangle$, $\langle D, G \rangle$, $\langle E, G \rangle$, $\langle F, G \rangle$, $\langle G, D, E, F, C \rangle$, $\langle H, C \rangle$.

5.2.5.7 Child+Ancestor

This feature template is a 2-tuple consisting of (1) a child node, and (2) one of its ancestor nodes. Tamura et al. (2007) reported that this kind of information was useful to improve accuracy of Japanese dependency parsing.

Example (Fig. 5.1): $\langle A, B \rangle$, $\langle A, C \rangle$, $\langle B, C \rangle$, $\langle D, G \rangle$, $\langle D, C \rangle$, $\langle E, G \rangle$, $\langle E, C \rangle$, $\langle F, G \rangle$, $\langle F, C \rangle$, $\langle G, C \rangle$, $\langle H, C \rangle$.

5.2.5.8 Acyclic

This feature type has one of two values, *true* if the dependency graph is acyclic and *false* otherwise.

Example (Fig. 5.1): *true*.

5.2.5.9 Projective

This feature type has one of two values, *true* if the dependency tree is projective and *false* otherwise.

Example (Fig. 5.1): *true*.

5.3 Dependency Relation Labeling

The method explained in the previous section determines unlabeled dependency structures only. The labels of the edges in the dependency tree are attached using Support Vector Machines afterwards.

5.3.1 *Model*

Dependency relation labeling can be handled as a multi-class classification problem, and Support Vector Machines (SVMs) are used for this task. Solving large-scale multi-class classification problem with SVMs requires substantial computational resources, so the revision learning method (Nakagawa et al., 2002) is used. The revision learning method combines a probabilistic model, which has a smaller computational cost, with a binary classifier, which has a higher generalization capacity. The latter classifier revises the output of the former model to conduct multi-class classification with higher accuracy at a reasonable computational cost. In this study, maximum entropy (ME) models are used for the probabilistic model and SVMs with the second order polynomial kernel for the binary classifier. The dependency relation label of each edge is determined independently of the labeling of other edges.

5.3.2 *Features*

For the features for SVMs to predict the dependency relation label between the i-th token and its parent, the lexical forms and POS tags of the i-th and h_i-th tokens are used. The lexical forms and POS tags of the tokens surrounding and in between them (i.e. the j-th token where $j \in \{j | \min\{i, h_i\} - 1 \leq j \leq \max\{i, h_i\} + 1\}$), the grandparent ($h_{h_i}$-th) token, the sibling tokens of i (the j'-th token where $j' \in \{j' | h_{j'} = h_i, j' \neq i\}$), and the child tokens of i (the j''-th token where $j'' \in \{j'' | h_{j''} = i\}$), are used as well. As for the features for ME models, a subset is used as ME models are simply for reducing the search space in the revision learning method, and thus do not need so many features.

5.4 Experiments

Experiments were conducted on the CoNLL 2007 shared task dataset, the CoNLL-X shared task dataset, and the Penn Treebank WSJ corpus. For the two CoNLL shared task datasets, the following measures were used to evaluate parsing performance.

$$\textit{Labeled Attachment Score (LAS)} = \frac{\langle \text{\# of tokens with correct heads and labels} \rangle}{\langle \text{\# of tokens} \rangle},$$

$$\textit{Unlabeled Attachment Score (UAS)} = \frac{\langle \text{\# of tokens with correct heads} \rangle}{\langle \text{\# of tokens} \rangle}.$$

For the WSJ corpus, the following measures were used:

$$\textit{Dependency Accuracy (DA)} = \frac{\langle \text{\# of tokens with correct heads} \rangle}{\langle \text{\# of tokens} \rangle},$$

$$\textit{Root Accuracy (RA)} = \frac{\langle \text{\# of sentences whose root nodes are correctly identified} \rangle}{\langle \text{\# of sentences} \rangle},$$

$$\textit{Complete Match (CM)} = \frac{\langle \text{\# of correctly parsed sentences} \rangle}{\langle \text{\# of sentences} \rangle}.$$

In the calculation of the above measures, punctuation marks were taken into account for the CoNLL 2007 dataset but ignored for the CoNLL-X dataset and the WSJ corpus. These evaluation methods conform to those used in previous studies (Yamada and Matsumoto, 2003; Buchholz and Marsi, 2006; Nivre et al., 2007).

5.4.1 Experiments on the CoNLL 2007 Shared Task Dataset

Experiments were conducted on the CoNLL 2007 shared task dataset (Nivre et al., 2007) which consists of corpora of 10 languages (Hajič et al., 2004; Aduriz et al., 2003; Martí et al., 2007; Chen et al., 2003; Böhmová et al., 2003; Marcus et al., 1993; Johansson and Nugues, 2007; Prokopidis et al., 2005; Csendes et al., 2005; Montemagni et al., 2003; Oflazer et al., 2003). In order to tune the hyper-parameters of the models, each training data set was split into two parts; the first half was used for training and the remaining half for testing in development. The values of the fixed parameters were set at $R = 500$, $S = 200$, $\sigma = 0.25$, and $\sigma' = 0.25$. The CLE algorithm was used for the Basque, Czech, Hungarian and Turkish languages; the Eisner algorithm was used for the others. Some corpora have information of both the word form and the lemma for each token; lemmas were used for Catalan, Czech, Greek, and Italian, and word forms for all others. With these parameter settings, training took 247 h, and testing took 343 min on an Opteron 250 processor.

Table 5.1 shows the evaluation results of the test sets. Compared to the parsing systems which participated in the shared task, the proposed method obtained the second-best average accuracy in the LAS, and the best average accuracy in the UAS (Nivre et al., 2007). Compared with the others, the gap between the labeled and unlabeled scores for the proposed method was relatively large. In this study, the labeling of dependency relations was performed in a separate post-processing step, and each label was predicted independently. The labeled scores may improve if the parsing process and the labeling process are performed simultaneously and dependencies among labels are taken into account.

Experiments were conducted with different settings. Table 5.2 shows the results measured using the UAS. In the table, **Eisner** and **CLE** indicate that the Eisner algorithm and the CLE algorithm respectively were used in decoding, and **Local**

Table 5.1 Results of dependency parsing on the CoNLL 2007 dataset

	Arabic	Basque	Catalan	Chinese	Czech	English	Greek	Hungar.	Italian	Turkish	Average
LAS(%)	75.08	72.56	87.90	83.84	80.19	88.41	76.31	76.74	83.61	78.22	80.29
UAS(%)	86.09	81.04	92.86	88.88	86.28	90.13	84.08	82.49	87.91	85.77	86.55

Table 5.2 Unlabeled attachment scores in different settings (bold: highest scores)

Algorithm	Features	Arabic	Basque	Catalan	Chinese	Czech	English	Greek	Hungar.	Italian	Turkish
Eisner	Local	85.15	80.20	91.75	86.75	84.19	88.65	83.31	80.27	86.72	84.82
(proj.)	+Global	**86.09**	81.00	**92.86**	**88.88**	85.99	**90.13**	**84.08**	81.55	87.91	84.82
CLE	Local	84.80	80.39	91.23	86.71	84.21	88.07	83.03	81.15	86.85	85.35
(non-proj.)	+Global	85.83	**81.04**	92.64	88.84	**86.28**	90.05	83.87	**82.49**	**87.97**	**85.77**

and **+Global** respectively indicate that local features, and local and global features together were used. The CLE algorithm performed better than the Eisner algorithm for Basque, Czech, Hungarian, Italian and Turkish. All of the data except for Italian contained relatively large numbers of non-projective sentences (the percentage of sentences with at least one non-projective relation in the training data was over 20% (Nivre et al., 2007)), though the Greek data, on which the Eisner algorithm performed better, also contains many non-projective sentences (20.3%).

By using the global features, the accuracy was improved in all the cases except for Turkish (Eisner) (Table 5.2). The increase in accuracy was significantly large in Chinese and Czech. When the global features were used in these languages, the dependency accuracy for tokens whose heads had conjunctions as parts of speech notably improved: from 80.5 to 86.0% in Chinese (Eisner) and from 73.2 to 77.6% in Czech (CLE). The trained parameters of the global features were investigated, and *Parent+All Children* features, whose parents were conjunctions and whose children had compatible classes, were found to have had large positive weights, and those whose children had incompatible classes had large negative weights. A feature with a larger weight is generally more influential. Riedel and Clarke (2006) proposed to use linguistic constraints such as "arguments of a coordination must have compatible word classes," and such constraints seemed to be represented by the features in the proposed models.

5.4.2 Experiments on the CoNLL-X Shared Task Dataset

Experiments were conducted on the CoNLL-X shared task dataset (Buchholz and Marsi, 2006), using the data for Danish, Dutch, Portuguese and Swedish.[5](Kromann, 2003; van der Beek et al., 2002; Afonso et al., 2002; Nilsson

[5] Although 13 languages were handled in the shared task, only the four languages were used because the corpora of the four languages are freely available.
(`http://nextens.uvt.nl/~conll/`)

Table 5.3 Labeled attachment scores on the CoNLL-X dataset

Algorithm (features)	Danish	Dutch	Portuguese	Swedish
Eisner (local)	84.07	76.93	86.38	81.88
Eisner (+global)	85.13	78.03	86.78	82.73
CLE (local)	84.11	79.79	86.32	81.74
CLE (+global)	**85.39**	**81.11**	87.00	82.49
CoNLL 1st	84.79	79.19	**87.60**	**84.58**
CoNLL 2nd	84.77	78.59	86.82	82.55
CoNLL 3rd	83.63	78.59	86.01	82.31

Table 5.4 Unlabeled attachment scores on the CoNLL-X dataset

Algorithm (features)	Danish	Dutch	Portuguese	Swedish
Eisner (local)	89.94	80.73	90.84	88.83
Eisner (+global)	90.92	81.81	91.36	**89.82**
CLE (local)	90.04	83.71	90.66	88.73
CLE (+global)	**91.24**	**85.33**	**91.44**	89.48
CoNLL 1st	90.58	83.57	91.36	89.54
CoNLL 2nd	89.80	82.91	91.22	89.50
CoNLL 3rd	89.66	81.73	90.30	89.05

et al., 2005) The hyper-parameters of the models were set to the same ones in Section 5.4.1.

Tables 5.3 and 5.4 show the results measured with the LAS and the UAS respectively. These results were compared to those of the top three systems which participated in the shared task (*CoNLL 1st, 2nd, 3rd*). The method proposed in this chapter had the best labeled attachment scores for Danish and Dutch, and had the best unlabeled attachment scores for all the languages.

5.4.3 Experiments on the WSJ Corpus

Experiments were conducted on the Penn Treebank WSJ corpus. Dependency structures were extracted from the corpus using the Yamada and Matsumoto (2003) head rules. Dependency edges in this corpus have no labels, and no dependency relation labeling was conducted. Sections 2–21 were used for training and Section 23 for evaluation. POS tags of the evaluation data were attached using an SVM-based POS tagger (Nakagawa et al., 2002) which was trained with the training data (tagging accuracy for the evaluation data was 97.1%). The hyper-parameters of the models were set to the values described in Section 5.4.1. The number of token-level local features was 14,910,831, and the number of sentence-level global features was 6,352,939.

The results are shown in Table 5.5. The method was then compared to MSTParser version 0.2. The parser can handle both projective dependency parsing (McDonald et al., 2005a) and non-projective dependency parsing (McDonald et al., 2005b), and also can use second order features (one of sentence-level global features)

Table 5.5 Results of dependency parsing on the WSJ corpus

Algorithm	DA (%)	RA (%)	CM (%)
Eisner (local)	90.7	95.2	35.6
Eisner (+global)	**91.8**	95.3	**42.6**
CLE (local)	90.3	**95.6**	33.7
CLE (+global)	91.6	95.4	41.5
MSTParser proj. (1st. order)	91.0	93.8	37.5
MSTParser proj. (+2nd. order)	91.7	94.9	**42.6**
MSTParser non-proj. (1st. order)	90.4	94.2	34.3
MSTParser non-proj. (+2nd. order)	91.5	94.4	40.6

(McDonald and Pereira, 2006) as well as first order features (token-level local features). The dependency accuracy of the proposed method was improved by using the global features and was slightly superior to MSTParser.

Other experiments were conducted in order to investigate the contribution of each global feature. The results are shown in Table 5.6, which were obtained using the Eisner algorithm. For each global feature, experiments were conducted with two settings: one using only one particular feature (*When Included*), and the other using all the features except that one (**When Excluded**). The accuracy always improved as each feature was included, except for the acyclic feature and the projective feature. When each feature was removed the accuracy did not decrease so much, indicating that these features have much redundancy.

The proposed method employs approximate calculation using randomly generated samples. S samples are used for the static Monte Carlo method in training, and R samples are used for Gibbs sampling in testing. Experiments were conducted for various values of S and R, in order to investigate the influence of the number of samples. Table 5.7 shows the results obtained with the Eisner algorithm. For both S and R, the parsing performance tended to be higher when the number of samples was larger.

Table 5.6 Results of dependency parsing with/without each global feature: two cases were examined for each feature; one is a case using only the feature, and the other is a case using all features other than that one

	DA (%)/CM (%)		
Feature	When included	When excluded	Number of features
None	90.7/35.6	91.8/42.6	0
All	91.8/42.6	90.7/35.6	6,352,939
Child Unigram+Parent+Grandparent	91.1/37.5	91.8/42.3	760,477
Child Bigram+Parent	91.3/39.2	91.8/42.3	622,525
Child Bigram+Parent+Grandparent	91.5/39.9	91.7/42.0	2,442,343
Child Trigram+Parent	91.4/40.0	91.7/41.8	1,680,397
Parent+All Children	91.0/37.2	91.8/42.0	139,167
Parent+All Children+Grandparent	91.0/37.0	91.7/42.3	222,197
Child+Ancestor	91.0/36.6	91.7/42.0	485,829
Acyclic	90.7/35.2	91.7/42.3	2
Projective	90.7/35.6	91.8/42.5	2

Table 5.7 Results of dependency parsing using different numbers of samples

DA (%)/CM (%)					
	S				
R	10	20	50	100	200
10	91.0/38.9	91.1/39.1	91.2/39.7	91.3/39.8	91.3/40.0
20	91.2/39.7	91.3/40.4	91.3/40.0	91.5/41.2	91.5/41.2
50	91.3/40.6	91.5/41.3	91.6/41.7	91.6/41.9	91.6/41.7
100	91.5/41.0	91.5/41.6	91.6/42.0	91.7/42.0	91.7/41.8
200	91.5/41.2	91.5/41.3	91.6/41.8	91.7/42.1	91.7/42.3
500	91.5/41.1	91.6/41.7	91.7/41.8	91.7/42.2	**91.8/42.6**
1000	91.5/41.0	91.6/41.7	91.7/42.2	**91.8**/42.1	**91.8**/42.4
2000	91.5/40.9	91.6/41.4	91.7/42.0	**91.8**/42.1	**91.8**/42.4

5.5 Related Work

There have been several studies on dependency parsing which attempted to use features without assuming independence among the heads of tokens. Kudo and Matsumoto (2002) studied deterministic Japanese dependency parsing, and Yamada and Matsumoto (2003) studied deterministic English dependency parsing. In their methods, sentences were parsed in a deterministic manner, and information of already determined heads was used as features. They reported that such features significantly improved parsing accuracy. These features can be used without extra computational cost in deterministic parsers; however, deterministic methods are based upon local decisions, which may fail for sentences with local ambiguities, and available features with the methods are limited to those that are in the already determined structures.

McDonald and Pereira (2006) proposed a dependency parsing algorithm which can incorporate *second-order features* (features relate to two neighboring child nodes and their parent node in dependency trees). They used the second-order projective Eisner algorithm for projective dependency parsing. In the case of non-projective dependency parsing, they rearranged the resulting projective tree using a greedy algorithm to obtain a better non-projective tree. The method is efficient and highly accurate, but it seems difficult to use even higher-order features in the framework.

Riedel and Clarke (2006) presented a method for non-projective dependency parsing using integer linear programming (Roth and Yih, 2004). They used integer linear programming for decoding in order to incorporate global linguistic constraints, such as "arguments of a coordination must have compatible word classes." Their method can incorporate a wide variety of sentence-level information; however, the method does not seem to be robust for noisy data because global information is used not as features but as hard constraints.

Collins and Koo (2005) proposed a reranking approach for phrase structure parsing. In their method, a fixed number of candidates were generated first for a given sentence by a base parser, and then reranked by another model using features in the candidate trees. The reranker can use any sentence-level global feature, and they reported that the parsing accuracy of the existing base parser was boosted with the method. However, correct solutions can not be obtained unless the base parser, which usually uses only local features, outputs the correct solutions among the candidates. Hall (2007) studied a reranking method for dependency parsing. In the study, k-best maximum spanning tree algorithm was used, which can efficiently generate k-best candidates of non-projective dependency trees. Global features such as valency and great grandparent information were used in reranking.

Johnson et al. (1999) studied exponential models for unification-based grammars. Global features were incorporated in their models, and a pseudo-likelihood estimator was used for parameter estimation. Rosenfeld et al. (2001) studied whole-sentence exponential language models. They used exponential models in order to use any sentence-level feature for language modeling, and used Gibbs sampling and other sampling methods for inference.

5.6 Conclusion

In this chapter, a method for dependency parsing using global features was presented. This method can incorporate any sentence-level global feature as well as token-level local features. It used the maximum spanning tree framework, and edge scores were calculated as marginal probabilities using Gibbs sampling. Experimental results showed that the method had high accuracy with such features. Future work will involve improving the dependency relation labeling.

Acknowledgements The author would like to thank Professor Yuji Matsumoto at Nara Institute of Science and Technology and Dr. Hiroyasu Yamada at JustSystems Corporation for their help.

References

Abeillé, A. (Ed.) (2003). *Treebanks: Building and Using Parsed Corpora*. Dordrecht: Kluwer.

Aduriz, I., M.J. Aranzabe, J.M. Arriola, A. Atutxa, A.D. de Ilarraza, A. Garmendia, and M. Oronoz (2003). Construction of a Basque dependency treebank. In *Proceedings of the 2nd Workshop on Treebanks and Linguistic Theories (TLT)*, pp. 201–204.

Afonso, S., E. Bick, R. Haber, and D. Santos (2002). "Floresta sintá(c)tica": a treebank for Portuguese. In *Proceedings of LREC 2002*, pp. 1698–1703.

Andrieu, C., N. de Freitas, A. Doucet, and M.I. Jordan (2003). An introduction to MCMC for machine learning. *Machine Learning 50*, 5–43.

Böhmová, A., J. Hajič, E. Hajičová, and B. Hladká (2003). The PDT: a 3-level annotation scenario. See Abeillé (2003), Chapter 7, pp. 103–127.

Buchholz, S. and E. Marsi (2006). Conll-x shared task on multilingual dependency parsing. In *Proceedings of CoNLL 2006*, New York, NY, pp. 149–164.

Chen, K., C. Luo, M. Chang, F. Chen, C. Chen, C. Huang, and Z. Gao (2003). Sinica treebank: Design criteria, representational issues and implementation. See Abeillé (2003), Chapter 13, pp. 231–248.

Collins, M. and T. Koo (2005). Discriminative reranking for natural language parsing. *Computational Linguistics 31*(1), 25–69.
Covington, M.A. (2001). A fundamental algorithm for dependency parsing. In *Proceedings of ACM Southeast Conference 2001*, pp. 95–102.
Csendes, D., J. Csirik, T. Gyimóthy, and A. Kocsor (2005). *The Szeged Treebank*. Springer.
Eisner, J. (1996). Three new probabilistic models for dependency parsing: an exploration. In *Proceedings of COLING '96*, pp. 340–345.
Hajič, J., O. Smrž, P. Zemánek, J. Šnaidauf, and E. Beška (2004). Prague Arabic dependency treebank: Development in data and tools. In *Proceedings of the NEMLAR International Conference on Arabic Language Resources and Tools*, pp. 110–117.
Hall, K. (2007). K-best spanning tree parsing. In *Proceedings of ACL 2007*, pp. 392–399.
Johansson, R. and P. Nugues (2007). Extended constituent-to-dependency conversion for English. In *Proceedings of the 16th Nordic Conference on Computational Linguistics (NODALIDA)*.
Johnson, M., S. Geman, S. Canon, Z. Chi, and S. Riezler (1999). Estimators for stochastic "unification-based" grammars. In *Proceedings of ACL'99*, pp. 535–541.
Kromann, M.T. (2003). The Danish dependency treebank and the underlying linguistic theory. In *Proceedings of the 2nd Workshop on Treebanks and Linguistic Theories (TLT)*.
Kudo, T. and Y. Matsumoto (2002). Japanese dependency analysis using cascaded chunking. In *Proceedings of CoNLL 2002*, pp. 63–69.
Liu, D.C. and J. Nocedal (1989). On the limited memory BFGS method for large scale optimization. *Mathematical Programming 45*(3), 503–528.
Marcus, M., B. Santorini, and M. Marcinkiewicz (1993). Building a large annotated corpus of English: the Penn Treebank. *Computational Linguistics 19*(2), 313–330.
Martí, M.A., M. Taulé, L. Màrquez, and M. Bertran (2007). CESS-ECE: A multilingual and multilevel annotated corpus. Available for download from: http://www.lsi.upc.edu/~mbertran/cess-ece/.
McDonald, R., K. Crammer, and F. Pereira (2005a). Online large-margin training of dependency parsers. In *Proceedings of ACL 2005*, pp. 91–98.
McDonald, R. and F. Pereira (2006). Online learning of approximate dependency parsing algorithms. In *Proceedings of EACL 2006*, pp. 81–88.
McDonald, R., F. Pereira, K. Ribarow, and J. Hajic (2005b). Non-projective dependency parsing using spanning tree algorithms. In *Proceedings of HLT/EMNLP 2005*, pp. 523–530.
Montemagni, S., F. Barsotti, M. Battista, N. Calzolari, O. Corazzari, A. Lenci, A. Zampolli, F. Fanciulli, M. Massetani, R. Raffaelli, R. Basili, M.T. Pazienza, D. Saracino, F. Zanzotto, N. Nana, F. Pianesi, and R. Delmonte (2003). Building the Italian syntactic-semantic treebank. See Abeillé (2003), Chapter 11, pp. 189–210.
Nakagawa, T., T. Kudo, and Y. Matsumoto (2002). Revision learning and its application to part-of-speech tagging. In *Proceedings of ACL 2002*, pp. 497–504.
Nilsson, J., J. Hall, and J. Nivre (2005). MAMBA meets TIGER: reconstructing a Swedish treebank from antiquity. In *Proceedings of the NODALIDA Special Session on Treebanks*.
Nivre, J. (2003). An efficient algorithm for projective dependency parsing. In *Proceedings of IWPT 2003*, pp. 149–160.
Nivre, J., J. Hall, S. Kübler, R. McDonald, J. Nilsson, S. Riedel, and D. Yuret (2007). The CoNLL 2007 shared task on dependency parsing. In *Proceedings of the CoNLL 2007 Shared Task. Joint Conference on Empirical Methods in Natural Language Processing and Computational Natural Language Learning (EMNLP-CoNLL)*.
Oflazer, K., B. Say, D.Z. Hakkani-Tür, and G. Tür (2003). Building a Turkish treebank. See Abeillé (2003), Chapter 15, pp. 261–277.
Prokopidis, P., E. Desypri, M. Koutsombogera, H. Papageorgiou, and S. Piperidis (2005). Theoretical and practical issues in the construction of a Greek dependency treebank. In *Proceedings of the 4th Workshop on Treebanks and Linguistic Theories (TLT)*, pp. 149–160.
Riedel, S. and J. Clarke (2006). Incremental integer linear programming for non-projective dependency parsing. In *Proceedings of EMNLP 2006*, pp. 129–137.

Rosenfeld, R., S.F. Chen, and X. Zhu (2001). Whole-sentence exponential language models: a vehicle for linguistic-statistical integration. *Computers Speech and Language 15*(1), 55–73.

Roth, D. and W. Yih (2004). A linear programming formulation for global inference in natural language tasks. In *Proceedings of CoNLL 2004*, pp. 1–8.

Tamura, A., H. Takamura, and M. Okumura (2007). Japanese dependency analysis using ancestor-descendant relations. In *Proceedings of EMNLP-CoNLL 2007*, pp. 600–609.

van der Beek, L., G. Bouma, R. Malouf, and G. van Noord (2002). The Alpino dependency treebank. In M. Theune, A. Nijholt, H. Hondorp (eds.),*Computational Linguistics in the Netherlands* 2001. (http://www.rodopi.nl/senj.asp?BookId=LC+45).

Yamada, H. and Y. Matsumoto (2003). Statistical dependency analysis with support vector machines. In *Proceedings of IWPT 2003*, pp. 195–206.

Chapter 6
Dependency Parsing with Second-Order Feature Maps and Annotated Semantic Information

Massimiliano Ciaramita and Giuseppe Attardi

6.1 Introduction

Dependency trees represent sentences as labeled directed graphs encoding syntactic relations between words. The labels on the arcs represent grammatical relations such as “subject”, “object”, various types of modifiers etc. Dependency trees capture grammatical structures that are easy to interpret and can be useful in several language processing tasks such as information extraction (Culotta and Sorensen, 2004), knowledge acquisition (Ciaramita et al., 2005), machine translation (Ding and Palmer, 2005) and information retrieval (Surdeanu et al., 2008). Dependency treebanks are becoming available in many languages. Several approaches to dependency parsing on multiple languages have been evaluated in the CoNLL 2006 and 2007 shared tasks (Buchholz and Marsi, 2006; Nivre et al., 2007), and in conjunction with semantic role labeling as a joint learning problem in the CoNLL 2008 shared task (Surdeanu et al., 2008).

Dependency parsing defines a simpler problem than constituency parsing, since dependency trees do not include extra non-terminal nodes and there is no need for a full phrase structure grammar to generate them. Popular approaches to statistical dependency parsing either generate such trees by considering all possible spanning trees (McDonald et al., 2005), or build a single tree by means of shift-reduce parsing actions (Yamada and Matsumoto, 2003). Deterministic parsers which run in linear time have also been developed (Nivre and Scholz, 2004; Attardi, 2006). These parsers process the sentence sequentially with an efficiency suitable for processing large amounts of text, as required, for example, in information retrieval applications.

The accuracy of statistical dependency parsers can be improved, at some additional computational cost, by using rich feature sets and higher-order modeling. McDonald and Pereira (2006), for instance, incorporate second order features relating to adjacent edge pairs in their maximum spanning tree parser (MST). This second-order MST algorithm has cubic time complexity. For non-projective structures the problem is NP-hard and McDonald and Pereira (2006) introduce

M. Ciaramita (✉)
Yahoo! Research, S-08018 Barcelona, Catalonia, Spain
e-mail: massi@alumni.brown.edu

H. Bunt et al. (eds.), *Trends in Parsing Technology*, Text, Speech and Language Technology 43, DOI 10.1007/978-90-481-9352-3_6,

an approximate algorithm to handle such cases. Yamada and Matsumoto (2003) showed that learning a Support Vector Machine (SVM) model in the dual space with polynomial kernel functions significantly improves the accuracy of a parser based on a linear SVM. However, when the training set is large, it is not practical to train a single SVM model, hence Yamada and Matsumoto (see also Hall et al., 2006) resort to partitioning the training data into multiple sets, on the basis of parts of speech (POS), and train a dual SVM model on each. While this approach simplifies the learning task, it makes the parser more sensitive to the error rate of the POS tagger.

In this chapter we investigate shift-reduce parsing with second-order feature maps, which explicitly represent all pairs of features from the input space. The augmented feature space increases the computational costs. However, a good efficiency/accuracy trade-off can be achieved by using the perceptron algorithm, without the need to resort to approximations, producing high-accuracy classifiers based on a single model. Models learned with such methods tend to have large memory footprints, however several simple options for optimization are available.

We also evaluate a novel set of features for parsing. Recently various forms of shallow semantic processing have been investigated such as named-entity recognition (NER), semantic role labeling (SRL) and relation extraction. Syntactic parsing can provide useful features for these tasks; e.g., Punyakanok et al. (2005) show that full parsing is effective for semantic role labeling (see also related approaches evaluated within the CoNLL 2005 shared task: Carreras and Màrquez, 2005). However, no significant evidence has been provided so far that annotated semantic information can be leveraged for improving parser performance. We report experiments showing that adding features extracted by a named entity tagger improves the accuracy of the dependency parser.

6.2 Dependency Parsing

A dependency parser takes as input a sentence s and returns a dependency graph d. Fig. 6.1 shows a dependency tree for the sentence "Last week CBS Inc. canceled 'The People Next Door'.".[1] Dependencies are represented as labeled arrows from the *head* of the relation to the *modifier* word; thus, in the example, "Inc." is a modifier, the subject, of the verb "canceled".

In statistical syntactic parsing a generator (e.g., a PCFG) is used to produce a number of candidate trees (Collins, 2000) with associated probabilities. This approach has been used also for dependency parsing, generating spanning trees as candidates and computing the maximum spanning tree (MST) using discriminative learning algorithms (McDonald et al., 2005). Yamada and Matsumoto (2003) proposed a deterministic classifier-based parser. Instead of learning directly which tree to assign to a sentence, the parser learns which *Shift/Reduce* actions to use in building the tree. Parsing is cast as a classification problem: at each step the parser applies a classifier to the features representing its current state to predict which

[1] The figure also contains entity annotations which will be explained below in Section 6.4.1.

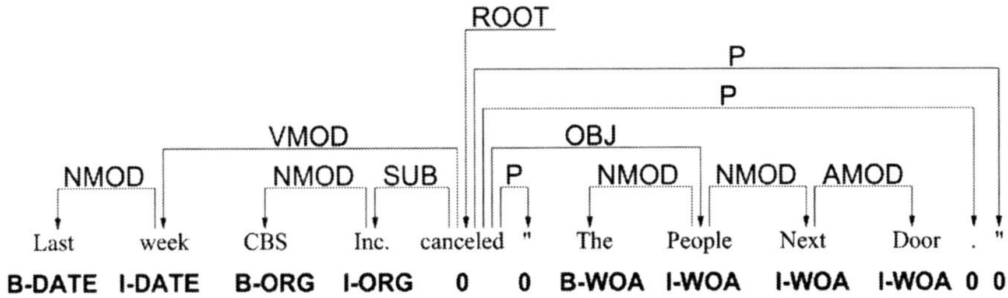

Fig. 6.1 A dependency tree from the Penn Treebank, with additional entity annotation from the BBN corpus

action to perform on the tree. Similar deterministic approaches to parsing have been investigated also in the context of constituent parsing (Wong and Wu, 1999; Kalt, 2004).

Nivre and Scholz (2004) proposed a variant of the model of Yamada and Matsumoto that reduces the complexity, from the worst case quadratic to linear. Attardi (2006) proposed a variant of the rules that handle non-projective relations while parsing deterministically in a single pass. Shift-reduce algorithms are simple and efficient, yet competitive in terms of accuracy: in the CoNLL-X shared task, for several languages, there was no statistically significant difference between second-order MST parsers and shift-reduce parsers.

6.3 A Shift-Reduce Parser

There are a few available implementations of shift-reduce dependency parsers: MaltParser (Nivre and Scholz, 2004), IDP (Titov and Henderson, 2007). Our experiments are based on DeSR, the shift-reduce parser described in Attardi (2006).[2] This parser builds dependency trees while scanning input sentences in a single left-to-right pass and performing shift/reduce parsing actions. The parsing algorithm is fully deterministic and has linear complexity. The parser behavior can be described as repeatedly selecting and applying a parsing rule to transform its state, while advancing through the sentence. Each token is analyzed once and a local decision is made concerning the action to take, without considering global properties of the tree being built.

6.3.1 Parsing Algorithm

The state of the parser is represented by a triple $\langle S, I, A\rangle$, where S is the stack, I is the list of input tokens that remain to be processed and A is the arc relation for the dependency graph, which consists of a set of labeled arcs (w_i, w_j, r), where

[2] Available from http://desr.sourceforge.net

$w_i, w_j \in W$ (the set of tokens), $r \in R$ (the set of dependencies); w_i is called the *head* and w_j is the *dependent*. Given an input sentence $\mathbf{w}$, the parser is initialized to $\langle \emptyset, \mathbf{w}, \emptyset \rangle$, and terminates at configuration $\langle \mathbf{w}, \emptyset, A \rangle$. The parser uses three rule schemata:

$$\text{Shift} \quad \frac{\langle S, n|I, A \rangle}{\langle n|S, I, A \rangle} \tag{1}$$

$$\text{Right}_r \quad \frac{\langle t|S, n|I, A \rangle}{\langle S, n|I, A \cup \{(n, t, r)\} \rangle} \tag{2}$$

$$\text{Left}_r \quad \frac{\langle t|S, n|I, A \rangle}{\langle S, t|I, A \cup \{(t, n, r)\} \rangle} \tag{3}$$

The Shift rule advances on the input; each Left_r and Right_r rule creates a link r between the next input token n and the top token on the stack t. For producing labeled dependencies the rules Left_r and Right_r are instantiated once for each dependency label r. Additional parsing actions (cf. Attardi, 2006) have been introduced for handling non-projective dependency trees: i.e., trees that cannot be drawn in the plane without crossing edges. However, they are not needed in the experiments reported here, because in the Penn Treebank used in our experiments dependencies are extracted without considering empty nodes and the resulting trees are all projective.[3]

The pseudo code in Algorithm 1 schematically reproduces the parsing process. The function getContext() extracts a vector of features $\mathbf{x}$ from the current state, typically considering just a subset of I, S and A, representing the context of the current input token.

Algorithm 1: DeSR: Dependency Shift Reduce parser

```
input: w = w_1, w_2, ..., w_n
begin
    S ← ⟨⟩
    I ← ⟨w_1, w_2, ..., w_n⟩
    A ← ⟨⟩
    while I ≠ ⟨⟩ do
        x ← getContext(S, I, A)
        y ← estimateAction(x, α)
        performAction(y, S, I, A)
end
```

The step estimateAction() predicts a parsing action y, given a trained model α and $\mathbf{x}$. The step performAction() updates the state according to the predicted parsing rule y.

[3] By contrast, the version of the Penn Treebank used for the CoNLL 2007 shared task includes also non-projective representations.

6.3.2 Features

The set of features used in this chapter were chosen with a few experiments on the development data as variants of a generic model. The only token features used are "Lemma", "Pos" and "Dep": "Lemma" refers to the morphologically simplified form of the token, "Pos" is the part of speech and "Dep" is the label on a dependency. "Child" refers to the child of a node (right or left): up to two furthest children of a node are considered. Table 6.1 lists which feature is extracted for which token: negative numbers refer to tokens on the stack, non-negative numbers refer to input tokens. As an example, Pos -1 is the part of speech of the token on top of the stack, while Lemma 0 is the lemma of the next token in the input, Pos leftChild(-1) extracts the part of speech of the leftmost child of the token on the top of the stack, etc.

Table 6.1 Configuration of the feature parameters used in the experiments

	Token	
Features	Stack	Input
Lemma	−2 −1 leftChild(−1) rightChild(−1)	0 1 2 3 leftChild(0) rightChild(0) prev(0)
Pos	−2 −1 leftChild(−1) rightChild(−1) succ(−1)	0 1 2 3 leftChild(0)
Dep	leftChild(−1) rightChild(−1)	leftChild(0) rightChild(0)

6.3.3 Learning a Parsing Model with the Perceptron

The problem of learning a parsing model can be framed as that of learning a classifier where each class $y_i \in \mathcal{Y}$ represents one of k possible parsing actions. Each such action is associated with a weight vector $\alpha_k \in \mathbb{R}^d$. Given a datapoint $\mathbf{x} \in \mathcal{X}$, a d-dimensional vector of binary features in the input space $\mathcal{X}$, a parsing action is chosen with a winner-take-all discriminant function:

$$\text{estimateAction}(\mathbf{x}, \alpha) = \arg\max_k f(\mathbf{x}, \alpha_k) \tag{4}$$

when using a linear classifier, such as the perceptron or SVM, $f(\mathbf{u}, \mathbf{v}) = \langle \mathbf{u}, \mathbf{v} \rangle$ is the inner product between vectors $\mathbf{u}$ and $\mathbf{v}$.

We learn the parameters α from the training data with the perceptron (Rosenblatt, 1958), in the on-line multiclass formulation of the algorithm (Crammer and Singer, 2003) with uniform negative updates. The perceptron has been used in previous work on dependency parsing by Carreras et al. (2006), with a parser based on Eisner's algorithm (Eisner, 2000), and also on incremental constituent parsing (Collins and Roark, 2004). Also the MST parser of McDonald uses a variant of the perceptron algorithm (McDonald, 2006). The choice is motivated by the simplicity and performance of perceptrons, which have proved competitive on a number of tasks, e.g., in shallow parsing, where the perceptron performance is comparable to that of the Conditional Random Field models (Sha and Pereira, 2003).

The only adjustable parameter of the model is the number of instances T to use for training. We fixed T using the development portion of the data. In our experiments, the best value is between 20 and 30 times the size of the training data. To regularize the model we take as the final model the average of all weight vectors posited during training (Collins, 2002). The perceptron learning procedure is listed in Algorithm 2. The final average model can be computed efficiently during training without storing the individual α vectors (e.g., see Ciaramita and Johnson, 2003).

Algorithm 2: Average multiclass perceptron

input : $\mathcal{S} = (\mathbf{x}_i, y_i)^N; \alpha_k^0 = \vec{\mathbf{0}}, \ \forall k \in \mathcal{Y}$
for $t = 1$ **to** T **do**
  choose j
  $E^t = \{r \in \mathcal{Y} : \langle \mathbf{x}_j, \alpha_r^t \rangle \geq \langle \mathbf{x}_j, \alpha_{y_j}^t \rangle\}$
  if $|E^t| > 0$ **then**
    $\alpha_r^{t+1} = \alpha_r^t - \frac{\mathbf{x}_j}{|E^t|}, \ \forall r \in E^t \ \alpha_{y_j}^{t+1} = \alpha_{y_j}^t + \mathbf{x}_j$

output: $\alpha_k = \frac{1}{T} \sum_t \alpha_k^t, \ \forall k \in \mathcal{Y}$

6.3.4 Higher-Order Feature Spaces

Higher-order feature representations and modeling can improve parsing accuracy, although at significant computational costs. To make SVM training feasible in the dual model with polynomial kernels, Yamada and Matsumoto (2003) split the training data into several sets, based on POS tags, and train a parsing model for each set. The second-order MST parser of McDonald and Pereira (2006) has $O(n^3)$ complexity, while for handling non-projective trees, otherwise an NP-hard problem, the authors resort to an approximate algorithm. Here we investigate how the feature representation can be enriched to improve parsing while maintaining the simplicity of the shift-reduce architecture, and performing discriminative learning without partitioning the training data.

The linear classifier (Equation 4) learned with the perceptron is inherently limited in the types of solutions it can learn. As originally pointed out by Minsky and Papert (1969), certain problems require non-linear solutions that cannot be learned by such models. A simple workaround for this limitation relies on feature maps $\Phi : \mathbb{R}^d \rightarrow \mathbb{R}^h$ that map the input vectors $\mathbf{x} \in \mathcal{X}$ into some higher h-dimensional representation $\Phi(\mathcal{X}) \subset \mathbb{R}^h$, the feature space. The feature space can represent, for example, all combinations of individual features in the input space. We define a feature map which extracts all second order features of the form $x_i x_j$; i.e.,

$$\Phi(\mathbf{x}) = (x_i x_j | i = 1, \dots, d, \ j = i, \dots, d). \tag{5}$$

The linear perceptron working in $\Phi(\mathcal{X})$ effectively implements a non-linear classifier in the original input space $\mathcal{X}$. One shortcoming of this approach is that it inflates considerably the feature representation and might not scale well. In general, the number of features of degree g over an input space of dimension d is $\binom{d+g-1}{g}$. In practice, a second-order feature map can be handled with reasonable efficiency by the perceptron. This so called 2nd-order model uses a modified scoring function:

$$g(\mathbf{x}, \alpha_k) = f(\Phi(\mathbf{x}), \alpha_k) \tag{6}$$

where also α_k is h-dimensional. The proposed feature map is equivalent to a polynomial kernel function of degree two $K(\mathbf{x}, \mathbf{z}) = \langle \mathbf{x}, \mathbf{z} \rangle^2$ (e.g., see Shawe-Taylor and Cristianini (2004)):

$$\begin{aligned} \langle \Phi(\mathbf{x}), \Phi(\mathbf{z}) \rangle &= \sum_{i=1}^{d} \sum_{j=1}^{d} x_i x_j z_i z_j \\ &= \sum_{i=1}^{d} x_i z_i \sum_{j=1}^{d} x_j z_j = \langle \mathbf{x}, \mathbf{z} \rangle^2 \end{aligned} \tag{7}$$

Notice that the second index j in Eq. (5) starts from i, rather than 1. The two formulations yield almost identical results, although the formulation in Eq. (5) is significantly more compact. Yamada and Matsumoto (2003) have shown that the degree two polynomial kernel has better accuracy than the linear model and polynomial kernels of higher degrees. However, using the dual model is not always practical for dependency parsing. The discriminant function of the dual model is defined as:

$$f'(\mathbf{x}, \alpha) = \arg\max_{k} \sum_{i=1}^{N} \alpha_{k,i} \langle \mathbf{x}, \mathbf{x}_i \rangle^g \tag{8}$$

where the weights α are associated with class-instance pairs rather than class-feature pairs. With respect to the discriminant function of Equation (4) there is an additional summation. In principle, the inner products can be cached in a kernel matrix to speed up training.

There are two shortcomings to using such a model in dependency parsing. First, if the amount of training data is large it might not be feasible to store the kernel matrix, which requires $O(N^3)$ computations and $O(N^2)$ space, for a dataset of size N. As an example, the number of training instances N used by the parser for the Penn Treebank is over 1.8 million: caching the kernel matrix would require several Terabytes of space. The second shortcoming is independent of training. In predicting a tree for unseen sentences the model will have to recompute the inner products between the observation and all the support vectors, i.e., all class-instance pairs with $\alpha_{k,i} > 0$. The second-order feature map with the perceptron is more efficient and allows faster training and prediction. Training a single parsing model avoids a potential loss of accuracy that occurs when using the technique of partitioning the training data according to the POS. Inaccurate predictions of the POS can significantly affect the accuracy of the actions predicted, while the single model is more robust, since the POS is just one of the many features used in prediction.

It is worth mentioning that there is significant work on optimizing SVMs for large-scale problems; e.g., by focusing on primal formulations. Keerthi and DeCoste (2005) introduce a (primal) Newton method for sparse linear SVMs, while Chapelle (2007) presents the primal point of view, both for linear and non-linear SVMs. However, these methods do not seem practical yet for the parsing task in which both the size of the training data and the dimensionality of the feature space are large.

6.4 Semantic Features

Semantic information is used implicitly in parsing. For example, conditioning on lexical heads provides a source of semantic information. There have been a few attempts at using semantic information more explicitly. Charniak's 1997 parser (Charniak, 1997), defined probability estimates backed off to word clusters. Collins and Koo (2005) introduced an improved reranking model for parsing which includes a hidden layer of semantic features. Yi and Palmer (2005) retrained a constituent parser in which phrases were annotated with argument information to improve SRL. However, this didn't improve over the output of the basic parser.

Several semantic annotation tasks are being tackled with the goal of identifying semantic information from documents, such as named-entity recognition, semantic role labeling and relation extraction. There is evidence that dependency and constituency parsing can be helpful in these and similar tasks, for instance in question classification and semantic role labeling using tree kernels (Zhang and Less, 2003; Moschitti, 2006).

It is natural to ask if also the opposite holds: whether semantic annotations can be used to improve parsing. In particular, it would be interesting to know if entity-like tags can be used for this purpose. One reason for this is that entity tagging is efficient and does not seem to need parsing for achieving top performance. Beyond improving traditional parsing, independently learned semantic tags might be helpful in adapting a parser to a new domain. To the best of our knowledge, no evidence has been produced yet that annotated semantic information can improve parsing. In the following we investigate adding entity tags as features of our parser.

6.4.1 BBN Entity Corpus

The BBN corpus[4] supplements the Wall Street Journal Penn Treebank with annotation of a large set of entity types. The corpus includes annotation of 12 named entity

---

[4] BBN Pronoun Coreference and Entity Type Corpus, 2005. Linguistic Data Consortium (LDC) catalog number LDC2005T33.

types (Person, Facility, Organization, GPE, Location, Nationality, Product, Event, Work of Art, Law, Language, and Contact-Info), nine nominal entity types (Person, Facility, Organization, GPE, Product, Plant, Animal, Substance, Disease and Game), and seven numeric types (Date, Time, Percent, Money, Quantity, Ordinal and Cardinal). Several of these types are further divided into subtypes.[5] This corpus provides adequate support for experimenting with semantic features for parsing. Figure 6.1 illustrates the annotation layer provided by the BBN corpus.[6]

The combination of semantic tags and dependencies appears to have an interesting property. If we consider segments composed of several words corresponding to entities there is exactly one dependency arc connecting a token outside the segment to a token inside the segment: e.g., "CBS Inc." is connected outside only through the token "Inc.", the subject of the main verb. With respect to the rest of the tree, entities tend to form units, with their own internal structure. Intuitively, this information seems relevant for parsing. This locally-structured patterns could help particularly Shift/Reduce algorithms, which have limited knowledge of the global structure being built.

Table 6.2 lists the 40 most frequent categories in Sections 2–21 of the BBN corpus, and the percentage of all entities they represent—altogether more than 97%. Sections 2–21 comprise 949,853 tokens, 23.5% of which have a non-null BBN entity tag: on average one out of four tokens is tagged. The total number of entities is 139,029, 70.5% of which are named entities and nominal concepts, 17% are numerical types and the remaining 12.5% describe time entities.

We designed three new features which extract simple properties of entities from the semantic annotation information:

- EOS: Distance to the end of the segment; e.g., EOS("Last") = 1, EOS("canceled") = 0;
- IOB: The first character of the BBN label for a token; e.g., IOB("CBS") = "B", and IOB("canceled") = 0;
- TAG: Full BBN tag for the token; e.g., TAG("CBS") = "B-ORG:Corporation", TAG("week") = "I-DATE".

The feature EOS provides information about the relative position of the token within a segment with respect to the end of the segment. The feature IOB discriminates tokens with no semantic annotation associated from tokens within a segment and tokens which start a segment. Finally, the feature TAG identifies the full semantic tag associated with the token. With respect to the former two features this bears the most fine-grained semantics.

Table 6.3 summarizes six additional models we implemented. The first three use all additional features together, applied to different sets of tokens, while the last three apply only one feature, on top of the base model, relative to the next token in the input, the following two tokens in the input, and the previous two tokens on the stack.

---

[5] BBN Corpus documentation.

[6] The full label for "ORG" is "ORG:Corporation", and "WOA" stands for "WorkOfArt:Other".

Table 6.2 The 40 most frequent labels in Sections 2–21 of the Wall Street Journal BBN Corpus and the percentage of tags occurrences

WSJ-BBN corpus categories

Tag	%	Tag	%	Tag	%	Tag	%
PER_DESC	15.5	ORG:CORP	13.7	DATE:DATE	9.2	ORG_DESC:CORP	8.9
PERSON	8.13	MONEY	6.5	CARDINAL	6.0	PERCENT	3.5
GPE:CITY	3.12	GPE:COUNTRY	2.9	ORG:GOV	2.6	NORP:NATION-TY	1.9
DATE:DURATION	1.8	GPE:PROVINCE	1.5	ORG_DESC:GOV	1.4	FAC_DESC:BLDG	1.1
ORG:OTHER	0.7	PROD_DESC:VEHICLE	0.7	ORG_DESC:OTHER	0.6	ORDINAL	0.6
TIME	0.5	GPE_DESC:COUNTRY	0.5	SUBST:OTHER	0.5	SUBST:FOOD	0.5
DATE:OTHER	0.4	NORP:POLITICAL	0.4	DATE:AGE	0.4	LOC:REGION	0.3
SUBST:CHEM	0.3	WOA:OTHER	0.3	FAC_DESC:OTHER	0.3	SUBST:DRUG	0.3
ANIMAL	0.3	GPE_DESC:PROVINCE	0.2	PROD:VEHICLE	0.2	GPE_DESC:CITY	0.2
PRODUCT:OTHER	0.2	LAW	0.2	ORG:POLITICAL	0.2	ORG:EDU	0.2

Table 6.3 Additional configurations for the models with BBN entity features

	Token				
Features	Stack		Input		
AS-0 = EOS + IOB + TAG			0		
AS-1 = EOS + IOB + TAG		−1	0	1	
AS-2 = EOS + IOB + TAG	−2	−1	0	1	2
EOS	−2	−1	0	1	2
IOB	−2	−1	0	1	2
TAG	−2	−1	0	1	2

6.4.2 Corpus Pre-processing

The original BBN corpus has its own tokenization which often does not reflect the Penn Treebank tokenization; e.g., when an entity intersects a hyphenated compound, thus "third-highest" becomes "third$_{ORDINAL}$-highest". This is problematic for combining entity annotation and dependency trees. Since our main focus is parsing we re-aligned the BBN Corpus with the Treebank tokenization. Thus, for example, when an entity splits a Treebank token, we extend the entity boundary to contain the whole original Treebank token, thus obtaining "third-highest$_{ORDINAL}$" in the example above.

6.4.3 Semantic Tagger

We treated semantic tags as POS tags. A tagger was trained on the BBN gold standard annotation and used to annotate development and evaluation data. We briefly describe the tagger (see Ciaramita and Altun, 2006, for more details), a Hidden Markov Model trained with the perceptron algorithm introduced in Collins (2002). Label to label dependencies are limited to the previous tag (first order HMM). A generic feature set for NER based on words, lemmas, POS tags, and word shape features was used.

The tagger is trained on Sections 2–21 of the BBN corpus. As before, Section 22 of the BBN corpus is used for choosing the perceptron's parameter T. The tagger model is regularized as described for Algorithm 2. The full BBN tagset comprises 105 classes organized hierarchically. We ignored the hierarchical organization and treated each tag as an independent class in the standard IOB encoding. The tagger evaluated on Section 23 achieves an F-score of 86.8%. The parts of speech for the evaluation/development sections were produced with TreeTagger. As a final remark we notice that the tagger complexity, linear in the length of the sentence, preserves the parser complexity.

6.5 Parsing Experiments

6.5.1 Data and Setup

We used the standard partitions of the Wall Street Journal Penn Treebank (Marcus et al., 1993), i.e., Sections 2–21 for training, Section 22 for development and Section 23 for evaluation. The constituent trees were transformed into dependency trees by means of a program created by Joakim Nivre that implements the rules proposed by Yamada and Matsumoto, which in turn are based on the head rules of Collins' parser (Collins, 1999).[7] The lemma for each token was produced using the "morph" function of the WordNet (Fellbaum, 1998) library.[8] The data in the WSJ Sections 22 and 23, both for the parser and for the semantic tagger, was POS-tagged using TreeTagger,[9] which has an accuracy of 97.0% on Section 23.

Training a parsing model on the Wall Street Journal requires a set of 22 classes: 10 of the 11 labels in the dependency corpus generated from the Penn Treebank (e.g., subj, obj, sbar, vmod, nmod, root, etc.) are paired with both Left and Right actions. In addition, there is in one rule for the "root" label and one for the Shift action. The total number of features found in training ranges from two hundred thousand for the 1st-order model to approximately 20 million for the 2nd-order models.

We evaluated several models, each trained with 1st-order and 2nd-order features. The base model (BASE) only uses the traditional set of features (cf. Table 6.1). Models EOS, IOB and TAG each use only one type of semantic feature with the configuration described in Table 6.3. Models AS-0, AS-1, and AS-2 use all three semantic features for the token on the stack in AS-0, plus the previous token on the stack and the new token in the input in AS-1, plus an additional token from the stack and an additional token from the input for AS-2 (cf. Table 6.3).

6.5.2 Results for 2nd-Order Models

Table 6.4 summarizes the results of all experiments. We report the following scores, obtained with the CoNLL-X scoring script: labeled attachment score (LAS), unlabeled attachment score (UAS) and label accuracy score (LAC). For the UAS score, the most frequently reported, we include the improvement in relative error reduction.

The 2nd-order base model improves on all measures over the 1st-order model by approximately 5% absolute. The UAS score is 90.55%, with an improvement of 4.9%. The magnitude of the improvement reflects the 4.6% improvement that Yamada and Matsumoto (2003) report going from the linear SVM to the polynomial

[7] The script is available from http://w3.msi.vxu.se/%7enivre/research/Penn2Malt.html

[8] http://wordnet.princeton.edu

[9] Tree Tagger is available from http://www.ims.uni-stuttgart.de/projekte/corplex/TreeTagger/

Table 6.4 Results of the different models on WSJ Section 23 using the CoNLL scores Labeled attachment score (LAS), Unlabeled attachment score (UAS), and Label accuracy score (LAC). The column labeled "Imp" reports the improvement in terms of relative error reduction with respect to the BASE model for the UAS score. In bold the best results

	1st-order scores				2nd-order scores			
DeSR model	LAS	UAS	Imp	LAC	LAS	UAS	Imp	LAC
BASE	84.01	85.56	–	88.24	89.20	90.55	–	92.22
EOS	84.89	86.37	+5.6	88.94	89.36	90.64	+1.0	92.37
IOB	84.95	86.37	+6.6	89.06	89.63	90.89	+3.6	92.55
TAG	84.76	86.26	+4.8	88.80	89.54	90.81	+2.8	92.55
AS-0	84.40	85.95	+2.7	88.38	89.41	90.72	+1.8	92.38
AS-1	85.13	86.52	+6.6	89.11	89.57	90.77	+2.3	92.49
AS-2	85.32	86.71	+8.0	89.25	**89.87**	**91.10**	+5.8	**92.68**

of degree two. Our base model accuracy (90.55% UAS) compares well with the accuracy of the parsers based on the polynomial kernel trained with SVM of Yamada and Matsumoto (UAS 90.3%), and Hall et al. (2006) (UAS 89.4%). We notice in particular that, given the lack of non-projective cases/rules, the parser of Hall et al. (2006) is almost identical to our parser, hence the difference in accuracy (+1.1%) might effectively be due to the classifier. Yamada and Matsumoto's parser is slightly more complex than our parser, and has quadratic worst-case complexity. Overall, the accuracy of the 2nd-order parser is comparable to that of the 1st-order MST parser (90.7%).

There is no direct evidence that our perceptron produces better classifiers than SVM. Rather, the pattern of results produced by the perceptron seems comparable to that of SVM (Yamada and Matsumoto, 2003). This is a useful finding in itself, given that the former is more efficient: the perceptron's update is linear while SVM solves a quadratic problem at each update. However, one major difference between the two approaches lies in the fact that learning with the primal model does not require splitting the model by POS, or other means. As a consequence, beyond the greater simplicity, our method might benefit from not depending so strongly on the quality of POS tagging. POS information is encoded as a feature and contributes its weight to the selection of the parsing action, together with all additionally available information. In the SVM-trained methods the model that makes the prediction for the parsing rule is essentially chosen by an oracle, the prediction of the POS tagger. Furthermore, it might be argued that learning a single model makes better use of the training data by exploiting the correlations between all datapoints, while in the dual split-training case the interaction is limited to datapoints in the same partition. In any case, second-order feature maps can be used also with SVM or other classifiers. The advantage of using the perceptron lies in the unchallenged accuracy/efficiency trade-off. Finally, we recall that training in the primal model can be performed fully on-line without affecting the resulting model nor the complexity of the algorithm.

6.5.3 Results for Models with Semantic Features

All models based on semantic features improve over the base model on all measures. The best configuration is that of model AS-2 which extracts all semantic features from the widest context. In the 1st-order AS-2 model the improvement, 86.71% UAS (+8% relative error reduction), is more marked than in the 2nd-order AS-2 model, 91.1% UAS (+5.8% error reduction). A possible simple explanation is that some information captured by the semantic features is correlated with other higher-order features which do not occur in the 1st-order encoding. Overall the accuracy of the DeSR parser with semantic information is slightly inferior to that of the second-order MST parser (McDonald and Pereira, 2006) (91.5% UAS). The best results on this dataset to date (approximately 93% UAS) are those achieved with ensemble techniques (McDonald, 2006; Sagae and Lavie, 2006) combining the predictions of several pre-existing parsers. Table 6.5 lists the main results on the version of the Penn Treebank for the dependency parsing task considered in this chapter.

In Table 6.4 we also evaluate the gain obtained by adding one semantic feature type at a time (cf. rows EOS/IOB/TAG). These results show that all semantic features provide some improvement (with the dubious case of EOS in the 2nd-order model). The IOB encoding seems to produce the most accurate features. This could be promising because it suggests that the benefit does not depend only on the specific tags, but that the segmentation in itself is important. Hence tagging could improve the adaptation of parsers to new domains even if only generic tagging methods are available.

Table 6.5 Comparison of main results on the Penn Treebank dataset

Parser	UAS
Hall et al. (2006)	89.4
Yamada and Matsumoto (2003)	90.3
DeSR	90.5
McDonald and Pereira 1st-order MST	90.7
DeSR AS-2	91.1
McDonald and Pereira 2nd-order MST	91.5

6.5.4 Remarks on Efficiency

All experiments were performed on a 2.4 GHz AMD Opteron CPU machine with 32 GB RAM. The 2nd-order parser uses almost 3 GB of memory. While it is several times slower and larger than the 1st-order model[10] the 2nd-order model performance is still competitive. It takes 3 min (user time) to parse Section 23, POS tagging included. In training, the model takes about 1 h to process the full dataset once. As a comparison, Hall et al. (2006) reports 1.5 h for training the partitioned SVM model

[10] The 1st-order parser takes 7 s (user time) to process Section 23.

Table 6.6 Parsing times for the CoNLL 2007 English and Chinese datasets for MST and DeSR

	Parsing time/s	
Parser	English	Chinese
MST 2n-order	97.52	59.05
MST 1st-order	76.62	49.13
DeSR	36.90	21.22

and 10 min for parsing the evaluation set on the same Penn Treebank data. We also compared directly the parsing time of our parser with that of the MST parser using the version 0.4.3 of MSTParser.[11] For these experiments we used two datasets from the CoNLL 2007 shared task for English and Chinese. Table 6.6 reports the times, in seconds, to parse the test sets for these languages on a 3.3 GHz Xeon machine with 4 GB Ram, of the MST 1st and 2nd-order parser and DeSR parser (without semantic features).

The architecture of the model presented here offers several options for optimization. For example, implementing the α models with full vectors rather than hash tables speeds up parsing by a factor of three, at the expense of memory. Alternatively, memory load in training can be reduced, at the expense of time, by using on-line training. However, the most valuable option for space reduction might be to filter out low-frequency second-order features. Since the frequency of such features seems to follow a power law distribution, this reduces significantly the feature space size even for low thresholds at small accuracy expense. In this chapter, however, we focused on the full model, and no approximations were required to run the experiments.

6.6 Conclusion

We explored the design space of a dependency parser by modeling and extending the feature representation, while adopting one of the simplest parsing architectures: a single-pass deterministic shift-reduce algorithm trained with a regularized multiclass perceptron. We showed that with the perceptron it is feasible to adopt higher-order feature maps equivalent to polynomial kernels without resorting to an approximate model (although this remains an option for optimization). The resulting models achieve accuracies at least comparable to more complex architectures based on dual SVM training, while parsing unseen data is typically faster. With respect to learning, more sophisticated formulations of the perceptron (e.g., MIRA Crammer and Singer, 2003) might provide further gains in accuracy, as shown with the MST parser (McDonald et al., 2005).

We also experimented with novel types of semantic features, extracted from the annotations produced by an entity tagger trained on the BBN corpus. This model

[11] Available from sourceforge.net

further improves over the standard model yielding an additional 5.8% relative error reduction. Although the magnitude of the improvement is not striking, to the best of our knowledge this is one of the first encouraging pieces of evidence that annotated semantic information can improve parsing and suggests several options for further research. For example, this finding might indicate that this type of approach, which combines semantic tagging and parsing, is viable for the adaptation of parsing to new domains for which semantic taggers exist. Semantic features could also be easily included in other types of dependency parsing algorithms, e.g., MST, and in current reranking methods for constituency parsing (Collins, 2000; Charniak and Johnson, 2005).

For future research several issues concerning the semantic features might be tackled. More complex semantic features might be designed and evaluated. For example, it might be useful to guess the "head" of segments with simple heuristics, i.e., guessing the node which is most likely to connect the segment with the rest of the tree, which all internal components of the entity depend upon. It would also be interesting to extract semantic features from taggers trained on different datasets and based on different tagsets.

Acknowledgements The first author would like to thank Thomas Hofmann for useful discussions concerning the issue of higher-order feature representations of Section 6.3.4. We would also like to thank Brian Roark and the editors for useful comments and references to related work.

References

Attardi, G. (2006). Experiments with a multilanguage non-projective dependency parser. In *Proceedings of the 10th Conference on Computational Natural Language Learning*, New York, NY, pp. 166–170.

Buchholz, S. and E. Marsi (2006). Introduction to CoNLL-X shared task on multilingual dependency parsing. In *Proceedings of the 10th Conference on Computational Natural Language Learning*, New York, NY, pp. 149–164.

Carreras, X. and L. Màrquez (2005). Introduction to the CoNLL-2005 shared task: semantic role labeling. In *Proceedings of the 9th Conference on Computational Natural Language Learning*, Ann Arbor, MI, pp. 152–154.

Carreras, X., M. Surdeanu, and L. Màrquez (2006). Projective dependency parsing with perceptron. In *Proceedings of the 10th Conference on Computational Natural Language Learning*, New York, NY, pp 181–185.

Chapelle, O. (2007). Training a support vector machine in the primal. *Neural Computation 19*, Cambridge, MA, MIT Press, 1155–1178.

Charniak, E. (1997). Statistical parsing with a context-free grammar and word statistics. In *Proceedings of the 14th National Conference on Artificial Intelligence AAAI*, Providence, RI, pp. 598–603.

Charniak, E. and M. Johnson (2005). Coarse-to-fine n-best parsing and maxent discriminative reranking. In *Proceedings of the 43rd Annual Meeting of the Association for Computational Linguistics*, Ann Arbar, MI, pp. 173–180.

Ciaramita, M. and Y. Altun (2006). Broad-coverage sense disambiguation and information extraction with a supersense sequence tagger. In *Proceedings of the 2006 Conference on Empirical Methods in Natural Language Processing*, Sydney, pp. 594–602.

Ciaramita, M., A. Gangemi, E. Ratsch, J. Šarić, and I. Rojas (2005). Unsupervised learning of semantic relations between concepts of a molecular biology ontology. In *Proceedings of the 19th International Joint Conference on Artificial Intelligence*, Edinburgh, pp. 659–664.

Ciaramita, M. and M. Johnson (2003). Supersense tagging of unknown nouns in wordnet. In *Proceedings of the 2003 Conference on Empirical Methods in Natural Language Processing*, Sapporo, pp. 168–175.

Collins, M. (1999). Head-driven statistical models for natural language parsing. Ph. D. thesis, University of Pennsylvania, Philadelphia, PA.

Collins, M. (2000). Discriminative reranking for natural language parsing. In *Proceedings of the 17th International Conference on Machine Learning*, Stanford, CA, pp. 175–182.

Collins, M. (2002). Discriminative training methods for Hidden Markov Models: theory and experiments with perceptron algorithms. In *Proceedings of the 2002 Conference on Empirical Methods in Natural Language Processing*, Philadelphia, PA, pp. 1–8.

Collins, M. and T. Koo (2005). Hidden-variable models for discriminative reranking. In *Proceedings of the 2005 Conference on Empirical Methods in Natural Language Processing*, Vancouver, pp. 507–514.

Collins, M. and B. Roark (2004). Incremental parsing with the perceptron algorithm. In *Proceedings of the 42nd Annual Meeting on Association for Computational Linguistics*, Barcelona, pp. 111–118.

Crammer, K. and Y. Singer (2003). Ultraconservative online algorithms for multiclass problems. *Journal of Machine Learning Research*, Cambridge, MA, MIT Press, pp. 951–991.

Culotta, A. and J. Sorensen (2004). Dependency tree kernels for relation extraction. In *Proceedings of the 42nd Annual Meeting on Association for Computational Linguistics*, Barcelona pp. 728–736..

Ding, Y. and M. Palmer (2005). Machine translation using probabilistic synchronous dependency insertion grammars. In *Proceedings of the 43rd Annual Meeting on Association for Computational Linguistics*, Ann Arbor, MI, pp. 541–548.

Eisner, J. (2000). Bilexical grammars and their cubic-time parsing algorithms. In H. Bunt and A. Nijholt (Eds.), *New Developments in Natural Language Parsing*. Kluwer Academic Publishers, pp. 29–62.

Fellbaum, C. (1998). *WordNet: An Electronic Lexical Database*. Cambridge, MA: MIT Press.

Hall, J., J. Nivre, and J. Nilsson (2006). Discriminative classifiers for deterministic dependency parsing. In *Proceedings of the COLING/ACL 2006 Main Conference Poster Sessions*, Sydney, pp. 316–323.

Kalt, T. (2004). Induction of greedy controllers for deterministic treebank parsers. In *Proceedings of the 2004 Conference on Empirical Methods in Natural Language*, Barcelona, pp. 17–24.

Keerthi, S. and D. DeCoste (2005). A modified finite newton method for fast solution of large scale linear SVMs. *Journal of Machine Learning Research* 6, Cambridge, MA, MIT Press, pp. 341–361.

Marcus, M., B. Santorini, and M. Marcinkiewicz (1993). Building a large annotated corpus of english: The penn treebank. *Computational Linguistics 19*(2), 313–330.

McDonald, R. (2006). Discriminative training and spanning tree algorithms for dependency parsing. Ph. D. thesis, University of Pennsylvania, Philadelphia, PA.

McDonald, R. and F. Pereira (2006). Online learning of approximate dependency parsing algorithms. In *Proceedings of the 11th Conference of the European Chapter of the Association for Computational Linguistics*, Trente, Italy, pp. 81–88.

McDonald, R., F. Pereira, K. Ribarov, and J. Hajič (2005). Non-projective dependency parsing using spanning tree algorithms. In *Proceedings of Human Language Technology Conference and Conference on Empirical Methods in Natural Language Processing*, Vancouver, pp. 523–530.

Minsky, M. and S. Papert (1969). *Perceptrons: An Introduction to Computational Geometry*. Cambridge, MA: MIT Press.

Moschitti, A. (2006). Efficient convolution kernels for dependency and constituent syntactic trees. In *Proceedings of the 17th European Conference on Machine Learning and the 10th European*

Conference on Principles and Practice of Knowledge Discovery in Databases , Philadelphia, PA, pp. 318–329.

Nivre, J., J. Hall, S. Kübler, R. McDonald, J. Nilsson, D. S. Riedel, and D. Yuret (2007). The CoNLL 2007 shared task on dependency parsing. In *Proceedings of the CoNLL Shared Task Session of EMNLP-CoNLL 2007*, New York, NY, pp. 915–932.

Nivre, J. and M. Scholz (2004). Deterministic dependency parsing of english text. In *Proceedings of COLING 2004*, Geneva, pp. 64–70.

Punyakanok, V., D. Roth, and W. Yih (2005). The necessity of syntactic parsing for semantic role labeling. In *Proceedings of the International Joint Conference on Artificial Intelligence*, Edinburgh, pp. 1117–1123.

Rosenblatt, F. (1958). The perceptron: a probabilistic model for information storage and organization in the brain. *Psychological Review*, pp. 386–408.

Sagae, K. and A. Lavie (2006). Parser combination by reparsing. In *Proceedings of the Human Language Technology Conference of the NAACL, Companion Volume: Short Papers*, New York, NY, pp. 129–132.

Sha, F. and F. Pereira (2003). Shallow parsing with conditional random fields. In *Proceedings of the 2003 Conference of the North American Chapter of the Association for Computational Linguistics on Human Language Technology*, Edmonton, pp. 134–141.

Shawe-Taylor, J. and N. Cristianini (2004). *Kernel Methods for Pattern Analysis*. Cambridge, UK: Cambridge University Press.

Surdeanu, M., M. Ciaramita, and H. Zaragoza (2008). Learning to rank answers on large online QA collections. In *Proceedings of the 46th Annual Meeting on Association for Computational Linguistics: Human Language Technologies*, Columbus, OH, pp. 719–727.

Surdeanu, M., R. Johansson, A. Meyers, L. Màrquez, and J. Nivre (2008). The CoNLL 2008 shared task on joint parsing of syntactic and semantic dependencies. In *Proceedings of the 12th Conference on Computational Natural Language Learning*, Manchester, pp. 159–177.

Titov, I. and J. Henderson (2007). A latent variable model for generative dependency parsing. In *Proceedings of the 10th International Conference on Parsing Technologies*, Prague, Czech Republic, pp. 144–155.

Wong, A. and D. Wu (1999). Learning a lightweight deterministic parser. In *Proceedings of the 6th European Conference on Speech Communication and Technology*, Budapest, Hungary, pp. 2047–2050.

Yamada, H. and Y. Matsumoto (2003). Statistical dependency analysis with support vector machines. In *Proceedings of the 8th International Workshop on Parsing Technologies*, Nancy, pp. 195–206.

Yi, S. and M. Palmer (2005). The integration of syntactic parsing and semantic role labeling. In *Proceedings of the 9th Conference on Computational Natural Language Learning*, Ann Arbor, MI, pp. 237–240.

Zhang, D. and W. Less (2003). Question classification using support vector machines. In *Proceedings of the 26th Annual International ACM SIGIR Conference on Research and Development in Informaion Retrieval*, Toronto, pp. 26–32.

Chapter 7
Strictly Lexicalised Dependency Parsing

Qin Iris Wang, Dale Schuurmans, and Dekang Lin

7.1 Introduction

There has been a great deal of progress in statistical parsing in the past decade (Collins, 1996, 1997; Charniak, 2000). A common characteristic of these previous generative parsers is their use of lexical statistics. However, it was subsequently discovered that bi-lexical statistics (parameters that involve two words) actually play a much smaller role than previously believed. It has been found by Gildea (2001) that the removal of bi-lexical statistics from a state-of-the-art PCFG parser resulted in little change in the output. Bikel (2004) observes that only 1.49% of the bi-lexical statistics needed in parsing were found in the training corpus. When considering only bigram statistics involved in the highest probability parse, this percentage becomes 28.8%. However, even when bi-lexical statistics do get used, they are remarkably similar to their back-off values using part-of-speech tags. Therefore, the utility of bi-lexical statistics becomes rather questionable. Klein and Manning (2003) present an unlexicalized parser that eliminates all lexical parameters, with a performance score close to the state-of-the-art lexicalised parsers.

We present a generative approach that employs Maximum Likelihood Markov Network training for dependency parsing. In particular, we present a statistical dependency parser that represents the other end of the spectrum where all statistical parameters are lexical and the parser does not require part-of-speech tags or grammatical categories. This is called *strictly lexicalised parsing*. A part-of-speech lexicon has always been considered to be a necessary component in any natural language parser. This is true in early rule-based as well as modern statistical parsers and in dependency parsers as well as constituency parsers. The need for part-of-speech tags arises from the sparseness of natural language data. They provide generalizations of words that are critical for parsers to deal with the sparseness. Words belonging to the same part-of-speech are expected to have the same syntactic behavior.

Q.I. Wang (✉)
Yahoo! Inc., Santa Clara, CA 95054, USA
e-mail: wangqin@gmail.com

H. Bunt et al. (eds.), *Trends in Parsing Technology*, Text, Speech and Language Technology 43, DOI 10.1007/978-90-481-9352-3_7,

Instead of relying on part-of-speech tags, we use *distributional word similarities* computed automatically from a large unannotated corpus. One of the benefits of strictly lexicalised parsing is that the parser can be trained with a treebank that only contains dependency relationships between words. The annotators do not need to annotate parts-of-speech or non-terminal symbols (they do not even have to know about them), making the construction of treebanks easier. Strictly lexicalised parsing is especially beneficial for languages such as Chinese, where parts-of-speech are not as clearly defined as English. In Chinese, clear indicators of a word's part-of-speech, such as suffixes *-ment, -ous* or function words, such as *the*, are largely absent. In fact, monolingual Chinese dictionaries intended for native speakers almost never contain part-of-speech information.

In the remainder of this chapter, we first present a method for modeling the probabilities of dependency trees. Next, in Sections 7.3 and 7.4, we apply a similarity-based smoothing technique to the probability model to deal with data sparseness. Then we describe a dependency parsing algorithm we use for experimental evaluation in Section 7.5. Finally, we present dependency parsing results on the Chinese Treebank 4.0 in Section 7.6 and discuss related work in Section 7.7.

7.2 A Probabilistic Dependency Parsing Model

Let X be a given sentence and Y be its dependency tree (shown in Fig. 7.1). Y is a directed tree connecting all the words in X. Each link in the tree represents a dependency relationship between two words, known as the head and the modifier. The direction of the link is from the head to the modifier. We add an artificial root node ($\perp$) at the beginning of each sentence and a dependency link from ($\perp$) to the head of the sentence so that the head of the sentence can be treated in the same manner as other words.

A triple (u, v, d) specifies a dependency link l, where u and v are the indices ($u < v$) of the words connected by l, and d specifies the direction of the link l. The value of d is either L or R. If $d = L$, v is the index of the head word; otherwise, u is the index of the head word.

We assume dependency trees are projective (without crossing arcs),[1] which means that if there is an arc from h to m, h is then an ancestor of all the words between h and m. Let $\Phi(X)$ be the set of possible directed, projective trees spanning

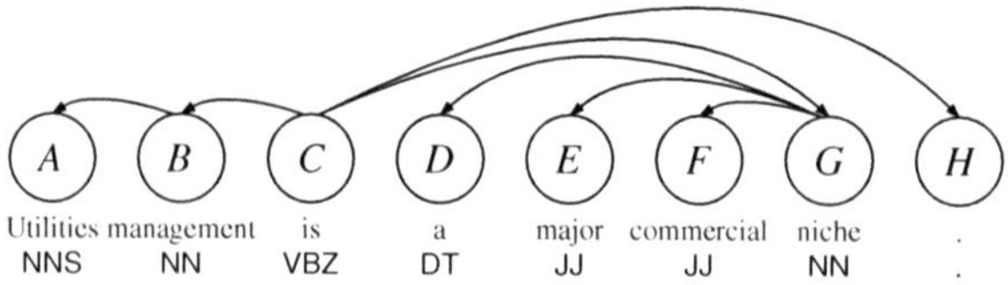

Fig. 7.1 A dependency tree

[1] Although non-projective trees exist, the dependency trees used in our experiments are projective trees that are converted from the Penn Chinese Treebank.

the sentence X. The parser's goal is then to find the most preferredparse; that is, a projective tree, $Y \in \Phi(X)$, that obtains the highest "score". In particular, one assumes that the score of a complete spanning tree Y for a given sentence, whether probabilistically motivated or not, can be decomposed as a sum of local scores for each link (a word pair) (Eisner, 1996; Eisner and Satta, 1999; McDonald et al., 2005). Given this assumption, the parsing problem reduces to

$$\begin{aligned} Y^* &= \arg \max_{Y \in \Phi(X)} score(Y|X) \\ &= \arg \max_{Y \in \Phi(X)} \sum_{(x_i \to x_j) \in Y} score(x_i \to x_j) \end{aligned} \quad (1)$$

where the $score(x_i \to x_j)$ can depend on any measurable property of x_i and x_j within the sentence X. This formulation is sufficiently general to capture many dependency parsing models, including the probabilistic dependency models of Eisner (1996), non-probabilistic models (McDonald et al., 2005), and our own work in this chapter.

The parsing problem defined in Equation (1) is to maximize the sum of all the link scores in a candidate tree. Here, the score will be log conditional probabilities. Thus finding the tree with highest probability would be equivalent to finding the tree with a maximum score in Equation (1).

Generative parsing models are usually defined recursively from top down, even though the decoders (parsers) for such models almost always take a bottom-up approach. The model proposed here is a bottom-up one. Like previous approaches, the generation of a parse tree can be decomposed into a sequence of steps. The probability of the tree is simply the product of the probabilities of the steps involved in the generation process. This scheme requires that different sequences of the steps must not lead to the same tree. This can be achieved by defining a canonical ordering of the links in a dependency tree. Each generation step corresponds to the construction of a dependency link in the canonical order.

Given two dependency links l and l' with the heads being h and h' and the modifiers being m and m', respectively, the order between l and l' is determined as follows:

- If $h \neq h'$ and there is a directed path from one (say h) to the other (say h'), then l' precedes l.
- If $h \neq h'$ and there does not exist a directed path between h and h', the order between l and l' is determined by the order of h and h' in the sentence (h precedes $h' \Rightarrow l$ precedes l').
- If $h = h'$ and the modifiers m and m' are on different sides of h, the link with modifier on the right precedes the other.
- If $h = h'$ and the modifiers m and m' are on the same side of the head h, the link with its modifier closer to h precedes the other one.

For example, if we add indices 1, 2, 3, ... to the words in Fig. 7.1 (index 0 is for the dummy node at the beginning of the sentence), the canonical order of the links in the dependency tree is: (4, 5, R), (7, 8, L), (6, 8, R), (4, 6, R), (3, 4, R), (2, 3, R), (1, 2, L), (0, 2, R).

The generation process according to the canonical order is similar to the head outward generation process in Collins (1999), except that it is bottom-up whereas Collins' models are top-down. Suppose a dependency tree Y is constructed in steps $G_1, \ldots, G_N$ in the canonical order of the dependency links, where N is the number of words in the sentence. The conditional probability of Y given the input sentence X can be computed as

$$P(Y|X) = P(G_1, G_2, \ldots, G_N|X) = \prod_{i=1}^{N} P(G_i|X, G_1, \ldots, G_{i-1}) \quad (2)$$

To search for a parse tree with the highest probability is equivalent to search for a tree with the highest sum of scores over all dependency links in the logarithmic space.

$$\begin{aligned} Y^* &= \arg \max_{Y \in \Phi(X)} P(Y|X) \\ &= \arg \max_{Y \in \Phi(X)} log(P(Y|X)) \\ &= \arg \max_{Y \in \Phi(X)} \sum_{i=1}^{N} log(P(G_i|X, G_1, \ldots, G_{i-1})) \end{aligned} \quad (3)$$

Following Klein and Manning (2004), we require that the creation of a dependency link from head h to modifier m be preceded by placing a left STOP and a right STOP around the modifier m and ¬STOP between h and m. The STOP events are crucial for modeling the number of dependents. Without them, a parse tree often contains some "obvious" errors, such as determiners taking arguments, or prepositions having arguments on their left (instead of right).

Let E_w^L (and E_w^R) denote the event that there are no more modifiers on the left (and right) of a word w. Suppose the dependency link created in the step i is (u, v, d). If $d = L$, G_i is the conjunction of the four events: E_u^R, E_u^L, $\neg E_v^L$ and $link_L(u, v)$. If $d = R$, G_i consists of four events: E_v^R, E_v^L, $\neg E_u^R$ and $link_R(u, v)$. The event G_i is conditioned on $X, G_1, \ldots, G_{i-1}$, which are the words in the sentence and a forest of trees constructed up to step $i-1$. Let C_w^L (and C_w^R) be the number of modifiers of w on its left (and right). We make the following independence assumptions:

- Whether there are any more modifiers of w on side d depends only on the number of modifiers already found on side d of w. That is, E_w^d depends only on w and C_w^d.
- Whether there is a dependency link from a word h to another word m depends only on the words h and m and the number of modifiers of h between m and h. That is,
  - $link_R(u,v)$ depends only on u, v, and C_u^R.
  - $link_L(u,v)$ depends only on u, v, and C_v^L.

Suppose G_i corresponds to a dependency link (u, v, L). The probability can be computed as:

$$\begin{aligned} & P\left(G_i|S, G_1, \ldots, G_{i-1}\right) \\ & = P\left(E_u^L, E_u^R, \neg E_v^L, link_L\left(u, v\right)|S, G_1, \ldots, G_{i-1}\right) \\ & = P\left(E_u^L|u, C_u^L\right) \times P\left(E_u^R|u, C_u^R\right) \times \left(1 - P\left(E_v^L|v, C_v^L\right)\right) \\ & \quad \times P\left(link_L\left(u, v\right)|u, v, C_v^L\right) \end{aligned} \tag{4}$$

The events E_w^R and E_w^L correspond to the STOP events in Collins (1999) and Klein and Manning (2004). This model requires three types of parameters:

- $P\left(E_w^d|w, C_w^d\right)$, where w is a word, d is a direction (left or right). This is the probability of a STOP after taking C_w^d modifiers on the d side.
- $P\left(link_R\left(u, v\right)|u, v, C_u^R\right)$ is the probability of v being the $(C_u^R + 1)$'th modifier of u on the right.
- $P\left(link_L\left(u, v\right)|u, v, C_v^L\right)$ is the probability of u being the $(C_v^L + 1)$'th modifier of v on the left.

The maximum likelihood estimations of these parameters can be obtained from the frequency counts in the training corpus:

- $C(w, c, d)$: the frequency count of w with c modifiers on the d side.
- $C(u, v, c, d)$: If $d = L$, this is the frequency count of words u and v co-occurring in a sentence and v has c modifiers between itself and u. If $d = R$, this is the frequency count words u and v co-occurring in a sentence and u has c modifiers between itself and v.
- $K(u, v, c, d)$: similar to $C(u, v, c, d)$ with an additional constraint that $link_d(u, v)$ is true.

$$\begin{aligned} P\left(E_w^d|w, C_w^d\right) &= \frac{C\left(w, c, d\right)}{\sum_{c' \geq c} C\left(w, c', d\right)}, \quad where \quad c = C_w^d; \\ P\left(link_R\left(u, v\right)|u, v, C_u^R\right) &= \frac{K\left(u, v, c, R\right)}{C\left(u, v, c, R\right)}, \quad where \quad c = C_u^R; \\ P\left(link_L\left(u, v\right)|u, v, C_v^L\right) &= \frac{K\left(u, v, c, L\right)}{C\left(u, v, c, L\right)}, \quad where \quad c = C_v^L. \end{aligned}$$

All the parameters in the model are conditional probabilities of the tree given the sentence, where the variables on the left side of the conditioning bar are binary. Taking logs of these probabilities one can then obtain a local scoring function that uses non-local features. This scoring function still decomposes in a way that allows one to use a dynamic programming parsing algorithm (similar to chart parsing) to parse sentences. The algorithm builds a packed parse forest from bottom up according to the canonical order introduced above. It attaches all the right dependents before attaching the left ones to maintain the canonical order as required by the model.

7.3 Similarity-Based Smoothing

The sparse data problem is very common in NLP. For learning a parser from data, the feature set is far too large to yield uniformly reliable estimates. Abstraction (e.g. using parts-of-speech) and smoothing are two standard techniques for mitigating the sparse data problem. Note that in dependency parsing, most features correspond to words or pairs of words. The weights on these features can be smoothed based on *similarity* determined on an auxiliary, unannotated corpus.

7.3.1 Distributional Word Similarity

Words that tend to appear in the same contexts tend to have similar meanings. This is known as the Distributional Hypothesis in linguistics (Harris, 1968). For example, the words *test* and *exam* are similar because both of them follow verbs such as *administer, cancel, cheat on, conduct,* etc. and both of them can be preceded by adjectives such as *academic, comprehensive, diagnostic, difficult,* etc.

Many methods have been proposed to compute distributional similarity between words (Hindle, 1990; Pereira et al., 1993; Grefenstette, 1994; Lin, 1998). Almost all of those methods represent a word by a feature vector where each feature corresponds to a type of context in which the word appears. They differ in how the feature vectors are constructed and how the similarity between two feature vectors is computed.

7.3.2 Similarity Measures

The most popular method is to use *point-wise mutual information* (PMI) to compute word similarity (Manning and Schutze, 1999). In this method, each word is presented as a feature vector f of contexts. The contexts of a word w are defined to be the set of words that occur within a small context window of w in a large corpus. The contexts of an instance of w consist of the closest *non-stop-words* on each side of w and the *stop-words* in between. Usually, the set of stop-words are defined as the top k most frequent words in the corpus. The value of a feature c is then defined as the point-wise mutual information between c and w:

$$f_w(c) = PMI\,(w, c) = \log\left(\frac{P\,(w, c)}{P\,(w)\,P\,(c)}\right) \tag{5}$$

where $P(w, c)$ is the probability of w and c co-occur in a context window.

centrepiece 0.28, figment 0.27, fulcrum 0.21, culmination 0.20, albatross 0.19, bane 0.19, pariahs 0.18, lifeblood 0.18, crux 0.18, redoubling 0.17, apotheosis 0.17, cornerstones 0.17, perpetuation 0.16, forerunners 0.16, shirking 0.16, cornerstone 0.16, birthright 0.15, hallmark 0.15, centerpiece 0.15, evidenced 0.15, germane 0.15, gist 0.14, reassessing 0.14, engrossed 0.14, Thorn 0.14, biding 0.14, narrowness 0.14, linchpin 0.14, enamored 0.14, formalised 0.14, tenths 0.13, testament 0.13, certainties 0.13, forerunner 0.13, re-evaluating 0.13, antithetical 0.12, extinct 0.12, rarest 0.12, imperiled 0.12, remiss 0.12, hindrance 0.12, detriment 0.12, prouder 0.12, upshot 0.12, cosponsor 0.12, hiccups 0.12, premised 0.12, perversion 0.12, destabilisation 0.12, prefaced 0.11, ...

Fig. 7.2 Words similar to *keystone*

Once the feature vectors have been determined, the *similarity* between two words w_1 and w_2 is then computed as the cosine of the corresponding feature vectors:

$$Sim(w_1, w_2) = \frac{\mathbf{f}_{w_1} \cdot \mathbf{f}_{w_2}}{\|\mathbf{f}_{w_1}\| \|\mathbf{f}_{w_2}\|} \quad (6)$$

For example, Fig. 7.2 shows the top similar words and corresponding similarities for the word *keystone*. They are computed from the English Gigaword corpus (Graff, 2003), which is a raw, unannotated newswire text data containing about one billion English words.

7.3.3 Similarity-Based Smoothing

Similarity-based smoothing is used in Dagan et al. (1999) to estimate word co-occurrence probabilities. Their method performs almost 40% better than the more commonly used back-off method. Unfortunately, similarity-based smoothing has not been successfully applied to statistical parsing up to now. We show how similarity-based smoothing can be used to improve the accuracy of generative learning approaches for parsing in Section 7.4 below.

In the original application of similarity-based smoothing (Dagan et al., 1999), bigram probabilities P($w_2|w_1$) were computed as the weighted average of the conditional probability of w_2 given words similar to w_1:

$$P_{SIM}\left(w_2|w_1\right) = \sum_{w'_1 \in S(w_1)} \frac{Sim\left(w_1, w'_1\right)}{norm\left(w_1\right)} P_{MLE}\left(w_2|w'_1\right) \quad (7)$$

where $Sim(w_1, w'_1)$ denotes the similarity (or an increasing function of the similarity) between w_1 and w'_1, and $S(w_1)$ denotes the set of words that are most similar to w_1. The normalization factor *norm*(w_1) is computed as

$$norm\left(w_1\right) = \sum_{w'_1 \in S(w_1)} Sim\left(w_1, w'_1\right)$$

The underlying assumption of this smoothing scheme is that a word is more likely to occur after w_1 if it tends to occur after words similar to w_1.

Similarity-based smoothing has turned out to be an important smoothing approach in many areas of natural language processing, which allows one to tap into unlimited auxiliary sources of raw unannotated text. By using similarity-based smoothing, one can easily estimate parameters for words that have never appeared in the training corpus. One of the goals of our work has been to obtain similar advantages on parsing.

7.4 Similarity-Based Smoothing in Dependency Parsing

We now introduce similarity-based smoothing into the dependency parsing framework outlined above, which to the best of our knowledge, is novel. The parameters in the model consist of conditional probabilities $\mathrm{P}(E|C)$ where E is the binary variable $link_d(u, v)$ or E_w^d and the context C is either $[w, C_w^d]$ or $[u, v, C_w^d]$, which involves one or two words in the input sentence. Due to the sparseness of natural language data, the contexts observed in the training data only cover a tiny fraction of the contexts whose probability distributions are needed during parsing. The standard approach is to back off to the probability of word classes (such as part-of-speech tags). In this chapter, we take a different approach: the training data is searched to find a set of similar contexts to C, and the probability of E is estimated based on its probabilities in the similar contexts observed in the training corpus.

Section 7.3.3 introduced the smoothing method of Dagan et al. (1999). The underlying assumption of their smoothing scheme is that a word is more likely to occur after w if it tends to occur after words similar to w. Here we make a similar assumption: the probability $\mathrm{P}(E|C)$ of event E given the context C is computed as the weighted average of $\mathrm{P}(E|C')$ where C' is a context similar to C and is attested in the training corpus:

$$P_{SIM}(E|C) = \sum_{C' \in S(C) \cap O} \frac{Sim(C, C')}{norm(C)} P_{MLE}(E|C') \tag{8}$$

Here $\mathrm{S}(C)$ is the set of the top k contexts most similar to C (in the experiments reported in this chapter, $k = 50$); O is the set of contexts observed in the training corpus, $Sim(C, C')$ is the similarity between two contexts and $norm(C)$ is the normalization factor.

Here, a context is either $[w, C_w^d]$ or $[u, v, C_w^d]$ and their similar contexts are defined as:

$$S([w, C_w^d]) = \{[w', C_{w'}^d] \mid w' \in S(w)\}$$
$$S([u, v, C_w^d]) = \{[u', v', C_w^d] \mid u' \in S(u), v' \in S(v)\}$$

where $S(w)$ is the set of the top k words most similar to w ($k = 50$).

Since all contexts used in the model contain at least one word, the similarity between two contexts, Sim(C, C'), is computed as the geometric average of the similarities between corresponding words:

$$Sim\left(\left[w, C^d_w\right], \left[w', C^d_{w'}\right]\right) = Sim\left(w, w'\right)$$
$$Sim\left(\left[u, v, C^d_w\right], \left[u', v', C^d_{w'}\right]\right) = \sqrt{Sim\left(u, u'\right) Sim\left(v, v'\right)}$$

Note that using a similarity-smoothed probability estimate is only necessary when the frequency count of the context C in the training corpus is low. Therefore the final probability is computed as the linear interpolation of the MLE probability and the similarity-based probability:

$$P\left(E|C\right) = \alpha P_{MLE}(E|C) + (1-\alpha)P_{SIM}(E|C) \tag{9}$$

where the smoothing factor $\alpha = \frac{|C|+1}{|C|+5}$ and $|C|$ is the frequency count of the context C in the training data. The purpose of α is to dynamically scale the smoothing, based on the frequency of the pair.

A difference between the similarity-based smoothing approach of Dagan et al. (1999) and the approach proposed here is that this model only computes probability distributions of binary variables. Words only appear as parts of contexts on the right side of the conditioning bar. This has two important implications. First, when a context contains two words, one can use the cross product of similar words, whereas Dagan et al. (1999) can only use the words similar to one of the words. This turns out to have significant impact on accuracy (see Section 7.6). Second, in Dagan et al. (1999), the distribution P$(.|w'_1)$ may itself be sparsely observed. When $\mathrm{P}_{MLE}(w_2|w'_1)$ is 0, it is often due to data sparseness. Their smoothing scheme therefore tends to under-estimate such probability values. This problem is avoided with the approach presented here. If a context does not occur in the training data, it is not included in Equation (9). If it does occur, the maximum likelihood estimation is reasonably accurate even if the context only occurs a few times, since the entropy of the probability distribution is upper-bounded by log 2.

7.5 Dependency Parsing Algorithms

Before presenting experimental results, we first describe the dependency parsing algorithm used in the experimental evaluation, which is adapted from a standard CKY parsing algorithm (Jurafsky and Martin, 2000). Although the output of the parser is a dependency tree, internally, it works similarly to a chart parsing algorithm for Context Free Grammars. Specifically, in a dependency parsing algorithm, the parser constructs a set of chart items, each of which has a head word. Each chart item is a 4-tuple: (*low, head, high, score*) where *low*, *head* and *high* (*low* $\leq$ *head* $\leq$ *high*) are positions of words in a sentence and *score* is non-negative. This means that there exists a dependency tree that spans the words from *low* to *high* with the given *score*, and rooted at the position *head*. Initially, the parsing algorithm creates a chart item for each individual word in the input sentence. The items are then combined with the existing items that are adjacent items to their left. The combined item has the span of the union of the two components and may take either item's head as its head. Thus, a dependency tree for the whole sentence can then be built up in a bottom-up manner, by successively combining adjacent chart items into bigger ones. A dependency parsing algorithm implemented in this way has $O(n^5)$ complexity in the worst case. An algorithm outline is given in Fig. 7.3. This dependency parsing algorithm is essentially a modified CKY parsing algorithm. We use this algorithm in the experimental evaluation in this chapter.

The novel probabilistic dependency parsing algorithm described in Eisner (1996) is a modified chart-parsing algorithm, with $O(n^3)$ complexity. The modification is that instead of storing spans of subtrees, it stores spans of half subtrees. A span is defined as a substring such that no interior word links to any word outside the span. The underlying idea is that in a span, only the end-words are active, i.e., those that still need a head. Either one or both of the end-words can be active.

The difference between these algorithms has to do with the linguistic constraints they can enforce and the types of features they can use during dynamic

```
Parse() {
  for (h = 0; h < N; ++h) {
    AddItem(new Item(h, h, h, 0));
    for l from h down to 0 do {
      foreach item t in items(l, h) {
        MergeAsModifier(t);
        MergeAsHead(t);
      }
    }
  }
}

MergeAsHead(item) {
  h = item.high;  mid = item.low - 1;
  for l from mid down to 0 do {
    m = argmax_{t in items(l, mid)} combined_score(h, t)
    AddItem(new Item(m.low, item.head, item.high, Combined_score(h, m)));
  }
}

MergeAsModifier(item) {
  h = item.high;  mid = item.low - 1;
  for l from mid down to 0 do {
    foreach item m in items(l, mid) without a pre-head modifier
      AddItem(new Item(m.low, m.head, item.high, Combined_score(m, item);
  }
}

AddItem(item) {
  if not exist t in item(l, h) s.t. t.head==item.head and
     t.score > item.score
  then add item to items(item.low, item.high);
}
```

Fig. 7.3 A dependency parsing algorithm

programming. Faster algorithms enforce fewer linguistic constraints and need to use a more restricted class of features. For example, when attaching a preposition, Eisner's $O(n^3)$ parser cannot access the noun after the preposition, whereas an $O(n^5)$ chart parser is able to do so and can therefore correctly disambiguate some prepositional phrase attachments that the cheaper $O(n^3)$ parser cannot handle appropriately.

7.6 Experimental Results

We evaluated the proposed learning technique developed in this chapter on the Penn Chinese Treebank 4.0 (CTB4). CTB4 contains constituency trees for each training sentence. The conversion from constituency structures to dependency trees is based on the rules described in Bikel (2004). We use the data split of Bikel (2004): Sections 1–270 and 400–931 for training, Sections 301–325 for development and Sections 271–300 for test. We tested on the sets of data with different sentence length: CTB4-10, CTB4-15, CTB4-20 and CTB4-40, which contain test sentences with up to 10, 15, 20 and 40 words respectively. Parsing Chinese generally involves segmentation as a pre-processing step. We used the gold standard segmentation in the CTB4. The distributional similarities between words are computed using the Chinese Gigaword corpus (Graff and Chen, 2003). We did not segment the corpus when computing the word similarities.

We measured the quality of the parser by undirected dependency accuracy, which is defined as the number of correct undirected dependency links divided by the total number of dependency links in the corpus (the treebank parse and the parser output always have the same number of links).[2] The results are summarized in Table 7.1. These results show that the performance of the parser is highly correlated with the length of sentences, due to the fact that the number of possible parse trees increases exponentially with sentence length.

We also experimented with several alternative models. Table 7.2 summarizes the results of these models on the test corpus with sentences with less than or equal to 40 words.

One of the characteristics of the parser developed here is that it uses words similar to both the head and the modifier for smoothing. The similarity-based smoothing method in Dagan et al. (1999) uses the words similar to only one of the words in a

Table 7.1 Evaluation results on Chinese Treebank 4.0

Test data	CTB4-10	CTB4-15	CTB4-20	CTB4-40
Undirected accuracy (%)	90.8	85.6	84.0	79.9

[2] We also computed directed dependency accuracy, which is defined as the percentage of words that have the correct head. We observed that the directed dependency accuracy is only slightly lower than the undirected one.

Table 7.2 Performance of alternative models

Models	Accuracy (%)
(a) Strictly lexicalised conditional model	79.9
(b) At most one word is different in a similar context	77.7
(c) Strictly lexicalised joint model	66.3
(d) Unlexicalized conditional models	71.1
(e) Unlexicalized joint models	71.1

bigram. The definition of similar context can be changed as follows so that only one word in a context similar to C may be different from a word in C (see Model (b) in Table 7.2):

$$S\left(\left[u, v, C_w^d\right]\right) = \left\{\left[u', v, C_w^d\right] \mid u' \in S(u)\right\} \cup \left\{\left[u, v', C_w^d\right] \mid v' \in S(v)\right\}$$

where w is either v or u depending on whether d is L or R. This change leads to a 2.2% drop in accuracy (compared with Model (a) in Table 7.2), which is probably due to the fact that many contexts do not have similar contexts in the training corpus.

Since most previous parsing models maximize the joint probability of the sentence and the parse tree P(X, Y) instead of the conditional probability of P($Y|X$), we also implemented a joint model (see Model (c) in Table 7.2):

$$\begin{aligned} P(X, Y) = \prod_{i=1}^{N} & P(E_{m_i}^L | m_i, C_{m_i}^L) \times P(E_{m_i}^R | m_i, C_{m_i}^R) \\ & \times \left(1 - P(E_{h_i}^d | h_i, C_{h_i}^d)\right) \times P(m_i | h_i, C_{h_i}^{d_i}) \end{aligned}$$

where h_i and m_i are the head and the modifier of the i'th dependency link. The probability $P\left(m_i | h_i, C_{h_i}^{d_i}\right)$ is smoothed by averaging the probabilities $P\left(m_i | h_i, C_{h_i'}^{d_i}\right)$, where h_i' is a word similar to h_i, as in Dagan et al. (1999). This change of using a joint model causes a dramatic decrease in accuracy, from 79.9% for the conditional model to 66.3% for the joint model.

In the model proposed here, the use of distributional word similarity can be viewed as assigning soft clusters to words. In contrast, parts-of-speech can be viewed as a hard cluster of words. Both the conditional and joint models can be modified to use part-of-speech tags instead of words. Since there are only a small number of tags, the modified models use maximum likelihood estimation without any smoothing except for a small probability constant for unseen events. Without smoothing, maximizing the conditional model is equivalent to maximizing the joint model. The accuracy of the unlexicalized models (see Model (d) and Model (e) in Table 7.2) is 71.1% which is considerably lower than the strictly lexicalised conditional model we have proposed, but higher than the strictly lexicalised joint model. This demonstrates that soft clusters obtained through distributional word similarity perform better than the part-of-speech tags, when used appropriately.

7.7 Related Work

Previous probabilistic parsing models (Collins, 1997; Charniak, 2000) maximize the joint probability $P(X, Y)$ of a sentence X and its parse tree Y. This chapter considers an approach that maximizes the conditional probability $P(Y|X)$. The use of conditional model allows us to take advantage of similarity-based smoothing.

Clark et al. (2002) also compute a conditional probability of dependency structures. While the probability space considered in this chapter consists of all possible projective dependency trees, their probability space is constrained to be all dependency structures that are allowed by a Combinatory Categorial Grammar (CCG) (**?**) and a category dictionary (lexicon). They therefore do not need the STOP markers in their model. Another major difference between the model presented here and Clark et al. (2002) is that the parameters used here consist exclusively of conditional probabilities of binary variables.

Ratnaparkhi's maximum entropy model (Ratnaparkhi, 1999) is also a conditional model. However, his model maximizes the probability of the action during each step of the parsing process, instead of overall quality of the parse tree. Yamada and Matsumoto (2003) presented a deterministic dependency parsing algorithm. It performs multi-pass scans of a partially built dependency structure (the initial structure is simply the input text). At each point, it focuses on a pair of adjacent heads in the partial dependency structure and uses a support vector machine to decide whether to create a dependency link between them or to shift the focus to the next pair of heads. The worse case complexity of the algorithm is $O(n^2)$ because it takes up to $n - 1$ passes to construct a complete dependency tree.

The MaltParser (Nivre et al., 2007) is an efficient deterministic dependency parser that is gaining popularity. Similar to Yamada and Matsumoto (2003), the MaltParser relies on a discriminative classifier to choose its actions. However, by employing the arc-eager algorithm presented in (Nivre, 2003), the parser can build the complete parse tree in a single pass and therefore it guarantees $O(n)$ complexity in the worst case.

In many dependency parsing models such as Eisner (1996) and McDonald et al. (2005), the score of a dependency tree is the sum of the scores of the dependency links, which are computed independently of other links. An undesirable consequence of this is that the parser often creates multiple dependency links that are separately likely but jointly improbable (or even impossible). For example, there is nothing in such models to prevent the parser from assigning two subjects to a verb. In the DMV model (Klein and Manning, 2004), the probability of a dependency link is partly conditioned on whether or not there is a head word of the link that already has a modifier. The model proposed in this chapter is quite similar to the DMV model, except that it computes the conditional probability of the parse tree given the sentence, instead of the joint probability of the parse tree and the sentence.

There have been several previous approaches to parsing Chinese with the Penn Chinese Treebank (Bikel and Chiang, 2000; Levy and Manning, 2003). Both of these approaches employ phrase-structure joint models and use part-of-speech tags in back-off smoothing. Their results were evaluated with the precision and recall of the brackets implied in the phrase structure parse trees. In contrast, the accuracy of the proposed model is measured in terms of the dependency relationships. A dependency tree may correspond to more than one constituency trees. Our results are therefore not directly comparable with the precision and recall values in previous research. Moreover, it was argued in Lin (1995) that dependency based evaluation is much more meaningful for the applications that use parse trees, since the semantic relationships are generally embedded in the dependency relationships.

7.8 Contributions

In this chapter, we present a generative approach that employs Maximum Likelihood Markov Network training for dependency parsing. This model is similar to the maximum entropy Markov models (MEMMs). In both MEMMs and the model presented here, the goal is to maximize the conditional probability given the observations and previous state. The probability parsing model we presented is also very closely related to the score-based parsing model (McDonald et al., 2005), since the product of link probabilities can be converted to a sum of scores in the log space. Instead of relying on part-of-speech tags or grammatical categories, similarity-based smoothing was applied to deal with data sparseness, which has not been applied to parsing before.

7.9 Conclusion

To the best of our knowledge, all previous natural language parsers have to rely on part-of-speech tags. In this chapter we present a strictly lexicalised model for dependency parsing that only relies on word statistics. We compared the resulting parser with an unlexicalized parser that employs the same probabilistic model except that the parameters are estimated using gold standard tags in the Chinese Treebank. The experimental results show that the strictly lexicalised parser significantly outperformed its unlexicalized counterpart.

An important distinction between the proposed statistical model and previous parsing models is that all the parameters in the model presented here are conditional probabilities of binary variables. This allows us to take advantage of similarity-based smoothing, which has not been successfully applied to parsing before.

Acknowledgements We would like to thank Mark Steedman for suggesting the comparison with unlexicalised parsing in Section 7.6 and the anonymous reviewers for their useful comments. This work was supported by NSERC, the Alberta Ingenuity Center for Machine Learning, and the Canada Research Chairs program. The first author was also supported by iCORE Scholarship.

References

Bikel, D.M. (2004). Intricacies of Collins' parsing model. *Computational Linguistics 30*(4), 479–511.

Bikel, D.M. and D. Chiang (2000). Two statistical parsing models applied to the chinese treebank. In *Proceedings of the 2nd Chinese Language Processing Workshop*, Hong Kong.

Charniak, E. (2000). A maximum entropy inspired parser. In *Proceedings of North American Annual Meeting of the Association for Computational Linguistics*, Seattle, Washington, pp. 132–139.

Clark, S., J. Hockenmaier, and M. Steedman (2002). Building deep dependency structures with a wide-coverage CCG parser. In *Proceedings of the Annual Meeting of the Association for Computational Linguistics*, Philadelphia, PA.

Collins, M. (1996). A new statistical parser based on bigram lexical dependencies. In *Proceedings of the Annual Meeting of the Association for Computational Linguistics*, Santa Cruz, California, pp. 184–191.

Collins, M. (1997). Three generative, lexicalized models for statistical parsing. In *Proceedings of the Annual Meeting of the Association for Computational Linguistics*, Madrid, pp. 16–23.

Collins, M. (1999). Head-driven statistical models for natural language parsing. Ph. D. thesis, University of Pennsylvania, Pennsylvania, PA.

Dagan, I., L. Lee, and F. Pereira (1999). Similarity-based models of word cooccurrence probabilities. *Machine Learning 34*(1–3), 43–69.

Eisner, J. (1996). Three new probabilistic models for dependency parsing: an exploration. In *Proceedings of the International Conference on Computational Linguistics*, Copenhagen.

Eisner, J. and G. Satta (1999). Efficient parsing for bilexical context-free grammars and head-automaton grammars. In *Proceedings of the Annual Meeting of the Association for Computational Linguistics*, Maryland.

Gildea, D. (2001). Corpus variation and parser performance. In *Proceedings of the Conference on Empirical Methods in Natural Language Processing*, Pittsburgh, PA.

Graff, D. (2003). *English Gigaword*. Philadelphia, PA: Linguistic Data Consortium.

Graff, D. and K. Chen (2003). *Chinese Gigaword*. Philadelphia, PA: Linguistic Data Consortium.

Grefenstette, G. (1994). Corpus-derived first, second and third-order word affinities. In *Proceedings of Euralex*, Amsterdam.

Harris, Z. (1968). *Mathematical Structures of Language*. New York, NY: Wiley.

Hindle, D. (1990). Noun classification from predicate-argument structures. In *Proceedings of the Annual Meeting of the Association for Computational Linguistics*, Pittsburgh, PA, pp. 268–275.

Jurafsky, D. and J. Martin (2000). *Speech and Language Processing*. Upper Saddle River, NJ: Prentice Hall.

Klein, D. and C. Manning (2003). Accurate unlexicalized parsing. In *Proceedings of the Annual Meeting of the Association for Computational Linguistics*, Sapporo.

Klein, D. and C. Manning (2004). Corpus-based induction of syntactic structure: models of dependency and constituency. In *Proceedings of the Annual Meeting of the Association for Computational Linguistics*, Barcelona.

Levy, R. and C.D. Manning (2003). Is it harder to parse chinese, or the chinese treebank? In *Proceedings of the Annual Meeting of the Association for Computational Linguistics 2003*, Sapporo, Hokkaido.

Lin, D. (1995). A dependency-based method for evaluating broad-coverage parsers. In *Proceedings of the International Joint Conference on Artificial Intelligence*, Montreal, Quebec, pp. 1420–1425.

Lin, D. (1998). Automatic retrieval and clustering of similar words. In *Proceedings of the International Conference on Computational Linguistics and the Annual Meeting of the Association for Computational Linguistics*, Montreal, Quebec, pp. 768–774.

Manning, C. and H. Schutze (1999). *Foundations of Statistical Natural Language Processing*. Cambridge, MA: MIT Press.

McDonald, R., K. Crammer, and F. Pereira (2005). Online large-margin training of dependency parsers. In *Proceedings of the Annual Meeting of the Association for Computational Linguistics*, Ann Arbor, Michigan.

Nivre, J. (2003). An efficient algorithm for projective dependency parsing. In *Proceedings of the 8th International Workshop on Parsing Technologies*, Nancy, pp. 149–160.

Nivre, J., J. Hall, J. Nilsson, A. Chanev, G. Eryigit, S. kubler, S. Marinov, and E. Marsi (2007). Maltparser: a language-independent system for data-driven dependency parsing. *Natural Language Engineering 13*, 95–135.

Pereira, F., N. Tishby, and L. Lee (1993). Distributional clustering of English words. In *Proceedings of the Annual Meeting of the Association for Computational Linguistics*, Columbus, Ohio, pp. 183–190.

Ratnaparkhi, A. (1999). Learning to parse natural language with maximum entropy models. *Machine Learning 34*(1–3), 151–175.

Yamada, H. and Y. Matsumoto (2003). Statistical dependency analysis with support vector machines. In *Proceedings of the International Workshop on Parsing Technologies*, Nancy.

Chapter 8
Favor Short Dependencies: Parsing with Soft and Hard Constraints on Dependency Length

Jason Eisner and Noah A. Smith

8.1 Introduction

Many modern parsers identify the head word of each constituent they find. This makes it possible to identify the word-to-word dependencies implicit in a parse.[1] Some parsers, known as dependency parsers, even return these dependencies as their primary output. Why bother to identify dependencies? The typical reason is to model the fact that some word pairs are more likely than others to engage in a dependency relationship.[2] In this paper, we propose a different reason to identify dependencies in candidate parses: to evaluate not the dependency's word pair but its *length* (i.e., the *string distance* between the two words). Dependency lengths differ from typical parsing features in that they cannot be determined from tree-local information. Though lengths are not usually considered, we will see that bilexical dynamic-programming parsing algorithms can easily consider them as they build the parse.

Soft constraints. Like any other feature of trees, dependency lengths can be explicitly used as features in a probability model that chooses among trees. Such a model will tend to disfavor long dependencies (at least of some kinds), as these are empirically rare. In the first part of the paper, we show that such features improve a simple baseline dependency parser.

Hard constraints. If the bias against long dependencies is strengthened into a hard constraint that absolutely prohibits long dependencies, then the parser turns into a partial parser with only finite-state power. In the second part of the paper, we show how to perform chart parsing in asymptotic linear time with a low grammar

J. Eisner (✉)
Johns Hopkins University, Baltimore, MD, USA
e-mail: jason@cs.jhu.edu

[1] In a phrase-structure parse, if phrase X headed by word token x is a subconstituent of phrase Y headed by word token $y \neq x$, then x is said to depend on y. In a more powerful compositional formalism like LTAG or CCG, dependencies can be extracted from the derivation tree.

[2] It has recently been questioned whether these "bilexical" features actually contribute much to parsing performance (Klein and Manning, 2003b; Bikel, 2004), at least when one has only a million words of training data.

H. Bunt et al. (eds.), *Trends in Parsing Technology*, Text, Speech and Language Technology 43, DOI 10.1007/978-90-481-9352-3_8,

constant. Such a partial parser does less work than a full parser in practice, and in many cases recovers a more precise set of dependencies (with little loss in recall).

8.2 Short Dependencies in Language

We assume that correct parses exhibit a "short-dependency preference": a word's dependents tend to be close to it in the string.[3] If the jth word of a sentence depends on the ith word, then $|i - j|$ tends to be small. This implies that neither i nor j is modified by complex phrases that fall between i and j. In terms of phrase structure, it implies that the *phrases* modifying word i from a given side tend to be (1) few in number, (2) ordered so that the longer phrases fall farther from i, and (3) internally structured so that the bulk of each phrase falls on the side of j away from i.

These principles have been blamed for several linguistic phenomena across languages, both by traditional linguists (Hawkins, 1994) and by computational linguists (Gildea and Temperley, 2007; Temperley, 2007). For example, (1) helps explain the "late closure" or "attach low" heuristic, whereby a modifier such as a PP is more likely to attach to the closest appropriate head (Frazier, 1979; Hobbs and Bear, 1990, for example). (2) helps account for heavy-shift: when an NP is long and complex, *take NP out*, *put NP on the table*, and *give NP to Mary* are likely to be rephrased as *take out NP*, *put on the table NP*, and *give Mary NP*. (3) explains certain non-canonical word orders: in English, a noun's left modifier must become a right modifier if and only if it is right-heavy (*a taller politician* vs. *a politician taller than all her rivals*[4]), and a verb's left modifier may extrapose its right-heavy portion (*An aardvark walked in who had circumnavigated the globe*[5]).

Why should sentences prefer short dependencies? Such sentences may be easier for humans to produce and comprehend. Each word can quickly "discharge its responsibilities," emitting or finding all its dependents soon after it is uttered or heard; then it can be dropped from working memory (Church, 1980; Gibson,

---

[3] In this paper, we consider only a crude notion of "closeness": the number of intervening words. Other distance measures could be substituted or added (following the literature on heavy-shift and sentence comprehension), including the phonological, morphological, syntactic, or referential (given/new) complexity of the intervening material (Gibson, 1998). In parsing, the most relevant previous work is due to Collins (1997), Klein and Manning (2003c), and McDonald et al. (2005), discussed in more detail in Section 8.7.

[4] Whereas **a politician taller* and **a taller-than-all-her-rivals politician* are not allowed. The phenomenon is pervasive. Other examples: *a sleeping baby* vs. *a baby sleeping in a crib*; *a gun-toting honcho* vs. *a honcho toting a gun*; *recently seen friends* vs. *friends seen recently*.

[5] This actually splits the heavy left dependent *[an aardvark who . . .]* into two non-adjacent pieces, moving the heavy second piece. By slightly stretching the *aardvark-who* dependency in this way, it greatly shortens *aardvark-walked*. The same is possible for heavy, non-final right dependents: *I met an aardvark yesterday who had circumnavigated the globe* again stretches *aardvark-who*, which greatly shortens *met-yesterday*. These examples illustrate (3) and (2) respectively. However, the resulting non-contiguous constituents lead to non-projective parses that are beyond the scope of this paper; see Section 8.8.

1998). Such sentences also succumb nicely to disambiguation heuristics that *assume* short dependencies, such as low attachment. Thus, to improve comprehensibility, a speaker can make stylistic choices that shorten dependencies (e.g., heavy-shift), and a language can categorically prohibit some structures that lead to long dependencies (**a taller-than-all-her-rivals politician*; **the sentence that another sentence that had center-embedding was inside was incomprehensible*).

Such functionalist pressures are not all-powerful. For example, many languages use SOV basic word order where SVO (or OVS) would give shorter dependencies. However, where the data exhibit some short-dependency preference, computer parsers as well as human parsers can obtain speed and accuracy benefits by exploiting that fact.

8.3 Soft Constraints on Dependency Length

We now enhance simple baseline probabilistic parsers for English, Chinese, and German so that they consider dependency lengths. We confine ourselves (throughout the paper) to parsing part-of-speech (POS) tag sequences. This allows us to ignore data sparseness, out-of-vocabulary, smoothing, and pruning issues, but it means that our accuracy measures are not state-of-the-art. Our techniques could be straightforwardly adapted to (bi)lexicalized parsers on actual word sequences, though not necessarily with the same success.

8.3.1 Grammar Formalism

Throughout this paper we will use split bilexical grammars, or SBGs (Eisner, 2000), a notationally simpler variant of split head-automaton grammars, or SHAGs (Eisner and Satta, 1999). The formalism is context-free and only allows projective parses (those that are free of crossing dependencies). We define here a probabilistic version,[6] which we use for the baseline models in our experiments. They are only baselines because the SBG generative process does *not* take note of dependency length.

An SBG is an tuple $\mathcal{G} = (\Sigma, \$, L, R)$. Σ is an alphabet of words. (In our experiments, we parse only POS tag sequences, so Σ is actually an alphabet of tags.) $\$ \notin \Sigma$ is a distinguished root symbol; let $\bar{\Sigma} = \Sigma \cup \{\$\}$. L and R are functions from $\bar{\Sigma}$ to probabilistic ϵ-free finite-state automata over Σ. Thus, for each $w \in \bar{\Sigma}$, the SBG specifies "left" and "right" probabilistic FSAs, L_w and R_w.

We use $\mathcal{L}_w(\mathcal{G}) : \bar{\Sigma}^* \to [0, 1]$ to denote the probabilistic context-free language of phrases headed by w. $\mathcal{L}_w(\mathcal{G})$ is defined by the following simple top-down for sampling from it:

---

[6] There is a straightforward generalization to *weighted* SBGs, which need not have a stochastic generative model.

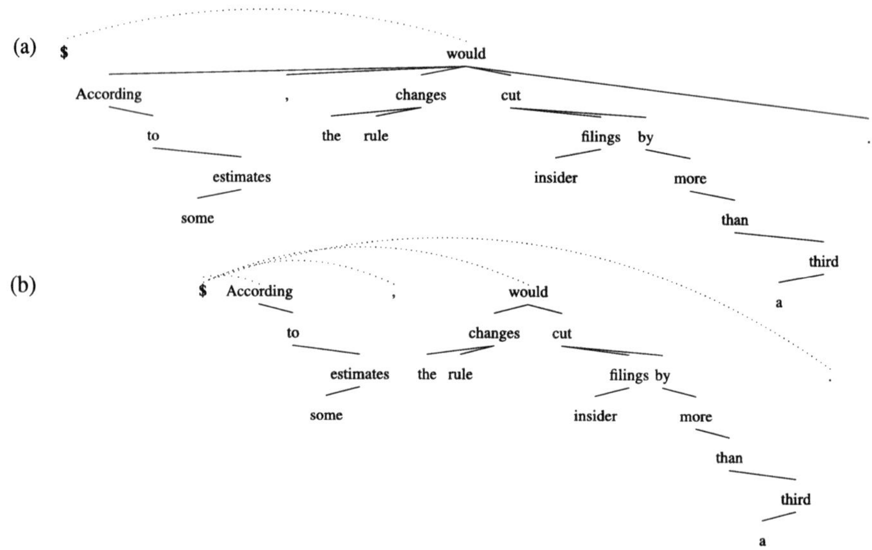

Fig. 8.1 **a** A dependency tree on words. (Our experiments use only POS tags.) **b** A partial parse for the same sentence retaining only tree dependencies of length $\leq k = 3$. The roots of the 4 resulting parse fragments are now connected only by their *dotted-line* "vine dependencies" on **$**. Transforming **(a)** into **(b)** involves grafting subtrees rooted at "*According*", ",", and "." onto the vine

1. Sample from the finite-state language $\mathcal{L}(L_w)$ a sequence $\lambda = w_{-1}w_{-2}\ldots w_{-\ell} \in \Sigma^*$ of left children, and from $\mathcal{L}(R_w)$ a sequence $\rho = w_1 w_2 \ldots w_r \in \Sigma^*$ of right children. Each sequence is found by a random walk on its probabilistic FSA. We say the children *depend* on w.
2. For each i from $-\ell$ to r with $i \neq 0$, recursively sample $\alpha_i \in \Sigma^*$ from the context-free language $\mathcal{L}_{w_i}(\mathcal{G})$. It is this step that indirectly determines dependency lengths.
3. Return $\alpha_{-\ell}\ldots\alpha_{-2}\alpha_{-1}w\alpha_1\alpha_2\ldots\alpha_r \in \bar{\Sigma}^*$, a concatenation of strings.

Notice that w's left children λ were generated in reverse order, so w_{-1} and w_1 are its closest children while $w_{-\ell}$ and w_r are the farthest.

Given an input sentence $\omega = w_1 w_2 \ldots w_n \in \Sigma^*$, a parser attempts to recover the highest-probability derivation by which $\$\omega$ could have been generated from $\mathcal{L}_{\$}(\mathcal{G})$. Thus, $\$$ plays the role of w_0. A sample derivation is shown in Fig. 8.1a. Typically, $L_{\$}$ and $R_{\$}$ are defined so that $\$$ must have no left children ($\ell = 0$) and at most one right child ($r \leq 1$), the latter serving as the conventional root of the parse.

8.3.2 Baseline Models

In the experiments reported here, we defined only very simple automata for L_w and R_w ($w \in \Sigma$). However, we tried three automaton types, of varying quality, so as to evaluate the benefit of adding length-sensitivity at three different levels of baseline performance.

In model A (the worst), each automaton has topology $\circledcirc\!\circlearrowleft$, with a single state q_1, so token w's left dependents are conditionally independent of one another given w. In model C (the best), each automaton $\circledcirc\!\longrightarrow\!\circledcirc\!\circlearrowleft$ has an extra state q_0 that allows the first (closest) dependent to be chosen differently from the rest. Model B is a compromise[7]: it is like model A, but each type $w \in \Sigma$ may have an elevated or reduced probability of having no dependents at all. This is accomplished by using automata $\circledcirc\!\longrightarrow\!\circledcirc\!\circlearrowleft$ as in model C, which allows the stopping probabilities $p(\text{STOP} \mid q_0)$ and $p(\text{STOP} \mid q_1)$ to differ, but tying the conditional distributions $p(q_0 \xrightarrow{w} q_1 \mid q_0, \neg\text{STOP})$ and $p(q_1 \xrightarrow{w} q_1 \mid q_1, \neg\text{STOP})$.

Finally, throughout Section 8.3, $L_\$$ and $R_\$$ are restricted as above, so $R_\$$ gives a probability distribution over Σ only.

8.3.3 Length-Sensitive Models

None of the baseline models A–C *explicitly* model the distance between a head and child. We enhanced them by multiplying in some extra length-sensitive factors when computing a tree's probability. For each dependency, an extra factor $p(\Delta \mid \ldots)$ is multiplied in for the probability of the dependency's length $\Delta = |i - j|$, where i and j are the positions of the head and child in the *surface* string. In practice, this especially penalizes trees with long dependencies, because large values of Δ are empirically unlikely.

Note that this is a crude procedure. Each legal tree—whether its dependencies are long or short—has had its probability reduced by some extra factors $p(\Delta \mid \ldots) \leq 1$. Thus, the resulting model is *deficient* (does not sum to 1). (The remaining probability mass goes to impossible trees whose putative dependency lengths Δ are inconsistent with the tree structure.) One could develop non-deficient models (either log-linear or generative), but we will see that even the present crude approach helps.

Again we tried three variants. In one version, this new probability $p(\Delta \mid \ldots)$ is conditioned only on the direction $d = \text{sign}(i - j)$ of the dependency. In another version, it is conditioned only on the POS tag h of the head. In a third version, it is conditioned on d, h, and the POS tag c of the child.

8.3.4 Parsing Algorithm

Figure 8.2 gives a variant of Eisner and Satta's (1999) SHAG parsing algorithm, adapted to SBGs, which are easier to understand.[8] (We will modify this algorithm later in Section 8.5.) The algorithm obtains $O(n^3)$ runtime, despite the need

[7] It is equivalent to the "dependency!model with valence" of Klein and Manning (2004).

[8] The SHAG notation was designed to highlight the connection to *non*-split HAGs.

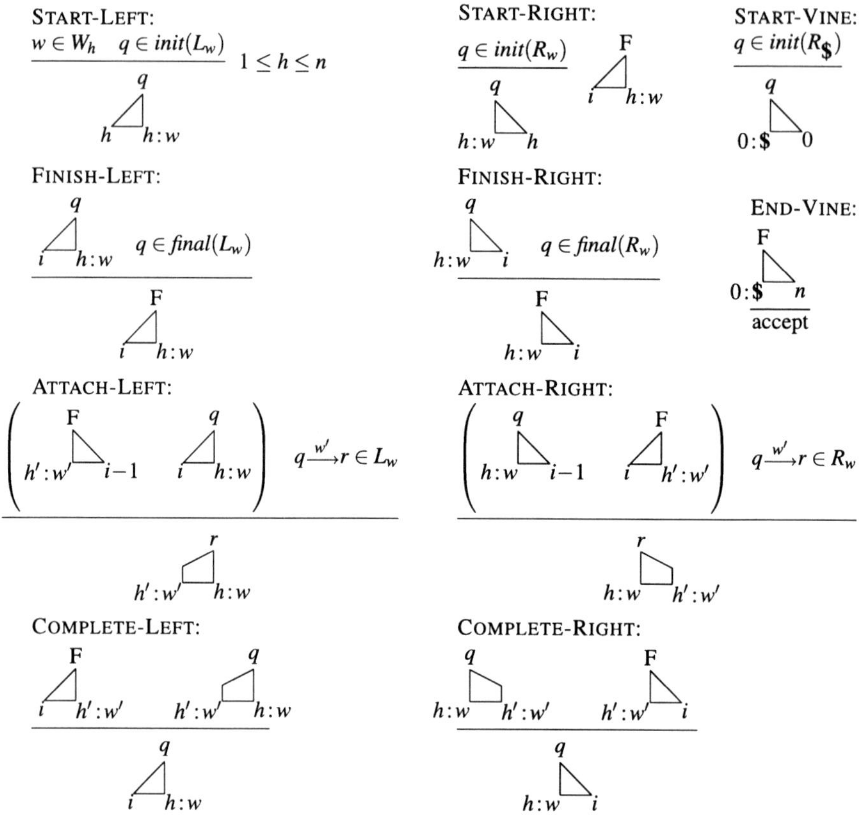

Fig. 8.2 An algorithm that parses $W_1 \dots W_n$ in cubic time $O(n^2(n+t')tg^2)$. Adapted with improvements from (Eisner and Satta, 1999, Fig. 3); see footnote 9 for a further practical speedup that delays the disambiguation of word senses. The algorithm is specified as a collection of deductive inference rules. Once one has derived all antecedent items above the *horizontal line* and any side conditions to the right of the *line*, one may derive the consequent item below the *line*. The parentheses in the ATTACH rules indicate the deduction of an intermediate item that "forgets" i. Weighted agenda-based deduction is handled in the usual way (Goodman, 1999): i.e., the weight of a consequent item is the product of the weights of its antecedents (not including side conditions), maximized (or summed) over all ways of deriving that consequent. The probabilities governing the automaton L_w, namely $p(\text{start at}q)$, $p(q \xrightarrow{w'} r \mid q)$, and $p(\text{stop} \mid q)$, respectively give the weights of the axiomatic items $q \in init(L_w)$, $q \xrightarrow{w'} r \in L_w$, and $q \in final(L_w)$; similarly for R_w. The weight of the axiomatic item $w \in W_h$ is 1, but could be modified to define a penalty (not mentioned in Section 8.3.5) for generating w rather than some other element of W_h

to track the position of head words, by exploiting the conditional independence between a head's left children and its right children (given the head). It builds "half-constituents" denoted by  (a head word together with some modifying phrases on the right, i.e., $w\alpha_1 \dots \alpha_r$) and 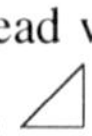 (a head word together with some modifying phrases on the left, i.e., $\alpha_{-\ell} \dots \alpha_{-1} w$). A new dependency is introduced when

 +  are combined to get the "trapezoid"  or 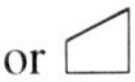 (a pair of linked head words with all the intervening phrases, i.e., $w\alpha_1 \dots \alpha_r \alpha'_{-\ell'} \dots \alpha'_{-1} w'$, where w is respectively the parent or child of w'). One can then combine  +  = , or 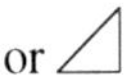 + 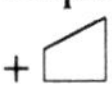 = 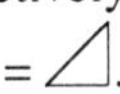. Only $O(n^3)$ combinations are possible in total when parsing a length-n sentence.

8.3.5 A Note on Word Senses

A remark is necessary about $:w$ and $:w'$ in Fig. 8.2, which represent *senses* of the words at positions h and h'. Like past algorithms for SBGs (Eisner, 2000), Fig. 8.2 is designed to be a bit more general and integrate sense disambiguation into parsing.[9] It formally runs on an input $\Omega = W_1 \dots W_n \subseteq \Sigma^*$, where each $W_i \subseteq \Sigma$ is a "confusion!set" over possible values of the ith word w_i. Thus Ω is a "confusion!network." The algorithm recovers the highest-probability derivation that generates $\$\omega$ for *some* $\omega \in \Omega$ (i.e., $\omega = w_1 \dots w_n$ with $(\forall i) w_i \in W_i$).

This extra level of generality is not needed for any of our experiments, but without it, SBG parsers would not be as flexible as SHAG parsers. We include it in this paper to broaden the applicability of both Fig. 8.2 and our extension of it in Section 8.5.

---

[9] In the present paper, we adopt the simpler and slightly more flexible SBG formalism of Eisner (2000), which allows explicit word senses, but follow the asymptotically more efficient SHAG parsing algorithm of Eisner and Satta (1999), in order to save a factor of g in our runtimes. Thus Fig. 8.2 presents a version of the Eisner–Satta SHAG algorithm that has been converted to work with SBGs, exactly as sketched and motivated in footnote 6 of Eisner and Satta (1999).

This conversion preserves the *asymptotic* runtime of the Eisner-Satta algorithm. However, notice that the version in Fig. 8.2 does have a *practical* inefficiency, in that START-LEFT nondeterministically guesses each possible sense $w \in W_h$, and these g senses are pursued separately. This inefficiency can be repaired as follows. We should not need to commit to one of a word's g senses until we have seen all its left children (in order to match the behavior of the Eisner–Satta algorithm, which arrives at one of g "flip states" in the word's FSA only by accepting a sequence of children). Thus, the left triangles and left trapezoids of Fig. 8.2 should be simplified so that they do not carry a sense $:w$ at all, except in the case of the completed left triangle (marked F) that is produced by FINISH-LEFT. The FINISH-LEFT rule should nondeterministically choose a sense w of W_h according to the final state q, which reflects knowledge of W_h's sequence of left children.

For this strategy to work, the transitions in L_w (used by ATTACH-LEFT) clearly may not depend on the particular sense $w \in W_h$ but only on W_h. In other words, all $L_w : w \in W_h$ are really copies of a shared L_{W_h}, except that they may have different final states. This slightly inelegant restriction on the SBG involves no loss of generality, since the nondeterministic shared L_{W_h} is free to branch as soon as it likes onto paths that commit to the various senses w.

We remark without details that this modification to Fig. 8.2, which defers the choice of w for as long as possible, could be obtained mechanically as an instance of the speculation transformation of Eisner and Blatz (2007). Speculation could similarly be used to extend the trick to the lattice parsing of Section 8.3.7, where a left triangle would commit immediately to the initial state of its head arc but defer committing to the full head arc for as long as possible.

The "senses" can be used in an SBG to pass a finite amount of information between the left and right children of a word (Eisner, 2000). For example, to model the fronting of a direct object, an SBG might use a special sense of a verb, whose automata tend to generate both one more noun in the left child sequence λ and one fewer noun in the right child sequence ρ.

Senses can also be used to pass information between parents and children. Important uses are to encode lexical senses, or to enrich the dependency parse with constituent labels, dependency labels, or supertags (Bangalore and Joshi, 1999; Eisner, 2000). For example, the input token $W_i = \{bank_1/N/NP, bank_2/N/NP, bank_3/V/VP, bank_3/V/S\} \subset \Sigma$ allows four "senses" of bank, namely two nominal meanings, and two *syntactically different* versions of the verbal meaning, whose automata require them to expand into VP and S phrases respectively.

The cubic runtime is proportional to the number of ways of instantiating the inference rules in Fig. 8.2: $O(n^2(n+t')tg^2)$, where $n = |\Omega|$ is the input length, $g = \max_{i=1}^{n} |W_i|$ bounds the size of a confusion!set, t bounds the number of states per automaton, and $t' \leq t$ bounds the number of automaton transitions from a state that emit the same word. For deterministic automata, $t' = 1$.

8.3.6 Probabilistic Parsing

It is easy to make the algorithm of Fig. 8.2 length-sensitive. When a new dependency is added by an ATTACH rule that combines ◺ + ◿, the annotations on ◺ and ◿ suffice to determine the dependency's length $\Delta = |h - h'|$, direction $d = \text{sign}(h - h')$, head word w, and child word w'.

So the additional cost of such a dependency, e.g. $p(\Delta \mid d, w, w')$, can be included as the weight of an extra antecedent to the rule, and so included in the weight of the resulting ⏢ or ⏥.

To execute the inference rules in Fig. 8.2, common practice is to use a prioritized agenda (Eisner et al., 2005), at the price of an additional logarithmic factor in the runtime for maintaining the priority queue. In our experiments, derived items such as ◺, ◿, ⏢, and ⏥ are prioritized by their Viterbi-inside probabilities. This is known as *uniform-cost search* or *shortest-hyperpath search* (Nederhof, 2003). We halt as soon as a full parse (the special *accept* item) pops from the agenda, since uniform-cost search (as a special case of the A* algorithm) guarantees this to be the maximum-probability parse. No other pruning is done.

With a prioritized agenda, a probability model that more sharply discriminates among parses will typically lead to a faster parser. (Low-probability constituents languish at the back of the agenda and are never pursued.) We will see that the length-sensitive models do run faster for this reason.[10]

[10] A better priority function that estimated outside costs would further improve performance (Caraballo and Charniak, 1998; Charniak et al., 1998; Klein and Manning, 2003a).

8.3.7 A Note on Lattice Parsing

A lattice is an acyclic FSA. Often parsing a weighted lattice is useful—for example, the output of a speech recognition or machine translation system. The parser extracts a good path through the lattice (i.e., one that explains the acoustic or source-language data) that also admits a good syntax tree (i.e., its string is likely under a generative syntactic language model, given by Section 8.3.1).

More generally, we may wish to parse an *arbitrary* FSA. For example, if we apply our inference rules using the inside semiring (Goodman, 1999), we obtain the total weight of all parses of all paths in the FSA. This provides a normalizing constant that is useful in learning, if the FSA is Σ^* or a "neighborhood" (contrast set) of distorted variants of the observed string (Smith and Eisner, 2005; Smith, 2006).

Thus, for completeness, we now present algorithms for the case where we are given an arbitrary FSA as input. A parse now consists of a choice of path through the given FSA together with an SBG dependency tree on the string accepted by that path. In the weighted case, the weight of the parse is the product of the respective FSA and SBG weights.

Section 8.3.5 already described a special case—the confusion network $\Omega = W_1 \ldots W_n$, which may be regarded as a particular unweighted lattice with n states and ng arcs. The confusion-network parsing algorithm of Fig. 8.2 can easily be generalized to parse an arbitrary weighted FSA, Ω:

- In general, the derivation tree of a triangle or trapezoid item now explains a path in Ω. The lower left corner of the item specifies the leftmost state or arc on that path, while the lower right corner specifies the rightmost state or arc. If the lower left corner specifies an arc, the weight of this leftmost arc is not included in the weight of the derivation tree (it will be added in by a later COMPLETE step).
- Each position h in Fig. 8.2 that is paired with a word w (i.e., $h:w$) now denotes an arc in Ω that is labeled with w. Similarly for $h':w'$.
- The special position 0, which is paired with the non-word \$, denotes the initial state of Ω (rather than an arc).
- Each unpaired position i now denotes a state in Ω. In the ATTACH rules, $i-1$ should be modified to equal i. In END-VINE, the unpaired position n should be constrained by a new antecedent to be a final state of Ω, whose stopping weight is the weight of this antecedent.
- In the START-LEFT (respectively START-RIGHT) rule, where h in $h : w$ now denotes an arc, the unpaired h should be replaced by the start (respectively end) state of this arc.
- In the START-LEFT rule, the antecedent $w \in W_h$ is replaced by a new antecedent requiring that h is an arc of Ω, labeled with w. The weight of this arc is the weight of the new antecedent.
- We add the following rule to handle arcs of Ω that are labeled with ε rather than with a word: TRAVERSE-ε

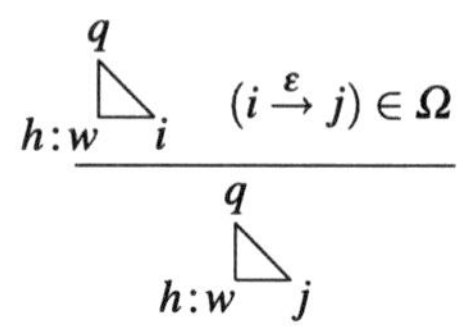

- If Ω is cyclic, it is possible to obtain cyclic derivations (analogous to unary rule cycles in CFG parsing) in which an item is used to help derive itself. However, this is essentially unproblematic if this cyclic derivation always has worse probability than the original acyclic one, and hence does not improve the weight of the item (Goodman, 1999).

The resulting algorithm has runtime $O(m^2(n+t')t)$ for a lattice of n states and m arcs. In the confusion!network case, where $m = ng$, this reduces to our earlier runtime of $O(n^2(n+t')tg^2)$ from Section 8.3.5.

The situation becomes somewhat trickier, however, when we wish to consider dependency lengths. For our soft constraints in Section 8.3.6, we needed to determine the length Δ of a new dependency that is added by an ATTACH rule. Unfortunately the distance $\Delta = |h - h'|$ is no longer well-defined now that h and h' denote arcs in an FSA rather than integer positions in a sentence. Different paths from h to h' might cover different numbers of words.

Before proceeding, let us generalize the notion of dependency length. Assume that each arc in the input FSA, Ω, comes equipped with a length. Recall that a parse specifies a finite path $h_1 h_2 \ldots h_n$ through Ω and a set of dependencies among the word tokens that label that path. If there is a leftward or rightward dependency between the word tokens that label arcs h_ℓ and h_r, where $\ell < r$, we define the length of this dependency to be the total length of the subpath $h_{\ell+1} h_{\ell+2} \ldots h_r$.[11]

When an ATTACH rule builds a trapezoid item, it adds a dependency. Our goal is to determine the length Δ of that dependency from the "width" of the trapezoid, so that the ATTACH rule can multiply in the appropriate penalty. The problem is that the width of an *item* is not well-defined: rather, each *derivation* (proof tree) of a triangle or trapezoid item has a possibly different width.

We define a derivation's width to be the total length of the subpath of Ω that is covered by the derivation, but excluding the leftmost arc of the subpath iff the item itself specifies that arc.[12] In other words, let i denote the item's leftmost state or the *end* state of its leftmost arc if specified, and j denote its rightmost state or the

[11] It is an arbitrary decision for a dependency's length to include the length of its right word but not the length of its left word. We adopt that convention only for consistency with our earlier definition of dependency length, and to simplify the relationship between dependency length and derivation width. It might however be justified in terms of incremental parsing, since it encodes the wait time once the left word has been heard until the right word is fully available to link to it.

[12] This exclusion ensures that when we combine two such derivations using COMPLETE or ATTACH, then the consequent derivation's width is always the sum of its antecedent derivations' widths. Recall from the first bullet point above that the same exclusion was used when defining the *weight* of an item, and for the same reason.

start state of its rightmost arc if specified. The derivation's width is the length of the subpath from i to j, plus the length of the rightmost arc if specified. Unfortunately, the item does not record this subpath, which differs by derivation; it only records i and j.

There are several possible attacks on the problem of defining the widths of triangle and trapezoid items:

Redefine length. One option is to ensure that all derivations of an item do have equal widths. This may be done by defining the arc lengths in Ω in a "consistent" way. Where Ω is an acoustic lattice derived from a speech signal, we can meaningfully associate a time $t(i)$ with each state $i \in \Omega$, and define the length of an arc to be the difference between its start and end times. Then *all* paths from state i to state j have the same length, namely $t(j) - t(i)$. In short, the problem goes away if we measure dependency length in acoustic milliseconds.

However, Ω is not necessarily an acoustic lattice. To measure a dependency's length by its string distance in words, as we have been doing thus far, we must define each arc's length to be be 1 or 0 according to whether it accepts a word or ε.[13] In this case, different paths from i to j do have different lengths.

Specialize the items. A second option is to augment each triangle or trapezoid item with a specific width Δ. In other words, we split an item that already specifies i and j into several more specific items, each of which allows only derivations of a particular width. The width of a consequent item can be determined easily by summing the widths of its antecedents.

Unfortunately, this exact method leads to more items and increased runtime (though only to the extent that there really are paths of many different lengths between i and j). In particular, it leads to infinitely many items if the input FSA Ω is cyclic.[14]

Use a lower bound based on shortest path. A third option is to *approximate* by using only a lower bound on dependency length. The ATTACH rule can consider the width of a trapezoid to be a lower bound on the widths of its derivations, specifically, the *shortest* path in Ω from i to j.[15] In other words, when evaluating a parse, we will define a dependency between arcs h_ℓ and h_r to be be "short" if these arcs are close on some path, though not necessarily on the path actually chosen by the parse.

Notice that one can improve this lower bound at the expense of greater runtime, by modifying Ω to use more states and less structure-sharing. A reasonable trick

---

[13] One could change the arc lengths to measure not in words but in one of the other measurement units from footnote 3.

[14] Although uniform-cost search will still terminate, provided that all cycles in Ω have positive cost. All sufficiently wide items will then have a cost worse than that of the best parse, so only finitely many items will pop from the priority queue.

[15] The shortest-path distances between all state pairs can be precomputed in $O(n^3 + m)$ time using the Floyd–Warshall algorithm. This preprocessing time is asymptotically dominated by the runtime of Fig. 8.2.

is to intersect Ω with an FSA that accepts Σ^* and has the topology of a simple 4-cycle. This does not change the weighted language accepted by Ω, but it splits states of Ω so that two paths from i to j must accept the same number of words, modulo 4. For many practical lattices, this will often ensure that all short paths from i to j accept exactly the same number of words. It increases n by a factor of ≤ 4 and does not increase m at all.[16]

Partially specialize the items. By combining the previous two methods, we can keep the number of items finite. Fix a constant $k \geq 0$. Each item either records a specific width $\Delta \in [0, k]$, or else records that it has width $> k$. The former items conside only derivations of a particular width, while for the latter items we can use a lower bound.

Coarse to fine. There is another way to combine these methods. The lower-bounding method can be run as a "coarse pass," followed by the exact specialized-items method as a "fine pass." If shorter dependencies are always more likely than longer ones, then the Viterbi outside probabilities from the coarse pass are upper bounds on the Viterbi outside probabilities from the fine pass, and hence can be used as an admissible A* heuristic to prioritize derivations on the fine pass.

Aggregate over derivations. A final option is to approximate more tightly. Each triangle and each trapezoid can dynamically maintain an estimate $\bar{\Delta}$ of the *minimum* (or the *expected*) width of its derivations. Whenever an inference rule derives or rederives the item, it can update this $\bar{\Delta}$ estimate based on the current estimates $\bar{\Delta}$ at its antecedents.[17] When deriving a trapezoid, the ATTACH rule can estimate the dependency length that it needs as the total current $\bar{\Delta}$ of its antecedents.[18]

This may give a lower bound that is tighter than the one given earlier, since it attempts to use the shortest i-to-j subpath that is covered by some actual derivation of the item in question, rather than the shortest i-to-j subpath overall. Unfortunately, if we wish to ensure that it is a true lower bound (i.e., considers *all* relevant i-to-j subpaths), then we must incur the extra overhead of updating it when new derivations are found. Specifically, we must consider reducing the $\bar{\Delta}$ of an item whenever the $\bar{\Delta}$ of one of its antecedents is reduced. Since a trapezoid's $\bar{\Delta}$ in turn affects its weight, this may in turn force us to propagate increases or other updates to item weights.

---

[16] A related trick is to convert Ω to a trie (if it is acyclic). This makes the lower bound exact by ensuring that there are never multiple paths from i to j, but potentially increases the size of Ω exponentially.

[17] For the expected-width case, each item must maintain both $\sum_d p(d)\Delta(d)$ and $\sum_d p(d)$, where d ranges over derivations. These quantities can be updated easily, and their ratio is the expected width.

[18] This is more precise than using the $\bar{\Delta}$ of the consequent, which is muddied by other derivations that are irrelevant to this dependency length.

8.4 Experiments with Soft Constraints

We trained models A–C, using unsmoothed maximum likelihood estimation, on three treebanks: the Penn (English) Treebank (split in the standard way, §2–21 train/§23 test, or 950K/57K words), the Penn Chinese Treebank (80% train/10% test or 508K/55K words), and the German TIGER corpus (80%/10% or 539K/68K words).[19] Estimation was a simple matter of counting automaton events and normalizing counts into probabilities. For each model, we also trained the three length-sensitive versions described in Section 8.3.3.

The German corpus contains some non-projective trees, whose dependencies cross. None of our parsers can recover these non-projective dependencies, nor can our models produce them (but see Section 8.8). This fact was ignored when counting events for maximum likelihood estimation: in particular, we always trained L_w and R_w on the sequence of w's immediate children, even in non-projective trees.

Our results (Table 8.1) show that sharpening the probabilities with the most sophisticated distance factors $p(\Delta \mid d, h, c)$, consistently improved the *speed* of all parsers.[20] The change to the code is trivial. The only overhead is the cost of looking up and multiplying in the extra distance factors.

Accuracy also improved over the baseline models of English and Chinese, as well as the simpler baseline models of German. Again, the most sophisticated distance factors helped most, but even the simplest distance factor usually obtained most of the accuracy benefit.

German model C fell slightly in accuracy. The speedup here suggests that the probabilities were sharpened, but often in favor of the wrong parses. We did not analyze the errors on German; it may be relevant that 25% of the German sentences contained a non-projective dependency between non-punctuation tokens.

Studying the parser output for English, we found that the length-sensitive models preferred closer attachments, with 19.7% of tags having a nearer parent in the best parse under model C with $p(\Delta \mid d, h, c)$ than in the original model C, 77.7% having a parent at the same distance, and only 2.5% having a farther parent. The surviving long dependencies (at any length > 1) tended to be much more accurate, while the (now more numerous) length-1 dependencies were slightly less accurate than before.

We caution, however, that the length-sensitive models improved accuracy only in the aggregate. They corrected many erroneous attachments, but also introduced

---

19 Heads were extracted for English using Michael Collins' rules and for Chinese using Fei Xia's rules (defaulting in both cases to right-most heads where the rules fail). German heads were extracted using the TIGER Java API; we discarded all resulting dependency structures that were cyclic or unconnected (6%).

20 In all cases, we measure runtime abstractly by the number of items built and pushed on the agenda, where multiple ways of building the same item are counted multiple times. The items in question are , , , , and in the case of Fig. 8.4, also  and 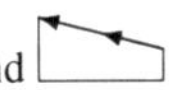.) Note that if the agenda is a general priority queue, then popping an item takes logarithmic time, although pushing an item can be achieved in constant time using a Fibonacci-heap implementation.

Table 8.1 Dependency parsing of POS tag sequences with simple probabilistic split bilexical grammars. The models differ only in how they weight the same candidate parse trees. Length-sensitive models are larger but can improve dependency accuracy and speed. (*Recall* is measured as the fraction of non-punctuation tags whose correct parent (if not the \$ symbol) was recovered by the parser; it equals precision, unless the parser left some sentences unparsed (or incompletely parsed, as in Section 8.5), in which case precision is higher. *Runtime* is measured abstractly as the average number of items built (see footnote 20). *Model size* is measured as the number of nonzero parameters)

	English (Penn Treebank)				Chinese (Chinese Treebank)				German (TIGER Corpus)			
	Recall (%)		Runtime	Model	Recall (%)		Runtime	Model	Recall (%)		Runtime	Model
model	Train	Test	Test	Size	Train	Test	Test	Size	Train	Test	Test	Size
A (1 state)	62.0	62.2	93.6	1, 878	50.7	49.3	146.7	782	70.9	72.0	53.4	1, 598
$+ p(\Delta \mid d)$	70.1	70.6	97.0	2, 032	59.0	58.0	161.9	1, 037	72.3	73.0	53.2	1, 763
$+ p(\Delta \mid h)$	70.5	71.0	94.7	3, 091	60.5	59.1	148.3	1, 759	73.1	74.0	48.3	2, 575
$+ p(\Delta \mid d, h, c)$	72.8	73.1	70.4	16, 305	62.2	60.6	106.7	7, 828	75.0	75.1	31.6	12, 325
B (2 states, tied arcs)	69.7	70.4	93.5	2, 106	56.7	56.2	151.4	928	73.7	75.1	52.9	1, 845
$+ p(\Delta \mid d)$	72.6	73.2	95.3	2, 260	60.2	59.5	156.9	1, 183	72.9	73.9	52.6	2, 010
$+ p(\Delta \mid h)$	73.1	73.7	92.1	3, 319	61.6	60.7	144.2	1, 905	74.1	75.3	47.6	2, 822
$+ p(\Delta \mid d, h, c)$	75.3	75.6	67.7	16, 533	62.9	61.6	104.0	7, 974	75.2	75.5	31.5	12, 572
C (2 states)	72.7	73.1	90.3	3, 233	61.8	61.0	148.3	1, 314	75.6	76.9	48.5	2, 638
$+ p(\Delta \mid d)$	73.9	74.5	91.7	3, 387	61.5	60.6	154.7	1, 569	74.3	75.0	48.9	2, 803
$+ p(\Delta \mid h)$	74.3	75.0	88.6	4, 446	63.1	61.9	141.9	2, 291	75.2	76.3	44.3	3, 615
$+ p(\Delta \mid d, h, c)$	75.3	75.5	66.6	17, 660	63.4	61.8	103.4	8, 360	75.1	75.2	31.0	13, 365

new errors. We also caution that length sensitivity's most dramatic improvements to accuracy were on the worse baseline models, which had more room to improve. The better baseline models (B and C) were already able to indirectly capture some preference for short dependencies, by learning that some parts of speech were unlikely to have multiple left or multiple right dependents. Enhancing B and C therefore contributed less, and indeed may have had some harmful effect by over-penalizing some structures that were already appropriately penalized.[21] It remains to be seen, therefore, whether distance features would help state-of-the art parsers that are already much better than model C. Such parsers may already incorporate features that indirectly impose a good model of distance (see Section 8.7), though perhaps not as cheaply.

8.5 Hard Dependency-Length Constraints

We have seen how an explicit model of distance can improve the speed and accuracy of a simple probabilistic dependency parser. Another way to capitalize on the fact that most dependencies are local is to impose a *hard constraint* that simply forbids long dependencies.

The dependency trees that satisfy this constraint yield a regular string language.[22] The constraint prevents arbitrarily deep center-embedding, as well as arbitrarily many direct dependents on a given head, either of which would allow the non-regular language $\{a^n bc^n : 0 < n < \infty\}$. However, it *does* allow arbitrarily deep right- or left-branching structures.

8.5.1 Vine Grammars

The tighter the bound on dependency length, the fewer parse trees we allow and the faster we can find them using an algorithm similar to Fig. 8.2 (as we will see). If the bound is too tight to allow the correct parse of some sentence, we would still like to allow an accurate partial parse: a sequence of accurate parse fragments (Hindle, 1990; Abney, 1991; Appelt et al., 1993; Chen, 1995; Grefenstette, 1996). Furthermore, we would like to use the fact that some fragment sequences are presumably more likely than others.

Our partial parses will look like the one in Fig. 8.1b. where four subtrees rather than just one are dependent on \$. This is easy to arrange in the SBG formalism.

---

[21] Owing to our deficient model. A log-linear or discriminative model would be trained to correct for overlapping penalties and would avoid this risk. Non-deficient generative models are also possible to design, along lines similar to footnote 22.

[22] One proof is to construct a strongly equivalent CFG without center-embedding (Nederhof, 2000). Each nonterminal has the form $\langle w, q, i, j\rangle$, where $w \in \Sigma$, q is a state of L_w or R_w, and $i, j \in \{0, 1, \ldots k-1, \geq k\}$. We leave the details as an exercise.

We merely need to construct our SBG so that the automaton $R_{\$}$ is now permitted to generate multiple children—the roots of parse fragments.

This $R_{\$}$ is a probabilistic finite-state automaton that describes legal or likely root sequences in Σ^*. In our experiments in this section, we will train it to be a first-order (bigram) Markov model. (Thus we construct $R_{\$}$ in the usual way to have $|\Sigma| + 1$ states, and train it on data like the other left and right automata. During generation, its state remembers the previously generated root, if any. Recall that we are working with POS tag sequences, so the roots, like all other words, are tags in Σ.)

The 4 subtrees in Fig. 8.1b appear as so many bunches of grapes hanging off a vine. We refer to the dotted dependencies upon **$** as *vine dependencies*, and the remaining, bilexical dependencies as *tree dependencies*.

One might informally use the term "vine grammar" (VG) for any generative formalism, intended for partial parsing, in which a parse is a constrained sequence of trees that cover the sentence. In general, a VG might use a two-part generative process: first generate a finite-state sequence of roots, then expand the roots according to some more powerful formalism. Conveniently, however, SBGs and other dependency grammars can integrate these two steps into a single formalism.

8.5.2 Feasible Parsing

Now, for both speed and accuracy, we will restrict the trees that may hang from the vine. We define a *feasible* parse under our SBG to be one in which all *tree* dependencies are short, i.e., their length never exceeds some hard bound k. The vine dependencies may have unbounded length, of course, as in Fig. 8.1b.

Sentences with feasible parses form a regular language. This would also be true under other definitions of feasibility: e.g., we could have limited the depth or width of each tree on the vine. However, that would have ruled out deeply right-branching trees, which are very common in language, and are also the traditional way to describe finite-state sublanguages within a context-free grammar. By contrast, our limitation on dependency length ensures regularity while still allowing (for any bound $k \geq 1$) arbitrarily wide and deep trees, such as $a \rightarrow b \rightarrow \ldots \rightarrow$ *root* $\leftarrow \ldots \leftarrow y \leftarrow z$.

Our goal is to find the *best feasible* parse (if any). (In our scenario, one will typically exist—at worse, just a vine of tiny single-word trees.) Rather than transform the grammar as in footnote 22, our strategy is to modify the parser so that it only considers feasible parses. The interesting problem is to achieve linear-time parsing with a grammar constant that is as small as for ordinary parsing.

One could enforce this restriction by modifying either the grammar $\mathcal{G}$ or the parser. In this paper, we leave the grammar alone, but restrict the parser so that it is only permitted to find *short* within-tree dependencies. Other parses may be permitted by the vine grammar but are not found by our parser.

We also correspondingly modify the training data so that we only train on feasible parses. That is, we break any long dependencies and thereby fragment each training parse (a single tree) into a vine of one or more restricted trees. When we break a child-to-parent dependency, we reattach the child to **$**.[23] This process, *grafting*, is illustrated in Fig. 8.1. Although this new parse may score less than 100% recall of the original dependencies, it is the best feasible parse, so we would like to train the parser to find it.[24] By training on the modified data, we learn more appropriate statistics for both $R_\$$ and the other automata. If we trained on the original trees, we would inaptly learn that $R_\$$ always generates a single root rather than a certain kind of sequence of roots.

For evaluation, we score tree dependencies in our feasible parses against the tree dependencies in the *unmodified* gold standard parses, which are not necessarily feasible. We also show oracle performance.

8.5.2.1 Approach #1: FSA Parsing

Since we are now dealing with a regular or rational string language, it is possible in principle to construct a weighted finite-state automaton (FSA) and use it to search for the best feasible parse. The idea is to find the highest-weighted path that accepts the input string $\omega = w_1 w_2 \ldots w_n$. Using the Viterbi algorithm, this takes time $O(n)$.

The trouble is that this linear runtime hides a constant factor, which depends on the size of the relevant part of the FSA and may be enormous for any correct FSA.[25] Consider an example from Fig. 8.1b. After nondeterministically reading $w_1 \ldots w_{11}$ = *According*...*insider* along the *correct* path, the FSA state must record (at least) that *insider* has no parent yet and that $R_\$$, R_{would}, and R_{cut} are in particular states that may still accept more children. Else the FSA cannot know whether to accept the continuation $w_{12} \ldots w_n$ = *filings by more than a third*.

In general, after parsing a prefix $w_1 \ldots w_j$, the FSA state must somehow record information about all incompletely linked words in the past. It must record the sequence of past words w_i $(i \leq j)$ that still need a parent or child in the future; if w_i still needs a child, it must also record the state of R_{w_i}.

Our restriction to dependency length $\leq k$ is what allows us to build a weighted *finite*-state automaton (as opposed to some kind of pushdown automaton with an unbounded number of configurations). We need only build the *finitely* many states in which the incompletely linked words are limited to at most w_0 = **$** and the k most recent words, $w_{j-k+1} \ldots w_j$. Other states cannot extend into a feasible parse, and can be pruned.

---

[23] Any dependency *covering* the child must also be broken to preserve projectivity. This case arises later; see footnote 34.

[24] Although our projective parser will still not be able to find it if it is non-projective (possible in German). Arguably we should have defined a more aggressive grafting procedure that produced projective parses, but we did not. See Section 8.8 for discussion of non-projective vine grammar parsing, which would always be able to recover the best feasible parse.

[25] The full runtime is $O(nE)$, where E is the number of FSA edges, or for a tighter estimate, the number of FSA edges that can be traversed by reading ω.

However, this still allows the FSA to be in $O(2^k t^{k+1})$ different states after nondeterministically reading $w_1 \ldots w_j$. Then the runtime of the Viterbi algorithm, though linear in n, is exponential in k.

8.5.2.2 Approach #2: Ordinary Chart Parsing

A much better idea for most purposes is to use a chart parser. This allows the usual dynamic programming techniques for reusing computation. (The FSA in the previous section failed to exploit many such opportunities: exponentially many states would have proceeded redundantly by building the same $w_{j+1}w_{j+2}w_{j+3}$ constituent.)

It is simple to restrict our algorithm of Fig. 8.2 to find only feasible parses. It is the ATTACH rules  +  that add dependencies: simply use a side condition to block them from applying unless $|h - h'| \leq k$ (short tree dependency) or $h = 0$ (vine dependency). This ensures that all  and  will have width $\leq k$ or have their left edge at 0. One might now incorrectly expect runtime linear in n. Unfortunately, the number of possible ATTACH combinations, which add new dependencies, is reduced from $O(n^3)$ to $O(nk^2)$, because i and h' are now restricted to a narrow range given h. Unfortunately, the half-constituents  and  may still be arbitrarily wide, thanks to arbitrary right- and left-branching: a feasible vine parse may be a sequence of wide trees 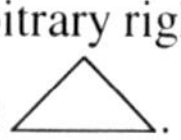. Thus there are $O(n^2k)$ possible COMPLETE combinations, not to mention $O(n^2)$ ATTACH-RIGHT combinations for which $h = 0$. So the runtime remains quadratic. We now fix this problem.

8.5.2.3 Approach #3: Specialized Chart Parsing

How, then, do we get linear runtime *and* a reasonable grammar constant? We give two ways to achieve runtime of $O(nk^2)$.

First, we observe without details that we can easily achieve this by starting instead with the algorithm of Eisner (2000),[26] rather than Eisner and Satta (1999), and again refusing to add long tree dependencies. That algorithm effectively concatenates only trapezoids, not triangles (i.e., half-constituents). Each is spanned by a single dependency and so has width $\leq k$. The vine dependencies do lead to wide trapezoids, but these are constrained to start at 0, where \$ is. So the algorithm tries at most $O(nk^2)$ trapezoid combinations of the form hi + ij (like the ATTACH combinations above) and $O(nk)$ combinations of the form 0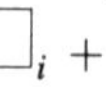i + i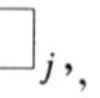j, where $i - h \leq k$, $j - i \leq k$. The precise runtime is $O(nk(k + t')tg^3)$, in terms of the parameters of Section 8.3.5. In the unrestricted case where $k = n$, we recover exactly the algorithm of Eisner (2000) and its runtime.

[26] With a small change that when two items are combined, the *right* item (rather than the left) must be simple (in the terms of Eisner (2000)).

We now propose a hybrid linear-time algorithm that further improves asymptotic runtime to $O(nk(k+t')tg^2)$, saving a factor of g in the grammar constant. While we will still build trapezoids as in Eisner (2000), the factor-of-g savings will come from building the internal structure of a trapezoid from both ends inward rather than from left to right. In the unrestricted case where $k = n$, this improved *runtime* exactly matches that of Eisner and Satta (1999) and Fig. 8.2 (as given in Section 8.3.5)—although the new *algorithm* itself is a hybrid of Eisner and Satta (1999) and Eisner (2000), since we already saw in Section 8.5.2.2 that simply restricting Eisner and Satta (1999) would not give linear runtime.

We observe that since within-tree dependencies must have length $\leq k$, they can all be captured within Eisner–Satta trapezoids of width $\leq k$. So our vine grammar parse  can be assembled by simply *concatenating* a sequence of the form  of these narrow trapezoids interspersed with width-0 triangles. As this is a *regular* sequence, we can assemble it in linear time from left to right (rather than in the order of Eisner and Satta (1999)), multiplying the items' probabilities together. Whenever we start adding the right half  of a tree along the vine, we have discovered that tree's root, so we multiply in the probability of a $\$ \leftarrow$ root vine dependency.

Formally, our hybrid parsing algorithm restricts the original rules of Fig. 8.2 to build only trapezoids of width $\leq k$ and triangles of width $< k$.[27] The additional inference rules in Fig. 8.3 then assemble the final VG parse from left to right as just described.

Specifically, the sequence 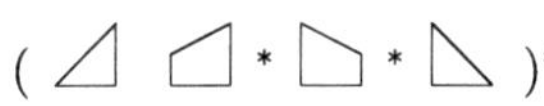 (all with F at the apex) is attached from left to right by the sequence of rules TREE-START TREE-LEFT* GRAFT-VINE TREE-RIGHT* TREE-END in Fig. 8.3. It is helpful to regard these rules as carrying out transitions in a small FSA whose state set is 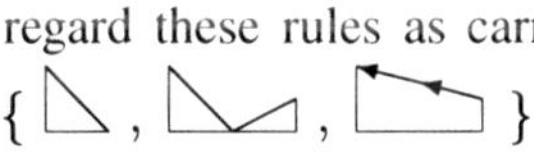 (all with 0 : $ at the left edge; these pictorially represent the state of the vine built so far). TREE-START is the arc 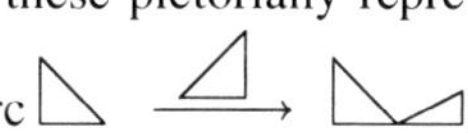; TREE-LEFT is the self-loop 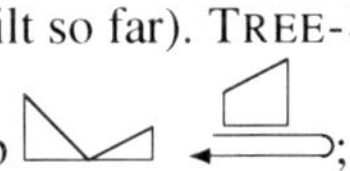; GRAFT-VINE is the ε-transition from 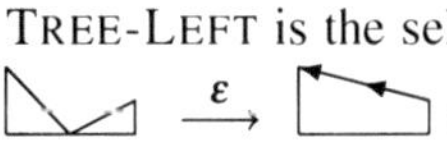 that is weighted by the vine dependency probability $p(\$ \leftarrow$ root); TREE-RIGHT is the self-loop 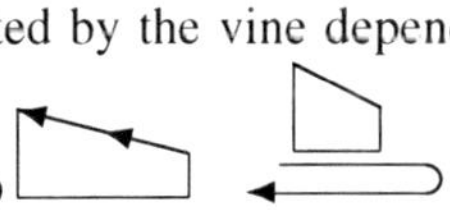; finally, TREE-END is the transition 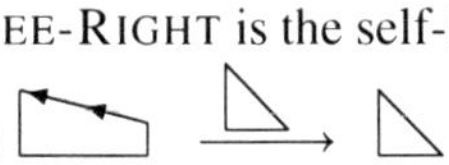 that loops back to the start state to accept the next fragment tree.

To understand the SEAL-LEFT rule in Fig. 8.3, notice that if a left trapezoid headed by $h : w$ has already received all its left children, there are two ways that

[27] For the experiments of Section 8.6.1, where k varied by type, we restricted these rules as tightly as possible given h and h'.

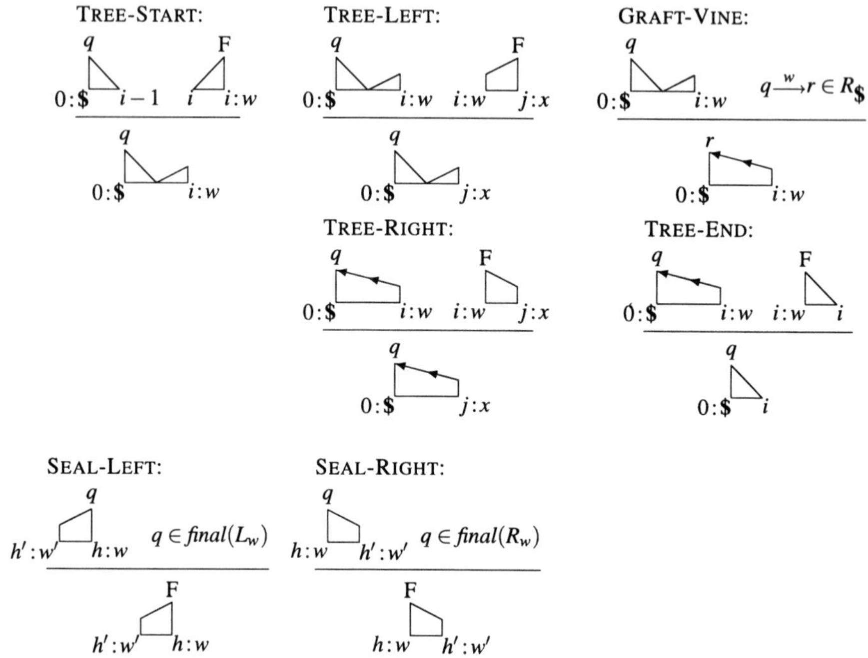

Fig. 8.3 Extension to the algorithm in Fig. 8.2. If the ATTACH rules (Fig. 8.2) are restricted to apply only when $|h - h'| \leq k$, and the COMPLETE rules (Fig. 8.2) only when $|h - i| < k$, then the additional rules above will assemble the resulting fragments into a vine parse. In this case, ATTACH-RIGHT should also be restricted to $h > 0$, to prevent duplicate derivations (spurious ambiguity). The runtime is $O(nk(k+t')tg^2)$, dominated by the ATTACH rules from Fig. 8.2; the additional rules above require only $O(nktg^2 + ngtt')$ additional time

it can be combined with its stopping weight from L_w. Following Fig. 8.2, we can use COMPLETE-LEFT to turn it into a left triangle for the last time, after which FINISH-LEFT will incorporate its stopping weight, changing its apex state to F. (Word w then combines with its parent using ATTACH-RIGHT or COMPLETE-LEFT, according to whether the parent is to the left or right of h.) However, these rules may not be permitted if their outputs are too wide. The alternative is to incorporate the left trapezoid directly into the vine parse using TREE-LEFT from Fig. 8.3. In this case, SEAL-LEFT must be used to incorporate the stopping weight, since we have bypassed FINISH-LEFT. (Word w then combines with its parent using GRAFT-VINE or another instance of TREE-LEFT, according to whether the parent is to the left of h (i.e., \$) or the right of h.) SEAL-RIGHT behaves similarly.

8.5.2.4 Lattice Parsing

Again, for completeness, we explain how to extend the final linear-time algorithm of Section 8.5.2.3 to parse a lattice or other input FSA, Ω.

We modify Fig. 8.2 to handle lattice parsing, exactly as in Section 8.3.7, and modify Fig. 8.3 similarly. Now, much as in Section 8.5.2.3, we restrict the ATTACH and COMPLETE rules in the modified Fig. 8.2 to apply only when the total width of the two triangle or trapezoid antecedents is $\leq k$. We then assemble the resulting fragments using the modified Fig. 8.3, as before.

But how do we define the width of a triangle or trapezoid? The simplest approach is to specialize these items as proposed in Section 8.3.7. Each such item records a explicit width $\Delta \in [0, k]$. Because of our hard constraints, we never need to build specialize items that are wider than that.[28]

The runtime of this algorithm depends on properties of Ω and its arc lengths. Let n be the number of states and m be the number of arcs. Define M' to be an upper bound, for all states $i \in \Omega$, on the size of the set $\{(j, \Delta) : \Omega$ contains a path of the form $i \ldots j$ having length $\Delta \leq k\}$. Define M similarly except that now j ranges over Ω's arcs rather than its states; note that $M \in [M', M'm]$. An upper bound on the runtime is then $O(mM(M'+t')t)$. In the confusion!network case, with n states, $m = ng$ arcs, $M' = O(k)$, $M = O(kg)$, this reduces to our earlier runtime of $O(nk(k+t')tg^2)$ from Section 8.5.2.3.

An alternative approach is at least as efficient, both asymptotically and practically. To avoid specializing the triangle or trapezoid items to record explicit widths, we define their widths using the shortest-path-based lower bounds from Section 8.3.7.[29] We are willing to combine two such items iff the sum of their widths is $\leq k$.[30]

The resulting search may consider some infeasible parses. In other words, it is possible that the search will return a parse that contains some dependencies that cover string distance $> k$, if this infeasible parse happens to score better than any of the feasible parses.[31] However, this is unproblematic if our goal is simply to prune infeasible parses in the interest of speed. If our pruning is incomplete and we can still maintain linear-time parsing, so much the better. That is, we are not required to consider infeasible parses (since we suppose that they will usually be suboptimal), but neither are we forbidden to consider them or allow them to win on the merits.

---

[28] We do not specialize the vine items, i.e., items whose left boundary is 0:\$. Vine items can have unbounded width $\Delta > k$, but it is unnecessary for them to record this width because it never comes into play.

[29] As in footnote 15, we may precompute the shortest-path distances between all state pairs, but here we only need to do this for the mM pairs whose distances are $\leq k$. Using a simple agenda-based relaxation algorithm that derives all such pairs together with their shortest-path distances, this takes time $O(mMb)$, where $b \leq M'$ is an upper bound on a state's number of outgoing transitions of length $\leq k$. This preprocessing time is asymptotically dominated by the runtime of the main algorithm.

[30] This test is more efficient to implement in a chart parser than requiring the width of the consequent to be $\leq k$. It rules out more combinations, since with lower-bound widths, a consequent of width $\leq k$ could be produced from two antecedents of total width $> k$. (The shortest path connecting its endpoints may not pass through the midpoint where the antecedents are joined.)

[31] For instance, suppose the best derivation of an item of width 3 happens to cover a subpath in Ω of length 5. The item will nonetheless permitted to combine with an adjacent item of width $k - 3$, perhaps resulting in the best parse overall, with a dependency of length $k + 2$.

If we really wish to consider only feasible parses, it may still be efficient to run the lower-bounding method first, as part of an A* algorithm (cf. Section 8.3.7). Since the lower-bounding method considers too many derivations, it produces optimistic probability estimates relative to the feasible-only parser that specializes the items. Thus, run the lower-bounding parser first. If this returns an infeasible parse, then compute its Viterbi-outside probabilities, and use them as an admissible A* heuristic when reparsing with the feasible-only parser.

8.6 Experiments with Hard Constraints

Our experiments used the asymptotically fast hybrid parsing algorithm of Section 8.5.2.3. We used the same left and right automata as in model C, the best-performing model from Section 8.3.2. However, we now define $R_\$$ to be a first-order (bigram) Markov model (Section 8.5.1). We trained and tested on the same headed treebanks as before (Section 8.4), except that we modified the *training* trees to make them feasible (Section 8.5.2).

Results with hard constraints are shown in Fig. 8.4, showing both the precision/recall tradeoff (upper left) and the speed/accuracy tradeoff (other graphs), for $k \in \{1, 2, \ldots, 10, 15, 20\}$. Dots correspond to different values of k. Tighter bounds k typically improve precision at the expense of recall, with the result that on English and Chinese, $k = 7$ (for example) actually achieves better F-measure accuracy than the $k = \infty$ unbounded parser (shown with +), not merely greater speed.

We observed separately that changing $R_\$$ from a bigram to a unigram model significantly hurt accuracy. This shows that it is in fact useful to empirically model likely *sequences* of parse fragments, as our vine grammar does.

Note that we continue to report runtime in terms of items built (see footnote 20). The absolute runtimes are not comparable across parsers because our prototype implementations of the different kinds of parser (baseline, soft constraints, single-bound, and the type-specific bounds in the next section) are known to suffer from different inefficiencies. However, to give a general idea, 60-word English sentences parsed in around 300 ms with no bounds, but at around 200 ms with either a distance model $p(\Delta \mid d, h, c)$ or a generous hard bound of $k = 10$.

8.6.1 Finer-Grained Hard Constraints

The dependency length bound k need not be a single value. Substantially better accuracy can be retained if each dependency type—each (h, c, d) = (head tag, child tag, direction) tuple—has its own bound $k(h, c, d)$.[32] We call these *type-specific*

---

[32] Note that $k(h, c, \text{right}) = 7$ bounds the width of . For a finer-grained approach, we could instead separately bound the widths of  and , say by $k_r(h, c, \text{right}) = 4$ and $k_l(h, c, \text{right}) = 2$.

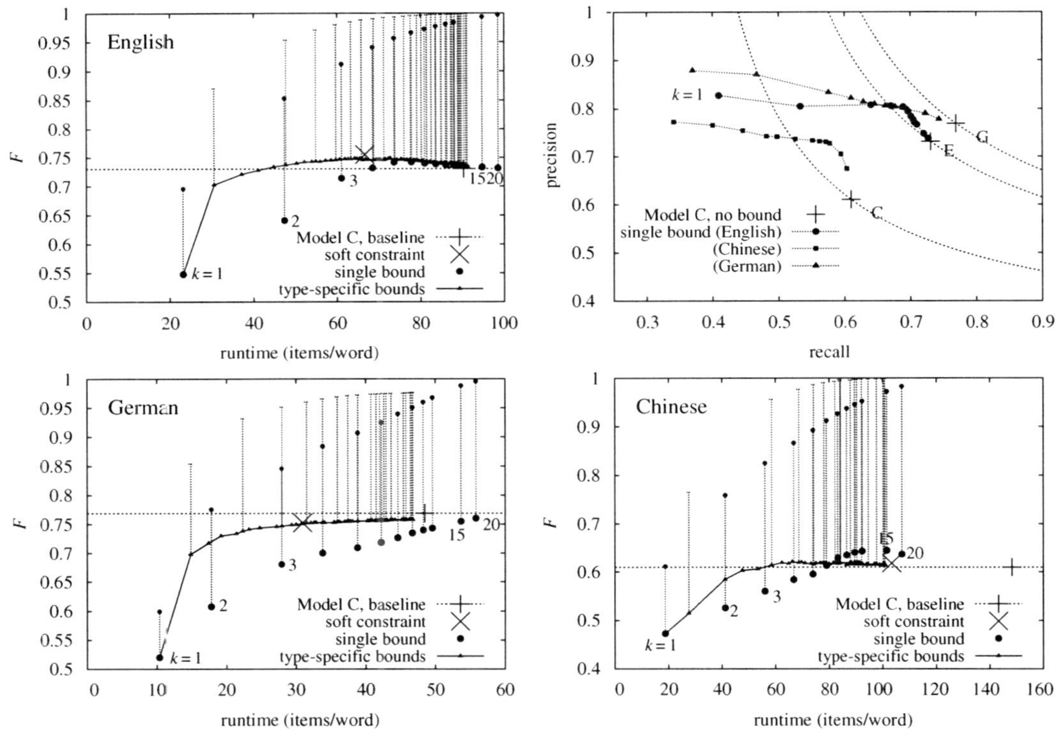

Fig. 8.4 *(upper left)* Trading recall for precision: Imposing bounds can improve precision at the expense of recall, for English and Chinese. German performance suffers more. Bounds shown are $k = \{1, 2, \ldots, 10, 15, 20\}$. The *dotted lines* show constant F-measure of the unbounded model. *(remaining graphs)* Trading accuracy for speed by varying the set of feasible parses: The baseline (no length bound) is shown as $+$. Tighter bounds always improve speed, except for the most lax bounds, for which vine construction overhead incurs a slowdown. Type-specific bounds (Section 8.6.1) tend to maintain good F-measure at higher speeds than the single-bound approach. The vertical bars connect each experiment to its "oracle" accuracy (i.e., the F-measure if we had recovered the best feasible parse, as constructed from the gold-standard parse by grafting: see Section 8.5.2). The "soft constraint" point marked with $\times$ shows the $p(\Delta \mid d, h, c)$-augmented model of Section 8.3

bounds: they create a many-dimensional space of possible parsers. We measured speed and accuracy along a sensible path through this space, gradually tightening the bounds using the following process:

1. Initialize each bound $k(h, c, d)$ to the maximum distance observed in training (or 1 for unseen triples).[33]
2. Greedily choose a bound $k(h, c, d)$ such that, if its value is decremented and trees that violate the new bound are accordingly broken, the *fewest* dependencies will be broken.[34]
3. Decrement the bound $k(h, c, d)$ and modify the training data to respect the bound by breaking dependencies that violate the bound and "grafting" the loose portion onto the vine. Retrain the parser on the training data.
4. If all bounds are not equal to 1, go to step 2.

The performance of every 200th model along the trajectory of this search is plotted in Fig. 8.4. The graph shows that type-specific bounds can speed up the parser to a given level with less loss in accuracy.

8.7 Related Work

An earlier version of this chapter was originally published as Eisner and Smith (2005). Since then, it has become more common to consider soft dependency-length features in dependency parsing. Indeed, at the same time as our 2005 paper, McDonald et al. (2005) used length features within a discriminatively trained model (versus our deficient generative model that redundantly generates dependency lengths). Furthermore, they considered not only approximately how many words intervened between a child and its parent, but also the POS tags of these words. These length and length-like features were very helpful, and variants were used in a subsequent extension by Hall (2007). Turian and Melamed's history-based parser (Turian and Melamed, 2006) also considered various kinds of length features when making its decisions.

There is also relevant work on soft length constraints that predates ours, and which like our present paper uses generative models. Klein and Manning (2003c) conditioned child generation at a given position on whether the position was adjacent to the parent, and they conditioned stopping on whether the position was 0, 1, 2–5, 6–10, or more than 11 words away from the parent, which is essentially a length feature. Even earlier, Collins (1997) used three binary features of the intervening material as conditioning context for generating a child: did the intervening material

[33] In the case of the German TIGER corpus, which contains non-projective dependencies, we first make the training trees into projective vines by raising all non-projective child nodes to become heads on the vine.

[34] Not counting dependencies that must be broken indirectly in order to maintain projectivity. (If word 4 depends on word 7 which depends on word 2, and the $4 \rightarrow 7$ dependency is broken, making 4 a root, then we must also break the $2 \rightarrow 7$ dependency.)

contain (a) any word tokens at all, (b) any verbs, (c) any commas or colons? Note that (b) is effective because it measures the length of a dependency in terms of the number of alternative attachment sites that the dependent skipped over, a notion that was generalized by the intervening POS features of McDonald et al. (2005), mentioned above.

Not all parsers evaluate directly whether a parse respects the short-dependency preference, but they do have other features that address some of the phenomena in Section 8.2. For example, Charniak and Johnson's reranker for phrase-structure parses (Charniak and Johnson, 2005) has "Heavy" features that can learn to favor late placement of *large constituents* in English, e.g., for heavy-shift. However, these other features make rather different distinctions and generalizations than ours do. It would be interesting to compare their empirical benefit.

We have subsequently applied our own soft constraint model to *unsupervised* parsing. By imposing a bias against long dependencies during unsupervised learning, we obtained substantial improvements in accuracy over plain Expectation-Maximization and other previous methods. Further improvements were obtained by gradually relaxing ("annealing") this bias as learning proceeded (Smith and Eisner, 2006; Smith, 2006).

As for hard constraints (Section 8.5), our limitation on dependency length can be regarded as approximating a context-free language by a subset that is a regular language. Our "vines" then let us concatenate several strings in this subset, which typically yields a superset of the original context-free language.

Subset and superset approximations of (weighted) CFLs by (weighted) regular languages, usually by preventing center-embedding, have been widely explored; Nederhof (2000) gives a thorough review. Our approach limits *all* dependency lengths (not just center-embedding).[35] Further, we derive weights from a modified treebank rather than by approximating the true weights. And though representing a regular language by a finite-state automaton (FSA) is useful for other purposes, we argued that the FSA in this case can be large, and that recognition and parsing are much more efficient with a modified version of a context-free chart parsing algorithm.

Bertsch and Nederhof (1999) gave a linear-time recognition algorithm for the recognition of the regular closure of deterministic context-free languages. Our result is slightly related, since a vine grammar is the Kleene closure of a different kind of restricted CFL (not deterministic, but restricted in its dependency length, hence regular).

Empirically, the algorithms described above were applied in Dreyer et al. (2006) to the construction of more interesting dependency parsing models. While the performance of those models was not competitive, that paper presents further evidence that hard bounds on dependency length need not harm the parser's precision.

[35] Of course, this still allows right-branching or left-branching to unbounded depth.

8.8 Future Work

The simple POS-sequence models we used as an experimental baseline are certainly not among the best parsers available today. They were chosen to illustrate how modeling and exploiting distance in syntax can affect various performance measures. Our approach may be helpful for other parsing situations as well.

First, we hope that our results will generalize to more expressively weighted grammars, such as log-linear models that can include head-child distance alongside and in conjunction with other rich features.

Second, fast approximate parsing may play a role in more accurate parsing. It might be used to rapidly compute approximate outside-probability estimates to prioritize best-first search (Caraballo and Charniak, 1998, for example). It might also be used to speed up the early iterations of training a weighted parsing model, which for modern training methods tends to require repeated parsing (either for the best parse, as in Taskar et al. (2004), or all parses, as in Miyao and Tsujii (2002)). Note that our algorithms also admit *inside–outside* variants (Goodman, 1999), allowing iterative estimation methods for log-linear models such as Miyao and Tsujii (2002).

Third, it would be useful to investigate algorithmic techniques and empirical benefits for limiting dependency length in more powerful grammar formalisms. Our runtime reduction from $O(n^3) \rightarrow O(nk^2)$ for a length-k bound applies only to a "split" bilexical grammar.[36] More expressive grammar formalisms include lexicalized CFG, CCG, and TAG (see footnote 1). Furthermore, various kinds of *synchronous* grammars (Shieber and Schabes, 1990; Wu, 1997) have seen a resurgence in statistical machine translation since the work of Chiang (2005). Their high runtime complexity might be reduced by limiting monolingual dependency length (Schafer and Yarowsky, 2003).

One tool in deriving further algorithms of this sort is to apply general-purpose transformations (Sikkel, 1997; Eisner and Blatz, 2007) to logical algorithm specifications such as the inference rules shown in Figs. 8.2 and 8.3. For example, Eisner and Blatz (2007) showed how to derive (a variant of) the $O(n^3)$ algorithm of Fig. 8.2 by transforming a naive $O(n^5)$ algorithm. Further transformations might be able to continue by deriving Fig. 8.3, and these transformations might generalize to other grammar formalisms.

Fourth, it would be useful to try limiting the dependency length in *non-projective* parsing, specifically for the tractable "edge-factored" case where $t = 1$ and $g = 1$ (as in our "model A" experiments). Here we can easily show a runtime reduction from $O(n^2) \rightarrow O(kn \log n)$ for a length-k bound. The $O(n^2)$ result for edge-factored non-projective parsing is due to McDonald et al. (2005), who directly applied a directed minimum spanning tree algorithm of Tarjan (1977) to the dense directed graph of all $O(n^2)$ possible dependency edges. Our "vine grammar" restric-

---

[36] The obvious reduction for unsplit head automaton grammars, say, is only $O(n^4) \rightarrow O(n^3k)$, following Eisner and Satta (1999). Alternatively, one can convert the unsplit HAG to a split one that preserves the set of feasible (length $\leq k$) parses, but then g becomes prohibitively large in the worst case.

tion would simply strip this graph down to a sparser graph of only $m = O(kn)$ possible edges (namely, the edges of length $\leq k$ together with the edges from \$). Another algorithm also in Tarjan (1977) can then find the desired non-projective tree in only $O(m \log n)$ time ($=O(kn \log n)$). It remains an empirical question whether this would lead to a desirable speed-accuracy tradeoff for non-projective dependency parsing.

Fifth, an obvious application of our algorithms is for linear-time, on-the-fly parsing or language modeling of long streams of tokens. Even though sentence boundaries can be accurately identified on the fly in newspaper text (Reynar and Ratnaparkhi, 1997), this is harder in informal genres and in speech, particularly given the lack of punctuation (Liu et al., 2005). Thus, one might want the syntactic model to help determine the segmentation. This is what a vine grammar does, permitting unboundedly long parsed fragments (which in practice would typically be the top-level sentences) as long as they do not contain long dependencies. For parsing such streams, our $O(nk^2)$ algorithm can be easily adapted to do *incremental* chart parsing in this situation, in linear time and space, perhaps using a k that is fairly generous (but still $\ll n$). For syntactic language modeling, an inside-algorithm version can be modified without too much difficulty so that it finds the probability of a given prefix string (or lattice state) under a vine grammar, summing over just the feasible prefix parses.[37] This modest vine approximation to Stolcke's exact PCFG syntactic language model (Stolcke, 1995) could make it more practical by speeding it up from cubic to linear time, as an alternative to switching to the history-based models and approximate multistack decoders of subsequent work on syntactic language modeling (Chelba and Jelinek, 2000, *et seq.*).

8.9 Conclusion

We have described a novel reason for identifying headword-to-headword dependencies while parsing: to consider their length. We have demonstrated that simple bilexical parsers of English, Chinese, and German can exploit a "short-dependency preference" to improve parsing runtime and dependency precision and the expense of recall. Notably, *soft* constraints on dependency length can improve both speed and accuracy, and *hard* constraints allow improved precision and speed with some loss in recall (on English and Chinese, remarkably little loss). Further, for the hard constraint "length $\leq k$," we have given an $O(nk^2)$ partial parsing algorithm for split bilexical grammars; the grammar constant is no worse than for state-of-the-art $O(n^3)$ algorithms. This algorithm strings together the partial trees' roots along a "vine." We extended this algorithm to the case where the input is a finite-state

[37] Note that the vine grammar as we have presented it is a deficient model, since unless we reparameterize it to consider dependency lengths, it also allocates some probability to infeasible parses that are not included in this sum. However, the short-dependency preference suggests that these infeasible parses should not usually contribute much to the total probability that we seek.

automaton such as a confusion network, a lattice, or Σ^*. We also noted a non-projective variant that runs in time $O(kn \log n)$.

Our approach might be adapted to richer parsing formalisms, including synchronous ones, and should be helpful as an approximation to full parsing when fast, high-precision recovery of syntactic information is needed, or when the input stream is very long.

Acknowledgements This work was supported by NSF ITR grant IIS-0313193 to the first author and a fellowship from the Fannie and John Hertz Foundation to the second author. The views expressed are not necessarily endorsed by the sponsors. The authors thank Mark Johnson, Eugene Charniak, Charles Schafer, Keith Hall, and John Hale for helpful discussion and Elliott Drábek and Markus Dreyer for insights on (respectively) Chinese and German parsing. They also thank an anonymous reviewer for suggesting the German experiments.

References

Abney, S.P. (1991). Parsing by chunks. In R. Berwick, S. Abney, and C. Tenny (eds.), *Principle-Based Parsing: Computation and Psycholinguistics*. Dordrecht: Kluwer.

Appelt, D.E., J.R. Hobbs, J. Bear, D. Israel, and M. Tyson (1993). FASTUS: A finite-state processor for information extraction from real-world text. In *Proceedings of the 13th International Joint Conference on Artificial Intelligence (IJCAI)*, Chambery, pp. 1172–1178.

Bangalore, S. and A.K. Joshi (1999). Supertagging: an approach to almost parsing. *Computational Linguistics 25*(2), 237–265.

Bertsch, E. and M.-J. Nederhof (1999). Regular closure of deterministic languages. *SIAM Journal on Computing 29*(1), 81–102.

Bikel, D. (2004). A distributional analysis of a lexicalized statistical parsing model. In *Proceedings of 2004 Conference on Empirical Methods in Natural Language Processing (EMNLP)*, Barcelona.

Caraballo, S.A. and E. Charniak (1998). New figures of merit for best-first probabilistic chart parsing. *Computational Linguistics 24*(2), 275–98.

Charniak, E., S. Goldwater, and M. Johnson (1998). Edge-based best-first chart parsing. In *Proceedings of 6th Workshop on Very Large* Corpora, *Montreal*, pp. 127–133.

Charniak, E. and M. Johnson (2005). Coarse-to-fine n-best parsing and maxent discriminative reranking. In *Proceedings of 43rd Annual Meeting of the Association for Computational Linguistics (ACL)*, Ann Arbor, Michigan, pp. 173–180.

Chelba, C. and F. Jelinek (2000). Structured language modeling. *Computer Speech and Language 14*, 283–332.

Chen, S. (1995). Bayesian grammar induction for language modeling. In *Proceedings of 33rd Annual Meeting of the Association for Computational Linguistics (ACL)*, Cambridge, Massachussetts, pp. 228–235.

Chiang, D. (2005). A hierarchical phrase-based model for statistical machine translation. In *Proceedings of 43rd Annual Meeting of the Association for Computational Linguistics (ACL)*, Ann Arbor, Michigan, pp. 263–270.

Church, K.W. (1980). On memory limitations in natural language processing. Master's thesis, MIT.

Collins, M. (1997). Three generative, lexicalised models for statistical parsing. In *Proceedings of 33rd Annual Meeting of the Association for Computational Linguistics (ACL)*, Madrid, pp. 16–23.

Dreyer, M., D.A. Smith, and N.A. Smith (2006). Vine parsing and minimum risk reranking for speed and precision. In *Proceedings of 10th Conference on Computational Natural Language Learning*, New York.

Eisner, J. (2000). Bilexical grammars and their cubic-time parsing algorithms. In H. Bunt and A. Nijholt (eds.), *Advances in Probabilistic and Other Parsing Technologies*. Dordrecht: Kluwer, pp. 29–61.

Eisner, J. and J. Blatz (2007). Program transformations for optimization of parsing algorithms and other weighted logic programs. In *Proceedings of FG*.

Eisner, J., E. Goldlust, and N.A. Smith (2005). Compiling Comp Ling: practical weighted dynamic programming and the Dyna language. In *Proceedings of Human Language Technology and Conference on Empirical Methods in Natural Language Processing (HLT/EMNLP)*, Vancouver, pp. 281–290.

Eisner, J. and G. Satta (1999). Efficient parsing for bilexical CFGs and head automaton grammars. In *Proceedings of 37th Annual Meeting of the Association for Computational Linguistics (ACL)*, University of Maryland, pp. 457–480.

Eisner, J. and N.A. Smith (2005). Parsing with soft and hard constraints on dependency length. In *Proceedings of the 9th International Workshop on Parsing Technologies (IWPT)*, Vancouver, pp. 30–41.

Frazier, L. (1979). *On Comprehending Sentences: Syntactic Parsing Strategies*. Ph. D. thesis, University of Massachusetts.

Gibson, E. (1998). Linguistic complexity: Locality of syntactic dependencies. *Cognition 68*, 1–76.

Gildea, D. and D. Temperley (2007). Optimizing grammars for minimum dependency length. In *Proceedings of 45th Annual Meeting of the Association for Computational Linguistics (ACL)*, Prague, pp. 184–191.

Goodman, J. (1999). Semiring parsing. *Computational Linguistics 25*(4), 573–605.

Grefenstette, G. (1996). Light parsing as finite-state filtering. In *Proceedings of the ECAI Workshop on Extended Finite-State Models of Language*, Budapest, pp. 20–25.

Hall, K. (2007). k-best spanning tree parsing. In *Proceedings of 45th Annual Meeting of the Association for Computational Linguistics (ACL)*, Prague, pp. 392–399.

Hawkins, J. (1994). *A Performance Theory of Order and Constituency*. Cambridge: Cambridge University Press.

Hindle, D. (1990). Noun classification from predicate-argument structure. In *Proceedings of 28th Annual Meeting of the Association for Computational Linguistics (ACL)*, Pittsburgh, pp. 268–275.

Hobbs, J.R. and J. Bear (1990). Two principles of parse preference. In *Proceedings of the 13th International Conference on Computational Linguistics (COLING)*, Helsinki, pp. 162–167.

Klein, D. and C.D. Manning (2003a). A* parsing: Fast exact viterbi parse selection. In *Proceedings of the Conference on Human Language Technology and the North Amercan Chapter of the Association for Computational Linguistics (HLT-NAACL)*, Edmonton, pp. 40–47.

Klein, D. and C.D. Manning (2003b). Accurate unlexicalized parsing. In *Proceedings of 41st Annual Meeting of the Association for Computational Linguistics (ACL)*, Sapporo, pp. 423–430.

Klein, D. and C.D. Manning (2003c). Fast exact inference with a factored model for natural language parsing. In S. Becker, S. Thrun, and K.Obermayer (eds.), *Advances in Neural Information Processing Systems (NIPS 2002)*, MIT Press, Cambridge, MA, pp. 3–10.

Klein, D. and C.D. Manning (2004). Corpus-based induction of syntactic structure: models of dependency and constituency. In *Proceedings of the 42nd Annual Meeting of the Association for Computational Linguistics (ACL)*, Barcelona, pp. 479–486.

Liu, Y., A. Stolcke, E. Shriberg, and M. Harper (2005). Using conditional random fields for sentence boundary detection in speech. In *Proceedings of 43rd Annual Meeting of the Association for Computational linguistics (ACL)*, Ann Arbor, Michigan, pp. 451–458.

McDonald, R., K. Crammer, and F. Pereira (2005). Online large-margin training of dependency parsers. In *Proceedings of 43rd Annual Meeting of the Association for Computational Linguistics (ACL)*, Ann Arbor, Michigan, pp. 91–98.

McDonald, R., F. Pereira, K. Ribarov, and J. Hajič (2005). Non-projective dependency parsing using spanning tree algorithms. In *Proceedings of Human Language Technology and Conference on Empirical Methods in Natural Language Processing (HLT/EMNLP)*, Vancouver, pp. 523–530.

Miyao, Y. and J. Tsujii (2002). Maximum entropy estimation for feature forests. In *Proceedings of the Conference on Human Language Technology (HLT)*, Edmonton, pp. 1–8.

Nederhof, M.-J. (2000). Practical experiments with regular approximation of context-free languages. *Computational Linguistics 26*(1), 17–44.

Nederhof, M.-J. (2003). Weighted deductive parsing and Knuth's algorithm. *Computational Linguistics 29*(1), 135–143.

Reynar, J.C. and A. Ratnaparkhi (1997). A maximum entropy approach to identifying sentence boundaries. In *Proceedings of the 5th Applied Natural Language Conference*, Washington, pp. 16–19.

Schafer, C. and D. Yarowsky (2003). A two-level syntax-based approach to Arabic-English statistical machine translation. In *Proceedings of the Workshop on Machine Translation for Semitic Languages*, New Orleans.

Shieber, S. and Y. Schabes (1990). Synchronous tree adjoining grammars. In *Proceedings of the 13th International Conference on Computational Linguistics (COLING)*, Helsinki.

Sikkel, K. (1997). *Parsing Schemata: A Framework for Specification and Analysis of Parsing Algorithms*. Texts in Theoretical Computer Science. Berlin, Heidelberg, New York: Springer.

Smith, N.A. (2006). *Novel Estimation Methods for Unsupervised Discovery of Latent Structure in Natural Language Text*. Ph. D. thesis, Johns Hopkins University.

Smith, N.A. and J. Eisner (2005). Contrastive estimation: Training log-linear models on unlabeled data. In *Proceedings of 43rd Annual Meeting of the Association for Computational Linguistics (ACL)*, Ann Arbor, Michigan, pp. 354–362.

Smith, N.A. and J. Eisner (2006). Annealing structural bias in multilingual weighted grammar induction. In *Proceedings of 21st International Conference on Computational Linguistics and 44th Annual Meeting of the Association for Computational Linguistics (COLING-ACL)*, Sydney, pp. 569–576.

Stolcke, A. (1995). An efficient probabilistic context-free parsing algorithm that computes prefix probabilities. *Computational Linguistics 21*(2), 165–201.

Tarjan, R.E. (1977). Finding optimum branchings. *Networks 7*(1), 25–35.

Taskar, B., D. Klein, M. Collins, D. Koller, and C. Manning (2004). Max-margin parsing. In *Proceedings of 2004 Conference on Empirical Methods in Natural Language Processing (EMNLP)*, Barcelona, pp. 1–8.

Temperley, D. (2007). Minimization of dependency length in written English. *Cognition 105*, 300–333.

Turian, J. and I.D. Melamed (2006). Advances in discriminative parsing. In *Proceedings of 21st International Conference on Computational Linguistics and 44th Annual Meeting of the Association for Computational Linguistics (COLING-ACL)*, Sydney, pp. 873–880.

Wu, D. (1997). Stochastic inversion transduction grammars and bilingual parsing of parallel corpora. *Computational Linguistics 23*(3), 377–404.

Chapter 9
Corrective Dependency Parsing

Keith Hall and Václav Novák

9.1 Introduction

This chapter presents a discriminative modeling technique which corrects the errors made by an automatic parser. The model is similar to reranking; however, it does not require the generation of k-best lists as in MCDonald et al. (2005), McDonald and Pereira (2006), Charniak and Johnson (2005), and Hall (2007). The *corrective* strategy employed by our technique is to explore a set of candidate parses which are constructed by making structurally—local perturbations to an automatically generated parse tree. We train a model which makes local, corrective decisions in order to optimize for parsing performance. The technique is independent of the parser generating the first set of parses. We show in this chapter that the only requirement for this technique is the ability to define a local neighborhood in which a large number of the errors occur.

The original motivation for the corrective technique was to extend the state-of-the-art dependency parsing technique based on constituency parsing (Collins et al. 1990). Statistical parsing models have been shown to be successful in recovering labeled constituencies (Collins, 2003; Charniak and Johnson, 2005; Roark and Collins, 2004) as well as recovering dependency relationships (Collins et al., 1990; Levy and Manning, 2004; Dubey and Keller, 2003; McDonald et al., 2005). The most effective models are lexicalized and include predictive models based on local context (e.g., the lexicalized probabilistic context-free grammars (PCFGs) used by Collins (2003) and Charniak (2000)). The embedded-bracketing constraint of constituency analysis restricts the types of dependency structures that can be encoded in derived trees.[1] A shortcoming of the most common context-free, constituency-based paradigm for parsing is that it is inherently incapable of representing non-projective dependency trees (we define non-projectivity in the following section).

K. Hall (✉)
Google Research, Zurich, Switzerland
e-mail: kbhall@google.com

[1] In order to correctly capture the dependency structure, co-indexed movement *traces* are used in a form similar to Government and Binding theory, GPSG, etc.

H. Bunt et al. (eds.), *Trends in Parsing Technology*, Text, Speech and Language Technology 43, DOI 10.1007/978-90-481-9352-3_9,

This is particularly problematic when parsing free word-order languages, such as Czech, due to the frequency of sentences with non-projective constructions.

We explore a corrective model which recovers non-projective dependency structures by training a classifier to select correct dependency pairs from a set of candidates based on parses generated by an automatic parser. We chose to use this model due to the observations that the dependency errors made by all of the parsers considered are commonly local errors. For the nodes with incorrect dependency links in the parser output, the correct governor of a node is often found within a local context of the proposed governor. By considering alternative dependencies based on local deviations of the parser output we constrain the set of candidate governors for each node during the corrective procedure. We present our previous results for two state-of-the-art constituency-based parsers (the Collins Czech parser (1990) and a version of the Charniak parser (2001) that was modified to parse Czech). We also present results in this chapter for experiments using state-of-the art dependency parsers, a projective parser based on the Eisner algorithm (Eisner, 1996) and a maximum spanning tree (MST) based non-projective parser as presented in McDonald et al. (2005) and McDonald et al. (2005). In this work, we only explore techniques where exhaustive parsing[2] is used to generate the base set of parse trees. Additionally, there are greedy shift-reduce-based parsers which perform equally as well as the exhaustive techniques (Attardi, 2006; Nivre, 2006).

The technique proposed in this chapter is similar to that of recent parser reranking approaches (Collins, 2000; Charniak and Johnson, 2005; Hall, 2007). However, while reranking approaches allow a parser to generate a likely candidate set according to a generative model, we consider a set of candidates based on local perturbations of the single most likely tree generated. The primary reason for such an approach is that we allow dependency structures which would never be hypothesized by the parser. Specifically, we allow for non-projective dependencies.

The corrective algorithm proposed in this chapter shares the motivation of the transformation-based learning work (Brill, 1995). We do consider local transformations of the dependency trees; however, the technique presented here is based on a generative model that maximizes the likelihood of good dependents. We consider a finite set of local perturbations of the tree and use a fixed model to select the best tree by independently choosing optimal dependency links.

In the next section we present an overview of the types of syntactic dependency trees we address in our experiments, specifically the Prague Dependency Treebank (PDT). In Section 9.3 we review the techniques used to adapt constituency parsers for dependency parsing as well as a brief overview of the other dependency parsing techniques we use. Section 9.4 describes corrective modeling as used in this work and Section 9.2 describes the model features with which we have experimented. Section 9.5 presents the results of a set of experiments we performed on data from the PDT with various baseline parsers.

---

[2] Exhaustive parsing assumes that the optimal parse under the model has been chosen; this is in contrast to greedy techniques, where the parse may not be optimal under the model.

9.2 Syntactic Dependency Trees

A dependency tree is a set of nodes $\Omega = \{w_0, w_1, \ldots, w_k\}$ where w_0 is the imaginary root node[3] and a set of dependency links $G = \{g_1, \ldots, g_k\}$ where g_i is an index into Ω representing the governor of w_i. In other words, $g_3 = 1$ indicates that the governor of w_3 is w_1. Finally, every node has exactly one governor except for w_0, which has no governor (the tree constraints).[4] The index of the nodes represents the surface order of the nodes in the sequence (i.e., w_i precedes w_j in the sentence if $i < j$).

A tree is *projective* if for every three nodes: w_a, w_b, and w_c where $a < b < c$; if w_a is governed by w_c then w_b is transitively governed by w_c or if w_c is governed by w_a then w_b is transitively governed by w_a.[5] Figure 9.1 shows examples of projective and non-projective trees. The rightmost tree, which is non-projective, contains a subtree consisting of w_a and w_c but not w_b; however, w_b occurs between w_a and w_c in the linear ordering of the nodes. Projectivity in a dependency tree is akin to the continuity constraint in a constituency tree; that is, the words within a constituent appear contiguously in the surface string. Such a constraint is implicitly imposed by trees generated from context free grammars (CFGs).

Strict word-order languages, such as English, exhibit non-projective dependency structures in a relatively constrained set of syntactic configurations (e.g., right-node raising). Traditionally, these movements are encoded in constituency analyses as *traces*. In languages with free word-order, such as Czech, constituency-based representations are overly constrained (Sgall et al., 1986); this causes word-order choice to influence the complexity of the syntactic analysis. Alternatively, syntactic dependency trees encode syntactic subordination relationships allowing the structure to be non-specific about the *surface word-order*. The relationship between a node and its subordinates expresses a sense of syntactic (functional) entailment.

In this work we explore the dependency structures encoded in the Prague Dependency Treebank (Böhmová et al., 2002). The PDT analytical layer is a set of Czech syntactic dependency trees; the nodes of which contain the word forms,

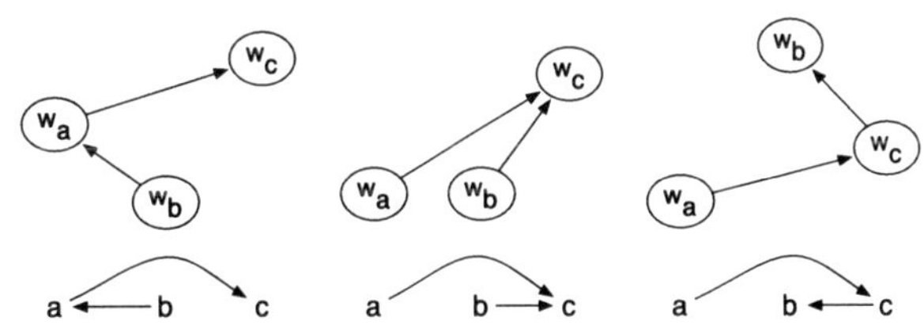

Fig. 9.1 Examples of projective and non-projective trees, using two different notations. The trees on the *left* and *center* are both projective. The tree on the *right* is non-projective

---

[3] The imaginary root node simplifies notation.

[4] The dependency structures here are very similar to those described by Mel'čuk (1988); however the nodes of the dependency trees discussed in this chapter are limited to the words of the sentence and are always ordered according to the surface word-order.

[5] Node w_a is said to transitively govern node w_b if w_b is a descendant of w_a in the dependency tree.

morphological features, and syntactic annotations. The trees were annotated by hand and are intended as an intermediate stage in the annotation of the Tectogrammatical Representation (TR), a *deep-syntactic* or syntacto-semantic layer in the theory of language (Sgall et al., 1986). All current automatic techniques for generating TR structures are based on syntactic dependency parsing. We report results on two sets of data in order to make comparisons with relevant parsers. The PDT 1.0 data is used to compare the results of corrective models for constituency-based parsers. For corrective modeling results for dependency-based parsers we use the CoNLL 2007 version of the PDT 2.0 (Nivre et al., 2007).

When evaluating the accuracy of dependency trees, we present unlabeled dependency scores. The current model specifically targets correcting the dependency structure and not relabeling the dependency edge.

9.3 Dependency Parsing Techniques

We review two approaches to dependency parsing for which we have examined the corrective modeling approach. The first is based on constituency analysis and the second on two varieties of dependency parsing. Exploring more than one framework for parsing, allows us to better understand the benefits of the corrective modeling paradigm.

9.3.1 Constituency Parsing for Dependency Trees

In Hall and Novák (2005) we motivate the use of constituency parses pragmatically; at the time the Collins and Charniak parsers were more accurate on the PDT than available dependency parsers. Note that both Charniak's and Collins' generative probabilistic models contain lexicalized dependency features.[6] From a generative modeling perspective, we use the constraints imposed by constituents (i.e., projectivity) to enable the encapsulation of syntactic substructures. This directly leads to efficient parsing algorithms such as the CKY algorithm and related agenda-based parsing algorithms (Manning and Schütze, 1999). Additionally, this allows for the efficient computation of the scores for the dynamic-programming state variables (i.e., the inside and outside probabilities) that are used in these statistical parsers. The computational complexity advantages of dynamic programming techniques along with efficient search techniques (Caraballo and Charniak, 1998; Klein and Manning, 2003) allow for richer predictive models which include local contextual information.

---

[6] Bilexical dependencies are components of both the Collins and Charniak parsers and model the types of syntactic subordination that we encode in a dependency tree. (Bilexical models were also proposed by Eisner (1996)). In the absence of lexicalization, both parsers have dependency features that are encoded as head-constituent to sibling features.

In an attempt to extend a constituency-based parsing model to train on dependency trees, Collins and colleagues transform the PDT dependency trees into constituency trees (Collins et al., 1990). In order to accomplish this task, they first normalize the trees to remove non-projectivities. Then, they create artificial constituents based on the parts-of-speech of the words associated with each dependency node. The mapping from dependency tree to constituency tree is not one-to-one. They describe a heuristic for choosing trees that works well with this parsing model.

9.3.1.1 Training a Constituency-Based Dependency Parser

We consider two approaches to creating projective trees from dependency trees exhibiting non-projectivities. The first is based on word-reordering and is the model that was used with the Collins parser. This algorithm identifies non-projective structures and deterministically reorders the words of the sentence to create projective trees. An alternative method, used by Charniak in the adaptation of his parser for Czech[7] and used by Nivre and Nilsson (2005), alters the dependency links by raising the governor to a higher node in the tree whenever a non-projectivity is observed. The trees are then transformed into Penn-Treebank-style constituencies using the technique described in Collins et al. (1990).

Both of these techniques have advantages and disadvantages which we briefly outline here:

Reordering: The dependency structure is preserved, but the training procedure will learn statistics for structures over word-strings that may not be part of the language. The parser, however, may be capable of constructing parses for any string of words if a smoothed grammar is being used.

Governor–Raising: The dependency structure is corrupted leading the parser to incorporate arbitrary dependency statistics into the model. However, the parser is trained on true sentences, the words of which are in the correct linear order. We expect the parser to predict similar incorrect dependencies when sentences similar to the training data are observed.

Although the results presented in Collins et al. (1990) used the reordering technique, we have experimented with his parser using the governor—raising technique and observed an increase in dependency accuracy. For the remainder of the chapter, we assume the governor—raising technique.

The process of generating dependency trees from parsed constituency trees is relatively straightforward. Both the Collins and Charniak parsers provide head-word annotation on each constituent. This is precisely the information that we encode in an unlabeled dependency tree, so the dependency structure can simply be extracted from the parsed constituency trees. Furthermore, the constituency labels can be used

[7] This information was provided by Eugene Charniak in a personal communication.

to identify the dependency labels; however, we do not attempt to identify correct dependency labels in this work.

9.3.2 Dependency Parsing

Corrective modeling is robust in the sense that it is not constrained by the type of baseline parser being used. In our previous work, we focused on constituency-based dependency parsing and here we extend this to the output of other parsers. Note that our technique can be used for non-statistical (even unweighted) parsing techniques as it need only be given a proposed parse tree and the gold standard for training. Eisner (1996) introduced a model for dependency parsing based on CKY parsing which is a direct dependency parsing technique. The CKY algorithm, and all dynamic-programming algorithms, require a factorization of the search space that allows for the recursive definition of sub-problems. The Eisner algorithm is limited to generating projective dependency structures in the same way as the constituency-based techniques. However, the models used for dependency parsing can differ quite a bit from those used in constituency parsing. McDonald et al. (2005) present accurate dependency parsing models for an implementation of the Eisner algorithm.

Non-projective parsing can be restated as a graph search problem, where the goal of finding a maximum directed spanning tree (MST) is equivalent to finding the maximum scoring parse. McDonald et al. (2005) introduced this approach along with effective graph-based models for dependency parsing. The short-coming of the MST approach is that the model scores must be *edge-factored*, meaning that the score for one edge cannot be conditioned on the existence of any other edge in the graph. This limits the expressivity of the models and has been shown to be a limiting factor in MST parsing (McDonald et al., 2006; Hall, 2007).

9.3.3 Dependency Errors

We now discuss a quantitative measure for the types of dependency errors made by dependency parsing techniques. For node w_i and the correct governor $w_{g_i^*}$ the *distance* between the two nodes in the hypothesized dependency tree is:

$$dist(w_i, w_{g_i^*}) = \begin{cases} d(w_i, w_{g_i^*}) & \text{iff } w_{g_i^*} \text{ is ancestor of } w_i \\ d(w_i, w_{g_i^*}) & \text{iff } w_{g_i^*} \text{ is sibling/cousin of } w_i \\ -d(w_i, w_{g_i^*}) & \text{iff } w_{g_i^*} \text{ is descendant of } w_i \end{cases}$$

Ancestor, sibling, and descendant have the standard interpretation in the context of a tree.[8] The dependency distance $d(w_i, w_{g_i^*})$ is the length of the undirected shortest-path from w_i to $w_{g_i^*}$ in the hypothesized dependency tree. The definition of the

[8] A cousin is a descendant of an ancestor and not an ancestor itself, which subsumes the definition of sibling.

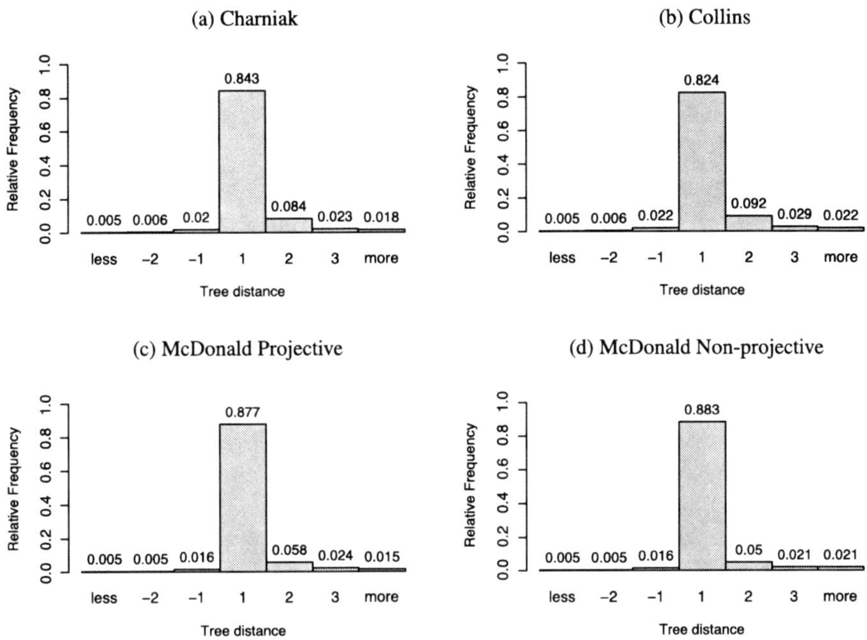

Fig. 9.2 Statistical distribution of correct governor positions in parsed output of the PDT development for the Charniak parser (**a**), Collins parser (**b**), McDonald projective (Eisner) parser (**c**), and McDonald non-projective (MST) parser (**d**)

dist function makes a distinction between paths through the parent of w_i (positive values) and paths through children of w_i (negative values). For all the parsers examined, we found that many of the correct governors were actually hypothesized as siblings or grandparents (a *dist* values of 2)—an extremely local error.

Figure 9.2 shows a histogram of the fraction of nodes whose correct governor was within a particular *dist* in the hypothesized tree. A *dist* of 1 indicates the correct governor was selected by the parser; in these graphs, the density at *dist* = 1 (on the x axis) shows the baseline dependency accuracy of each parser. For the constituency-based parsers (Charniak and Collins), if we repaired only the nodes that are within a *dist* of 2 (grandparents and siblings), we can recover more than 50% of the incorrect dependency links (a raw accuracy improvement of up to 9%). We believe this distribution to be indirectly caused by the governor-raising projectivization routine. In the cases where non-projective structures can be repaired by raising the node's governor to its parent, the correct governor becomes a sibling of the node.

9.4 Corrective Modeling

The error analysis of the previous section suggests that by looking only at a local neighborhood of the proposed governor in the hypothesized trees, we can correct many of the incorrect dependencies. This fact motivates the corrective modeling procedure employed here.

Table 9.1 Corrective modeling procedure

CORRECT (W)

- Parse sentence W using the constituency-based parser
- Generate a dependency structure from the constituency tree
- **for** $w_i \in W$
- **do for** $w_c \in \mathcal{N}(w_{g_i^h})$ *// Local neighborhood of proposed governor*
-   **do** $l(c) \leftarrow P(g_i^* = c | w_i, \mathcal{N}(w_{g_i^h}))$
-     $g_i' \leftarrow \arg\max_c l(c)$ *// Pick the governor in which we are most confident*

Table 9.1 presents the pseudo-code for the corrective procedure. The set g^h contains the indices of governors as predicted by the parser. The set of governors predicted by the corrective procedure is denoted as $g^{'}$. The procedure independently corrects each node of the parsed trees, meaning that there is potential for inconsistent governor relationships to exist in the proposed set; specifically, the resulting dependency graph may have cycles. We employ a greedy search to remove cycles when they are present in the output graph.

The final line of the algorithm picks the governor in which we are most confident. We use the correct-governor classification likelihood: $P(g_i^* = c | w_i, \mathcal{N}(w_{g_i^h}))$, as a measure of the confidence that w_c is the correct governor of w_i where the parser had proposed $w_{g_i^h}$ as the governor. In effect, we create a decision list using the most likely decision when it is valid (i.e., there are no cycles). If the dependency graph resulting from the most likely decisions does not result in a tree, we use the decision lists to greedily select the tree for which the product of the independent decisions is maximal. This is closely related to a greedy version of the Edmonds/Chu-Liu MST algorithm (see Tarjan 1977).

Training the corrective model requires pairs of dependency trees; each pair contains a manually-annotated tree (i.e., the gold standard tree) and a tree generated by the parser. This data is trivially transformed into per-node samples. For each node w_i in the tree, there are $|\mathcal{N}(w_{g_i^h})|$ samples; one for each governor candidate in the local neighborhood.

One advantage to the type of corrective algorithm presented here is that it is completely disconnected from the parser used to generate the tree hypotheses. This means that the original parser need not be statistical or even constituency based. However, in order for this technique to work, the distribution of dependency errors must be relatively local, as is the case with the errors made by the parsers we explore in the empirical section below. This can be determined via data analysis using the *dist* metric. Determining the size of the local neighborhood is data/parser dependent. If subordinate nodes are considered as candidate governors, then a more robust cycle removal technique is required.

9.4.1 Maximum Entropy Estimation

We have chosen a Maximum Entropy (MaxEnt) model to estimate the governor distributions: $P(g_i^* = c | w_i, \mathcal{N}(w_{g_i^h}))$. In the next section, we outline the feature set with which we have experimented, noting that the features are selected based on linguistic intuition. An advantage of the MaxEnt framework is that we need not describe the generative process in terms of factoring the interdependencies of the features.

The maximum entropy principle states that we wish to find an estimate of $p(y|x) \in \mathcal{C}$ that maximizes the entropy over a sample set X for some set of observations Y, where $x \in X$ is an observation and $y \in Y$ is a outcome label assigned to that observation,

$$H(p) \equiv - \sum_{x \in X, y \in Y} \tilde{p}(x) p(y|x) \log p(y|x)$$

The set $\mathcal{C}$ is the candidate set of distributions from which we wish to select $p(y|x)$. We define this set as the $p(y|x)$ that meets a feature-based expectation constraint. Specifically, we want the expected count of a feature, $f(x, y)$, to be equivalent under the distribution $p(y|x)$ and under the observed distribution $\tilde{p}(y|x)$.

$$\sum_{x \in X, y \in Y} \tilde{p}(x) p(y|x) f_i(x, y) = \sum_{x \in X, y \in Y} \tilde{p}(x) \tilde{p}(y|x) f_i(x, y)$$

$f_i(x, y)$ is a feature of our model with which we capture correlations between observations and outcomes. In the following section, we describe a set of features with which we have experimented to determine when a word is likely to be the correct governor of another word.

We incorporate the expected feature-count constraints into the maximum entropy objective using Lagrange multipliers additionally; constraints are added to ensure the distributions $p(y|x)$ are consistent probability distributions:

$$H(p) + \sum_i \alpha_i \sum_{x \in X, y \in Y} (\tilde{p}(x) p(y|x) f_i(x, y) - \tilde{p}(x) \tilde{p}(y|x) f_i(x, y)) + \gamma \sum_{y \in Y} p(y|x) - 1$$

Holding the α_i's constant, we compute the unconstrained maximum of the above Lagrangian form:

$$p_\alpha(y|x) = \frac{1}{Z_\alpha(x)} \exp\left(\sum_i \alpha_i f_i(x, y)\right)$$

$$Z_\alpha(x) = \sum_{y \in Y} \exp\left(\sum_i \alpha_i f_i(x, y)\right)$$

giving us the log-linear form of the distributions $p(y|x)$ in $\mathcal{C}$ (Z is a normalization constant). Finally, we compute the α_i's that maximize the objective function:

$$- \sum_{x \in X} \tilde{p}(x) \log Z_\alpha(x) + \sum_i \alpha_i \tilde{p}(x, y) f_i(x, y)$$

A number of algorithms have been proposed to efficiently compute the optimization described in this derivation. For a more detailed introduction to maximum entropy estimation see Berger et al. (1996).

9.4.2 Proposed Model

Given the above formulation of the MaxEnt estimation procedure, we define features over pairs of observations and outcomes. In our case, the observations are simply w_i, w_c, and $\mathcal{N}(w_{g_i^h})$ and the outcome is a binary variable indicating whether $c = g_i^*$ (i.e., w_c is the correct governor). In order to limit the dimensionality of the feature space, we consider feature functions over the outcome, the current node w_i, the candidate governor node w_c and the node proposed as the governor by the parser $w_{g_i^h}$.

Table 9.2 describes the general classes of features used. We write F_i to indicate the form of the current child node, F_c for the form of the candidate, and F_g as the form of the governor proposed by the parser. A combined feature is denoted as $L_i T_c$ and indicates that we observed a particular lemma for the current node with a particular tag of the candidate.

Table 9.2 Description of the classes of features used

Feature Type	Id	Description
Form	F	The fully inflected word form as it appears in the data
Lemma	L	The morphologically reduced lemma
MTag	T	A subset of the morphological tag as described in (Collins et al., 1990)
POS	P	Major part-of-speech tag (first field of the morphological tag)
ParserGov	G	True if candidate was proposed as governor by parser
ChildCount	C	The number of children
Agreement	$A(x, y)$	Check for case/number agreement between word x and y

In all models, we include features containing the form, the lemma, the morphological tag, and the ParserGov feature. We have experimented with different sets of feature combinations. Each combination set is intended to capture some intuitive linguistic correlation. For example, the feature component $L_i T_c$ will fire if a child's lemma L_i is observed with a candidate's morphological tag T_c. One intuition behind features of this sort is that it can capture phenomena surrounding particles; for example, in Czech, the governor of the reflexive particle *se* will likely be a verb.

9.4.3 Related Work

In Hall and Novák (2005), we proposed our corrective technique in order to improve upon the success of the constituency-based approach. Our approach is more general than the recovery of non-projective structure. In McDonald and Pereira (2006), a related technique is used to identify the optimal non-projective modification to a projective parser. In Attardi and Ciaramita (2007), a technique very similar to the one presented here was shown to improve the parsing quality of a greedy shift-reduce-based parser.

Nivre and Nilsson (2005) introduced a technique where the projectivization transformation is encoded in the non-terminals of constituents during parsing. This allows for a deterministic procedure that undoes the projectivization in the generated parse trees, creating non-projective structures. This technique could be incorporated into a statistical parsing framework; however, we believe that the sparsity of such non-projective configurations may be problematic when using smoothed, backed-off grammars. The deterministic procedure employed by Nivre and Nilsson enables their parser to greedily consider non-projective constructions when possible.

We mentioned above that our approach appears to be similar to that of reranking for statistical parsing (Collins, 2000; Charniak and Johnson, 2005; Hall, 2007). While it is true that we are improving upon the output of the automatic parser, we are not considering multiple alternate parses. Instead, we consider a complete set of alternate trees which are minimal perturbations of the best tree generated by the parser. In the context of dependency parsing, we do this in order to generate structures that constituency-based parsers are incapable of generating (i.e., non-projectivities).

Work by Smith and Eisner (2005) on *contrastive estimation* suggests similar techniques to generate local neighborhoods of a parse; however, the purpose in their work is to define an approximation to the partition function for log-linear estimation (e.g., the normalization factor in a MaxEnt model) to be used in unsupervised learning.

9.5 Empirical Results

In this section we report results from experiments on the PDT Czech dataset. Approximately 1.9% of the words' dependencies are non-projective and these occur in 23.2% of the sentences[9] (Hajičová et al., 2004). We repeat our previous results for the Charniak parser on PDT 1.0 and the Collins parsers on PDT 2.0. We use Ryan McDonald's parser[10] for both the projective (Eisner algorithm) and non-projective (MST algorithm) experiments on the CoNLL 2007 Czech datasets[11] (Nivre et al., 2007).

The Charniak parser was trained on the entire training set of the PDT 1.0 and then used to parse the same data. It is generally a problem to parse the training data, but in this case the Charniak parser performed only slightly better on the training data than on the development data. We train our model on the Collins trees generated

---

[9] These statistics are for the complete PDT 1.0 dataset.

[10] `http://sourceforge.net/projects/mstparser`

[11] The CoNLL07 shared-task data is a subset of the PDT 2.0 data.

via a 20-fold jack-knife training procedure.[12] We use Zhang Lee's implementation of the MaxEnt estimator using the L-BFGS optimization algorithms and Gaussian smoothing.[13]

9.5.1 Constituency-Based Corrective Models

Table 9.4 presents results on development data for the correction model applied to constituency-based parsers. The features of the *Simple* model are the form (F), lemma (L), and morphological tag (M) for each node, the parser-proposed governor node, and the candidate node; this model also contains the ParserGov feature. We show the results for the simple model augmented with feature sets of the categories described in Table 9.2. Table 9.3 provides a short description of each of the models. As we believe the *Simple* model provides the minimum information needed to perform this task, we experimented with the effect of each feature class being added to the model. The final row of Table 9.4 contains results for the model which includes all features from all other models.

We define *NonP Accuracy* as the accuracy for the nodes which were non-projective in the original trees. Although both the Charniak and the Collins parser can never produce non-projective trees, the baseline NonP accuracy is greater than zero; this is due to the parser making mistakes in the tree such that the originally non-projective node's dependency is correct and in a projective configuration.

Alternatively, we report the Non-Projective Precision and Recall for our experiment suite in Table 9.5. Here the numerator of the precision is the number of nodes that are non-projective in the correct tree and end up in a non-projective

Table 9.3 Model feature descriptions

Model	Features	Description
Count	ChildCount	Count of children for the three nodes
MTagL	$T_i T_c$, $L_i L_c$, $L_i T_c$, $T_i L_c$, $T_i P_g$	Conjunctions of MTag and Lemmas
MTagF	$T_i T_c$, $F_i F_c$, $F_i T_c$, $T_i F_c$, $T_i P_g$	Conjunctions of MTag and Forms
POSL	P_i, P_c, P_g, $P_i P_c P_g$, $P_i P_g$, $P_c L_c$	Conjunctions of POS and Lemma
TTT	$T_i T_c T_g$	Conjunction of tags for each of the three nodes
Agr	$A(T_i, T_c)$, $A(T_i, T_g)$	Binary feature if case/number agree
Trig	$L_i L_g T_c$, $T_i L_g T_c$, $L_i L_g L_c$	Trigrams of Lemma/Tag

[12] Jack-knife cross-validation is the process of splitting the data into m sets, training on $m - 1$ of these, and applying the trained model the remaining set. We do this m times, resulting in predictions for the entire training set while never using a model trained on the data for which we are making predictions.

[13] Using held-out development data, we determined a Gaussian prior parameter setting of 4 worked best. The optimal number of training iterations was chosen on held-out data for each experiment. This was generally in the order of a couple hundred iterations of L-BFGS. The MaxEnt modeling implementation can be found at `http://homepages.inf.ed.ac.uk/s0450736/maxent_toolkit.html`

Table 9.4 Comparative results for different versions of our model on the Charniak and Collins parse trees for the PDT development data

	Charniak parse trees		Collins parse trees	
Model	Devel. accuracy (%)	NonP accuracy (%)	Devel. accuracy (%)	NonP accuracy (%)
Baseline	84.3	15.9	82.4	12.0
Simple	84.3	16.0	82.5	12.2
Simple + Count	84.3	16.7	82.5	13.8
Simple + MtagL	84.8	43.5	83.2	44.1
Simple + MtagF	84.8	42.2	83.2	43.2
Simple + POS	84.3	16.0	82.4	12.1
Simple + TTT	84.3	16.0	82.5	12.2
Simple + Agr	84.3	16.2	82.5	12.2
Simple + Trig	84.9	47.9	83.1	47.7
All features	85.0	51.9	83.5	57.5

configuration; however, this new configuration may be based on incorrect dependencies. Recall is the obvious counterpart to precision. These values correspond to the NonP accuracy results reported in Table 9.4. From these tables, we see that the most effective features (when used in isolation) are the conjunctive MTag/Lemma, MTag/Form, and Trigram MTag/Lemma features.

Table 9.6 shows the results of the full model run on the evaluation data for the Collins and Charniak parse trees. It appears that the Charniak parser fares better on the evaluation data than does the Collins parser. However, the corrective model is still successful at recovering non-projective structures. Overall, we see a significant improvement in the dependency accuracy.

We have performed a review of the errors that the corrective process makes and observed that the model does a poor job dealing with punctuation. This is shown in Table 9.7 along with other types of nodes on which we performed well and poorly, respectively. Collins et al. (1990) explicitly added features to their parser to

Table 9.5 Alternative non-projectivity scores for different versions of our model on the Charniak and Collins parse trees

	Charniak parse trees			Collins parse trees		
Model	Precision (%)	Recall (%)	F-measure (%)	Precision (%)	Recall (%)	F-measure (%)
Baseline	N/A	0.0	0.0	N/A	0.0	0.0
Simple	22.6	0.3	0.6	5.0	0.2	0.4
Simple + Count	37.3	1.1	2.1	16.8	2.0	3.6
Simple + MtagL	78.0	29.7	43.0	62.4	35.0	44.8
Simple + MtagF	78.7	28.6	42.0	62.0	34.3	44.2
Simple + POS	23.3	0.3	0.6	2.5	0.1	0.2
Simple + TTT	20.7	0.3	0.6	6.1	0.2	0.4
Simple + Agr	40.0	0.5	1.0	5.7	0.2	0.4
Simple + Trig	74.6	35.0	47.6	52.3	40.2	45.5
All features	75.7	39.0	51.5	48.1	51.6	49.8

Table 9.6 Final results on PDT evaluation datasets for Collins' and Charniak's trees with and without the corrective model

Model	Dependency accuracy (%)	NonP accuracy (%)
Collins	81.6	N/A
Collins + Corrective	82.8	53.1
Charniak	84.4	N/A
Charniak + Corrective	85.1	53.9

Table 9.7 Categorization of corrections and errors made by our model on trees from the Charniak parser. *root* is the artificial root node of the PDT tree. For each node position (child, proposed parent, and correct parent), the top five words are reported (based on absolute count of occurrences). The particle "se" occurs frequently explaining why it occurs in the top five good and top five bad repairs

Top five words for good/bad repairs	
Well repaired child	se i si až jen
Well repaired false governor	v však li na o
Well repaired real governor	a je stát ba ,
Poorly repaired child	, se na že -
Poorly repaired false governor	a , však musí li
Poorly repaired real governor	*root* sklo , je -

improve punctuation accuracy. The PARSEVAL evaluation metric for constituency-based parsing explicitly ignores punctuation in determining the correct boundaries of constituents (Harrison et al., 1991) and so should the dependency evaluation. However, the reported results include punctuation for comparative purposes.

9.5.2 Dependency-Based Parsing

We explored the efficacy of our corrective modeling technique on the output of parsers that directly model and generate dependency structures. Recall that the maximum improvement achievable by allowing structurally local corrections (sibling and grandparent) is less than in the case of constituency parsers; this is depicted in graphs (c) and (d) of Fig. 9.2. The results of our experiments are presented in Table 9.8.[14] We explored the same feature-set as with the constituency-based parsers, and found that the simple model features performed best on the development data. The model hyper-parameters were selected to maximize performance on the development dataset. The model hyper-parameters are the maximum number of training iterations and the mixture of the Gaussian regularizer.

Interestingly, we were able to improve performance of the projective dependency-parser (a second-order feature model parser by the Eisner algorithm). The accuracy difference for the non-projective dependency-parser (a first-order

[14] The MaltEval (`http://w3.msi.vxu.se/~jni/malteval/`) tool was used for evaluation of the dependency-based parsers.

Table 9.8 Results for the corrective modeling approach on the dependency-based parsers. Scores are the unlabeled accuracy as reported by the MaltEval tools. Scores for the best hyper-parameter settings on the development data are reported in parentheses. Scores for the evaluation data are for the models which performed best on development data

Model	Baseline (development) evaluation	Unlabeled dependency accuracy (development) evaluation
Projective	(87.7) 82.9	(88.2) 83.1
Non-projective	(88.3) 83.5	(88.4) 83.4

model parsed by the MST algorithm) on both development and evaluation data are not significant. The current model is not robust enough to improve on the non-projective parser results.

9.5.3 Characterization of Corrective Decisions

The central goal of our technique is to learn a model which is able to discriminate between good and bad corrections. In Table 9.9 we present statistics for the repairs made on the evaluation datasets. Our model is relatively weak in the sense that it is usually only making good corrections on slightly more than 50% of the data (with the exception of the non-projective experiment where very few corrections were made). We believe that the simplicity of our model, especially the limited structural locality of our features, is not discriminative enough when selected from a set of candidates, even when that set is relatively small.

Table 9.9 Categorization of corrections made by our model on the evaluation datasets

	Charniak (%)	Collins (%)	Projective (%)	Non-projective (%)
Correct to incorrect	13.0	20.0	28.6	50.0
Incorrect to incorrect	21.5	25.8	19.0	17.5
Incorrect to correct	65.5	54.2	52.4	32.5

9.6 Conclusion

Corrective modeling is an approach to repair the output from a system where more information can be used in the model. In this chapter, we present a corrective model for dependency parsing using a Maximum Entropy trained discriminative classifier. We show that many of the errors are structurally local for a set of parsers parsing the Czech PDT data. Our algorithm presents a simple framework for modeling a corrective procedure; the model we proposed shows a gain in performance for most of the parsers examined. A key aspect of this modeling framework is the independence between this model and the baseline parser which generates the trees we correct.

Acknowledgements This work was partially supported by U.S. NSF grants IIS–9982329 and OISE–0530118, by the Czech Ministry of Education grant LC536 and Czech Academy of Sciences grant 1ET201120505.

References

Attardi, G. and M. Ciaramita (2007). Tree revision learning for dependency parsing. In *Proceedings of Human Language Technologies 2007: The Conference of the North American Chapter of the Association for Computational Linguistics*, Rochester, NY.

Berger, A.L., S.A.D. Pietra, and V.J.D. Pietra (1996). A maximum entropy approach to natural language processing. *Computational Linguistics 22*(1), 39–71.

Böhmová, A., J. Hajič, E. Hajičová, and B.V. Hladká (2002). The Prague Dependency Treebank: three-level annotation scenario. In A. Abeille (Ed.), *In Treebanks: Building and Using Syntactically Annotated Corpora*. Dordrecht: Kluwer Academic Publishers.

Brill, E. (1995, December). Transformation-based error-driven learning and natural language processing: a case study in part of speech tagging. *Computational Linguistics 21*(4), 543–565.

Caraballo, S. and E. Charniak (1998, June). New figures of merit for best-first probabilistic chart parsing. *Computational Linguistics 24*(2), 275–298.

Charniak, E. (2000). A maximum-entropy-inspired parser. In *Proceedings of the 2000 Conference of the North American Chapter of the Association for Computational Linguistics*, ACL, New Brunswick, NJ.

Charniak, E. (2001). Immediate-head parsing for language models. In *Proceedings of the 39th Annual Meeting of the Association for Computational Linguistics*, Toulouse, France.

Charniak, E. and M. Johnson (2005). Coarse-to-fine n-best parsing and MaxEnt discriminative reranking. In *Proceedings of the 43rd Annual Meeting of the Association for Computational Linguistics*, Ann Arbor, Michigan.

Collins, M. (2000). Discriminative reranking for natural language parsing. In *Proceedings of the 17th International Conference on Machine Learning 2000*, Stanford, CA.

Collins, M. (2003). Head-driven statistical models for natural language processing. *Computational Linguistics 29*(4), 589–637.

Collins, M., L. Ramshaw, J. Hajič, and C. Tillmann (1999). A statistical parser for Czech. In *Proceedings of the 37th Annual Meeting of the Association for Computational Linguistics*, College Park, MD. pp. 505–512.

Dubey, A. and F. Keller (2003). Probabilistic parsing for German using sister-head dependencies. In *Proceedings of the 41st Annual Meeting of the Association for Computational Linguistics*, Sapporo, Sapporo, Japan pp. 96–103.

Eisner, J. (1996). Three new probabilistic models for dependency parsing: an exploration. In *Proceedings of the 16th International Conference on Computational Linguistics (COLING)*, Copenhagen, Denmark pp. 340–345.

Hajič, J. (1998). Building a syntactically annotated corpus: The Prague Dependency Treebank. In *Issues of Valency and Meaning*. Praha: Karolinum, pp. 106–132.

Hajičová, E., J. Havelka, P. Sgall, K. Veselá, and D. Zeman (2004). Issues of projectivity in the Prague Dependency Treebank. *Prague Bulletin of Mathematical Linguistics 81*, 5–22.

Hall, K. (2007). k-best spanning tree parsing. In *Proceedings of the 45th Annual Meeting of the Association for Computational Linguistics*, Prague, Czech Republic.

Hall, K. and V. Novák (2005). Corrective modeling for non-projective dependency parsing. In *Proceedings of the 9th International Workshop on Parsing Technologies*, Vancouver, BC Canada.

Harrison, P., S. Abney, D. Fleckenger, C. Gdaniec, R. Grishman, D. Hindle, B. Ingria, M. Marcus, B. Santorini, and T. Strzalkowski (1991). Evaluating syntax performance of parser/grammars of english. In *Proceedings of the Workshop on Evaluating Natural Language Processing Systems, ACL*, Berkeley, CA.

Klein, D. and C.D. Manning (2003). Factored A* search for models over sequences and trees. In *Proceedings of IJCAI 2003*, Acapulco, Mexico.

Levy, R. and C. Manning (2004). Deep dependencies from context-free statistical parsers: correcting the surface dependency approximation. In *Proceedings of the 42nd Annual Meeting of the Association for Computational Linguistics*, Barcelona, Spain, pp. 327–334.

Manning, C.D. and H. Schütze (1999). *Foundations of Statistical Natural Language Processing*. Cambridge, MA: MIT Press.

McDonald, R., K. Crammer, and F. Pereira (2005). Online large-margin training of dependency parsers. In *Proceedings of the 43nd Annual Meeting of the Association for Computational Linguistics*, Ann Arbor, MI.

McDonald, R., K. Lerman, and F. Pereira (2006). Multilingual dependency parsing with a two-stage discriminative parser. In *Conference on Natural Language Learning*, New York, NY.

McDonald, R. and F. Pereira (2006). Online learning of approximate dependency parsing algorithms. In *Proceedings of the Annual Meeting of the European Association for Computational Linguistics*, Trento, Italy.

McDonald, R., F. Pereira, K. Ribarov, and J. Hajič (2005, October). Non-projective dependency parsing using spanning tree algorithms. In *Proceedings of Human Language Technology Conference and Conference on Empirical Methods in Natural Language Processing*, Vancouver, BC, Canada, pp. 523–530.

Mel'čuk, I. (1988). *Dependency Syntax: Theory and Practice*. Albany, NY: SUNY Press.

Nivre, J. (2006). *Inductive Dependency Parsing*, Text, Speech and Language Technology vol. 34. New York, NY: Springer.

Nivre, J., J. Hall, S. Kübler, R. McDonald, J. Nilsson, S. Riedel, and D. Yuret (2007). The CoNLL 2007 shared task on dependency parsing. In *Proceedings of the Joint Conference on Empirical Methods in Natural Language Processing and Computational Natural Language Learning (EMNLP-CoNLL)*, Prague, Czech Republic.

Nivre, J. and J. Nilsson (2005). Pseudo-projective dependency parsing. In *Proceedings of the 43rd Annual Meeting of the Association for Computational Linguistics*, Ann Arbor, MI, pp. 99–106.

Roark, B. and M. Collins (2004). Incremental parsing with the perceptron algorithm. In *Proceedings of the 42nd Annual Meeting of the Association for Computational Linguistics*, Barcelona.

Sgall, P., E. Hajičová, and J. Panevová (1986). *The Meaning of the Sentence in Its Semantic and Pragmatic Aspects*. Boston, MA: Kluwer Academic.

Smith, N.A. and J. Eisner (2005). Contrastive estimation: Training log-linear models on unlabeled data. In *Proceedings of the Association for Computational Linguistics (ACL 2005)*, Ann Arbor, MI.

Tarjan, R. (1977). Finding optimal branchings. *Networks 7*, 25–35.

Chapter 10
Inducing Lexicalised PCFGs with Latent Heads

Detlef Prescher

10.1 Introduction

State-of-the-art statistical parsers for natural language are based on probabilistic grammars acquired from transformed treebanks. The method of transforming the treebank is of major influence on the accuracy and coverage of the statistical parser. The most important treebank transformation in the literature is lexicalization: Each node in a tree is labeled with its head word, the most important word of the constituent under the node (Magerman, 1995; Collins, 1996; Charniak, 1997; Collins, 1997; Carroll and Rooth, 1998, etc.). It turns out, however, that lexicalization is not unproblematic: First, there is evidence that full lexicalization does not carry over across different treebanks for other languages, annotations or domains Dubey and Keller, 2003. Second, full lexicalization leads to a serious sparse-data problem, which can only be solved by sophisticated smoothing and pruning techniques.

Recently, Klein and Manning (2003) showed that a carefully performed linguistic mark-up of the treebank leads to almost the same performance results as lexicalization. This result is attractive since unlexicalized grammars are easy to estimate, easy to parse with, and time- and space-efficient: Klein and Manning (2003) do not smooth grammar-rule probabilities, except unknown-word probabilities, and they do not prune since they are able to determine the most probable parse of each *full* parse forest. Both facts are noteworthy in the context of statistical parsing with a treebank grammar. A drawback of their method is, however, that manual linguistic mark-up is not based on abstract rules but rather on individual linguistic intuition, which makes it difficult to repeat their experiment and to generalize their findings to languages other than English.

Is it possible to automatically acquire a more refined probabilistic grammar from a given treebank without resorting to full lexicalization? We present a novel method that is able to induce a parser that is located between two extremes:

D. Prescher (✉)
76307 Karlsbad, Czech Republic
e-mail: prescher@snlp.de

H. Bunt et al. (eds.), *Trends in Parsing Technology*, Text, Speech and Language Technology 43, DOI 10.1007/978-90-481-9352-3_10,

a fully-lexicalized parser on one side *versus* an accurate unlexicalized parser based on a manually refined treebank on the other side.

In short, our method is based on the same linguistic principles of headedness as other methods: We do believe that lexical information represents an important knowledge source. To circumvent data sparseness resulting from full lexicalization with words, we simply follow the suggestion of various advanced linguistic theories, e.g. Lexical-Functional Grammar (Kaplan and Bresnan, 1982), where more complex categories based on feature combinations represent the lexical effect. We complement this by a learning paradigm: lexical entries carry latent information to be used as head information, and this head information is induced from the treebank.

In this paper, we study two different latent-head models, as well as two different estimation methods: The first model is built around completely hidden heads, whereas the second one uses relatively fine-grained combinations of Part-Of-Speech (POS) tags with hidden extra-information; The first estimation method selects a head-driven probabilistic context-free grammar (PCFG) by exploiting latent-head distributions for each node in the treebank, whereas the second one is more traditional, reading off the grammar from the treebank annotated with the most probable latent heads only. In other words, both models and estimation methods differ in the degree of information incorporated into them as prior knowledge. In general, it can be expected that the better (sharper or richer, or more accurate) the information is, the better the induced grammar will be. Our empirical results, however, are surprising: First, estimation with latent-head distributions outperforms estimation with most-probable-head annotation. Second, modeling with completely hidden heads is almost as good as modeling with latent heads based on POS tags, and moreover, results in much smaller grammars.

We emphasize that our task is to automatically induce a more refined grammar based on a few linguistic principles. With automatic refinement it is harder to guarantee improved performance than with manual refinements (Klein and Manning, 2003) or with refinements based on direct lexicalization (Magerman, 1995; Collins, 1996, Charniak, 1997, etc.). If, however, our refinement provides improved performance then it has a clear advantage: it is automatically induced, which suggests that it is applicable across different domains, languages and treebank annotations.

Applying our method to the benchmark Penn treebank Wall-Street Journal, we obtain a refined probabilistic grammar that significantly improves over the original treebank grammar and that shows performance that is on par with early work on lexicalized probabilistic grammars. This is a promising result given the hard task of automatic induction of improved probabilistic grammars.

10.2 Head Lexicalization

As previously shown (Magerman, 1995; Collins, 1996; Charniak, 1997, etc.), Context-Free Grammars (CFGs) can be transformed to lexicalized CFGs, provided that a head-marking scheme for rules is given. The basic idea is that the head

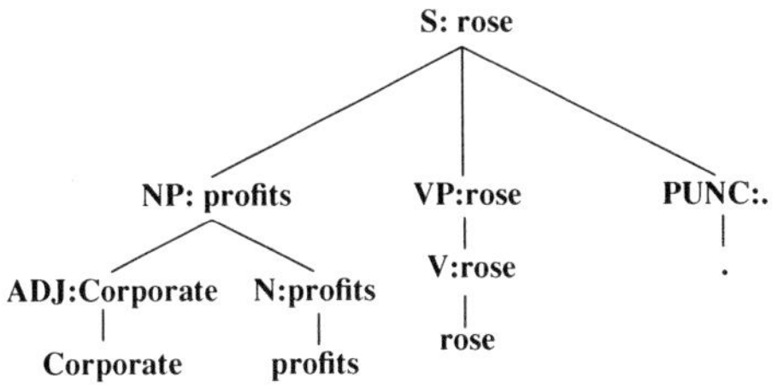

Internal Rules:
S:rose $\longrightarrow$ NP:profits VP:rose PUNC:.
NP:profits $\longrightarrow$ ADJ:Corporate N:profits
VP:rose $\longrightarrow$ V:rose
Lexical Rules:
ADJ:Corporate $\longrightarrow$ Corporate
N:profits $\longrightarrow$ profits
V:rose $\longrightarrow$ rose
PUNC:. $\longrightarrow$.

Fig. 10.1 Parse tree, and a list of the rules it contains (Charniak, 1997)

marking on rules is used to project lexical items up a chain of nodes. Figure 10.1 displays an example.

In this section, we focus on the approaches of Charniak (1997) and Carroll and Rooth (1998). These approaches are especially attractive for us for two reasons: First, both approaches make use of an *explicit linguistic grammar*. By contrast, alternative approaches, like Collins (1997), apply an additional transformation to each tree in the treebank, splitting each rule into small parts, which finally results in a new grammar covering many more sentences than the explicit one. Second, Charniak (1997) and Carroll and Rooth (1998) rely on almost the same lexicalization technique. In fact, the significant difference between them is that, in one case, a lexicalized version of the *treebank grammar* is learned from a corpus of trees (supervised learning), whereas, in the other case, a lexicalized version of a *manually written CFG* is learned from a text corpus (unsupervised learning). As we will see in Section 10.3, our approach is a blend of these approaches in that it aims at unsupervised learning of a (latent-head-) lexicalized version of the treebank grammar.

Starting with Charniak (1997), Fig. 10.2 displays an internal rule as it is used in the parse in Fig. 10.1, and its probability as defined by Charniak. Here, H is the head-child of the rule, which inherits the head h from its parent C. The children D_1:d_1, ..., D_m:d_m and D_{m+1}:d_{m+1}, ..., D_{m+n}:d_{m+n} are left and right modifiers of H. Either n or m may be zero, and $n = m = 0$ for unary rules. Because the probabilities occurring in Charniak's definition are already so specific that there is no real chance of obtaining the data empirically, they are smoothed by deleted interpolation.

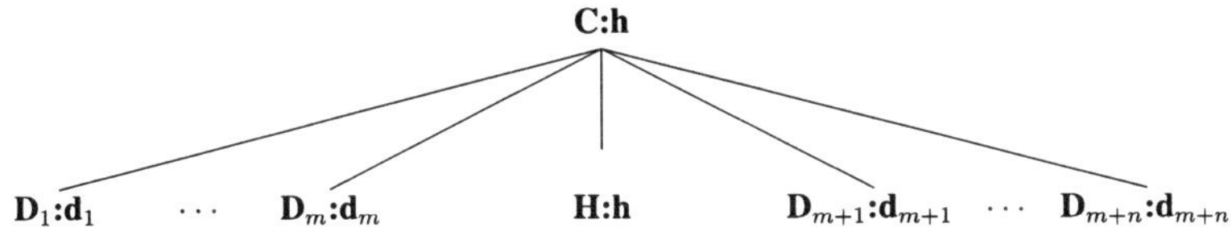

$$p_{\mathbf{CHARNIAK97}}(\text{ this local tree }) = p(\ r \mid \mathbf{C}, h, \mathbf{C}_p\ ) \times \prod_{i=1}^{n+m} p(\ d_i \mid \mathbf{D}_i, \mathbf{C}, h\ )$$

(r **is the** ***unlexicalized*** **rule,**
$\mathbf{C}_p$ **is C's parent category**)

Fig. 10.2 Internal rule, and its probability (Charniak, 1997)

Crucial smoothing of rule probabilities by Charniak (1997):

$$
\begin{aligned}
p(\,r \mid \mathrm{C}, h, \mathrm{C}_p\,) = \quad & \lambda_1 \cdot \hat{p}(\,r \mid \mathrm{C}, h, \mathrm{C}_p\,) \\
& + \lambda_2 \cdot \hat{p}(\,r \mid \mathrm{C}, h\,) \\
& + \lambda_3 \cdot \hat{p}(\,r \mid \mathrm{C}, \mathrm{class}(h)\,) \\
& + \lambda_4 \cdot \hat{p}(\,r \mid \mathrm{C}, \mathrm{C}_p\,) \\
& + \lambda_5 \cdot \hat{p}(\,r \mid \mathrm{C}\,)
\end{aligned}
$$

$$
\begin{aligned}
p(\,d \mid \mathrm{D}, \mathrm{C}, h\,) = \quad & \lambda_1 \cdot \hat{p}(\,d \mid \mathrm{D}, \mathrm{C}, h\,) \\
& + \lambda_2 \cdot \hat{p}(\,d \mid \mathrm{D}, \mathrm{C}, class(h)\,) \\
& + \lambda_3 \cdot \hat{p}(\,d \mid \mathrm{D}, \mathrm{C}\,) \\
& + \lambda_4 \cdot \hat{p}(\,d \mid \mathrm{D}\,)
\end{aligned}
$$

Here, class(h) denotes a class for the head word h. Charniak takes these word classes from an *external* distributional clustering model, but does not describe this model in detail.

An at a first glance different lexicalization technique is described in (Carroll and Rooth, 1998). In their approach, a grammar transformation is used to lexicalize a manually written grammar. The key step for understanding their model is to imagine that the rule in Fig. 10.2 is transformed to a *sub-tree*, the one displayed in Fig. 10.3. After this transformation, the sub-tree probability is simply calculated with the PCFG's standard model; The result is also displayed in the figure. Comparing this probability with the probability that Charniak assigns to the rule itself, we see that

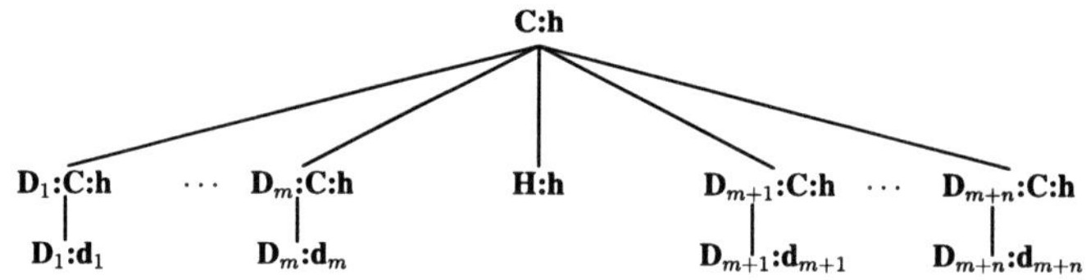

$p_{\text{STANDARD-PCFG}}(\ \textbf{this sub-tree}\ )$

$$
\begin{aligned}
&= p(\ \mathbf{D}_1{:}\mathbf{C}{:}h \ldots \mathbf{D}_m{:}\mathbf{C}{:}h\ \mathbf{H}{:}h\ \mathbf{D}_{m+1}{:}\mathbf{C}{:}h \ldots \mathbf{D}_{m+n}{:}\mathbf{C}{:}\,h \mid \mathbf{C}{:}h\ ) \times \textstyle\prod_{i=1}^{m+n} p(\ \mathbf{D}_i{:}d_i \mid \mathbf{D}_i{:}\mathbf{C}{:}h\ ) \\
&= p(\ \mathbf{D}_1 \ldots \mathbf{D}_m\ \mathbf{H}\ \mathbf{D}_{m+1} \ldots \mathbf{D}_{m+n} \mid \mathbf{C}, h\ ) \times \textstyle\prod_{i=1}^{m+n} p(\ d_i \mid \mathbf{D}_i, \mathbf{C}, h\ ) \\
&= p(\ r \mid \mathbf{C}, h\ ) \times \textstyle\prod_{i=1}^{m+n} p(\ d_i \mid \mathbf{D}_i, \mathbf{C}, h\ )
\end{aligned}
$$

(**r is the *unlexicalized* rule**)

Fig. 10.3 Transformed internal rule, and its standard-PCFG probability (Carroll and Rooth, 1998)

Table 10.1 Context-free rule types in the transform (Carroll and Rooth, 1998)

S → S:h	(Starting rules)
C:h → D_1:C:h … D_m:C:h H:h D_{m+1}:C:h … D_{m+n}:C:h	(Lexicalized rules)
D:C:h → D:d	(Dependencies)
C:w → w	(Lexical rules)

the subtree probability equals the rule probability.[1] In other words, both probability models are based on the same idea for lexicalization, but the type of the corpora they are estimated from differ (*trees* versus *sentences*).

In more detail, Table 10.1 displays all four grammar-rule types resulting from the grammar transformation of Carroll and Rooth (1998). The underlying entities from the original CFG are: The starting symbol S (also the starting symbol of the transform), the internal rule C $\longrightarrow$ $D_1 \ldots D_m$ H $D_{m+1} \ldots D_{m+n}$, and the lexical rule C $\longrightarrow$ w. From these, the context-free transforms are generated as displayed in the table (for all possible head words h and d, and for all non-head children D=D_1, …, D_{m+n}). Figure 10.4 displays an example parse on the basis of the transformed grammar. It is noteworthy that although Carroll and Rooth (1998) learn from a text corpus of about 50 million words, it is still necessary to smooth the rule probabilities of the transform. Unlike Charniak (1997), however, they do not use word classes in their back-off scheme.

To summarize, the major problem of full-lexicalization techniques is that they lead to serious sparse-data problems. For both models presented in this section, a large number $|T|$ of full word forms makes it difficult to reliably estimate the probability weights of the $O(|T|^2)$ dependencies and the $O(|T|)$ lexicalized rules.

A linguistically naive approach to this problem is to use POS tags as heads to decrease the number of heads. From a computational perspective, the sparse data problem would then be completely solved since the number |POS| of POS tags is

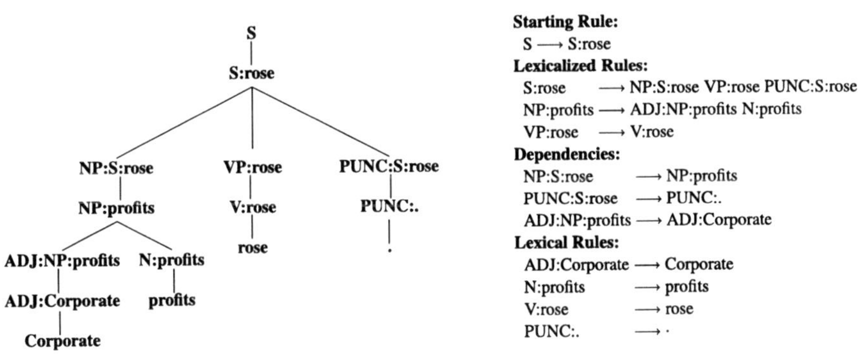

Fig. 10.4 Transformed parse tree, and a list of the rules it contains (Carroll and Rooth, 1998)

[1] At least, if we ignore Charniak's conditioning on C's parent category C_p for the moment. Note that C's parent category is available in the treebank, but may not occur in the left-hand sides of the rules of a manually written CFG.

tiny compared to the number $|T|$ of full-word forms. Although we will demonstrate that parsing results benefit already from this naive lexicalization routine, we expect that (computationally and linguistically) optimal head-lexicalized models are arranged around a number |HEADS| of head elements such that $|\text{POS}| \leq |\text{HEADS}| \ll |T|$.

10.3 Latent-Head Models

This section defines two probability models over the trees licensed by a head-lexicalized CFG with latent head-information, thereby exploiting three simple linguistic principles: (i) all rules have head markers, (ii) information is projected up a chain of categories marked as heads, (iii) lexical entries carry latent head values which can be learned. Moreover, two estimation methods for the latent-head models are described.

10.3.1 Head-Lexicalized CFGs with Latent Heads

Principles (i) and (ii) are satisfied by all head -lexicalized models we know of, and clearly, they are also satisfied by the model of Carroll and Rooth (1998). Principle (iii), however, deals with latent information for lexical entries, which is beyond the capability of this model. To see this, remember that lexical rules $\text{C} \longrightarrow w$ are unambiguously transformed to $\text{C}{:}w \longrightarrow w$. Because this transformation is unambiguous, latent information does not play a role in it. It is surprisingly simple, however, to satisfy principle (iii) with slightly modified versions of Carroll and Rooth's transformation of lexical rules. In the following, we present two of them:

Lexical-rule transformation (Model 1): Transform each lexical rule $\text{C} \longrightarrow w$ to a set of rules, having the form $\text{C}{:}h \longrightarrow w$, where $h \in \{1, \ldots, L\}$, and L is a free parameter.

Lexical-rule transformation (Model 2): Transform each lexical rule $\text{C} \longrightarrow w$ to a set of rules, having the form $\text{C}{:}h \longrightarrow w$, where $h \in \{\text{C}\} \times \{1, \ldots, L\}$, and L is a free parameter.

Both models introduce latent heads for lexical entries. The difference is that Model 1 introduces completely latent heads h, whereas Model 2 introduces heads h on the basis of the POS tag C of the word w: each such head is a combination of C with some abstract extra-information. Figure 10.5 gives an example. Because we still apply Carroll and Rooth's grammar transformation scheme to the non-lexical rules, latent heads are percolated up a path of categories marked as heads.

Although our modifications are small, their effect is remarkable. In contrast to Carroll and Rooth (1998), where an unlexicalized tree is unambiguously mapped to a *single* transform, our models map an unlexicalized tree to *multiple* transforms (for free parameters ≥ 2). Note also that although latent information is freely introduced

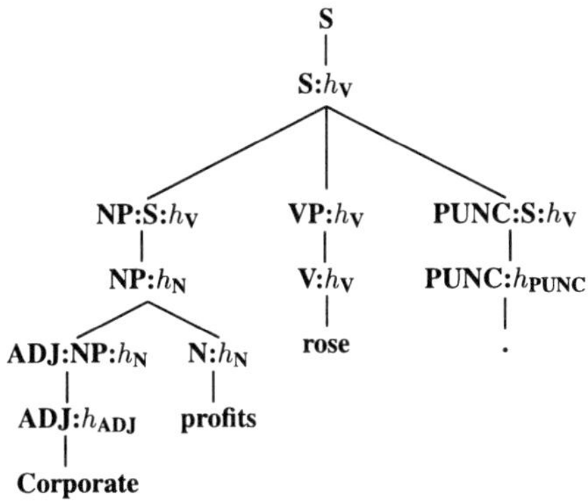

Starting Rule:
S $\longrightarrow$ S:h_V
Lexicalized Rules:
S:h_V $\longrightarrow$ NP:S:h_V VP:h_V PUNC:S:h_V
NP:h_N $\longrightarrow$ ADJ:NP:h_N N:h_N
VP:h_V $\longrightarrow$ V:h_V
Dependencies:
NP:S:h_V $\longrightarrow$ NP:h_N
PUNC:S:h_V $\longrightarrow$ PUNC:h_{PUNC}
ADJ:NP:h_N $\longrightarrow$ ADJ:h_{ADJ}
Lexical Rules:
ADJ:h_{ADJ} $\longrightarrow$ Corporate
N:h_N $\longrightarrow$ profits
V:h_V $\longrightarrow$ rose
PUNC:h_{PUNC} $\longrightarrow$.

Model 1 (Completely Latent Heads):
h_{ADJ}, h_N, h_V, and $h_{PUNC} \in \{1, \ldots, L\}$

Model 2 (Latent Heads Based on POS Tags):
$h_{ADJ} \in \{ADJ\} \times \{1, \ldots, L\}$
$h_N \in \{N\} \times \{1, \ldots, L\}$
$h_V \in \{V\} \times \{1, \ldots, L\}$
$h_{PUNC} \in \{PUNC\} \times \{1, \ldots, L\}$

Number of Latent-Head Types $= \begin{cases} L & \text{for Model 1} \\ |POS| \times L & \text{for Model 2} \end{cases}$ (L is a free parameter)

Fig. 10.5 Parse tree with latent heads, and a list of the rules it contains

at the lexical level, it is not freely distributed over the nodes of the tree. Rather, the space of latent heads for a tree is constrained according the linguistic principle of headedness. Finally, for the case $L = 1$, our models perform unambiguous transformations: in Model 1 the transformation makes no relevant changes, whereas Model 2 performs unambiguous lexicalization with POS tags. In the rest of the paper, we show how to learn models with hidden, richer, and more accurate head-information from a treebank, if $L \geq 2$.

10.3.2 Unsupervised Estimation of Head-Lexicalized CFGs with Latent Heads

In the following, we define two methods for estimating latent-head models. The main difficulty here is that the rules of a head-lexicalized CFG with latent heads cannot be directly estimated from the treebank (by counting rules) since the latent heads are not annotated in the trees. Faced with this incomplete-data problem, we apply the Expectation-Maximization (EM) algorithm developed for these type of problems Dempster et al. (1977). For details of the EM algorithm, we refer to the numerous tutorials on EM (e.g. Prescher, 2003). Here, it suffices to know that it is a sort of meta algorithm, resulting for each incomplete-data problem in an iterative estimation method that aims at maximum-likelihood estimation on the data. Disregarding the fact that we implement a dynamic-programming version for our experiments (running in linear time in the size of the trees in the treebank Prescher, 2005b),

Initialization: Generate a randomly initialized distribution p_0 for the rules of G_{LEX} (a head-lexicalized CFG with latent heads as previously defined).

Iterations:

(1) for each $i = 1, 2, 3, \ldots,$ *number_of_iterations* do

(2) set $p = p_{i-1}$

(3) **E step**: Generate a lexicalized tree-bank T_{LEX}, by
- running over all unlexicalized trees t of the original tree-bank
- generating the finite set $G_{\text{LEX}}(t)$ of the lexicalized transforms of t
- allocating the frequency $c(t') = c(t) \cdot p(\, t' \mid t\,)$ to the lexicalized trees $t' \in G_{\text{LEX}}(t)$

[Here, $c(t)$ is the frequency of t in the original tree-bank
]

(4) **M step**: Read the tree-bank grammar off T_{LEX}, by
- calculating relative frequencies $\hat{p}$ for all rules of G_{LEX} as occurring in T_{LEX}

(5) set $p_i = \hat{p}$

(6) end

Fig. 10.6 Grammar induction algorithm (EM algorithm)

the EM algorithm is here as displayed in Fig. 10.6. Beside this pure form of the EM algorithm, we also use a variant where the original treebank is annotated with most probable heads only. Here is a characterization of both estimation methods:

Estimation from latent-head distributions: The key steps of the EM algorithm produce a lexicalized treebank T_{LEX}, consisting of all lexicalized versions of the original trees (E-step), and calculate the probabilities for the rules of G_{LEX} on the basis of T_{LEX} (M-step). Clearly, all lexicalized trees in $G_{\text{LEX}}(t)$ differ only in the heads of their nodes. Thus, EM estimation uses the original treebank, where each node can be thought of as annotated with a *latent-head distribution*.

Estimation from most probable heads: By contrast, a quite different scheme is applied in (Klein and Manning, 2003): extensive manual annotation enriches the treebank with information, but no trees are added to the treebank. We borrow from this scheme in that we take the best EM model to calculate the most probable head-lexicalized versions of the trees in the original treebank. After collecting this Viterbi-style lexicalized treebank, the ordinary treebank estimation yields another estimate of G_{LEX}. Clearly, this estimation method uses the original treebank, where each node can be thought of annotated with the *most probable latent head*.

10.4 Experiments

This section presents empirical results across our models and estimation methods.

10.4.1 Data and Parameters

To facilitate comparison with previous work, we trained our models on Sections 2–21 of the WSJ section of the Penn treebank Marcus et al. (1993). All trees were modified such that the empty top node got the category TOP; node labels consisted solely of syntactic category information; empty nodes (i.e. nodes dominating the empty string) were deleted; and words in rules occurring less than 3 times in the treebank were replaced by (word-suffix based) unknown-word symbols. No other changes were made.

On this treebank, we trained several head-lexicalized CFGs with latent heads as described in Section 10.3, but smoothed the grammar rules using deleted interpolation. We also performed some preliminary experiments without smoothing, but after observing that about 3,000 trees of our training corpus were allocated a zero-probability (resulting from the fact that too many grammar rules got a zero-probability), we decided to smooth all rule probabilities.

We tried to find optimal starting parameters by repeating the whole training process multiple times, but we observed that starting parameters affect final results only up to 0.5%. We also tried to find optimal iteration numbers by evaluating our models after each iteration step on a held-out corpus, and observed that the best results were obtained with 70–130 iterations. Within a wide range from 50 to 200 iteration, however, iteration numbers affect final results only up to 0.5%.

10.4.2 Empirical Results

We evaluated on a parsing task performed on Section 22 of the WSJ section of the Penn treebank. For parsing, we mapped all unknown words to unknown word symbols, and applied the Viterbi algorithm as implemented in Schmid (2004), exploiting its ability to deal with highly-ambiguous grammars. That is, we did not use any pruning or smoothing routines for parsing sentences. We then de-transformed the resulting maximum-probability parses to the format described in the previous subsection. That is, we deleted the heads, the dependencies, and the starting rules. All grammars were able to exhaustively parse the evaluation corpus. Table 10.2 displays our results in terms of LP/LR F_1 Black et al. (1991). The largest number per column is printed in italics. The absolutely largest number is printed in boldface. The numbers in brackets are the number of grammar rules (without counting lexical rules). The gain in LP/LR F_1 per estimation method and per model is also displayed (Δ). Finally, the average training time per iteration ranges from 2 to 4 h (depending on

Table 10.2 Parsing results in LP/LR F_1 (the baseline is $L = 1$)

	Estimation from most probable heads		Estimation from head distributions	
	Model 1 (completely latent)	Model 2 (POS+latent)	Model 1 (completely latent)	Model 2 (POS+latent)
Baseline	(15,400) 73.5	(25,000) 78.9	(15,400) 73.5	(25,000) 78.9
$L = 2$	(17,900) 76.3	(32,300) 81.1	(25,900) 76.9	(49,500) 81.6
$L = 5$	(22,800) 80.7	(46,200) *83.3*	(49,200) 82.0	(116,300) 84.9
$L = 10$	(28,100) *83.3*	(58,900) 82.6	(79,200) *84.6*	(224,300) **85.7**
	$\Delta = 9.8$	$\Delta = 4.4$	$\Delta =$ **11.1**	$\Delta = 6.8$

both L and the type of the model). The average parsing time is 10 s per sentence, which is comparable to what is reported in Klein and Manning, 2003.

10.4.3 Latent Heads

Table 10.3 exemplifies the latent heads induced for Model 2 with a free parameter of $L = 10$. In this model, a latent head is a combination of a POS tag and a number between 1 and 10. In the following, we interpret each latent head as a head class, i.e. a set of head words, ordered by occurrence frequencies.

Among a total number of ten head classes per POS tag, Table 10.3 displays a selection of three head classes for the tags NN (nouns), JJ (adjectives), and CD (numbers), as well as four head classes for the POS tag CD (numbers). For example, the first entry "745.31 president" of the head class "NN-#1" in Table 10.3 belongs to the lexical rule "NN:NN-#1 $\rightarrow$ president" occurring 745.31 times in the WSJ section of the Penn treebank (where the count is estimated by the EM algorithm in Fig. 10.6). Each head class in the table is represented by eight such entries derived from the most frequent lexical rules. For a discussion of the selected latent heads, we refer to Section 10.5.

10.5 Discussion

First of all, all model instances outperform the baseline, i.e., the original grammar ($F_1 = 73.5$), and the head-lexicalized grammar with POS tags as heads ($F_1 = 78.9$). The only plausible explanation for these significant improvements is that useful head classes have been learned by our method. Moreover, increasing L consistently increases F_1 (except for Model 2 estimated from most probable heads; $L = 10$ is out of the row). We thus argue that the granularity of the current head classes is not fine enough; Further refinement may lead to even better latent-head statistics.

Second, Table 10.3 exemplifies that the latent heads are semantic in nature. For example, they can be interpreted as time expressions (NN-#9), quantifiers (JJ-#1), alpha-numeric expressions (CD-#3), fractions (CD-#4), or as verbal expressions indicating some sort of change (VBD-#2). Clearly, this does not come as a surprise: we infer latent heads on the basis of syntactic principles (head percolation), thereby generalising lexical information as much as possible.

Third, estimation from head distributions consistently outperforms estimation from most probable heads (for both models). Although coarse-grained models clearly benefit from POS information in the heads ($L = 1, 2, 5$), it is surprising that the *best* models with completely latent heads are on a par with or almost as good as the *best* ones using POS as head information.

Finally, our absolutely best model ($F_1 = 85.7$) combines POS tags with latent extra-information ($L = 10$) and is estimated from latent-head distributions. Although it also has the largest number of grammar rules (about 224,300), it is still much smaller than fully-lexicalized models. The best model with completely latent

Table 10.3 Induced latent heads for Model 2 (with free parameter $L = 10$) augmented by a linguistic interpretation such as "time", "quantifiers", "years/days", "change", etc

745.31 president	90.53 effort	2042.71 year
402.45 chairman	76.96 ability	680.71 quarter
302.29 director	65.32 plan	640.09 week
293.67 officer	55.07 decision	440.51 month
261.34 company	54.21 UNKNOWN	391.95 time
259.92 executive	53.39 right	260.37 end
237.89 analyst	50.37 attempt	222.5 day
222.27 unit	38.2 agreement	181.35 period
NN-#1 "functions"	NN-#8 "arrangements"	NN-#9 "time"

273.63 few	311.48 chief	964.61 last
194.22 many	170.92 composite	469.33 next
178.29 several	157.79 executive	457.56 first
117.5 other	126.95 senior	278.65 past
101.6 Many	88.47 financial	270.53 third
90.46 Other	77.6 federal	169.48 same
70.23 senior	72.22 familiar	164.46 recent
61.44 common	59.43 national	160.71 fiscal
JJ-#1 "quantifiers"	JJ-#6 "functions"	JJ-#10 "ranking"

354.39 1988	950.26 two	226.96 1/2	301.48 8
298.69 1989	566.07 three	205.92 3/4	258.63 1
254.56 1990	390.41 UNKNOWN	145.11 1/4	223.32 10
253.93 1987	329.33 five	121.61 5/8	185.07 15
137.89 1986	257.65 six	108.92 7/8	173.25 2
136.03 1	249.02 four	108.31 3/8	141.85 20
131.78 30	192.73 nine	97.29 1/8	137.92 30
105.26 31	166.11 10	37.73 11/16	132.87 9
CD-#1 "years/days"	CD-#3 "alpha-num"	CD-#4 "fractions"	CD-#10 "integers"

304.13 take	163.55 say	588.67 rose
204.42 buy	103.84 know	314.63 fell
203.93 sell	84.69 think	114.76 dropped
195.37 pay	53.91 see	101.14 increased
174.88 give	53.3 believe	84.41 gained
157.77 make	29.73 mean	82.48 jumped
131.68 provide	28.08 show	60.8 climbed
129.52 raise	26.76 decide	51.04 declined
VB-#7 "transaction"	VB-#9 "opinion"	VBD-#2 "change"

heads, however, leads to almost the same performance ($F_1 = 84.6$), and has the further advantage of having significantly fewer rules (only about 79,200). Moreover, it is the model which leads to the largest gain compared to the baseline ($\Delta = 11.1$).

In the rest of the section, we compare our method to related methods. To start with performance values, Table 10.4 displays previous results on parsing Section 23

Table 10.4 Comparison with other parsers (sentences of length ≤ 40)

	LP	LR	F_1	Exact	CB
Model 1 (this paper)	84.8	84.4	84.6	26.4	1.37
Magerman (1995)	84.9	84.6			1.26
Model 2 (this paper)	85.7	85.7	85.7	29.3	1.29
Collins (1996)	86.3	85.8			1.14
Matsuzaki et al. (2005)	86.6	86.7			1.19
Klein and Manning (2003)	86.9	85.7	86.3	30.9	1.10
Charniak (1997)	87.4	87.5			1.00
Collins (1997)	88.6	88.1			0.91

of the WSJ section of the Penn treebank. Comparison indicates that our best model is better than the early lexicalized model of Magerman (1995). It is a bit worse than the unlexicalized PCFGs of Klein and Manning (2003) and Matsuzaki et al. (2005), and of course, it is also worse than state-of-the-art lexicalized parsers (experience shows that evaluation results on Sections 22 and 23 do not differ much).

Beyond performance values, we believe our formalism and methodology have the following attractive features: first, our models incorporate context and lexical information collected from the whole treebank. Information is bundled into abstract heads of higher-order information, which results in a drastically reduced parameter space. In terms of Section 10.2, our approach does not aim at improving the approximation of rule probabilities $p(r|\mathrm{C}, h)$ and dependency probabilities $p(d|\mathrm{D}, \mathrm{C}, h)$ by smoothing. Rather, our approach induces head classes for the words h and d from the treebank and aims at an exact calculation of rule probabilities $p(r|\mathrm{C}, \mathrm{class}(h))$ and dependency probabilities $p(\mathrm{class}(d)|\mathrm{D}, \mathrm{C}, \mathrm{class}(h))$. This is in sharp contrast to the smoothed fixed-word statistics in most lexicalized parsing models derived from sparse data (Magerman, 1995; Collins, 1996; Charniak, 1997, etc.). Particularly, class-based dependency probabilities $p(\mathrm{class}(d)|\mathrm{D}, \mathrm{C}, \mathrm{class}(h))$ induced from the treebank are not exploited by most of these parsers.

Second, our method results in an *automatic* linguistic mark-up of treebank grammars. In contrast, manual linguistic mark-up of the treebank like in Klein and Manning (2003) is based on individual linguistic intuition and might be cost and time intensive.

Third, our method can be thought of as a new lexicalization scheme of CFG based on the notion of latent head-information, or as a successful attempt to incorporate lexical classes into parsers, combined with a new word clustering method based on the context represented by tree structure. It thus complements and extends the approach of Chiang and Bikel (2002), who aim at discovering latent head *markers* in treebanks to improve manually written head-percolation rules.

Finally, the method can also be viewed as an extension of *factorial HMMs* Ghahramani and Jordan (1995) to PCFGs: the node labels on trees are enriched with a latent variable and the latent variables are learned by EM. Matsuzaki et al. (2005) independently introduce a similar approach and present empirical results that rival ours. In contrast to us, they do not use an *explicit linguistic grammar*, and they do not attempt to *constrain* the space of latent variables *by linguistic principles*. As a consequence, our best models are three orders of magnitude more space efficient than theirs (with about 30,000,000 parameters). Therefore, parsing with their models requires sophisticated smoothing and pruning, whereas parsing with ours does not. Moreover, we calculate the most probable latent-head-decorated parse and delete the latent heads in a post-processing step. This is comparable to what they call "Viterbi complete tree" parsing. Under this regime, our parser is on a par with theirs ($F_1 = 85.5$). This suggests that both models have learned a comparable degree of information, which is surprising, because we learn latent heads only, whereas they aim at learning general features. Crucially, a final 1% improvement comes from selecting most-probable parses by bagging all complete parses with the same incomplete skeleton beforehand; Clearly, a solution to this NP-Complete problem (Sima'an, 2002) can/should be also incorporated into our parser.

10.6 Conclusion

We introduced a method for inducing a head-driven PCFG with latent-head statistics from a treebank. The automatically trained parser is time and space efficient and achieves a performance better than early lexicalized ones. This result suggests that our grammar-induction method can be successfully applied across domains, languages, and treebank annotations.

10.7 Further Reading

This paper is a slightly extended version of Prescher (2005a). New is Table 10.3 and the conclusion that the latent heads are semantic in nature. Starting with Matsuzaki et al. (2005) and Prescher (2005b), there are nowadays a bunch of excellent papers on "latent variable parsing", e.g. Petrov et al. (2006), Dreyer and Eisner (2006), Petrov and Klein (2007, 2008).

References

Black, E., S. Abney, D. Flickinger, C. Gdaniec, R. Grisham, P. Harrison, D. Hindle, R. Ingria, F. Jelinek, J. Klavans, M. Liberman, M. Marcus, S. Roukos, B. Santorini, and T. Strzalkowski (1991). A procedure for quantitatively comparing the syntactic coverage of English grammars. In *Proceedings of the DARPA Speech and Natural Language Workshop*, Pacific Grove, California, pp. 306–311.

Carroll, G. and M. Rooth (1998). Valence induction with a head-lexicalized PCFG. In *Proceedings of the 3rd Conference on Empirical Methods in Natural Language Processing*, Granada, pp. 36–45.

Charniak, E. (1997). Statistical parsing with a context-free grammar and word statistics. In *Proceedings of the 14th National Conference on Artificial Intelligence, Providence, Rhode Island*, AAAI Press/MIT Press, pp. 598–603.

Chiang, D. and D. Bikel (2002). Recovering latent information in treebanks. In *Proceedings of the 19th International Conference on Computational Linguistics* (COLING), Taipei, pp. 1–7.

Collins, M. (1996). A new statistical parser based on bigram lexical dependencies. In *Proceedings of the 34th Annual Meeting of the Association for Computational Linguistics*, Santa Cruz, California, pp. 184–191.

Collins, M. (1997). Three generative, lexicalised models for statistical parsing. In *Proceedings of the 35th Annual Meeting of the Association for Computational Linguistics and 8th Conference of the European Chapter of the Association for Computational Linguistics*, Madrid, pp. 16–23.

Dempster, A., N. Laird, and D. Rubin (1977). Maximum likelihood from incomplete data via the EM algorithm. *Journal of the Royal Statistical Society, Series B 39*(1):1–38.

Dreyer, M. and Eisner, J. (2006). Better informed training of latent syntactic features. In *Proceedings of the 2006 Conference on Empirical Methods in Natural Language Processing*, Sydney, pp. 317–326.

Dubey, A. and F. Keller (2003). Probabilistic parsing for German using sister-head dependencies. In *Proceedings of the 41st Annual Meeting on Association for Computational Linguistics*, Sapporo, pp. 96–103.

Ghahramani, Z. and M. Jordan (1995). Factorial hidden Markov models. MIT Technical Report, Vienna.

Kaplan, R. and J. Bresnan (1982). Lexical-functional grammar: a formal system for grammatical representation. In J. Bresnan (Ed.), *The Mental Representation of Grammatical Relations*. Cambridge, MA: MIT Press, pp. 173–281.

Klein, D. and C. Manning (2003). Accurate unlexicalized parsing. In *Proceedings of the 41st Annual Meeting of the Association for Computational Linguistics*, Sapporo, pp. 423–430.

Magerman, D. (1995). Statistical decision-tree models for parsing. In *Proceedings of the 33rd Annual Meeting on Association for Computational Linguistics*, Cambridge, MA, pp. 276–283.

Marcus, M., B. Santorini, and M. Marcinkiewicz (1993). Building a large annotated corpus of English: the Penn treebank. *Computational Linguistics 19*, 313–330.

Matsuzaki, T., Y. Miyao, and J. Tsujii (2005). Probabilistic CFG with latent annotations. In *Proceedings of the 43rd Annual Meeting on Association for Computational Linguistics*, Ann Arbor, MI, pp. 75–82.

Petrov, S., L. Barrett, R. Thibaux, and D. Klein (2006). Learning accurate, compact, and interpretable tree annotation. In *Proceedings of the 21st International Conference on Computational Linguistics and the 44th Annual Meeting of the Association for Computational Linguistics*, Sydney, pp. 433–440.

Petrov, S. and D. Klein (2007). Improved inference for unlexicalized parsing. In *Human Language Technologies 2007: The Conference of the North American Chapter of the Association for Computational Linguistics; Proceedings of the Main Conference*, Rochester, NY, pp. 404–411.

Petrov, S. and D. Klein (2008). Parsing German with latent variable grammars. In *Proceedings of the Workshop on Parsing German at the 46th Annual Meeting of the Association for Computational Linguistics: Human Language Technologies*, Columbus, OH, pp. 33–39.

Prescher, D. (2003). A tutorial on the expectation-maximization algorithm including maximum-likelihood estimation and EM training of probabilistic context-free grammars. *Presented at the 15th European Summer School in Logic, Language and Information (ESSLLI).*

Prescher, D. (2005a). Head-driven PCFGs with latent-head statistics. In *Proceedings of the 9th International Workshop on Parsing Technology*, Vancouver, pp. 115–124.

Prescher, D. (2005b). Inducing head-driven PCFGs with latent heads: refining a tree-bank grammar for parsing. In *Proceedings of the 16th European Conference on Machine Learning*, Porto, pp. 292–304.

Schmid, H. (2004). Efficient parsing of highly ambiguous context-free grammars with bit vectors. In *Proceedings of the 20th International Conference on Computational Linguistics*, Geneva, pp. 162–168.

Sima'an, K. (2002). Computational complexity of probabilistic disambiguation. *Grammars 5*(2), 125–151.

Chapter 11
Self-Trained Bilexical Preferences to Improve Disambiguation Accuracy

Gertjan van Noord

11.1 Motivation

In parse selection, the task is to select the correct syntactic analysis of a given sentence from a set of parses generated by some other mechanism. On the basis of correctly labeled examples, supervised parse selection techniques can be employed to obtain reasonable accuracy. Although parsing has improved enormously over the last few years, even the most successful parsers make very silly, sometimes embarrassing, mistakes. In our experiments with a large wide-coverage stochastic attribute-value grammar of Dutch, we noted that the system sometimes is insensitive to the naturalness of the various lexical combinations it has to consider. Although parsers often employ lexical features which are in principle able to represent preferences with respect to word combinations, the size of the manually labeled training data will be too small to be able to learn the relevance of such features.

In maximum-entropy parsing—the supervised parsing technique that we use in our experiments—arbitrary features can be defined which are employed to characterize different parses. So it is possible to construct features for any property that is thought to be important for disambiguation. However, such features can be useful for disambiguation only in case the training set contains a sufficient number of occurrences of these features. This is problematic, in practice, for features that encode bilexical preferences such as selection restrictions, because typical training sets are much too small to estimate the relevance of features representing co-occurrences of two words. As a simple example consider the ambiguous Dutch sentence

(1) Melk drinkt de baby niet
Milk drinks the baby not
The baby doesn't drink milk / Milk doesn't drink the baby

The standard model of the parser we experimented with employs a wide variety of features including syntactic features and lexical features. In particular, the model also includes features which encode whether or not the subject or the object is

G. van Noord (✉)
Faculty of Arts, University of Groningen, 9700 AS Groningen, The Netherlands
e-mail: G.J.M.van.Noord@rug.nl

H. Bunt et al. (eds.), *Trends in Parsing Technology*, Text, Speech and Language Technology 43, DOI 10.1007/978-90-481-9352-3_11,

fronted in a parse. Since subjects, in general, are fronted much more frequently than objects, the model has learned to prefer readings in which the fronted constituent is analyzed as the subject. Although the model also contains features to distinguish whether `milk` occurs as the subject or the object of `drink`, the model has not learned a preference for either of these features, since there were no sentences in the training data that involved both these two words.

To make this point more explicit, we found that in about 200 sentences of our parsed corpus of 27 million sentences `milk` is the head of the direct object of the verb `drink`. Suppose that we need at least perhaps 5–10 sentences in our training corpus in order to be able to learn the specific preference between `milk` and `drink`. The implication is that we would need a (manually labeled!) training corpus of approximately 1 million sentences (20 million words). In contrast, the disambiguation model of the Dutch parser we are reporting on in this paper is trained on a manually labeled corpus of slightly over 7,000 sentences (145,000 words). It appears that semi-supervised or un-supervised methods are required here.

Note that the problem not only occurs for artificial examples such as (1); here are a few misparsed examples actually encountered in a large parsed corpus:

(2) a. Campari moet **u** gedronken hebben
Campari must you drunk have
Campari must have drunk you / You must have drunk Campari

b. De wijn die **Elvis** zou hebben gedronken als hij wijn zou
The wine which Elvis would have drunk if he wine would
hebben gedronken
have drunk
The wine Elvis would have drunk if he had drunk wine/
The wine that would have drunk Elvis if he had drunk wine

c. De paus heeft **tweehonderd daklozen** te eten gehad
The pope has two-hundred homeless-people to eat had
The pope had two-hundred homeless people for dinner

In this paper, we describe an alternative approach in which we employ point-wise mutual information association score in the maximum entropy disambiguation model. The association scores used here are estimated using a very large parsed corpus of 500 million words (27 million sentences). We show that the incorporation of this additional knowledge source improves parsing accuracy.

11.2 Previous Research

Automatically learning selection restrictions from corpora using a parser goes back to Church et al. (1989); Church and Hanks (1990). They proposed the use of point-wise mutual information (Fano, 1961) to estimate the strength of association between verbs and head nouns of direct objects. Preprocessing of the corpus included the application of a robust parser (the Fidditch parser).

In Resnik (1993), an alternative association metric is formulated which takes into account classes of arguments. For instance, verbs are associated with preferences for particular classes of head nouns as direct objects, rather than individual nouns. A number of variants of Resnik's metric are described in Ribas (1995), and Ribas performs a number of experiments comparing these variants.

Clearly, the idea that selection restrictions ought to be useful for parsing accuracy is not new. However, as far as we know, this is the first time that automatically acquired selection restrictions have been shown to improve parsing accuracy results for a wide-coverage full parsing task. For instance, Ribas (1995) describes potential NLP tasks which could benefit from selectional restrictions, including syntactic ambiguity resolution. In his conclusions he mentions that "...the technique still seems far from practical application to NLP tasks...".

Earlier work *has* shown that selection restrictions can be good predictors for certain types of attachment ambiguity. Based on an empirical study, Whittemore et al. (1990) conclude that PP attachment decisions are predictable on the basis of lexical preferences of nouns, verbs and prepositions.

Furthermore, Gamallo et al. (2003) describes a corpus-based technique to learn so-called *co-restrictions* automatically, and the paper illustrate that these could be useful for parsing by showing that for a particular attachment resolution task, the availability of co-restrictions improves over a right association baseline.

Abekawa and Okumura (2006) and Kawahara and Kurohashi (2006) describe how statistical information between verbs and case elements is collected on the basis of large automatically analyzed corpora. In a recent paper Kawahara and Kurohashi (2008) they show that these case frames help disambiguate coordinations.

The association scores employed in this paper are estimated on the basis of a large corpus that is parsed by the parser that we aim to improve upon. Therefore, this technique can be described as a somewhat particular instance of self-training. Self-training has been investigated for statistical parsing before. Although naively adding self-labeled material to extend training data is normally not successful, there have been successful variants of self-learning for parsing as well. For instance, in McClosky et al. (2006) self-learning is used to improve a two-phase parser reranker, with very good results for the classical Wall Street Journal parsing task.

11.3 Background: Alpino Parser

The experiments are performed using the Alpino parser for Dutch. In this section we briefly describe the parser, as well as the corpora that we have used in the experiments described later.

11.3.1 Grammar and Lexicon

The Alpino system is a linguistically motivated, wide-coverage grammar and parser for Dutch in the tradition of HPSG. It consists of over 700 grammar rules and a large lexicon of over 100,000 lexemes and various rules to recognize special constructs such as named entities, temporal expressions, etc. The grammar takes a "constructional" approach, with rich lexical representations and a large number of detailed, construction specific rules. Both the lexicon and the rule component are organized in a multiple inheritance hierarchy. Heuristics have been implemented to deal with unknown words and word sequences, and ungrammatical or out-of-coverage sentences (which may nevertheless contain fragments that are analyzable). The Alpino system includes a POS-tagger which greatly reduces lexical ambiguity, without an observable decrease in parsing accuracy (Prins, 2005).

11.3.2 Parser

Based on the categories assigned to words, and the set of grammar rules compiled from the HPSG grammar, a left-corner parser finds the set of all parses, and stores this set compactly in a packed parse forest. All parses are rooted by an instance of the top category, which is a category that generalizes over all maximal projections (S, NP, VP, ADVP, AP, PP and some others). If there is no parse covering the complete input, the parser finds all parses for each sub-string. In such cases, the robustness component will then select the best sequence of non-overlapping parses (i.e., maximal projections) from this set.

In order to select the best parse from the compact parse forest, a best-first search algorithm is applied. The algorithm consults a maximum entropy disambiguation model to judge the quality of (partial) parses. Since the disambiguation model includes inherently non-local features, efficient dynamic programming solutions are not directly applicable. Instead, a best-first beam-search algorithm is employed (van Noord and Malouf, 2005; van Noord et al., 2006).

11.3.3 Maximum Entropy Disambiguation Model

The maximum entropy model is a conditional model which assigns a probability to a parse t for a given sentence s. Furthermore, $f_i(t)$ are the feature functions which count the occurrence of each feature i in a parse t. Each feature i has an associated weight λ_i. The score ϕ of a parse t is defined as the sum of the weighted feature counts:

$$\phi(t) = \sum_i \lambda_i f_i(t)$$

If t is a parse of s, the conditional probability is given by the following, where $T(s)$ are all parses of s:

$$P(t|s) = \frac{\exp(\phi(t))}{\sum_{u \in T(s)} \exp(\phi(u))}$$

If we only want to select the best parse we can ignore the actual probability, and use the score ϕ to rank competing parses.

The maximum entropy model employs a large set of features. The standard model uses about 42,000 features. Features describe various properties of parses. For instance, the model includes features which signal the application of particular grammar rules, as well as local configurations of grammar rules. There are features signaling specific POS-tags and subcategorization frames. Other features signal local or non-local occurrences of extraction (WH-movement, relative clauses etc.), the grammatical role of the extracted element (subject vs. non-subject etc.), features to represent the distance of a relative clause and the noun it modifies, features describing the amount of parallelism between conjuncts in a coordination, etc. In addition, there are lexical features which represent the co-occurrence of two specific words in a specific dependency, and the occurrence of a specific word as a specific dependent for a given POS-tag. Each parse is characterized by its feature vector (the counts for each of the 42,000 features). Once the model is trained, each feature is associated with its weight λ (a positive or negative number, typically close to 0). To find out which parse is the best parse according to the model, it suffices to multiply the frequency of each feature with its corresponding weight, and sum these weighted frequencies. The parse with the highest sum is the best parse. Formal details of the disambiguation model are presented in van Noord and Malouf (2005). For training the maximum entropy models, we use an implementation by Malouf (2002).

11.3.4 Dependency Structures

Although Alpino is not a dependency grammar in the traditional sense, dependency structures are generated by the lexicon and grammar rules as the value of a dedicated feature `dt`. The dependency structures are based on CGN (Corpus Gesproken Nederlands, Corpus of Spoken Dutch) (Hoekstra et al., 2003), D-Coi and LASSY (van Noord et al., 2006). Such dependency structures are somewhat idiosyncratic, as can be observed in the example in Fig. 11.1 for the sentence:

(3) waar en wanneer dronk Elvis wijn?
where and when drank Elvis wine?
Where and when did Elvis drink wine?

In such a CGN dependency structure, heads are represented as a daughter leaf node of an abstract non-terminal node. Different types of head receive a different relation label such as `hd` for ordinary heads and `whd` (for WH-phrases). Other types of heads include coordinators (`crd`), relative pronouns (`rhd`) and complementizers (`cmp`). Non-leaf nodes are decorated further with a category specification, and leaf-nodes similarly have a POS-tag.

As a further peculiarity, nodes can be linked to more than a single mother node. In such cases, dependency structures are really graphs. In CGN, the term *secondary edge* was used for such cases. As in attribute-value structures with reentrancies, such graphs are visualized by displaying trees where co-indexed nodes indicate sharing.

Fig. 11.1 Dependency graph example

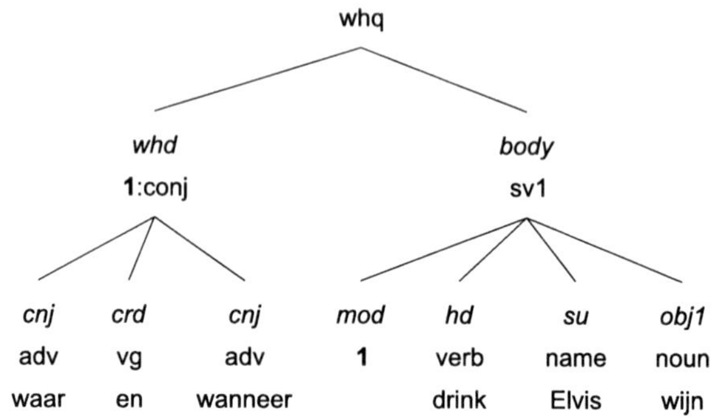

In this case, for example, the WH-phrase is both the *whd* element of the top-node, as well as a *mod* dependent of the verbal cluster headed by *drink*, as indicated by the index 1.

11.3.5 Named Dependency Relations

Often we do not work with the dependency structures themselves, but we extract named lexical dependencies from the dependency structure. The dependency graph in Fig. 11.1 is represented with the following set of dependencies:

crd/cnj(en, waar)	crd/cnj(en, wanneer)
whd/body(en, drink)	hd/mod(drink, en)
hd/obj1(drink, wijn)	hd/su(drink, Elvis)

For a given node in a dependency structure, a dependency exists between the root form associated with the head daughter (the daughter labeled with one of the designated labels indicating heads) and the root forms associated with each of the non-head daughters. The root form of a dependency structure for non-leaf nodes is the root form associated with the head daughter of that structure. A named lexical dependency is written as $r_1/r_2(w_1, w_2)$ where the head daughter has dependency label r_1, the non-head daughter has dependency label r_2, and the root forms associated with the head daughter and the non-head daughter are w_1 and w_2 respectively. Below, we often write $r(w_1, w_2)$ with the understanding that r is a pair such as `hd/obj1` or `whd/body`.

11.3.6 Evaluation

The output of the parser is evaluated by comparing the generated dependency structure for a corpus sentence to the gold standard dependency structure in a treebank. For this comparison, we represent the dependency structure as a set of named dependency relations, as illustrated in the previous paragraph.

Comparing these sets, we count the number of dependencies that are identical in the generated parse and the stored structure, which is expressed traditionally using precision, recall and f-score (Briscoe et al., 2002).

Let D_p^i be the number of dependencies produced by the parser for sentence i, D_g^i is the number of dependencies in the treebank parse, and D_o^i is the number of correct dependencies produced by the parser. If no superscript is used, we aggregate over all sentences of the test set, i.e.,:

$$D_p = \sum_i D_p^i \qquad D_o = \sum_i D_o^i \qquad D_g = \sum_i D_g^i$$

We define precision as the total number of correct dependencies returned by the parser, divided by the overall number of dependencies returned by the parser; recall is the number of correct system dependencies divided by the total number of dependencies in the treebank:

$$\text{precision} = \frac{D_o}{D_p} \qquad \text{recall} = \frac{D_o}{D_g}$$

As usual, precision and recall are combined in a single f-score metric:

$$\text{f-score} = \frac{2 * \text{precision} * \text{recall}}{\text{precision} + \text{recall}}$$

An alternative similarity score for dependency structures is based on the observation that for a given sentence of n words, a parser would be expected to return (about) n dependencies. In such cases, we can simply use the percentage of correct dependencies as a measure of accuracy. To allow for some discrepancies between the number of expected and returned dependencies, we divide by the maximum of both. This leads to the following definition of *concept accuracy*. A similar definition can be found, for instance, in Boros et al. (1996). The number of returned dependencies can be greater than the number of expected dependencies, in cases where the gold parse includes fewer secondary edges than the proposed parse.

$$\text{CA} = \frac{D_o}{\sum_i \max(D_g^i, D_p^i)}$$

The concept accuracy metric can be characterized as the mean of a per-sentence minimum of recall and precision. The resulting CA score therefore is typically slightly lower than the corresponding f-score.

The standard version of Alpino that we use here as baseline system is trained on the 145,000 word Alpino treebank, which contains dependency structures for the `cdbl` (newspaper) part of the Eindhoven corpus. The parameters for training the model are the same for the baseline model, as well as the model that includes the self-trained bilexical preferences (introduced below). These parameters include the Gaussian penalty, thresholds for feature selection, etc. Details of the training procedure are described in van Noord and Malouf (2005).

11.3.7 Parsed Corpora

Over the course of about a year, Alpino has been used to parse a large amount of sentences from various corpora. We included all Dutch newspaper texts from the Twente Newspaper Corpus (Ordelman et al., 2007), the full Dutch Wikipedia (the version made available to the CLEF2007 participants), and the Dutch part of Europarl (available from `www.statmt.org/europarl`).

We used the 200 node Beowulf Linux cluster of the High-Performance Computing center of the University of Groningen. The dependency structures are stored in XML. The XML files can be processed and searched in various ways, for instance, using XPATH, XSLT and Xquery (Bouma and Kloosterman, 2002, 2007). Some quantitative information of this parsed corpus is listed in Table 11.1. In the experiments described below, we do not distinguish between full and fragment parses; sentences without a parse are simply ignored.

Table 11.1 Approximate counts of the number of sentences and words in the parsed corpus. About 0.3% of the sentences did not get a parse, for computational reasons (out of memory, or maximum parse time exceeded)

Number of sentences	100.0%	30,000,000
Number of words		500,000,000
Number of sentences without parse	0.3%	100,000
Number of sentences with fragments	8.0%	2,500,000
Number of single full parse	92.0%	27,500,000

11.4 Bilexical Preferences

In this section, we describe how association scores for lexical dependencies are defined, and how the scores are applied in the disambiguation model.

In the first subsection, we show in detail how point-wise mutual information scores are computed on the basis of a large parsed corpus. In the second subsection, we extend lexical dependencies for an improved treatment of relative clauses and coordination. In the third subsection, we describe how the bilexical preferences are integrated in the disambiguation model.

11.4.1 Association Score

The parsed corpora described in the previous section have been used in order to compute association scores between lexical dependencies. The parses constructed

Table 11.2 Number of lexical dependencies in parsed corpora (approximate counts)

Tokens	480,000,000
Types	100,000,000
Types with frequency ≥ 20	2,350,000

by Alpino are dependency structures. From these dependency structures, we extract all named dependencies. In Table 11.2, we list the number of named dependencies extracted from the parsed corpora.

Named dependencies that occur fewer than 20 times are ignored, because the mutual information score that we use below is unreliable for low frequencies. An additional benefit of a frequency threshold is a manageable size of the resulting data-structures.

Bilexical preference between two root forms w_1 and w_2 is computed using an association score based on *point-wise mutual information*, as defined by Fano (1961) and used for a similar purpose in Church and Hanks (1990), as well as in many other studies in corpus linguistics. The association score is defined here as follows:

$$I(r(w_1, w_2)) = \log \frac{f(r(w_1, w_2))}{f(r(w_1, \_))f(\_(\_, w_2))}$$

where $f(X)$ is the relative frequency of X. In the above formula, the underscore is a place-holder for an arbitrary relation or an arbitrary word. The association score I compares the actual frequency of w_1 and w_2 with dependency r, with the frequency we would expect if the words were independent. For instance, to compute I(hd/obj1(`drink`, `melk`)) we look up the number of times `drink` occurs with a direct object out of all 462,250,644 dependencies (15,713) and the number of times `melk` occurs as a dependent (10,172). If we multiply the two corresponding relative frequencies, we get the expected relative frequency for hd/obj1(`drink`, `melk`). Multiplying the expected relative frequency with the corpus size (all 462M dependencies) gives an expected absolute frequency of 0.35. The actual frequency, 195, is about 560 times as big. Taking the log of 560 gives us the association score (6.33) for this bi-lexical dependency.

The pairs involving a direct object relationship with the highest scores are listed in Fig. 11.2. Focusing on the verbs `drinken` (to drink) and `eten` (to eat), we provide in Fig. 11.3 the corresponding highest scoring heads of objects.

bijltje gooi_neer, duimschroef draai_aan, goes by time, kostje scharrel, peentje zweet, traantje pink_weg, boontje dop, centje verdien_bij, champagne_fles ontkurk, dorst les, fikkie stook, gal spuw, garen spin, geld_kraan draai_dicht, graantje pik_mee, krediet_kraan, draai_dicht, kruis_band scheur_af, kruit verschiet, olie_kraan draai_open, onderspit delf, oven_schaal vet_in, pijp_steel regen, proef_ballonnetje laat_op, scepter zwaai, spuigat loop_uit, subsidie_kraan draai_dicht, vin verroer, wereld_zee bevaar, woordje spreek_mee

Fig. 11.2 Pairs involving a direct object relationship with the highest point-wise mutual information score biertje, borreltje, glaasje, pilsje, pintje, pint, wijntje, alcohol, bier, borrel, cappuccino, champage, chocolademelk, cola, espresso, koffie, kopje, limonade, liter, pils, slok, vruchtensap, whisky, wodka, cocktail, drankje, druppel, frisdrank, glas, jenever, liter, melk, sherry, slok, thee, wijn, blikje, bloed, drank, flesje, fles, kop, liter, urine, beker, dag, water, hoeveelheid, veel, wat

boterhammetje, hapje, Heart, mens_vlees, patatje, work, biefstuk, boer_kool, boterham, broodje, couscous, drop, frietje, friet, fruit, gebakje, hamburger, haring, home, ijsje, insect, kaas, kaviaar, kers, koolhydraat, kroket, mossel, oester, oliebol, pannenkoek, patat, pizza, rundvlees, slak, soep, spaghetti, spruitje, stam_pot, sushi, taartje, varkensvlees, vlees, aardappel, aardbei, appel, asperge, banaan, boon, brood, chocolade, chocola, garnaal, gerecht, gras, groente, hap, kalkoen, kilo, kip, koekje, kreeft, maaltijd, paling, pasta, portie, rijst, salade, sla, taart, toetje, vet, visje, vis, voedsel, voer, worst,bordje, bord, chip, dag, ei, gram, ijs, kilo, knoflook, koek, konijn, paddestoel, plant, service, stukje, thuis, tomaat, vrucht, wat, wild, zalm

Fig. 11.3 Pairs involving a direct object relationship with the highest point-wise mutual information score for the verbs `drink` (first list) and `eat` (second list)

Selection restrictions are often associated only with direct objects. We include bilexical association scores for all types of dependencies. We found that association scores for other types of dependencies also captures both collocational preferences as well as weaker co-occurrence preferences. Some examples including modifiers are listed in Fig. 11.4. Such preferences are useful for disambiguation as well. Consider the ambiguous Dutch sentence

(4) omdat we lauw bier dronken
because we cold-warm beer drank
because we drank warm beer / because we drank beer indifferently

The adjective `lauw` (cold, lukewarm, warm, indifferently) can be used to modify both nouns and verbs; this latter possibility is exemplified in:

(5) We hebben lauw gereageerd
We have cold-warm reacted
We reacted indifferently

If we incorporate bilexical preferences between heads and modifiers, then we can hope to disambiguate such cases as well.

Association scores can be negative if two words in a lexical dependency occur less frequently than one would expect if the words were independent. However, since association scores are unreliable for low frequencies (including, often,

overlangs snijd_door, ten hele dwaal, welig tier, dunnetjes doe_over, omver kegel, on_zedelijk betast, stief_moederlijk bedeel, stierlijk verveel, straal loop_voorbij, uitein rafel, aaneen smeed, bestraf spreek_toe, cum laude studeer_af, deerlijk vergis, des te meer klem, door en door verrot, glad strijk_af, glazig fruit, hermetisch grendel_af, ingespannen tuur, instemmend knik, kat_kwaad haal_uit, kostelijk amuseer, kwistig strooi, lijdzaam zie_toe, luchtig spatel, neer plof, neer vlij, on_geforceerd verfilm, ongenadig krijg_langs, on_heus bejegen, onverdroten ga_voort, oraal bevredig, rakelings scheer, reikhals kijk_uit, standrechtelijk executeer, ten halve keer, tussenuit knijp, vergenoegd wrijf, voort borduur, voort kabbel, wagenwijd zet_open, wijd sper_open, woord voor woord zing_mee

Fig. 11.4 Highest scoring pairs involving a modifier relationship between a verb and an adverbial frequencies of zero), and since such negative associations involve low frequencies by their nature, we only take into account positive association scores.

11.4.2 Extending Pairs

The CGN dependencies that we work with fail to relate pairs of words in certain syntactic constructions for which it can be reasonably assumed that bilexical preferences should be useful. We have identified two such constructions, namely relative clauses and coordination, and for these constructions we generalize our method, to take such dependencies into account too (both during dependency extraction from the parsed corpus, and during disambiguation). Consider coordinations such as:

(6) Bier of wijn drinkt Elvis niet
Beer or wine drinks Elvis not
Elvis does not drink beer or wine

The dependency structure of the intended analysis is given in Fig. 11.5. The set of named dependencies for this example illustrates that the coordinator is treated as the head of the conjunction:

hd/obj1(`drink`, `of`) crd/cnj(`of`, `bier`)
crd/cnj(`of`, `wijn`) hd/su(`drink`, `elvis`)
hd/mod(`drink`, `niet`)

So there are no direct dependencies between the verb and the individual conjuncts. For this reason, we add additional dependencies $r(A, C)$ for every pair of dependency $r(A, B)$, crd/cnj(B, C).

Relative clauses are another syntactic phenomenon where we extend the set of dependencies. For a noun phrase such as:

(7) Wijn die Elvis niet dronk
Wine which Elvis not drank
Wine which Elvis did not drink

there is no direct dependency between `wijn`

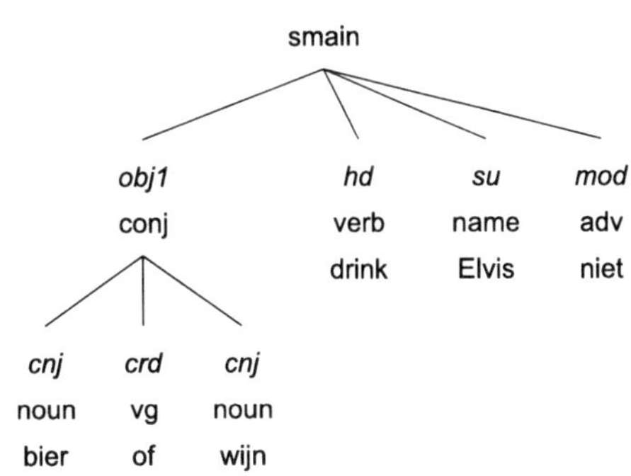

Fig. 11.5 Dependency structure produced for coordination

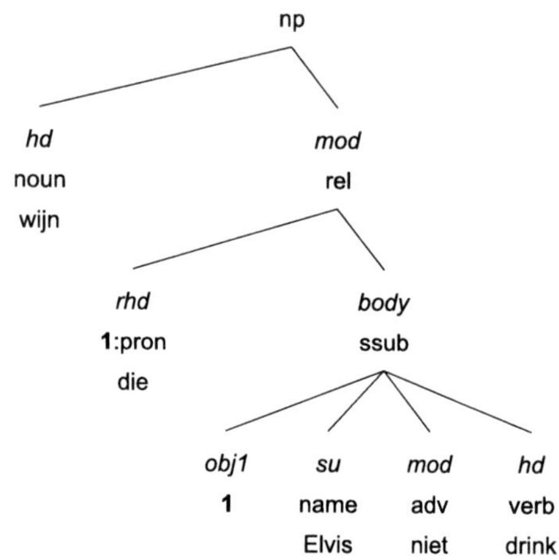

Fig. 11.6 Dependency structure produced for relative clause

and `drink`, as can be seen in the dependency structure given in Fig. 11.6. Sets of dependencies are extended in such cases, to make the relation between the noun and the role it plays in the relative clause explicit: if a noun w_2 is modified by a relative headed by a relative pronoun, and this pronoun is a dependent r of a verb w_1, then a new dependency $r(w_1, w_2)$ is added.

11.4.3 Using Association Scores as Features

The association scores for all dependencies are used in our disambiguation model by means of a technique developed by Johnson and Riezler (2000) to incorporate auxiliary distributions in stochastic attribute value grammar.

Auxiliary distributions offer the possibility to incorporate information from additional sources into a maximum entropy disambiguation model. In more detail, auxiliary distributions are integrated by considering the logarithm of the probability given by an auxiliary distribution as an additional, real-valued feature. More formally, given k auxiliary distributions $Q_i(t)$, then k new *auxiliary features* $f_{m+1}, \ldots, f_{m+k}$ are added such that

$$f_{m+i}(t) = \log Q_i(t)$$

In Johnson and Riezler (2000) it is noted that $Q_i(t)$ do not need to be proper probability distributions, however they must be strictly positive. In our case, we use auxiliary distributions $Q_{t,r}$ for each of the major POS-tag labels t (verb, noun, adjective, adverb, ...) and each of the dependency relations r (subject, object, ...).

More concretely, we introduce additional auxiliary features $z(t, r)$ for each of the major POS labels t and each of the dependency relations r. The "count" of such features is determined by the association scores for actually occuring dependency pairs. For example, if in a given parse a given verb v has a direct object dependent n, then we compute the association of this particular pair, and use the resulting number as the count of that feature. Of course, if there are multiple dependencies of this type in a single parse, the corresponding association scores are all summed, to arrive at the count for the feature $z(t, r)$.

To illustrate this technique, consider the dependency structure given earlier in Fig. 11.5. For this example, there are four of these new features with a non-zero count. The counts are given by the corresponding association scores as follows:

$$\begin{aligned} z(\text{verb}, \text{hd/su}) &= I(\text{hd/su}(\texttt{drink}, \texttt{elvis})) \\ z(\text{verb}, \text{hd/mod}) &= I(\text{hd/mod}(\texttt{drink}, \texttt{niet})) \\ z(\text{verb}, \text{hd/obj1}) &= I(\text{hd/obj1}(\texttt{drink}, \texttt{of})) \\ &+ I(\text{hd/obj1}(\texttt{drink}, \texttt{bier})) \\ &+ I(\text{hd/obj1}(\texttt{drink}, \texttt{wijn})) \\ z(\text{conj}, \text{crd/cnj}) &= I(\text{crd/cnj}(\texttt{of}, \texttt{bier})) \\ &+ I(\text{crd/cnj}(\texttt{of}, \texttt{wijn})) \end{aligned}$$

It is crucial to observe that the new features do not include any direct reference to actual words. This means that there will be only a fairly limited number of new features (depending on the number of tags t and relations r, in the experiments below there are slightly over 100 new features), and we can expect that these features are frequent enough to be able to estimate their weights in training material of limited size.

With the new features present, the model is re-trained on the original training data. As a result, the features including the new $z(t, r)$ features are assigned weights. These new weights can then be used in parse selection. As an example, consider the two parses in Fig. 11.7 for sentence (1), repeated here for convenience:

(8) Melk drinkt de baby niet
Milk drinks the baby not
The baby doesn't drink milk / Milk doesn't drink the baby

In Table 11.3 we show some of the relevant features to distinguish the two readings, with the corresponding counts and weights. In this example, the bias of the

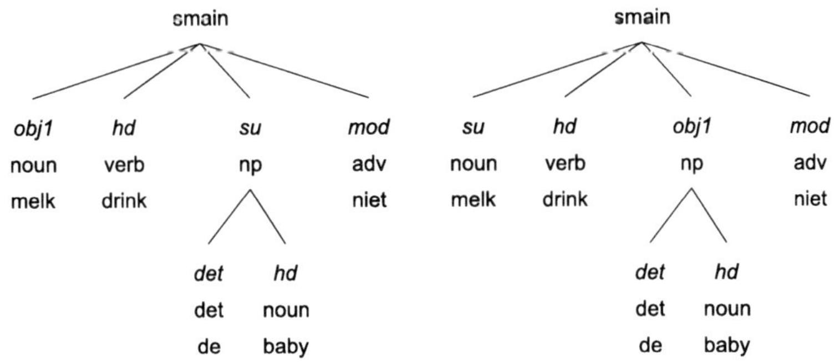

Fig. 11.7 Two competing dependency structures for the sentence *Melk drinkt de baby niet*

Table 11.3 Relevant features and their counts and weights for two readings of the sentence *Melk drinkt de baby niet*

Correct reading				Wrong reading			
Feature	Count	Weight	Sum	Feature	Count	Weight	Sum
Non-subj-topic	1	−0.015	−0.015	Subj-topic	1	+0.043	+0.043
z(verb,hd/obj1)	6	+0.009	+0.054				
z(verb,hd/su)	4	+0.010	+0.040				
		ϕ	+0.079			ϕ	+0.043

model for topicalized subjects is properly outweighted by the inclusion of the new lexical preference features. Therefore the model correctly selects the desired reading in this case.

11.5 Experiments

We report on two experiments. In the first experiment, we report on the results of ten-fold cross-validation on the Alpino treebank. This is the material that is standardly used for training and testing. For each of the sentences of this corpus, the system produces at most the first 1,000 parses. For every parse, we compute the quality by comparing its dependency structure with the gold standard dependency structure in the treebank. For training, at most 100 parses are selected randomly for each sentence. For (ten-fold cross-validated) testing, we use all available parses for a given sentence. In order to test the quality of the model, we check for each given sentence which of its 1,000 parses is selected by the disambiguation model. The quality of that parse is used in the computation of the accuracy, as listed in Table 11.4. The column labeled *exact* measures the proportion of sentences for which the model selected (one of) the best possible parse(s) (there can be multiple best possible parses). The *baseline* row reports on the quality of a disambiguation model which simply selects the first parse for each sentence. The *oracle* row reports on the quality of the best-possible disambiguation model, which would (by magic) always select the best possible parse (this number is lower than 100, because some parses are outside the coverage of the system, and some parses are generated only after more than 1,000 inferior parses). The *error reduction* column measures which part of the disambiguation problem (difference between the baseline and oracle scores) is solved by the model.[1]

The results show a small, but clear, increase in error reduction, if the standard model (without the association score features) is compared with a (retrained) model

[1] Note that the error reduction numbers presented in the table are lower than those presented in van Noord and Malouf (2005). The reason is that we report here on experiments in which parses are generated with a version of Alpino with the POS-tagger switched on. The POS-tagger already reduces the number of ambiguities, and in particular solves many of the "easy" cases. The resulting models, however, are more effective in practice (where the model also is applied after the POS-tagger).

Table 11.4 Results with ten-fold cross-validation on the Eindhoven-cdbl part of the Alpino treebank. In these experiments, the models are used to select a parse from a given set of at most 1,000 parses per sentence

	Fscore (%)	Error-reduction (%)	Exact (%)	CA (%)
Baseline	74.02	0.00	16.0	73.48
Oracle	91.97	100.00	100.0	91.67
Standard	87.41	74.60	52.0	87.02
+Bilexical preferences	87.91	77.38	54.8	87.51

that includes the association score features. The relatively large improvement of the *exact* score suggests that the bilexical preference features are particularly good at choosing between very good parses.

For the second experiment, we evaluate how well the resulting model performs in the full system. First of all, this is the only really convincing evaluation which measures progress for the system as a whole by virtue of including bilexical preferences. The second motivation for this experiment is for methodological reasons: we now test on a truly unseen test-set. The first experiment can be criticized on methodological grounds as follows. The Alpino treebank was used to train the disambiguation model which was used to construct the large parsed treebank from which we extracted the counts for the association scores. Those scores might somehow therefore indirectly reflect certain aspects of the Alpino treebank training data. Testing on that data later (with the inclusion of the association scores) is therefore not sound.

For this second experiment we used the WR-P-P-H (newspaper) part of the D-Coi corpus. This part contains 2,256 sentences from the newspaper Trouw (2001). In Table 11.5, we show the resulting f-score and CA for a system with and without the inclusion of the $z(t, r)$ features. The improvement found in the previous experiment is confirmed.

Table 11.5 Results on the WR-P-P-H part of the D-Coi corpus (2,267 sentences from the newspaper Trouw, from 2001). In these experiments, we report on the full system. In the full system, the disambiguation model is used to guide a best-first beam-search procedure which extracts a parse from the parse forest. Difference in CA was found to be significant (using paired T-test on the per sentence CA scores)

	Precision (%)	Recall (%)	Fscore (%)	CA (%)
Standard	90.77	90.49	90.63	90.32
+Bilexical preferences	91.19	90.89	91.01	90.73

11.6 Conclusion and Outlook

One might wonder why self-training works in the case of selection restrictions, at least in the set-up described above. One may argue that, in order to learn that *milk* is a good object for *drink*, the parser has to analyze examples of *drink milk* in the raw data correctly. But if the parser is capable of analyzing these examples, why does it need selection restrictions? The answer appears to be that the parser (without selection restrictions) is able to analyze the large majority of cases correctly. These cases include the many easy occurrences where no (difficult) ambiguities arise (case marking, number agreement, and other syntactic characteristics often force a particular reading). The easy cases outnumber the misparsed difficult cases, and therefore the selection restrictions can be learned. Using these selection restrictions as additional features, the parser is then able to also get some of the difficult, ambiguous, cases right.

There are various aspects of our method that need further investigation. First of all, existing techniques that involve selection restrictions Resnik (1993) typically assume classes of nouns, rather than individual nouns. In future work, we hope to generalize our method to take classes into account, where the aim is to learn class membership also on the basis of large parsed corpora.

Another aspect of the technique that needs further research involves the use of a threshold in establishing the association score, and perhaps related to this issue, the incorporation of negative association scores (for instance for cases where a large number of co-occurrences of a pair would be expected but where in fact none or very few were found).

There are also some more practical issues that perhaps had a negative impact on our results. First, the large parsed corpus was collected over a period of about a year, but during that period, the actual system was not stable. In particular, due to various improvements of the dictionary, the root form of words that was used by the system changed over time. Since we used root forms in the computation of the association scores, this could be harmful in some specific cases. A further practical issue concerns repeated sentences or even full paragraphs. This happens in typical newspaper material for instance in the case of short descriptions of movies that may be repeated weekly for as long as that movie is playing. Pairs of words that occur in such repeated sentences receive association scores that are much too high. The method should be adapted to take this into account, perhaps simply by removing duplicated sentences.

The association scores are defined with respect to root forms. This may not be optimal. In our dictionary, verbs are often associated with many different subcategorization frames. Sometimes, the meaning of a verb can be dependent on the choice of subcategorization frame. For instance, the meaning of the intransitive use of *eindigen* (to end) is quite different from its transitive use, as the following two examples illustrate:

(9) a. Het verhaal eindigt hier
The story ends here
The story ends here

b. Hij eindigde zijn voordracht
He ended his presentation
He ended his presentation

In the ideal case, we might want to have access to the information that, for this verb, the subject phrase in the intransitive use of the verb is thematically related to the direct object of the transitive use of the verb. Currently, this information is not available to the system; rather the subjects of both the intransitive as well as the transitive use of the verb are all treated together.

A better alternative might be to define mutual information scores with respect to pairs of root forms and subcategorization frames; however this would probably be harmful for cases such as *eten* (to eat), where the subject of both the transitive and intransitive use of the verb appear to share the thematic role. One interesting direction would be to try integrate the research on automatic, corpus-based, verb classification (Merlo and Stevenson, 2001; Schulte im Walde, 2009; McCarthy, 2001).

The insight that selection restrictions are useful for parsing is not new. However, as far as we know this is the first time that automatically acquired selection restrictions have been shown to improve parsing accuracy results for a wide-coverage full parsing task.

Acknowledgements This research was carried out in part in the context of the Lassy project. The Lassy project is carried out within the STEVIN programme which is funded by the Dutch and Flemish governments http://taalunieversum.org/taal/technologie/stevin.

References

Abekawa, T. and M. Okumura (2006). Japanese dependency parsing using co-occurrence information and a combination of case elements. In *Proceedings of the 21st International Conference on Computational Linguistics and 44th Annual Meeting of the Association for Computational Linguistics*, Association for Computational Linguistics, Sydney, pp. 833–840.

Boros, M., W. Eckert, F. Gallwitz, G. Görz, G. Hanrieder, and H. Niemann (1996). Towards understanding spontaneous speech: word accuracy vs. concept accuracy. In *Proceedings of the 4th International Conference on Spoken Language Processing (ICSLP 96)*, Philadelphia, PA, pp. 1009–1012.

Bouma, G. and G. Kloosterman (2002). Querying dependency treebanks in XML. In *Proceedings of the 3rd International Conference on Language Resources and Evaluation (LREC)*, Gran Canaria, pp. 1686–1691.

Bouma, G. and G. Kloosterman (2007). Mining syntactically annotated corpora using XQuery. In *Proceedings of the Linguistic Annotation Workshop, Proceedings of the Linguistic Annotation Workshop (ACL'07)*, Prague, pp. 17–24.

Briscoe, T., J. Carroll, J. Graham, and A. Copestake (2002). Relational evaluation schemes. In *Proceedings of the Beyond PARSEVAL Workshop at the 3rd International Conference on Language Resources and Evaluation*, Las Palmas, Gran Canaria, pp. 4–8.

Church, K.W., W.A. Gale, P. Hanks, and D. Hindle (1989). Parsing, word association and typical predicate argument relations. In *Proceedings of the 1st International Workshop on Parsing Technologies (IWPT '89)*, Carnegie Mellon University, Pittsburg, PA, pp. 389–398.

Church, K.W. and P. Hanks (1990). Word association norms, mutual information and lexicography. *Computational Linguistics 16*(1):22–29.

Fano, R.M. (1961). *Transmission of Information: A Statistical Theory of Communications*. Cambridge, MA: MIT Press.

Gamallo, P., A. Agustini, and G.P. Lopes (2003). Learning subcategorisation information to model a grammar with "co-restrictions". *TAL 44*(1):93–117.

Hoekstra, H., M. Moortgat, B. Renmans, M. Schouppe, I. Schuurman, and T. van derWouden (2003). CGN Syntactische Annotatie. CGN Internal Project Report, available at http://www.ccl.kuleuven.be/Papers/sa-man.DEF.pdf

Johnson, M. and S. Riezler (2000). Exploiting auxiliary distributions in stochastic unification-based grammars. In *Proceedings of the 1st Conference on North American Chapter of the Association for Computational Linguistics*, Morgan Kaufmann Publishers Inc., San Francisco, CA, pp. 154–161.

Kawahara, D. and S. Kurohashi (2006). A fully-lexicalized probabilistic model for Japanese syntactic and case structure analysis. In *Proceedings of the Main Conference on Human Language Technology Conference of the North American Chapter of the Association of Computational Linguistics*, Association for Computational Linguistics, Morristown, NJ, pp. 176–183.

Kawahara, D. and S. Kurohashi (2008). Coordination disambiguation without any similarities. In *Proceedings of the 22nd International Conference on Computational Linguistics (COLING 2008)*, Manchester, pp. 425–432.

Malouf, R. (2002). A comparison of algorithms for maximum entropy parameter estimation. In *Proceedings of the 6th Conference on Natural Language Learning (CoNLL-2002)*, Taipei, pp. 49–55.

McCarthy, D. (2001). Lexical acquisition at the syntax-semantics interface: diathesis alternations, subcategorization frames and selectional preferences. Ph.D. thesis, University of Sussex.

McClosky, D., E. Charniak, and M. Johnson (2006). Effective self-training for parsing. In *Proceedings of the Human Language Technology Conference of the NAACL, Main Conference*, Association for Computational Linguistics, New York City, NY, pp. 152–159.

Merlo, P. and S. Stevenson (2001). Automatic verb classification based on statistical distributions of argument structure. *Computational Linguistics 27*(3):373–408.

Ordelman, R., F. de Jong, A. van Hessen, and H. Hondorp (2007). TwNC: a multifaceted Dutch news corpus. *ELRA Newsletter 12*(3/4):4–7.

Prins, R. (2005). Finite-state pre-processing for natural language analysis. Ph.D. thesis, University of Groningen.

Resnik, P.S. (1993). Selection and information: a class-based approach to lexical relationships. Ph.D. thesis, University of Pennsylvania, Philadelphia, PA.

Ribas, F. (1995). On learning more appropriate selectional restrictions. In *Proceedings of the 7th Conference on European Chapter of the Association for Computational Linguistics*, Morgan Kaufmann Publishers Inc., San Francisco, CA, pp. 112–118, DOI http://dx.doi.org/10.3115/976973.976990

Schulte im Walde, S. (2009). The induction of verb frames and verb classes from corpora. In A. Lüdeling and M. Kytö (Eds.), *Corpus Linguistics. An International Handbook*. Berlin: Mouton de Gruyter.

van Noord, G. (2006). At last parsing is now operational. In *TALN 2006, Actes de la 13e Conference sur le Traitement Automatique des Langues Naturelles*, Leuven, pp. 20–42.

van Noord, G. and R. Malouf (2005). Wide coverage parsing with stochastic attribute value grammars, draft available from http://www.let.rug.nl/˜vannoord. A preliminary version of this paper was published in the *Proceedings of the IJCNLP Workshop Beyond Shallow Analyses*, Hainan, 2004.

van Noord, G., I. Schuurman, and V. Vandeghinste (2006). Syntactic annotation of large corpora in STEVIN. In *Proceedings of the 5th International Conference on Language Resources and Evaluation (LREC)*, Genoa.

Whittemore, G., K. Ferrara, and H. Brunner (1990). Empirical study of predictive powers of simple attachment schemes for post-modifier prepositional phrases. In *Proceedings of the 28th Annual Meeting of the Association for Computational Linguistics*, Association for Computational Linguistics, Pittsburgh, PA, pp. 23–30, DOI 10.3115/981823.981827.

Chapter 12
Are Very Large Context-Free Grammars Tractable?

Pierre Boullier and Benoît Sagot

12.1 Introduction

More and more often, in real-word natural language processing (NLP) applications based upon grammars, these grammars are no longer written by hand, but are automatically generated. This chapter will consider one of the consequences of this state of affairs: the generated grammars may be very large. Indeed, we aim to deal with grammars that might have over a million symbol occurrences and several hundred thousands rules. Traditional parsers are not usually prepared to handle them, either because these grammars are simply too big (the parser's internal structures blow up) or the time spent to analyze a sentence becomes prohibitive.

This chapter will concentrate on context-free grammars (CFG) and their associated parsers. However, virtually all Tree Adjoining Grammars (TAG, see for example Schabes, Abeillé, and Joshi (1988)) used in NLP applications can (almost) be seen as lexicalized Tree Insertion Grammars (TIG). Therefore, they can be converted into strongly equivalent CFGs (Schabes and Waters, 1995). Hence, the parsing techniques and tools described here can be applied to most TAGs used in NLP.[1] This is indeed what we have achieved with a TAG automatically extracted from Villemonte de La Clergerie (2005)'s large-coverage factorized French TAG, as we will see in Section 12.4. In fact, even (some kinds of) non CFGs may benefit from the ideas described in this chapter.

The reason why the run-time of context-free (CF) parsers for large CFGs is degraded relies on a theoretical result. It is well known that CF parsers may reach a worst-case running time of $\mathcal{O}(|G| \times n^3)$ where $|G|$ is the *size* of the CFG and n is the *length* of the source text. (These two notions will be defined precisely later on.) Typical NLP applications mainly work at the sentence level. For French, English

P. Boullier (✉)
INRIA-Rocquencourt, Domaine de Voluceau, 78153 Le Chesnay Cedex, France
e-mail: pierre.boullier@inria.fr

[1] In the general case, the original TAG cannot be considered as a TIG and therefore converted into a strongly equivalent CFG. However, an over-generating TIG can be trivially extracted from the TAG. Parsing with the corresponding CFG, using if necessary the techniques described in this chapter, provides an efficient guide to the TAG parser, in the sense of Boullier (2003).

H. Bunt et al. (eds.), *Trends in Parsing Technology*, Text, Speech and Language Technology 43, DOI 10.1007/978-90-481-9352-3_12,

and similar languages, the length of a sentence does not often exceed a value of say 100, while its average length is around 20–30 words. In these conditions, the size of the grammar, despite its linear impact on the complexity, may be the prevailing factor. This idea goes back to the early 80s (Berwick and Weinberg, 1984). More recently, it has been pointed out by Joshi (1997), who remarks that "the real limiting factor in practice is the size of the grammar".

The idea developed in this chapter is to split the parsing process in two passes. A first pass called *filtering* pass computes the sub-grammar of the large input grammar selected by the input sentence and various filtering strategies. The second pass is a traditional parser which works with the sub-grammar and the input sentence. The purpose is to find a filtering strategy which, in typical practical situations, minimizes on average the total run-time of the filtering pass followed by the parsing pass.

A filtering pass may be seen as a (filtering) function that uses the input sentence to select a sub-grammar out of a large input CFG. Our hope, using such a filter, is that the time saved by the parser pass which uses a (smaller) sub-grammar will not totally be used up by the filter pass to generate this sub-grammar. It must be clear that this method cannot improve the worst-case parse-time because there exists grammars for which the sub-grammar selected by the filtering pass is the input grammar itself. In such a case, the filtering pass is simply a waste of time. Our purpose in this chapter is to argue that this technique may take advantage of typical grammars used in NLP. To do that we put aside the theoretical point of view and we will consider instead the average behaviour of our processors. More precisely, we will study the behaviour of our filtering strategies on a set of test sentences in two large NLP CFGs. The purpose of this investigation is to choose the *best* filtering strategy, if any. By best, we mean the one which, on the average, minimizes the total run-time of both the filtering pass followed by the parsing pass.

Useful formal notions and notations are recalled in Section 12.2. The filtering strategies are presented in Section 12.3 while the associated experiments are reported in Section 12.4. This chapter ends with some concluding remarks in Section 12.5.

12.2 Preliminaries

This section sums up basic notions and notations that we will use throughout this chapter. We focus successively on CFGs, on finite-state automata, on directed acyclic graphs (DAGs) that will be used as parser input, and on an algorithm for computing the reduced form of a CFG.

12.2.1 Context-Free Grammars

A CFG G is a quadruple (N, T, P, S) where N is a non-empty finite set of *nonterminal symbols*, T is a finite set of *terminal symbols*, P is a finite set of (context-free rewriting) *rules* (or *productions*) and S is a distinguished nonterminal symbol called the *axiom*. The sets N and T are disjoint and $V = N \cup T$ is the *vocabulary*. The rules in P have the form $A \to \alpha$, with $A \in N$ and $\alpha \in V^*$.

For a given string $\alpha \in V^*$, its size (length) is noted $|\alpha|$. As an example, for the input string $w = a_1 \cdots a_n$, $a_i \in T$, we have $|w| = n$. The empty string is denoted ε and we have $|\varepsilon| = 0$. The *size* $|G|$ of a CFG G is defined by $|G| = \sum_{A \to \alpha \in P} |A\alpha|$.

For G, on strings of V^*, we define the binary relation *derive*, noted $\Rightarrow$, by $\gamma_1 A \gamma_2 \overset{A \to \alpha}{\underset{G}{\Rightarrow}} \gamma_1 \alpha \gamma_2$ if $A \to \alpha \in P$ and $\gamma_1, \gamma_2 \in V^*$. The subscript G or even the superscript $A \to \alpha$ may be omitted. As usual, its transitive (resp. reflexive transitive) closure is noted $\overset{+}{\underset{G}{\Rightarrow}}$ (resp. $\overset{*}{\underset{G}{\Rightarrow}}$). We call *derivation* any sequence of the form $\gamma_1 \underset{G}{\Rightarrow} \cdots \underset{G}{\Rightarrow} \gamma_2$. A *complete derivation* is a derivation which starts with the axiom and ends with a terminal string w. In that case we have $S \overset{*}{\underset{G}{\Rightarrow}} \gamma \overset{*}{\underset{G}{\Rightarrow}} w$, and γ is a *sentential form*.

The *string language* defined (generated, recognized) by G is the set of all the terminal strings that can be derived from the axiom: $\mathcal{L}(G) = \{w \mid S \overset{+}{\underset{G}{\Rightarrow}} w, w \in T^*\}$. We say that a CFG is empty if and only if its language is empty.

A nonterminal symbol A is *nullable* if and only if it can derive the empty string (i.e., $A \overset{+}{\underset{G}{\Rightarrow}} \varepsilon$). A CFG is *$\varepsilon$-free* if and only if its nonterminal symbols are non-nullable.

A CFG is *reduced* if and only if every symbol of every production is a symbol of at least one complete derivation. A reduced grammar is empty if and only if its production set is empty ($P = \emptyset$). We say that a non-empty reduced grammar is in *canonical form* if and only if its vocabulary only contains symbols that appear in the productions of P.[2] Note that the pair (P, S) completely defines a reduced CFG $G = (N, T, P, S)$ in canonical form since we have $N = \{X_0 \mid X_0 \to \alpha \in P\} \cup \{S\}$, $T = \{X_i \mid X_0 \to X_1 \cdots X_p \in P \wedge 1 \le i \le p\} \setminus N$. Thus, in what follows, we often note simply $G = (P, S)$ grammars in canonical form.

Two CFGs G and G' are *weakly equivalent* if and only if they generate the same string language. They are *strongly equivalent* if and only if they generate the same set of structural descriptions (i.e., parse trees). It is a well known result (see Section 12.2.4) that every CFG G can be transformed in time linear with respect to $|G|$ into a strongly equivalent (canonical) reduced CFG G'.

For a given input string $w \in T^*$, we define its *ranges* as the set $R^w = \{[i..j] \mid 1 \le i \le j \le |w| + 1\}$. If $w = w_1 t w_3 \in T^*$ is a terminal string, and if $t \in T \cup \{\varepsilon\}$ is a (terminal or empty) symbol, the *instantiation* of t in w is the triple noted $t[i..j]$ where $[i..j]$ is a range with $i = |w_1| + 1$ and $j = i + |t|$. More generally, the *instantiation* of the terminal string w_2 in $w_1 w_2 w_3$ is noted $w_2[i..j]$ with $i = |w_1| + 1$ and $j = i + |w_2|$. Obviously, the instantiation of w itself is then $w[1..1 + |w|]$.

---

[2] We may say that the canonical form of the empty reduced grammar is $(\{S\}, \emptyset, \emptyset, S)$ though the axiom S does not appear in any production.

Let us consider an input string $w = w_1w_2w_3$ and a CFG G. If we have a complete derivation $d = S \overset{*}{\underset{G}{\Rightarrow}} w_1Aw_3 \overset{A\to\alpha}{\underset{G}{\Rightarrow}} w_1\alpha w_3 \overset{*}{\underset{G}{\Rightarrow}} w_1w_2w_3$, we see that A derives w_2 (we have $A \overset{+}{\underset{G}{\Rightarrow}} w_2$). Moreover, in this complete derivation, we also know a range in R^w, namely $[i..j]$, which covers the substring w_2 which is derived by A ($i = |w_1|+1$ and $j = i + |w_2|$). This defines an *instantiated nonterminal symbol* that we denote by $A[i..j]$. In fact, each symbol which appears in a complete derivation may be transformed into its instantiated counterpart. We thus talk of instantiated productions or (complete) instantiated derivations. For a given input text w, and a CFG G, let P_G^w be the set of instantiated productions that appears in all complete instantiated derivations. For example, in the previous complete derivation d, let the right-hand side α be the (vocabulary) string $X_1 \cdots X_k \cdots X_p$ in which each symbol X_k derives the terminal string $x_k \in T^*$ (we have $X_k \overset{*}{\underset{G}{\Rightarrow}} x_k$ and $w_2 = x_1 \cdots x_k \cdots x_p$), then the instantiated production $A[i_0..i_p] \to X_1[i_0..i_1] \cdots X_k[i_{k-1}..i_k] \cdots X_p[i_{p-1}..i_p]$ with $i_0 = |w_1| + 1$, $i_1 = i_0 + |x_1|, \ldots, i_k = i_{k-1} + |x_k| \ldots$ and $i_p = i_0 + |w_2|$ is an element of P_G^w. The pair $(P_G^w, S[1..1 + |w|])$ is a CFG in canonical form called *shared parse forest*.[3]

12.2.2 Finite-State Automata

A *finite-state automaton* (FSA) is the 5-tuple $A = (Q, \Sigma, \delta, q_0, F)$ where Q is a non-empty finite set of *states*, Σ is a finite set of *terminal symbols*, δ is the transition relation $\delta = \{(q_i, t, q_j) \mid q_i, q_j \in Q \wedge t \in \Sigma \cup \{\varepsilon\}\}$, q_0 is a distinguished element of Q called the *initial state* and F is a subset of Q whose elements are called *final states*. The size of A is defined by $|A| = |\delta|$.

As usual, we define a *configuration* as an element of $Q \times \Sigma^*$ and *derive* a binary relation between configurations, noted $\underset{A}{\vdash}$, by $(q, tx) \underset{A}{\vdash} (q', x)$ if and only if $(q, t, q') \in \delta$. If $w'w'' \in \Sigma^*$, we call *derivation* any sequence of the form $(q', w'w'') \underset{A}{\vdash} \cdots \underset{A}{\vdash} (q'', w'')$. If $w \in \Sigma^*$, the *initial configuration* c_0 is the pair (q_0, w). A *final configuration* c_f has the form (q_f, ε) with $q_f \in F$. A *complete derivation* is a derivation which starts with c_0 and ends in a final configuration c_f. In that case we have $c_0 \overset{*}{\underset{A}{\vdash}} c_f$.

The *language* $\mathcal{L}(A)$ *defined* (*generated*, *recognized*) by the FSA A is the set of all terminal strings for which there exists a complete derivation. We say that an FSA is empty if and only if its language is empty. Two FSAs A and A' are *equivalent* if and only if they define the same language.

---

[3] The popular notion of shared forest mainly comes from Billot and Lang (1989). This notion generalizes straight-forwardly, when the input sentence, as assumed below, is not a linear string but a word DAG (see Section 12.2.3).

An FSA is *ε-free* if and only if its transition relation has the form $\delta = \{(q_i, t, q_j) \mid q_i, q_j \in Q, t \in \Sigma\}$, except perhaps for a distinguished transition, the *ε-transition* which has the form $(q_0, \varepsilon, q_f), q_f \in F$ and allows the empty string ε to be in $\mathcal{L}(A)$.[4] Every FSA can be transformed into an equivalent ε-free FSA.

An FSA $A = (Q, \Sigma, \delta, q_0, F)$ is *reduced* if and only if each element of δ appears in at least one complete derivation of at least one string $w \in \mathcal{L}(A)$. A reduced FSA is empty if and only if we have $\delta = \emptyset$. We say that a non-empty reduced FSA is in *canonical form* if and only if its set of states Q and its set of terminal symbols Σ only contain elements that appear in the transition relation δ.[5] It is a well known result that every FSA A can be transformed in time linear with $|A|$ into an equivalent (canonical) reduced FSA A'.

12.2.3 Input Strings and Input DAGs

In many NLP applications the source text cannot be considered as a (linear) string of terminal symbols, but rather it must be considered as a finite set of terminal strings, so as to encode not-yet-solved ambiguities in the input.[6] These sets are finite languages which can be defined by particular FSAs. These FSAs are called *directed-acyclic graphs* (DAGs). Informally, DAGs are FSAs that do not contain any loop. Therefore, all states of a DAG can be ordered in such a way that for every transition (i, t, j), the statement $i < j$ holds.

Formally, a DAG $w = (Q, \Sigma, \delta, q_0, F)$ is an FSA that satisfies the following constraints. The set Q of its states is a contiguous interval of positive integers: $Q = \{i \mid 1 \leq i \leq |Q|\}$. The initial state q_0 is 1, while the state $f = |Q|$ is the *only* final state in F.[7] We request that the initial state and the final state are distinct ($|Q| > 1$, and $\delta \neq \emptyset$), unless the DAG is the empty DAG. Without any loss of generality, it can be assumed that each transition $(i, t, j) \in \delta$ is such that $i < j$. Moreover, we will assume that DAGs are ε-free reduced FSAs in canonical form.[8] Any DAG w is fully described (and will be denoted) by the triple (Σ, δ, f), since its initial state is always 1 and its set of states is $Q = \{i \mid 1 \leq i \leq f\}$. In fact, w is fully described by δ only, since $\Sigma = \{t \neq \varepsilon \mid (i, t, j) \in \delta\}$ and $f = \max_{(i,t,j)\in\delta} j$.

---

[4] Instead of the classical definition without ε-transitions, we have chosen this definition for compatibility with our definition of ε-free DAGs (see Section 12.2.3). This difference in definitions has no impact on non-empty strings.

[5] We may say that the canonical form of the empty reduced FSA is $(\{q_0\}, \emptyset, \emptyset, q_0, \emptyset)$ though the initial state q_0 does not appear in any transition.

[6] This is particularly relevant in contexts such as speech processing, lexical ambiguity representation, ambiguous spelling correction, and others.

[7] This constraint is not included in the usual definition of DAGs, but it does not decrease their expressive power. It has some drawbacks that we shall not discuss here, but allows us to generalize usual parsing algorithms to DAGs with virtually no effort, as described in the remainder of this section.

[8] Where "ε-free" is to be understood according to the definition given above; if ε is in the language, the transition $(1, \varepsilon, f)$ is in δ.

For a given CFG $G = (N, T, P, S)$, the recognition of an input DAG $w = (\Sigma, \delta, f)$ is equivalent to the emptiness of its intersection with G. This problem can be solved in time linear in $|G|$ and cubic in f. In what follows, we assume that $\Sigma \subset T$.

If the input text is a DAG, the previous notions of range, instantiation and parse forest easily generalize: the subscripts i and j, which in the case of strings locate the positions of substrings, are changed in the DAG case into DAG states. For example, if $A[i_0..i_p] \to X_1[i_0..i_1] \cdots X_p[i_{p-1}..i_p]$ is an instantiated production of the parse forest for $G = (N, T, P, S)$ and $w = (\Sigma, \delta, f)$, we have $A \to X_1 \cdots X_p \in P$ and there is a path in the input DAG from state i_0 to state i_p through states $i_1, \ldots, i_{p-1}$.

Of course, any nonempty terminal string $w \in T^+$ may be viewed as a DAG (Σ, δ, f) where $\Sigma = \{t \mid w = w_1 t w_2 \wedge t \in T\}$, $\delta = \{(i, t, i+1) \mid w = w_1 t w_2 \wedge t \in T \wedge i = 1 + |w_1|\}$ and $f = 1 + |w|$. If the input string w is the empty string ε, the associated DAG is (Σ, δ, f) where $\Sigma = \emptyset$, $\delta = \{(1, \varepsilon, 2)\}$ and $f = 2$. Thus, in the rest of the chapter, we will assume that the inputs of our parsers are not strings but DAGs. As a consequence the size (or *length*) of a sentence is the size of its DAG (i.e., its number of transitions).

12.2.4 The Make-a-Reduced-Grammar *Algorithm*

An algorithm which takes as input any CFG $G = (N, T, P, S)$ and generates as output a strongly equivalent *reduced* CFG G' and which runs in $\mathcal{O}(|G|)$ can be found in many text books. (See Hopcroft and Ullman (1979) for example.) So as to eliminate from all our intermediate sub-grammars all useless productions, each filtering strategy will end by a call to such an algorithm, named *make-a-reduced-grammar*.

Usually, a symbol $X \in V$ is *productive* if and only if $X \overset{*}{\underset{G}{\Rightarrow}} w, w \in T^*$. A symbol $X \in V$ is *reachable* if and only if $S \overset{*}{\underset{G}{\Rightarrow}} w_1 X w_2, w_1 w_2 \in T^*$. A symbol is *useful* (otherwise *useless*) if it is both productive and reachable. A production $A \to X_1 \cdots X_p$ is *useful* (otherwise *useless*) if and only if all its symbols are useful.

The *make-a-reduced-grammar* algorithm works as follows. It first finds all productive symbols. Next, it finds all reachable symbols. A last scan over the grammar identifies and erases all useless productions, leaving the reduced form. The *canonical form* is reached by only retaining in the nonterminal and terminal sets of the sub-grammar the symbols which occur in the (useful) production set.

12.3 Filtering Strategies

This section introduces various strategies, or *filters* f, that can be used, given an input DAG w, to transform a CFG G into a smaller one called G_w^f (or G^f if the input w is implicit). The set of complete derivations of w according to both grammars is the same (any production used in at least one of w's derivations according to G has to be kept in G^f). We suppose that f uses the *make-a-reduced-grammar* algorithm, so that G^f is always a reduced CFG.

Filters can be used in sequence. Therefore, the input of a filter f is always a pair (G^σ, w), where $G^\sigma = (P^\sigma, S)$ is a reduced CFG in canonical form which has already been filtered by a previous (possibly empty) sequence σ of strategies. The filter f generates a reduced CFG in canonical form noted $G^{\sigma f} = (P^{\sigma f}, S)$. Of course it may happen that $G^{\sigma f}$ is identical to G^σ if the f-filter is not effective. A filtering strategy or a sequence of filtering strategies may be applied several times and lead to a filtered grammar of the form say G^{ba^2da} in which the sequence ba^2da makes explicit the order in which the filtering strategies b, a and d have been applied. We may even repeatedly apply a until a fixed point is reached before applying d, and thus obtain a grammar of the form $G^{ba^\infty d}$.

We are interested in (sequences of) strategies σ that are *time-optimal. Size-optimal* (sequences of) strategies σ (in the sense that P_w^σ is of minimal size) are not necessarily also time-optimal: the time taken at filtering-time to obtain a smaller grammar will not necessarily be won back at parse-time.

For a given CFG, a given input DAG and a given filtering strategy, we only have to plot both the runtimes of the filtering pass (the chosen sequence of filters) and the parsing pass to make some estimations on their average (median, decile) parse times, and then to decide which is the winner. However, these results do not necessarily apply to a new data-set: a strategy which was not considered the best with the sample of CFGs and the test sets tried could be the winner in another context.

12.3.1 Gold Strategy: g-Filter

Let $G = (N, T, P, S)$ be a CFG, $w = (\Sigma, \delta, f)$ be an input DAG of size $n = |\delta|$ and $\langle F_w \rangle = (\langle P_w \rangle, S[1..f])$ be the reduced output parse forest in canonical form. From $\langle P_w \rangle$, it is possible to extract a set of (reduced) uninstantiated productions $P_w^g = \{A \to X_1 \cdots X_p \mid A[i_0..i_p] \to X_1[i_0..i_1]\, X_2[i_1..i_2] \cdots X_p[i_{p-1}..i_p] \in \langle P_w \rangle\}$, which, together with the axiom S, defines a new reduced CFG $G_w^g = (P_w^g, S)$ in canonical form. This grammar is called the *gold* grammar of G for w, hence the superscript g. Now, if we use G_w^g to reparse the same input DAG w, we will get the same output forest $\langle F_w \rangle$. But in that case, we are sure that every production in P_w^g is used in at least one complete derivation. Now, if this process is viewed as a filtering strategy that computes a filtering function as introduced above, it is clear that this strategy is size-optimal, we call it the *gold* strategy and the associated gold filtering function is noted g.

Since, by definition, a filtering strategy cannot lose parses, the result $G_w^f = (P_w^f, S)$ of any filter f on any input w must be such that P_w^f is a superset of P_w^g. In other words, the *recall score* of any filtering function f must be 100%. This means that the parsing pass, which generates G_w^g, may be preceded by any filtering strategy f, making parsing (i.e., computing P_w^g) possible even with very large grammars.

The *precision score* (precision for short) of a filtering strategy f is defined in the usual way. For a given w, it is defined by the quotient $\frac{|P_w^g|}{|P_w^f|}$ which expresses the proportion of useful productions selected by f on w (for some G).

12.3.2 Basic Filtering Strategy: b-Filter

The basic filtering strategy (b-filter for short) which is described in this section will always be applied first. Thus, its input is the pair (G, w) where $G = (N, T, P, S)$ is the large initial CFG and the input w is a reduced DAG in canonical form $w = (\Sigma, \delta, f)$ of size n. The b-filter generates a reduced CFG in canonical form referred to as $G^b = (P^b, S)$, in which the reference to w is assumed.

The idea behind the b-filter is very simple and has been used widely in parsing with lexicalized formalisms, in particular in LTAG parsing (Schabes et al., 1988). The b-filter rejects productions of P which contain terminal symbols that do not occur in Σ (i.e., that are not terminal symbols of the DAG w) and thus takes $\mathcal{O}(|G|)$ time, if we assume that the access to the elements of the terminal set Σ is performed in constant time. *Unlexicalized* productions whose right-hand sides are in N^* are kept. Our b-filter also rejects productions in which several terminal symbols occur in an order which is not compatible with their ordering in w.

Consider for example the set of productions shown in Table 12.1 and assume that the source text is the terminal string ab. The b-filter will erase production 6, since c is not in the source text.

The execution of the b-filter produces a (non-reduced) CFG G' such that $|G'| \leq |G|$. However, it may be the case that some productions of G' are useless; it will thus be the task of the *make-a-reduced-grammar* algorithm to transform G' into its reduced canonical form G^b in time $\mathcal{O}(|G'|)$. The worst-case total running time of the whole b-filter pass is thus $\mathcal{O}(|G| \times n)$. We can notice that, after the execution of the b-filter, the set of terminal symbols of G^b is a subset of $T \cap \Sigma$.

Table 12.1 A simple grammar

$S \to AB$	(1)
$S \to BA$	(2)
$A \to a$	(3)
$A \to ab$	(4)
$B \to b$	(5)
$B \to bc$	(6)

12.3.3 Adjacent Filtering Strategy: a-Filter

As explained before, we assume that the input to the adjacent filtering strategy (a-filter for short) described in this section is a pair (G^c, w) where $G^c = (N^c, T^c, P^c, S)$ is a reduced CFG in canonical form. However, the a-filter would also work for a non-reduced CFG. As usual, we define the symbols of G^c as the elements of the vocabulary $V^c = N^c \cup T^c$.

The goal is to erase productions that cannot be part of any parses for w in using an adjacency criterion: if two symbols are adjacent in a rule, they must derive terminal symbols that are also adjacent in w. To give a (very) simple practical idea of what we mean by adjacency criterion, let us consider again the source string ab and the grammar defined in Table 12.1 in which the last production has already been erased by the b-filter. The fact that the B-production ends with a b, and that the A-productions all start with an a implies that production 2 is in a complete parse only if the source text is such that a b is immediately followed by an a. Since this is not the case, production 2 can be erased.

More generally, consider a production of the form $A \to \cdots XY \cdots$. If for each pair $(a, b) \in T^2$ in which a is a terminal symbol that can terminate (the terminal strings generated by) X and b is a terminal symbol that can lead (the terminal strings generated by) Y, there is no transition on b that can follow a transition on a in the DAG w, it is clear that the production $A \to \cdots XY \cdots$ can be safely erased. Now assume that we have the following (left) derivation

$$Y \stackrel{*}{\Rightarrow} Y_1\beta_1 \stackrel{*}{\Rightarrow} Y_i\beta_i \cdots \beta_1 \stackrel{*}{\Rightarrow} \cdots \stackrel{Y_{p-1}\to\alpha_p Y_p\beta_p}{\Rightarrow} \alpha_p Y_p \beta_p \cdots \beta_1$$
$$\stackrel{*}{\Rightarrow} Y_p\beta_p \cdots \beta_1,$$

with $\alpha_p \stackrel{*}{\Rightarrow} \varepsilon$. If for each pair (a, b') in which a has the previous definition and b' is a terminal symbol that can lead (the terminal strings generated by) Y_p, there is no transition on b' that can follow a transition on a in the DAG w, the production $Y_{p-1} \to \alpha_p Y_p \beta_p$ can be erased if it is not valid in another context. Moreover, consider a (right) derivation of the form

$$X \stackrel{*}{\Rightarrow} \alpha_1 X_1 \stackrel{*}{\Rightarrow} \alpha_1 \cdots \alpha_i X_i \stackrel{*}{\Rightarrow} \cdots \stackrel{X_{p-1}\to\alpha_p X_p\beta_p}{\Rightarrow} \alpha_1 \cdots \alpha_p X_p \beta_p$$
$$\stackrel{*}{\Rightarrow} \alpha_1 \cdots \alpha_p X_p,$$

with $\beta_p \stackrel{*}{\Rightarrow} \varepsilon$. If for each pair (a', b) in which b has the previous definition and a' is a terminal symbol that can terminate (the terminal strings generated by) X_p, there is no transition on b that can follow a transition on a' in the DAG w, the production $X_{p-1} \to \alpha_p X_p \beta_p$ can be erased, if it is not valid in another context.

In order to formalize these notions we define several binary relations together with their (reflexive) transitive closure. Within a CFG $G = (N, T, P, S)$, we first define *left-corner* noted $\llcorner$. Left-corner hereafter *LC*, is a well-known relation since many parsing strategies are based upon it (Nederhof, 1993; Moore, 2000). We say that X is in the LC of A and we write $A \llcorner X$ if and only if $(A, X) \in \{(B, Y) \mid B \to$

$\alpha Y\beta \in P \wedge \alpha \underset{G}{\overset{*}{\Rightarrow}} \varepsilon\}$. We can write $A \underset{A\to\alpha X\beta}{\llcorner} X$ to enforce how the pair (A, X) may be produced.

For its dual relation, *right-corner*, noted $\lrcorner$, we say that X is the right corner of A and we write $X \lrcorner A$ if and only if $(X, A) \in \{(Y, B) \mid B \to \alpha Y\beta \in P \wedge \beta \underset{G}{\overset{*}{\Rightarrow}} \varepsilon\}$. We can write $X \underset{A\to\alpha X\beta}{\lrcorner} A$ to enforce how the pair (X, A) may be produced.

We also define the *first* (resp. *last*) relation noted $\hookrightarrow_t$ (resp. $\hookleftarrow_t$) by:

$$\hookrightarrow_t = \{(X, t) \mid X \in V \wedge t \in T \wedge X \underset{G}{\overset{*}{\Rightarrow}} tx \wedge x \in T^*\}$$
$$\text{resp. } \hookleftarrow_t = \{(X, t) \mid X \in V \wedge t \in T \wedge X \underset{G}{\overset{*}{\Rightarrow}} xt \wedge x \in T^*\}.$$

We define the *adjacent* ternary relation on $V \times N^* \times V$ noted $\leftrightarrow$ and we write $X \overset{\sigma}{\leftrightarrow} Y$ if and only if $(X, \sigma, Y) \in \{(U, \beta, V) \mid A \to \alpha U\beta V\gamma \in P \wedge \beta \underset{G}{\overset{*}{\Rightarrow}} \varepsilon\}$. This means that X and Y occur in that order in the right-hand side of some production and are separated by a nullable string σ. Note that X or Y may or may not be nullable.

On the input DAG $w = (\Sigma, \delta, f)$, we define the *immediately precede* relation noted $<$ and we write $a < b$ for $a, b \in \Sigma$ if and only if $w_1abw_3 \in \mathcal{L}(w)$, $w_1, w_3 \in \Sigma^*$.

We also define the *precede* relation noted $\ll$ and we write $a \ll b$ for $a, b \in \Sigma$ if and only if $w_1aw_2bw_3 \in \mathcal{L}(w)$, $w_1, w_2, w_3 \in \Sigma^*$. We can note that $\ll$ is not the transitive closure of $<$. For example, consider the source string $bcab$ for which we have $a \overset{+}{<} c$, but not $a \ll c$.

For each production $A \to \alpha X_0X_1 \cdots X_{p-1}X_p\gamma$ in P^c and for each symbol pairs (X_0, X_p) of non-nullable symbols s.t. $X_1 \cdots X_{p-1} \underset{G^c}{\overset{*}{\Rightarrow}} \varepsilon$, we compute two sets A_1 and A_2 of pairs (a, b), $a, b \in T^c$ defined by

$$A_1 = \cup_{0<i\leq p}\{(a, b) \mid a \hookleftarrow_t X_0 \overset{X_1\cdots X_{i-1}}{\leftrightarrow} X_i \hookrightarrow_t b\}$$
$$\text{and } A_2 = \cup_{0\leq i<p}\{(a, b) \mid a \hookleftarrow_t X_i \overset{X_{i+1}\cdots X_{p-1}}{\leftrightarrow} X_p \hookrightarrow_t b\}.$$

Any pair (a, b) of A_1 is such that the terminal symbol a may terminate a phrase of X_0 while the terminal symbol b may lead a phrase of $X_1 \cdots X_p$. Since X_0 and X_p are not nullable, A_1 is not empty. If none of its elements (a, b) is such that $a < b$, the production $A \to \alpha X_0X_1 \cdots X_{p-1}X_p\gamma$ is useless and can be erased. Analogously, any pair (a, b) of A_2 is such that the terminal symbol a may terminate a phrase of $X_0X_1 \cdots X_{p-1}$ while the terminal symbol b may lead a phrase of X_p. Since X_0 and X_p are not nullable, A_2 is not empty. If none of its elements (a, b) is such that

$a < b$, the production $A \to \alpha X_0 X_1 \cdots X_{p-1} X_p \gamma$ is useless and can be erased. Of course if $X_1 \cdots X_{p-1} = \varepsilon$, we have $A_1 = A_2$.[9]

The previous method has checked some adjacent properties inside the right-hand sides of productions. The following will perform some analogous checks but at the beginning and at the end of the right-hand sides of productions.

Let us go back to Table 12.1 to illustrate our purpose. Recall that, with source text ab, productions 6 and 2 have already been erased. Consider production 4 whose left-hand side is an A, the terminal string ab that it generates ends by b. If we look for the occurrences of A in the right-hand sides of the (remaining) productions, we only find production 1 which indicates that A is followed by B. Since the phrases of B all start with b—see, for example, production 5—and since in the source text b does not immediately follow another b, production 4 can be erased.

In order to check that the input sentence w starts and ends by valid terminal symbols, we augment the adjacent relation with two elements $(\$, \varepsilon, S)$ and $(S, \varepsilon, \$)$ where \$ is a new terminal symbol which is supposed to start and to end every sentence.[10]

Let $Z \to \alpha U \beta$ be a production in P^c in which U is non-nullable and $\alpha \underset{G_c}{\overset{*}{\Rightarrow}} \varepsilon$. If X is a non-nullable symbol, we compute the set

$$L = \{(a, b) \mid a \hookleftarrow_t X \overset{\sigma}{\leftrightarrow} Y \overset{*}{\llcorner} Z \underset{Z \to \alpha U \beta}{\llcorner} U \hookrightarrow_t b\}.$$

Since G^c is reduced and since $\$ < S$, we are sure that the set $X \overset{\sigma}{\leftrightarrow} Y \overset{*}{\llcorner} Z$ is non-empty, thus L is also non-empty.[11]

We can associate with each pair $(a, b) \in L$ at least one (left) derivation of the form

$$\begin{array}{rl} X \sigma Y & \underset{G^c}{\overset{*}{\Rightarrow}} w_0 a w_1 \sigma Y \underset{G^c}{\overset{*}{\Rightarrow}} w_0 a w_1 w_2 Y \underset{G^c}{\overset{*}{\Rightarrow}} w_0 a w_1 w_2 w_3 Z \gamma_2 \\ & \underset{G^c}{\overset{Z \to \alpha U \beta}{\Rightarrow}} w_0 a w_1 w_2 w_3 \alpha U \beta \gamma_2 \underset{G^c}{\overset{*}{\Rightarrow}} w_0 a w_1 w_2 w_3 w_4 U \beta \gamma_2 \\ & \underset{G^c}{\overset{*}{\Rightarrow}} w_0 a w_1 w_2 w_3 w_4 w_5 b \gamma_1 \beta \gamma_2 \end{array}$$

in which $w_1 w_2 w_3 w_4 w_5 \in T^{c*}$. These derivations contains all possible usages of the production $Z \to \alpha U \beta$ in a parse. If for every pair $(a, b) \in L$, the statement $a \ll b$

[9] It can be shown that the previous check can be performed on (G^c, w) in worst-case time $\mathcal{O}(|G^c| \times |\Sigma|^3)$ (recall that $|\Sigma| \leq n$). This time reduces to $\mathcal{O}(|G^c| \times |\Sigma|^2)$ if the input sentence is not a DAG but a string.

[10] This is equivalent to assuming the existence in the grammar of a *super-production* whose right-hand side has the form $\$S\$$.

[11] This statement no longer holds if we exclude from P^c the productions that have been previously erased during the current a-filter. In that case, an empty set indicates that the production $Z \to \alpha U \beta$ can be erased.

does not hold, we can conclude that the production $Z \to \alpha U \beta$ is not used in any parse and can thus be deleted.

Analogously, we can check that the order of terminal symbols is compatible with both a production and its right grammatical context.

Let $Z \to \alpha U \beta$ be a production in P^c in which U is non-nullable and $\beta \overset{*}{\underset{G_c}{\Rightarrow}} \varepsilon$. If Y is a non-nullable symbol, we compute the set

$$R = \{(a, b) \mid a \hookleftarrow_t U \underset{Z \to \alpha U \beta}{\lrcorner} Z \overset{*}{\lrcorner} X \overset{\sigma}{\leftrightarrow} Y \hookrightarrow_t b\}.$$

Since G^c is reduced and since $S < \$$, we are sure that the set $Z \overset{*}{\lrcorner} X \overset{\sigma}{\leftrightarrow} Y$ is non-empty, thus R is also non-empty.[11]

To each pair $(a, b) \in R$ we can associate at least one (right) derivation of the form

$$\begin{aligned}
X\sigma Y &\overset{*}{\underset{G^c}{\Rightarrow}} X\sigma w_1 b w_0 \overset{*}{\underset{G^c}{\Rightarrow}} X w_2 w_1 b w_0 \overset{*}{\underset{G^c}{\Rightarrow}} \gamma_1 Z w_3 w_2 w_1 b w_0 \\
&\overset{Z \to \alpha U \beta}{\underset{G^c}{\Rightarrow}} \gamma_1 \alpha U \beta w_3 w_2 w_1 b w_0 \overset{*}{\underset{G^c}{\Rightarrow}} \gamma_1 \alpha U w_4 w_3 w_2 w_1 b w_0 \\
&\overset{*}{\underset{G^c}{\Rightarrow}} \gamma_1 \alpha \gamma_2 a w_5 w_4 w_3 w_2 w_1 b w_0
\end{aligned}$$

in which $w_5 w_4 w_3 w_2 w_1 \in T^{c*}$. These derivations contains all possible usages of the production $Z \to \alpha U \beta$ in a partial parse. If for every pair $(a, b) \in R$, the statement $a \ll b$ does not hold, we can conclude that the production $Z \to \alpha U \beta$ is not used in any parse and can thus be deleted.

Now, a call to the *make-a-reduced-grammar* algorithm produces a reduced CFG in canonical form named $G^{ca} = (N^{ca}, T^{ca}, P^{ca}, S)$.

12.3.4 Dynamic Set Automaton Filtering Strategy: d-Filter

In Boullier (2003), a method—called *dynamic set automaton* (DSA)—was presented that takes a CFG G and computes a FSA that defines a regular superset of $\mathcal{L}(G)$. However, this method would produce intractably large FSAs. Thus, the method is instead used to compute the FSA dynamically at parse time on a given source text. Based on experimental results, this use of DSA is shown to be tractable. The DSA method is used to *guide* an Earley parser (Earley, 1970) and shows improvements over the non-guided version. The DSA method can also be directly used as a filtering strategy, since the states of the underlying FSA are in fact sets of *items*. For a CFG $G = (N, T, P, S)$, an item (or dotted production) is an element of $\{[A \to \alpha \bullet \beta] \mid A \to \alpha\beta \in P\}$. A *complete* item has the form $[A \to \gamma \bullet]$, it indicates that the production $A \to \gamma$ has been, in some sense, recognized. Thus, the complete items of the DSA states gives the set of productions selected by the DSA. This selection can be further refined if we also use the mirror DSA which processes the source text from right to left and if we only select complete items that both belong to the DSA and to its mirror.

Thus, if we assume that the input to the DSA filtering strategy (d-filter) is a pair (G^c, w) where $G^c = (P^c, S)$ is a reduced CFG in canonical form, we will eventually obtain a set of productions which is a subset of P^c. If it is a strict subset, we then apply the *make-a-reduced-grammar* algorithm which produces a reduced CFG in canonical form named $G^{cd} = (P^{cd}, S)$. Section 12.4 will provide measures that may help compare the practical merits of the a and d-filtering strategies.

12.4 Experiments

We have implemented all filtering strategies presented in the previous section in our CFG parser. This parser is based on an extension of the Earley algorithm (Boullier, 2003), and is part of the SYNTAX parser generator.[12]

We have performed experiments with two large French grammars on a common corpus. We have evaluated our algorithms and implementation thereof in terms of precision and execution time of the filters, and more importantly in terms of global execution time. This allows us to draw preliminary conclusions on the efficiency and usefulness of the filtering strategies described above, and to give an answer to the question raised in the title of this chapter.

12.4.1 Grammars and Corpus

The two large grammars we used for our experiments are described below. The former is an automatically generated CFG, the latter is the CFG equivalent of a TIG automatically extracted from a factorized TAG.

The first grammar, named $G^{T>N}$, is a variant of the CFG backbone of a large-coverage Lexical-Functional Grammar (LFG) grammar for French, used in the French LFG parser described in Boullier and Sagot (2005). In this variant, the set T of terminal symbols is the whole set of French inflected forms present in the *Lefff*, a large-coverage syntactic lexicon for French (Sagot et al. 2006).[13] This leads to as many as 407,863 different terminal symbols and 520,711 lexicalized productions. The average number of categories—which are here non-terminal symbols—for an inflected form is 1.27. Moreover, this CFG entails a non-negligible amount of syntactic constraints, for instance checking of over-generating of sub-categorization frames. This gives rise to as many as $|P_u| = 19,028$ non-lexicalized productions. In total, $G^{T>N}$ has 539,739 productions. It is a highly ambiguous grammar, as shown

[12] The homepage of SYNTAX is http://syntax.gforge.inria.fr/. SYNTAX is freely available at http://gforge.inria.fr/projects/syntax

[13] The name $G^{T>N}$ comes from this construction process: the set T of terminal symbols of the original grammar has been turned into a subset of the non-terminal symbols N.

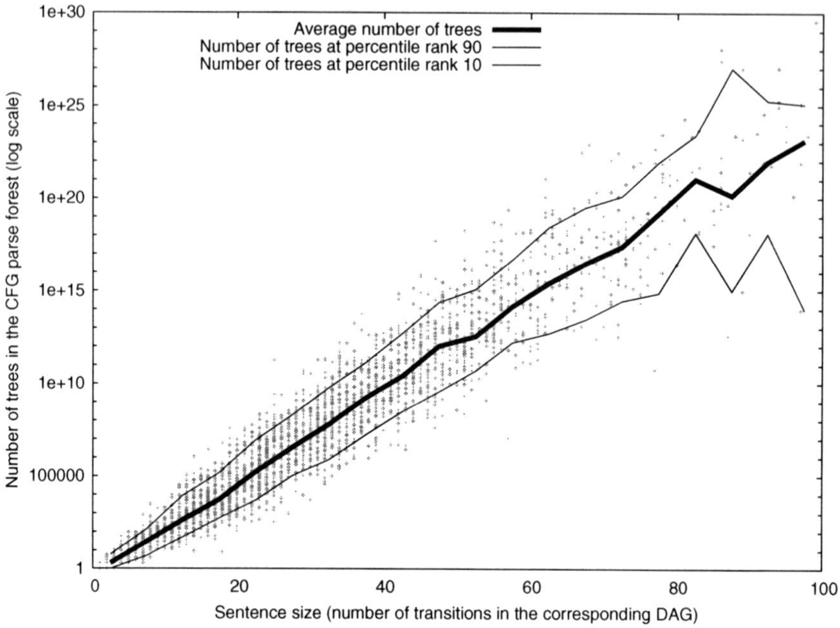

Fig. 12.1 Ambiguity of the $G^{T>N}$ grammar

by Fig. 12.1. This figure plots the number of parses (i.e., the number of trees in the parse forest) for each sentence of the corpus described below, as a function of its size (i.e., the number of transitions in the corresponding DAG). It also indicates the corresponding percentiles, computed on classes of sentences of length $10i$ to $10(i+1)-1$ and plotted with a centered x-coordinate $(10(i+1/2))$.[14] Empirically, it can be observed that the number of trees in the forest grows exponentially with respect to the sentence size.

The second grammar, named G^{TIG}, is a CFG which represents a TIG. To achieve this, we applied Boullier (2000)'s algorithm on the unfolded version of Villemonte de La Clergerie (2005)'s factorized TAG. The number of productions in G^{TIG} is comparable to that of $G^{T>N}$. However, these two grammars are completely different. First, G^{TIG} has many fewer terminal and non-terminal symbols than $G^{T>N}$. This means that the basic filter may be less efficient on G^{TIG} than on $G^{T>N}$.

[14] We use classes of sentences for smoothing purposes: they tackle the sparse data problem that arises when computing medians over sets of sentences of the same length. Indeed, given the modest size of the corpus we used, there are not so many sentences with a same given length, especially for large lengths.

Table 12.2 Sizes of the grammars $G^{T>N}$ and G^{TIG} used in our experiments

G	$\|N\|$	$\|T\|$	$\|P\|$	$\|P_u\|$	$\|G\|$
$G^{T>N}$	7,862	407,863	539,739	19,028	1,123,062
G^{TIG}	448	173	493,408	4,338	12,455,767

Second, the size[15] of G^{TIG} is enormous (more than 10 times that of $G^{T>N}$), which shows that right-hand sides of G^{TIG}'s productions are very large (the average number of right-hand side symbols is over 24). This may increase the usefulness of a- and d-filtering strategies. Global quantitative data about these grammars is shown in Table 12.2.

Both grammars, as mentioned in the introduction, have not been written by hand. On the contrary, they are automatically generated from a more abstract and more compact level:a meta-level over LFG for $G^{T>N}$, and a metagrammar for G^{TIG}. These grammars are not artificial grammars set up only for this experiment; they are very large realistice CFGs and are variants of grammars used in real NLP applications.

Our test suite is a set of 3,093 French journalistic sentences. These sentences are the *general_lemonde* part of the EASy parsing evaluation campaign corpus. Raw sentences have been turned into DAGs of word (more precisely, DAGs of inflected forms) known by both grammar/lexicon pairs.[16] This step has been achieved by the pre-syntactic processing chain SxPipe (Sagot and Boullier, 2005). Approximately 15% of these sentences were not recognized, and required error recovery techniques for one grammar or the other; we decided to discard them for this experiment. Therefore, all remaining sentences are recognized by both grammars. The resulting DAGs have a median size of 28 and an average size of 31.7. Note that the size of a DAG, as defined above, is slightly higher than the number of words (or tokens) of the underlying sentence, because of capitalization and tokenization (multi-word units) ambiguities.

Before going into details, let us give here the first important result of these experiments: it was actually possible to build parsers out of $G^{T>N}$ and G^{TIG} and to parse efficiently with the resulting parsers (we shall provide details on efficiency results later). Given the fact that we are dealing with grammars whose sizes are respectively over 1,000,000 and over 12,000,000, this is in itself a satisfying result.

[15] As already defined in Section 12.2.1, the *size* of a CFG is the number of (terminal or non-terminal) symbol occurrences in the set of all productions of the grammar. For example, a grammar made up of n binary rules has size $3n$.

[16] As seen above, inflected forms are directly terminal symbols of $G^{T>N}$, while G^{TIG} uses a *lexicon* to map these inflected forms into its own terminal symbols, thereby possibly introducing lexical ambiguity.

12.4.2 Precision Results

Let us recall informally that the precision of a filtering strategy is the proportion of productions in the resulting sub-grammar that are in the gold grammar, i.e., that have effectively instantiated counterparts in the final parse forest.

We have applied different strategies so as to compare their precisions. The results on $G^{T>N}$ and G^{TIG} are summarized in Table 12.3. First, as expected, the basic b-filter drastically reduces the size of the grammar. The result is even better on $G^{T>N}$ thanks to its large number of terminal symbols. Second, both the adjacency a-filter and the DSA d-filter efficiently reduce the size of the grammar; on $G^{T>N}$, the a-filter eliminates 20% of the productions it receives as input, a bit less for the d-filter. Indeed, on this test suite, the a-filter performs better than the d-filter introduced in Boullier (2003), at least as precision is concerned. We shall see later that this is still the case on global parsing times. However, applying the d-filter after the a-filter still removes a non-negligible amount of productions: each technique is able to eliminate productions that are kept by the other one. Although not reported here, applying the a before d leads to the same conclusion. The result of these filters is surprisingly good: on average, after all filters, only approximately 20% of the productions that have been kept will not be successfully instantiated in the final parse forest. Third, the adjacency filter can be used in its one-pass mode, since almost all the benefit from the full (fix-point) mode is already reached after the first application. This is practically a very valuable result, since the one-pass mode is obviously faster than the full mode.

However, all these filters do require computing time, and it is necessary to evaluate not only the precision of these filters, but also their execution times as well as the influence they have on the global (including filtering) parsing time.

Table 12.3 Average precision of six different filtering strategies on our test corpus with $G^{T>N}$ and G^{TIG}

	Average precision	
Strategy	$G^{T>N}$(%)	G^{TIG}(%)
No filter	0.04	0.03
b	62.87	39.43
bd	74.53	66.56
ba	77.31	66.94
ba^{∞}	77.48	67.48
bad	80.27	77.16
$ba^{\infty}d$	80.30	77.41
Gold	100	100

12.4.3 Parsing Time and Best Filter

Filter execution times[17] for the six filtering strategies introduced in Table 12.3 are illustrated for $G^{T>N}$ in Fig. 12.2. Percentiles are computed the same way as in Fig. 12.1. These graphs show three valuable pieces of information. First, filtering

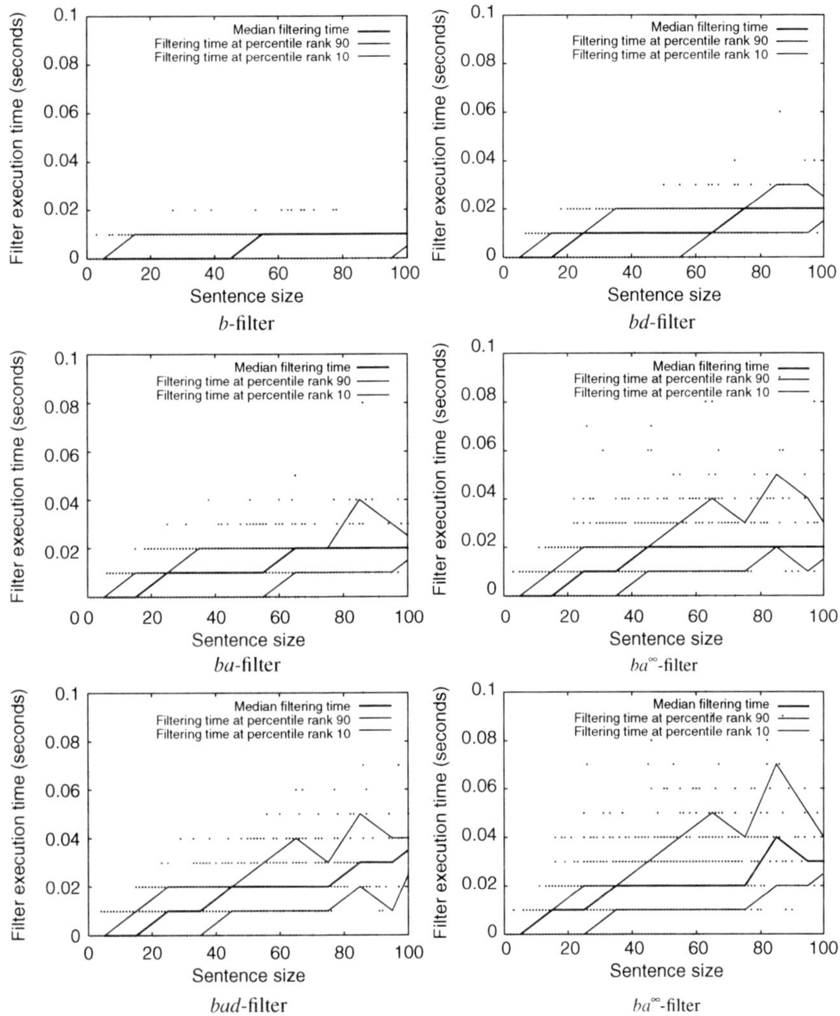

Fig. 12.2 Filtering times for six different strategies with $G^{T>N}$

[17] The measures presented in this section have been taken on a 1.7 GHz AMD Athlon PC with 1.5 Gb of RAM running Linux. All parsers are written in C and have been compiled with gcc 2.96 with the *O2* optimization flag.

times are extremely low: the average filtering time for the slowest filter ($ba^{\infty}d$, i.e., basic plus full adjacency plus DSA) on 40-word sentences is around 20 ms. Second, on small sentences, filtering times are virtually null. This is important, since it means that there is almost no fixed cost to pay when using these filters (let us recall that without any filter, building an efficient parser for such a huge grammar is highly problematic). Third, all these filters, at least when used with $G^{T>N}$, are executed in a time which is *linear* with respect to the size of the input sentence (i.e., the size of the input DAG).

The results on G^{TIG} lead to the same conclusions, with one exception: with this extremely huge grammar with such long right-hand sides, the basic filter is not as fast as on $G^{T>N}$. It is also not as precise, as we will see below. This property slows down the *make-a-reduced-grammar* algorithm, since the algorithm is applied on a larger filtered grammar). For example, the median execution time for the basic filter on sentences whose length is approximately 40 words is 0.25 s, to be compared with the 0.00 s reached on $G^{T>N}$; this zero value indicates a median time strictly lower than 0.01 s, which is the granularity of our time measurements.

Figures 12.3 and 12.4 show the global execution time for the 6 different filters. Global execution time is the sum of filtering and parsing time. We only show median times, computed the same way as in Fig. 12.1, but results with other percentiles or average times on the same classes draw the same overall picture.

One can see that these two figures are completely different from one another, showing a strong dependency on the characteristics of the grammar. In the case

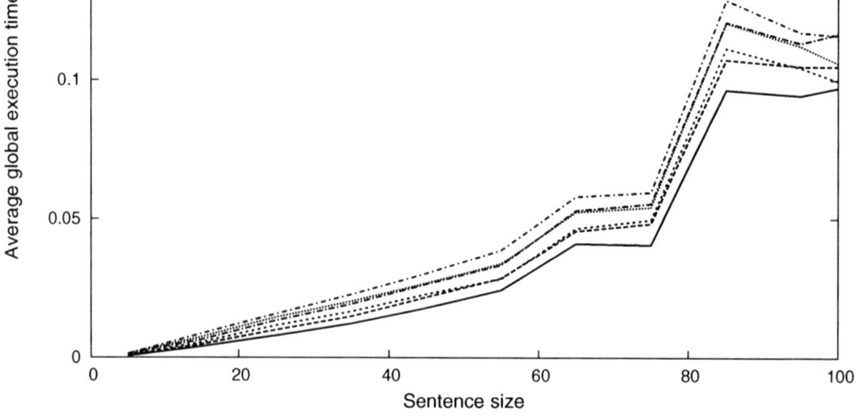

Fig. 12.3 Global (filtering+parsing) times for six different strategies with $G^{T>N}$

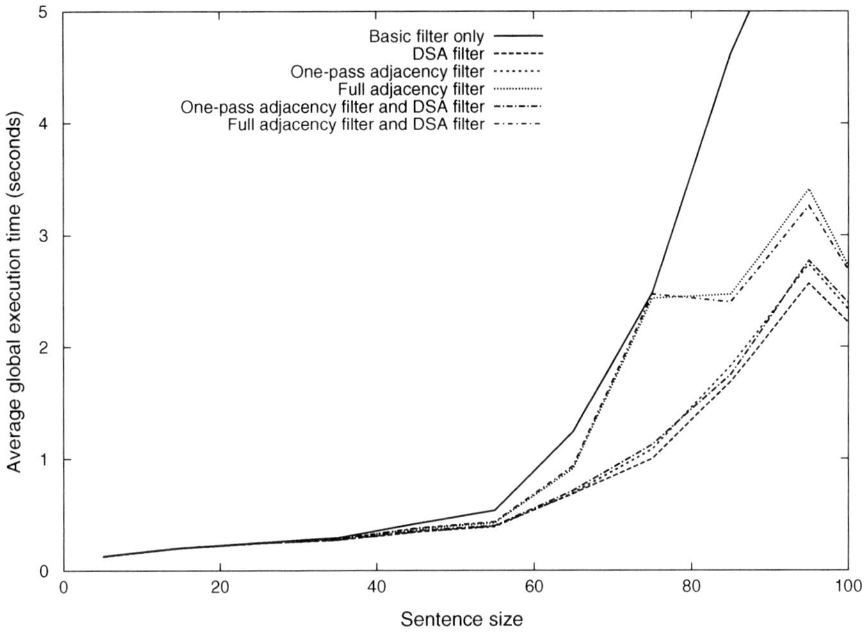

Fig. 12.4 Global (filtering+parsing) times for six different strategies with G^{TIG}

of $G^{T>N}$, the huge number of terminal symbols and the reasonable average size of right-hand sides of productions, the basic filtering strategy is the best strategy: although it is fast because relatively simple, it reduces the grammar extremely efficiently (it has a 60.56% precision, to be compared with the precision of the void filter which is 0.04%). Hence, for $G^{T>N}$, our only result is that this basic filter does allow us to build an efficient parser (the most efficient one), but that refined additional filtering strategies are not useful.

The picture is completely different with G^{TIG}. Contrary to $G^{T>N}$, this grammar has comparatively few terminal and non-terminal symbols, and very long right-hand sides. These two facts lead to a lower precision of the basic filter (39.43%), which keeps many more productions when applied to G^{TIG} than when applied to $G^{T>N}$, and leads, when applied alone, to the less efficient parser. This gives many more opportunities to the adjacency filter to improve the global execution time. However, the complexity of the grammar makes the construction of the DSA filter relatively costly despite its precision, leading to the following conclusion: on G^{TIG}, and probably on any grammar with similar characteristics, the best filtering strategy is the one-pass adjacency strategy. In particular, this filter leads to an improvement over the work of Boullier (2003) ,which only introduced the DSA filter. Incidentally, the extreme size of G^{TIG} leads to much longer parsing times, approximately 10 times longer than with $G^{T>N}$. This result is consistent with the ratio between the sizes of both grammars involved.

12.5 Conclusion

It is a well known result in optimization techniques that the key to practically improve a process is to reduce its search space. This is also the case in parsing and in particular in CF parsing.

Many parsers process their input from left to right, but we can find other parsing strategies in the literature. In particular, in NLP, van Noord (1997) and Satta and Stock (1994) propose bidirectional algorithms. These parsers have the reputation of exhibiting better efficiency than their left-to-right counterpart. This reputation is not only based upon experimental results van Noord (1997), but also on mathematical arguments (Nederhof and Satta, 2000). This is especially true when the productions of the CFG strongly depend on lexical information. In this case the parsing search space is reduced, because the constraints associated to lexical elements are evaluated as early as possible. We can notice that our filtering strategies try to reach the same purpose by totally different means: we reduce the parsing search space by eliminating as many productions as possible, including possibly non-lexicalized productions whose irrelevance to parse the current input cannot be directly deduced from that input.

We can also notice that our results are not in contradiction with the claims of Nederhof and Satta (2000) in which they argue that "Earley algorithm and related standard parsing techniques [...] cannot be directly extended to allow left-to-right and correct-prefix-property parsing in acceptable time bound".

First, as already noted in Section 12.1, our method does not work for any large CFG. In order to work well, the first step of our basic strategy must filter out a great amount of (lexicalized) productions. To do that, it is clear that the set of terminals in the input text must select a small ratio of lexicalized productions. To give a more concrete idea we advocate that the selected productions produce roughly a grammar of *normal* size out of the large grammar.

Second, our method as a whole clearly does not process the input text from left-to-right and thus does not enter in the categories studied in Nederhof and Satta (2000). Moreover, the authors put forth strong evidence that in case of polynomial-time off-line compilation of the grammar, left-to-right parsing cannot be performed in polynomial time, independently of the size of the lexicon. Once again, if our filter pass is viewed as an off-line processing of the large input grammar, our output is not a compilation of the large grammar, but a compilation of a smaller grammar, specialized in some abstractions of the source text only. In other words, their negative results do not necessarily apply to our specific case.

The experiments have been conducted in using an Earley-like parser.[18] We have also successfuly tried the coupling of our filtering strategies with a CYK parser (Kasami, 1967; Younger, 1967) as post-processor. However the coupling with a

[18] Contrarily to classical Earley parsers, its *predictor* phase uses a pre-computed structure which is roughly an LC relation. Note that this feature forces our filters to compute an LC relation on the generated sub-grammar. This also shows that LC parsers may also benefit from our filtering techniques.

GLR parser (see Satta, 1992 for example) may be more problematic since the time taken to build up the underlying nondeterministic LR automaton from the sub-grammar can be prohibitive.

Though no definitive answer can be given to the question asked in the title, we have shown that, in some cases, the answer can be *yes*.

References

Berwick, R.C. and A.S. Weinberg (1984, May). *The Grammatical Basis of Linguistic Performance – Language Use and Acquisition*. Cambridge, MA: MIT Press.

Billot, S. and B. Lang (1989). The structure of shared forests in ambiguous parsing. In *Proceedings of the 27th Annual Meeting of the Association for Computational Linguistics*, Vancouver, BC, pp. 143–151.

Boullier, P. (2000). On TAG parsing. *Traitement Automatique des Langues 41*(3), 759–793.

Boullier, P. (2003). Guided earley parsing. In *Proceedings of the 7th International Workshop on Parsing Technologies*, Nancy, pp. 43–54.

Boullier, P. and B. Sagot (2005). Efficient and robust LFG parsing: SxLFG. In *Proceedings of the 9th International Workshop on Parsing Technologies*, Vancouver, pp. 1–10.

Earley, J. (1970). An efficient context-free parsing algorithm. *Communication of the ACM 13*(2), 94–102.

Hopcroft, J.D. and J.E. Ullman (1979). *Introduction to Automata Theory, Languages, and Computation*. Reading, MA: Addison-Wesley.

Joshi, A. (1997). Parsing techniques. In *Survey of the State of the Art in Human Language Technology*, pp. 351–356. New York, NY: Cambridge University Press.

Kasami, T. (1967). An efficient recognition and syntax algorithm for context-free languages. Scientific Report AFCRL-65–758. Bedford, MA: Air Force Cambridge Research Laboratory.

Moore, R.C. (2000). Improved left-corner chart parsing for large context-free grammars. In *Proceedings of the 6th International Workshop on Parsing Technologies*, Trento, Italy, pp. 171–182. Revised version at http://www.cogs.susx.ac.uk/lab/nlp/carroll/cfg-resources/iwpt2000-rev2.ps

Nederhof, M.-J. (1993). Generalized left-corner parsing. In *Proceedings of the 6th Conference of the European Chapter of the Association for Computational Linguistics*, Morristown, NJ, pp. 305–314.

Nederhof, M.-J. and G. Satta (2000). Left-to-right parsing and bilexical context-free grammars. In *Proceedings of the 1st Conference of the North American Chapter of the Association for Computational Linguistics*, San Francisco, CA, pp. 272–279. Morgan Kaufmann Publishers Inc.

Sagot, B. and P. Boullier (2005). From raw corpus to word lattices: robust pre-parsing processing. In *Proceedings of the 2nd Language and Technology Conference*, Poznań, pp. 348–351.

Sagot, B., L. Clément, E. Villemonte de La Clergerie, and P. Boullier (2006). The Lefff 2 syntactic lexicon for french: architecture, acquisition, use. In *Proceedings of the 5th International Conference on Language Resources and Evaluation*, Genoa, pp. 1348–1351.

Satta, G. (1992). Review of "Generalized LR parsing" by Masaru Tomita. Kluwer Academic Publishers 1991. *Computational Linguistics 18*(3), 377–381.

Satta, G. and O. Stock (1994). Bidirectional context-free grammar parsing for natural language processing. *Artificial Intelligence 69*(1–2), 123–164.

Schabes, Y., A. Abeillé, and A. Joshi (1988). Parsing strategies with 'lexicalized' grammars: application to tree adjoining grammars. In *Proceedings of the 12th International Conference on Computational Linguistics*, Budapest, pp. 578–583.

Schabes, Y. and R.C. Waters (1995). Tree insertion grammar: cubic-time, parsable formalism that lexicalizes context-free grammar without changing the trees produced. *Computational Linguistics 21*(4), 479–513.

van Noord, G. (1997). An efficient implementation of the head-corner parser. *Computational Linguistics 23*(3), 425–456.

Villemonte de La Clergerie, E. (2005). From metagrammars to factorized TAG/TIG parsers. In *Proceedings of the 9th International Workshop on Parsing Technologies*, Vancouver, pp. 190–191.

Younger, D.H. (1967). Recognition and parsing of context-free languages in time n^3. *Information and Control 10*(2), 189–208.

Chapter 13
Efficiency in Unification-Based N-Best Parsing

Yi Zhang, Stephan Oepen, and John Carroll

13.1 Background and Motivation

Technology for natural language analysis using linguistically precise grammars has matured to a level of coverage and efficiency that enables parsing of large amounts of running text. Research groups working within grammatical frameworks like Combinatory Categorial Grammar (CCG; Clark and Curran, 2004), Lexical-Functional Grammar (LFG; Riezler et al., 2002), and Head-Driven Phrase Structure Grammar (HPSG; Malouf and van Noord, 2004; Oepen et al., 2004; Miyao et al., 2005) have successfully integrated broad-coverage computational grammars with sophisticated statistical parse selection models. The former delineate the space of possible analyses, while the latter provide a probability distribution over competing hypotheses. Parse selection approaches for these frameworks often use discriminative Maximum Entropy (ME) models, where the probability of each parse tree, given an input string, is estimated on the basis of select properties (called features) of the tree (Abney, 1997; Johnson et al., 1999). Such features, in principle, are not restricted in their domain of locality, and enable the parse selection process to take into account properties that extend beyond local contexts (i.e. sub-trees of depth one).

There is a trade-off in this set-up between the accuracy of the parse selection model on the one hand, and the efficiency of the search for the best solutions on the other hand. Extending the context size of ME features, within the bounds of available training data, enables increased parse selection accuracy. However, the interplay of the core parsing algorithm and the probabilistic ranking of alternate (sub-)hypotheses becomes considerably more complex and costly when the feature size exceeds the domain of locality (of depth-one trees) that is characteristic of phrase structure grammar-based formalisms. One current line of research focuses on

Y. Zhang (✉)
Language Technology Laboratory, Department of Computational Linguistics, Saarland University, DFKI GmbH, Saarbrücken, Germany
e-mail: yzhang@coli.uni-sb.de

H. Bunt et al. (eds.), *Trends in Parsing Technology*, Text, Speech and Language Technology 43, DOI 10.1007/978-90-481-9352-3_13,

finding the best balance between parsing efficiency and parse selection techniques of increasing complexity, aiming to identify the most probable solution(s) with minimal effort.

This chapter explores a range of techniques, combining a broad-coverage, high-efficiency HPSG parser with a series of parse selection models with varying context size of features. We sketch three general scenarios for the integration: (a) a baseline sequential configuration, where all results are enumerated first, and subsequently ranked; (b) an interleaved but approximative solution, performing a greedy search for an n-best list of results; and (c) a two-phase approach, where a complete packed forest is created and combined with a specialized graph search procedure to selectively enumerate results in (globally) correct rank order. Although conceptually simple, the second technique has not previously been evaluated for HPSG parsing (to the best of our knowledge). The last of these techniques, which we call *selective unpacking*, was first proposed by Carroll and Oepen (2005) in the context of chart-based generation. However, they only provide an account of the algorithm for local ME properties and assert that the technique should generalize to larger contexts straightforwardly. This chapter describes this generalization of selective unpacking, in its application to parsing, and demonstrates that the move from features that resemble a context-free domain of locality to features of, in principle, arbitrary context size can indeed be based on the same algorithm, but the required extensions are non-trivial.

The structure of the chapter is as follows. Section 13.2 summarizes some relevant properties of our descriptive formalism, grammars used, parse selection approach, and training and test data. Section 13.3 discusses the range of possibilities for structuring the process of statistical, grammar-based parsing, and Sections 13.4, 13.5 and 13.6 describe our approach to efficient n-best parsing. We present experimental results in Section 13.7, compare our approach to previous ones (Section 13.8), and finally conclude.

13.2 Overall Set-Up

While couched in the HPSG framework, the techniques explored here are applicable to the larger class of unification-based grammar formalisms. We make use of the DELPH-IN[1] reference formalism, as implemented by a variety of systems, including the LKB (Copestake, 2002) and PET (Callmeier, 2002). For the experiments discussed here, we adapted the open-source PET parsing engine in conjunction with two publicly available grammars, the English Resource Grammar (ERG; Flickinger, 2000) and the DFKI German Grammar (GG; Müller and Kasper, 2000; Crysmann, 2005). Our parse selection models were trained and evaluated on HPSG treebanks that are distributed with these grammars. The following paragraphs summarize relevant properties of the structures manipulated by the parser, followed by relevant background on parse selection.

[1] Deep Linguistic Processing with HPSG, an open-source repository of grammars and processing tools; see "http://www.delph-in.net/".

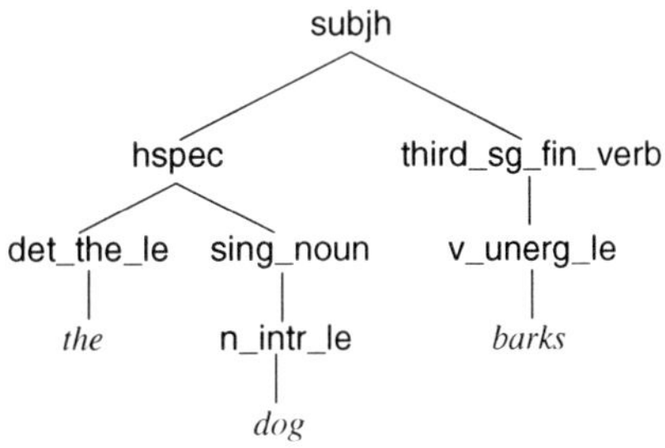

Fig. 13.1 Sample HPSG derivation tree for the sentence *the dog barks*. Phrasal nodes are labeled with identifiers of grammar rules, and (pre-terminal) lexical nodes with class names for types of lexical entries

Figure 13.1 shows an example ERG derivation tree. Internal tree nodes are labeled with identifiers of grammar rules, and leaves with lexical entries. The derivation tree provides complete information about the actual HPSG analysis, in the sense that it can be viewed as a recipe for computing it. Lexical entries and grammar rules alike are ultimately just feature structures, complex and highly-structured linguistic categories. When unified together in the configuration depicted by the derivation tree, the resulting feature structure yields an HPSG sign, a detailed representation of the syntactic and semantic properties of the input string. Just as the full derivation denotes a feature structure, so do its sub-trees, and for grammars like the ERG and GG each such structure will contain hundreds of feature–value pairs.

Because of the lexicalized nature of HPSG (and similar frameworks) our parsers search for well-formed derivations in a pure bottom-up fashion. Other than that, there are no hard-wired assumptions about the order of computation, i.e. the specific parsing strategy. Our basic set-up closely mimics that of Oepen and Carroll (2002), where edges indexed by sub-string positions in a chart represent the nodes of the tree, recording both a feature structure (as its category label) and the identity of the underlying lexical entry or rule in the grammar. Multiple edges derived for identical sub-strings can be "packed" into a single chart entry in case their feature structures are compatible, i.e. stand in an equivalence or subsumption relation. By virtue of having each edge keep back-pointers to its daughter edges—the immediate sub-nodes in the tree whose combination resulted in the mother edge—the parse forest provides a complete and *explicit* encoding of all possible results in a maximally compact form.[2] The basic CKY procedure (Kasami, 1965), for example, as well as many unification-based adaptations (e.g. the Core Language Engine; Moore and Alshawi, 1992) merely record the local category of each edge, which is sufficient for the recognition task and simplifies the search. However, reading out complete trees from the chart, then, amounts to a limited form of search, going back to the rules of the grammar itself to (re-)discover decomposition relations among chart entries. A simple unpacking procedure is obtained from the cross-multiplication of all local combinatorics, which is directly amenable to dynamic programming.

Figure 13.2 shows a hypothetical forest (on the left), where sets of edges exhibiting local ambiguity have been packed into a single "representative" edge, viz. the

[2] This property of parse forests is not a prerequisite of the chart parsing framework.

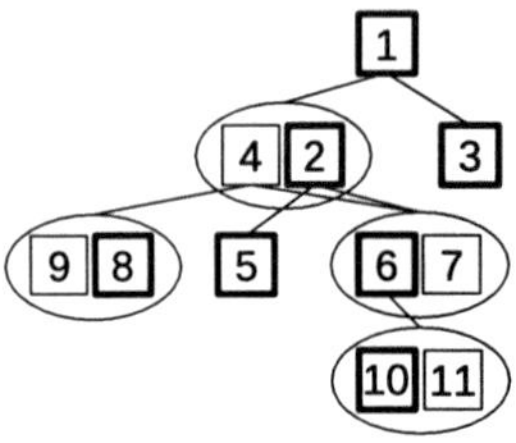

$$\boxed{1} \rightarrow \langle \boxed{2}\,\boxed{3} \rangle \mid \langle \boxed{4}\,\boxed{3} \rangle$$
$$\boxed{2} \rightarrow \langle \boxed{5}\,\boxed{6} \rangle \mid \langle \boxed{5}\,\boxed{7} \rangle$$
$$\boxed{4} \rightarrow \langle \boxed{8}\,\boxed{6} \rangle \mid \langle \boxed{8}\,\boxed{7} \rangle \mid \langle \boxed{9}\,\boxed{6} \rangle \mid \langle \boxed{9}\,\boxed{7} \rangle$$
$$\boxed{6} \rightarrow \langle \boxed{10} \rangle \mid \langle \boxed{11} \rangle$$

Fig. 13.2 Sample forest and sub-node decompositions: ovals in the forest (on the *left*) indicate packing of edges under subsumption, i.e. edges in *bold boxes* are in the chart proper, while other edges ($\boxed{4}$, $\boxed{7}$, $\boxed{9}$, and $\boxed{11}$) have been packed and removed from the chart. During unpacking, there will be multiple ways of instantiating a chart edge, each obtained from cross-multiplying alternate daughter sequences locally. The elements of this cross-product we call *decomposition*, and they are pivotal points both for stochastic scoring and dynamic programming in selective unpacking. The table on the *right* shows all non-leaf decompositions for our example packed forest: given two ways of decomposing $\boxed{6}$, there will be three candidate ways of instantiating $\boxed{2}$ and six for $\boxed{4}$, respectively, for a total of nine full trees

one in each set with one or more incoming dominance arcs.[3] Confirming the findings of Oepen and Carroll (2002), in our experiments packing under feature structure subsumption is much more effective than packing under mere equivalence, i.e. for each pair of edges (over identical sub-strings) that stand in a subsumption relation, a technique that Oepen and Carroll (2002) termed *retro-active packing* ensures that the more general of the two edges remains in the chart. When packing under subsumption, however, some of the cross-product of local ambiguities in the forest may not be globally consistent. Assume for example that, in Fig. 13.2, edges $\boxed{6}$ and $\boxed{8}$ subsume $\boxed{7}$ and $\boxed{9}$, respectively; combining $\boxed{7}$ and $\boxed{9}$ into the same tree during unpacking can in principle fail. Thus, unpacking effectively needs to deterministically replay unifications, but this extra expense in our experience is negligible when compared to the decreased cost of constructing the forest under subsumption. In Section 13.3 we argue that this very property, in addition to increasing parsing efficiency, interacts beneficially with parse selection and on-demand enumeration of results in rank order.

Following Johnson et al. (1999), a conditional ME model of the probabilities of trees $\{t_1 \ldots t_n\}$ for a string s, and assuming a set of feature functions $\{f_1 \ldots f_m\}$ with corresponding weights $\{\lambda_1 \ldots \lambda_m\}$, is defined as:

$$p(t_i|s) = \frac{\exp \sum_j \lambda_j f_j(t_i)}{\sum_{k=1}^{n} \exp \sum_j \lambda_j f_j(t_k)} \tag{1}$$

[3] Our graphical representation of the forest closely resembles the data structures actually used during parsing. Sets of packed edges (indicated by ovals) correspond to “or” (or disjunctive) nodes, when viewing the forest as a general *and–or graph*; in this view, the edges themselves (drawn as boxes in Fig. 13.2 correspond to “and” (or conjunctive) nodes. Conversely, “or” nodes are represented as vertexes in the conceptualization of parse forests as *hypergraphs* (Klein and Manning, 2001; Huang and Chiang, 2005), where hyperarcs correspond to “and” nodes.

Table 13.1 Examples of structural features extracted from the derivation tree in Fig. 13.1. The *Type* column indicates the template corresponding to each sample feature; the integer that starts each feature indicates the degree of grandparenting (in the case of type 1 and 2 features) or n-gram size (type 3 features). The symbols $\triangle$ and $\triangleleft$ denote the root of the tree and left periphery of the yield, respectively

Type	Sample features
1	⟨0 subjh hspec third_sg_fin_verb⟩
1	⟨1 △ subjh hspec third_sg_fin_verb⟩
1	⟨0 hspec det_the_le sing_noun⟩
1	⟨1 subjh hspec det_the_le sing_noun⟩
1	⟨2 △ subjh hspec det_the_le sing_noun⟩
2	⟨0 subjh third_sg_fin_verb⟩
2	⟨0 subjh hspce⟩
2	⟨1 subjh hspec det_the_le⟩
2	⟨1 subjh hspec sing_noun⟩
3	⟨1 n_intr_le *dog*⟩
3	⟨2 det_the_le n_intr_le *dog*⟩
3	⟨3 ◁ det_the_le n_intr_le *dog*⟩

Feature functions f_j can test for arbitrary structural properties of analyses t_i, and their value typically is the number of times a specific property is present in t_i. Toutanova et al. (2005) propose an inventory of features that perform well in HPSG parse selection; currently we restrict ourselves to the best-performing of these, of the form illustrated in Table 13.1, comprising depth-one sub-trees (or portions of these) with grammar-internal identifiers as node labels, plus optionally a chain of one or more dominating nodes (i.e. levels of grandparents). If a grandparents chain is present then the feature is non-local. For expository purposes, Table 13.1 includes another feature type, n-grams over leaf nodes of the derivation; in Section 13.5 below we speculate about the incorporation of these (and similar) features in our algorithm.

13.3 Interleaving Parsing and Ranking

At an abstract level, given a grammar and an associated ME parse selection model, there are three basic ways of combining them in order to find the single "best" or smallest set of n-best results.

The first way is a naïve sequential set-up, in which the parser first enumerates the full set of analyses, computes a score for each using the model, and returns the highest-ranking n results. For carefully crafted grammars and inputs of average complexity the approach can perform reasonably well.

Another mode of operation is to organize the parser's search according to an agenda (i.e. priority queue) that assigns numeric scores to parsing moves (Erbach, 1991). Each such move is an application of the fundamental rule of chart parsing, combining an active and a passive edge, and the scores represent the expected "figure of merit" (Caraballo and Charniak, 1998) of the resulting structure.

Assuming a parse selection model of the type sketched in Section 13.2, we can determine the agenda priority for a parsing move according to the (unnormalized) ME score of the derivation (sub-)tree that would result from its successful execution. Note that, unlike in probabilistic context-free grammars (PCFGs), ME scores of partial trees do not necessarily decrease as the tree size increases; instead, the distribution of feature weights is in the range $(-\infty, +\infty)$, centered around 0, where negative weights intuitively correspond to dis-preferred properties.

This lack of monotonicity in the scores associated with sub-trees, on the one hand, is beneficial, in that performing a greedy best-first search becomes practical: in contrast, with PCFGs and their monotonically decreasing probabilities on larger sub-trees, once the parser finds the first full tree the chart necessarily has been instantiated almost completely. On the other hand, the same property prohibits the application of exact best-first techniques like A* search, because there is no reliable future cost estimate; in this respect, our set-up differs fundamentally from that of Klein and Manning (2003) and related PCFG parsing work. Using the unnormalized sum of ME weights on a partial solution as its agenda score, effectively, means that sub-trees with low scores "sink" to the bottom of the agenda; highly-ranked partial constituents, in turn, instigate the immediate creation of larger structures, and ideally the bottom-up agenda-driven search will greedily steer the parser towards full analyses with high scores. Given its heuristic nature, this procedure cannot guarantee that its n-best list of results corresponds to the globally correct rank order, but it may in practice come reasonably close to it. While conceptually simple, greedy best-first search does not combine easily with ambiguity packing in the chart: (a) at least when packing under subsumption, it is not obvious how to accurately compute the agenda score of packed nodes, and (b) to the extent that the greedy search avoids exploration of dis-preferred local ambiguity, the need for packing should be greatly reduced. Unfortunately, in scoring bottom-up parsing moves, ME features involving grandparenting are not applicable, leading to a second potential source of reduced parse selection accuracy. In Section 13.7 below, we provide an empirical evaluation of both the naïve sequential and greedy best-first approaches.

13.4 Selective Unpacking

Carroll and Oepen (2005) observe that, at least for grammars like the ERG, the construction of the parse forest can be very efficient (with observed polynomial complexity), especially when packing edges under subsumption. Their selective unpacking procedure, originally proposed for the forest created by a chart *generator*, aims to unpack the n-best set of full trees from the forest, guaranteeing the globally correct rank order according to the probability distribution, with a minimal amount of search. The basic algorithm is a specialized graph search through the forest, with local contexts of optimization corresponding to packed nodes.

Each such node represents local combinatorics, and two key notions in the selective unpacking procedure are the concepts of (a) *decomposing* an edge locally into

[2]

```
procedure selectively-unpack-edge(edge, n) ≡
  results ← ⟨⟩; i ← 0;
  do
    hypothesis ← hypothesize-edge(edge, i); i ← i + 1;
    if (new ← instantiate-hypothesis(hypothesis)) then
      n ← n − 1; results ← results ⊕ ⟨new⟩;
  while (hypothesis and n ≥ 1)
  return results;
```

[2]

```
procedure hypothesize-edge(edge, i) ≡
  if (edge.hypotheses[i]) return edge.hypotheses[i];
  if (i = 0) then
    for each (decomposition in decompose-edge(edge)) do
      daughters ← ⟨⟩; indices ← ⟨⟩
      for each (edge in decomposition.rhs) do
        daughters ← daughters ⊕ ⟨hypothesize-edge(edge, 0)⟩;
        indices ← indices ⊕ ⟨0⟩;
      new-hypothesis(edge, decomposition, daughters, indices);
  if (hypothesis ← edge.agenda.pop()) then
    for each (indices in advance-indices(hypothesis.indices)) do
      if (indices ∈ hypothesis.decomposition.indices) then continue
      daughters ← ⟨⟩;
      for each (edge in hypothesis.decomposition.rhs) each (i in indices) do
        daughter ← hypothesize-edge(edge, i);
        if (not daughter) then daughters ← ⟨⟩; break
        daughters ← daughters ⊕ ⟨daughter⟩;
      if (daughters) then new-hypothesis(edge, hypothesis.decomposition, daughters,
indices)
    edge.hypotheses[i] ← hypothesis;
    return hypothesis;
```

[2]

```
procedure new-hypothesis(edge, decomposition, daughters, indices) ≡
  hypothesis ← new hypothesis(decomposition, daughters, indices);
  edge.agenda.insert(score-hypothesis(hypothesis), hypothesis);
  decomposition.indices ← decomposition.indices ∪ {indices};
```

Fig. 13.3 Selective unpacking procedure, enumerating the n best realizations for a top-level result *edge* from a packed forest. An auxiliary function decompose-edge() performs local cross-multiplication as shown in the examples in Fig. 13.2. Another utility function not shown in pseudo-code is advance-indices(), a "driver" routine searching for alternate instantiations of daughter edges, e.g. advance-indices(⟨0 2 1⟩) → {⟨1 2 1⟩ ⟨0 3 1⟩ ⟨0 2 2⟩}. Finally, instantiate-hypothesis() is the function that actually builds result trees, replaying the unifications of constructions from the grammar (as identified by chart edges) with the feature structures of daughter constituents candidate ways of instantiating it, and of (b) nested contexts of local search for ranked *hypotheses* (i.e. uninstantiated edges) about candidate subtrees. See Fig. 13.2 for examples of the decomposition of edges. Given one decomposition—i.e. a vector of candidate daughters for a particular rule—there can be multiple ways of instantiating each daughter: a parallel index vector $\mathbf{I} = \langle i_0 \ldots i_n \rangle$ serves to keep track of "vertical" search among daughter hypotheses, where each index i_j denotes the i-th best instantiation (hypothesis) of the daughter at position j. If we restrict ME features to a depth of one (i.e. without grandparenting), then given the additive nature of ME scores on complete derivations, it can be guaranteed that hypothesized trees including an edge e as an immediate daughter must use the best instantiation of e in their own best instantiation. Assuming a binary rule, the corresponding hypothesis would use daughter indices of $\langle 0\ 0 \rangle$. The second-best instantiation, in turn, can be obtained from moving to the second-best hypothesis for *one* of the elements in the (right-hand side of the) decomposition, e.g. indices $\langle 0\ 1 \rangle$ or $\langle 1\ 0 \rangle$ in the binary example. Hypotheses are associated with ME scores and ordered within each nested context by means of a local priority queue (stored in the original representative edge, for convenience). Therefore, nested local optimizations result in a top-down, breadth-first, exact n-best search through the packed forest, while avoiding exhaustive cross-multiplication of packed nodes.

Figure 13.3 shows the unchanged pseudo-code of Carroll and Oepen (2005). The main function hypothesize-edge() controls both the "horizontal" and "vertical" search, initializing the set of decompositions and pushing initial hypotheses onto the local agenda when called on an edge for the first time (lines 11–17). For each call, the procedure retrieves the current next-best hypothesis from the agenda (line 18), generates new hypotheses by advancing daughter indices (while skipping over configurations seen earlier) and calling itself recursively for each new index (lines 19–26), and, finally, arranging for the resulting hypothesis to be cached for later invocations on the same *edge* and i values (line 27). Note that unification (in instantiate-hypothesis()) is only invoked on complete, top-level hypotheses, as our structural ME features can actually be evaluated *prior* to building each full feature structure. However, as Carroll and Oepen (2005) suggest, the procedure could be adapted to perform instantiation of sub-hypotheses within each local search, should additional features require it. For better efficiency, the instantiate-hypothesis() routine applies dynamic programming (i.e. memoization) to intermediate results.

13.5 Generalizing the Algorithm

Carroll and Oepen (2005) offer no solution for selective unpacking with larger-context ME features. Yet, both Toutanova et al. (2005) and our own experiments (described in Section 13.7 below) suggest that properties of larger contexts and especially grandparenting can greatly improve parse selection accuracy. The following paragraphs outline how to generalize the basic selective unpacking procedure, while retaining its key properties: exact n-best enumeration with minimal search.

Our generalization of the algorithm distinguishes between "upward" contexts, with grandparenting with dominating nodes as a representative feature type, and "downward" extensions, which we discuss for the example of lexical n-gram features.

A naïve approach to selective unpacking with grandparenting might be extending the cross-multiplication of local ambiguity to trees of more than depth one. However, with multiple levels of grandparenting this approach would greatly increase the combinatorics to be explored, and it would pose the puzzle of overlapping local contexts of optimization. Choices made among the alternates for one packed node would interact with other ambiguity contexts in their internal nodes, rather than merely at the leaves of their decompositions. However, it is sufficient to keep the depth of decompositions to minimal sub-trees and rather contextualize each decomposition as a whole. Assuming our sample forest and set of decompositions from Fig. 13.2, let $\langle \boxed{1}\boxed{4} \rangle : \boxed{6} \rightarrow \langle \boxed{10} \rangle$ denote the decomposition of node $\boxed{6}$ in the context of $\boxed{4}$ and $\boxed{1}$ as its immediate parents. When descending through the forest, hypothesize-edge() can, without significant extra cost, maintain a vector $\mathbf{P} = \langle p_n \ \dots \ p_0 \rangle$ of parents of the current node, for n-level grandparenting. For each packed node, the bookkeeping elements of the graph search procedure need to be contextualized on **P**, viz. (a) the edge-local priority queue, (b) the record of index vectors hypothesized already, and (c) the cache of previous instantiations. Assuming each is stored in an associative array, then all references to edge.agenda in the original procedure can be replaced by edge.agenda[**P**], and likewise for other slots. With these extensions in place, the original control structure of nested, on-demand creation of hypotheses and dynamic programming of partial results can be retained, and for each packed node with multiple parents ($\boxed{6}$ in our sample forest) there will be parallel, contextualized partitions of optimization. Thus, extra combinatorics introduced in this generalized procedure are confined to only such nodes, which (intuitively at least) appears to establish the lower bound of added search needed—while keeping the algorithm non-approximative. Section 13.7 provides empirical data on the degradation of the procedure in growing levels of grandparenting and the number of n-best results to be extracted from the forest.

Finally, we turn to enlarged feature contexts that capture information from nodes *below* the elements of a local decomposition. Consider the example of feature type 3 in Table 13.1, n-grams (of various size) over properties of the yield of the parse tree. For now we only consider lexical *bi*-grams. For an edge e dominating a sub-string of n words $\langle w_i \ \dots \ w_{i+n-1} \rangle$ there will be $n-1$ bi-grams internal to e, and two bi-grams that interact with w_{i-1} and w_{i+n}—which will be determined by the left- and right-adjacent edges to e in a complete tree. The internal bi-grams are unproblematic, and we can assume that ME weights corresponding to these features have been included in the sum of weights associated to e. Seeing that e may occur in multiple trees, with different sister edges, the selective unpacking procedure has to take this variation into account when evaluating local contexts of optimization.

Let ${}_x e_y$ denote an edge e, with x and y as the lexical types of its leftmost and rightmost daughters, respectively. Returning to our sample forest, assume lexicalizations ${}_\beta\boxed{10}_\beta$ and ${}_\gamma\boxed{11}_\gamma$ (each spanning only one word), with $\beta \neq \gamma$. Obviously, when decomposing $\boxed{4}$ as $\langle \boxed{8}\boxed{6} \rangle$, its ME score, in turn, will depend on the choice made in the expansion of $\boxed{6}$: the sequences $\langle {}_{\alpha}\boxed{8}_{\alpha}\ {}_{\beta}\boxed{6}_{\beta} \rangle$ and $\langle {}_{\alpha}\boxed{8}_{\alpha}\ {}_{\gamma}\boxed{6}_{\gamma} \rangle$ will differ in (at least) the scores associated with the bi-grams $\langle \alpha\ \beta \rangle$ vs. $\langle \alpha\ \gamma \rangle$. Accordingly, when evaluating candidate decompositions of $\boxed{4}$, the number of hypotheses that need to be considered is doubled; as an immediate consequence, there can be up to eight distinct lexicalized variants for the decomposition $\boxed{1} \rightarrow \langle \boxed{4}\,\boxed{3} \rangle$ further up in the tree. It may look as if combinatorics will cross-multiply throughout the tree—in the worst case returning us to an exponential number of hypotheses—but this is fortunately not the case: regarding the external bi-grams of $\boxed{1}$, node $\boxed{6}$ no longer participates in its left- or rightmost periphery, so variation internal to $\boxed{6}$ is not a multiplicative factor at this level. This is essentially the observation of Langkilde (2000), and her bottom-up factoring of n-gram computation is easily incorporated into our top-down selective unpacking control structure. At the point where hypothesize-edge() invokes itself recursively (line 23 in Fig. 13.3), its return value is now a set of lexicalized alternates, and hypothesis creation (in line 26) can take into account the local cross-product of all such alternation. Including additional properties from non-local sub-trees (for example higher-order n-grams and head lexicalization) is a straightforward extension of this scheme, replacing our per-edge left- and rightmost periphery symbols with a generalized vector of externally relevant, internal properties. In addition to traditional (head) lexicalization as we have just discussed it, such extended "downward" properties on decompositions—percolated from daughters to mothers and cross-multiplied as appropriate—could include metrics of constituent weight too, for example to enable the ME model to prefer "balanced" coordination structures.

However, given that Toutanova et al. (2005) obtain only marginally improved parse selection accuracy from the inclusion of n-gram (and other lexical) ME features, we have left the implementation of lexicalization and empirical evaluation for future work.

13.6 Failure Caching and Propagation

As we pointed out at the end of Section 13.4, during the unpacking phase, unification is only replayed in instantiate-hypothesis() on the top-level hypotheses. It is only at this step that inconsistencies in the local combinatorics are discovered. However, such a discovery can be used to improve the unpacking routine by (a) avoiding further unification on hypotheses that have already failed to instantiate, (b) avoiding creating new hypotheses based on failed sub-hypotheses. This requires some changes to the routines instantiate-hypothesis() and hypothesize-edge(), as well as an extra boolean marker for each hypothesis.

The extended instantiate-hypothesis() starts by checking whether the hypothesis is already marked as failed. If it is not so marked, the routine recursively instantiates all sub-hypotheses. Any failure will again lead to instant return. Otherwise, unification is used to create a new edge from the outcome of the sub-hypothesis instantiations. If this unification fails, the current hypothesis is marked. Moreover, all its ancestor hypotheses are also marked (by recursively following the pointers to the direct parent hypotheses) as they are also guaranteed to fail.

Correspondingly, hypothesize-edge() needs to check the instantiation failure marker to avoid returning hypotheses that are guaranteed to fail. If a hypothesis coming out of the agenda is already marked as failed, it will be used to create new hypotheses (with advance-indices()), but dropped afterward. Subsequent hypotheses will be popped from the agenda until either a hypothesis that is not marked as failed is returned, or the agenda is empty.

Moreover, hypothesize-edge() also needs to avoid creating new hypotheses based on failed sub-hypotheses. When a failed sub-hypothesis is found, the creation of the new hypothesis is skipped. But the index vector **I** may not be simply discarded. Otherwise hypotheses based on advance-indices(**I**) will not be reachable in the search. On the other hand, simply adding every advance-indices(**I**) on to the pending creation list is not efficient either in the case where multiple sub-hypotheses fail.

To solve the problem, we compute a failure vector $\mathbf{F} = \langle f_0 \dots f_n \rangle$, where f_j is 1 when the sub-hypothesis at position j is known as failed, and 0 otherwise. If a sub-hypothesis at position j is failed then all the index vectors having value i_j at position j must also fail. By putting the result of $\mathbf{I} + \mathbf{F}$ on the pending creation list, we can safely skip the failed rows of sub-hypotheses, while not losing the reachability of the others. As an example, suppose we have a ternary index vector $\langle 3\ 1\ 2 \rangle$ for which a new hypothesis is to be created. By checking the instantiation failure marker of the sub-hypotheses, we find that the first and the third sub-hypotheses are already marked. The failure recording vector will then be $\langle 1\ 0\ 1 \rangle$. By putting $\langle 4\ 1\ 3 \rangle = \langle 3\ 1\ 2 \rangle + \langle 1\ 0\ 1 \rangle$ on to the pending hypothesis creation list, the failed sub-hypotheses are skipped.

We evaluate the effects of instantiation failure caching and propagation below in Section 13.7.

13.7 Empirical Results

To evaluate the performance of the selective unpacking algorithm, we carried out a series of empirical evaluations with the ERG and GG, in combination with a modified version of the PET parser. When running the ERG we used as our test set the *JH4* section of the LOGON treebank,[4] which contains 1,603 items with an average sentence length of 14.6 words. The remaining LOGON treebank (of around 8,000 items) was used in training the various ME parse disambiguation models. For the experiment with GG, we designated a 2,825-item portion of the DFKI Verb*mobil*

[4] The treebank comprises several booklets of edited, instructional texts on backcountry activities in Norway. The data is available from the LOGON web site at "http://www.emmtee.net".

treebank[5] for our tests, and trained ME models on the remaining 10,000 utterances. At only 7.4 words, the average sentence length is much shorter in the Verb*mobil* data.

We ran seven different configurations of the parser with different search strategies and (un-)packing mechanisms:

- Agenda driven greedy n-best parsing using the ME score without grandparenting features; no local ambiguity packing;
- Local ambiguity packing with exhaustive unpacking, without grandparenting features;
- Local ambiguity packing and selective unpacking for n-best parsing, with 0 through 4 levels of grandparenting (GP) features.

As a side-effect of differences in efficiency, some configurations could not complete parsing all sentences given reasonable memory constraints (which we set at a limit of 100k passive edges or 300 s processing time per item). The overall coverage and processing time of different configurations on *JH4* are given in Table 13.2.

The correlation between processing time and coverage is interesting. However, it makes the efficiency comparison difficult as parser behavior is not clearly defined when the memory limit is exceeded. To circumvent this problem, in the following experiments we average only over those 1,362 utterances from *JH4* that complete parsing within the resource limit in all seven configurations. Nevertheless, it must be noted that this restriction potentially reduces efficiency differences between configurations, as some of the more challenging inputs (which typically lead to the largest differences) are excluded.

Figure 13.4 compares the processing time of different configurations. The difference is much more significant for longer sentences (i.e. with more than 15 words). If the parser unpacks exhaustively, the time for unpacking grows with sentence length at a quickly increasing rate. In such cases, the efficiency gain with ambiguity

Table 13.2 Coverage on the ERG for different configurations, with fixed resource consumption limits (of 100k passive edges or 300 s). In all cases, up to ten "best" results were searched, and *Coverage* shows the percentage of inputs that succeed to parse within the available resource. *Time* shows the end-to-end processing time for each batch

Configuration	GP	Coverage (%)	Time (s)
Greedy best-first	0	91.6	3,889
Exhaustive unpacking	0	84.5	4,673
Selective unpacking	0	94.3	2,245
	1	94.3	2,529
	2	94.3	3,964
	3	94.2	3,199
	4	94.2	3,502

[5] The data in this treebank is taken from transcribed appointment scheduling dialogues; see "http://gg.dfki.de/" for further information on GG and its treebank.

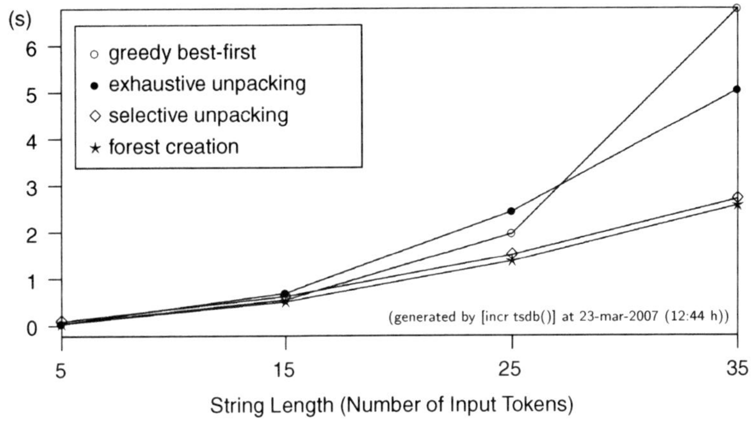

Fig. 13.4 Parsing times for different configurations using the ERG, in all three cases searching for up to ten results, without the use of grandparenting

packing in the parsing phase is mostly lost in the unpacking phase. The graph shows that greedy best-first parsing without packing outperforms exhaustive unpacking for sentences of less than 25 words. With sentences longer than 25 words, the packing mechanism helps the parser to overtake greedy best-first parsing, although the exhaustive unpacking time also grows fast.

With the selective unpacking algorithm presented in the previous sections, unpacking time is reduced, and grows only slowly as sentence length increases. Unpacking up to ten results, when contrasted with the timings for forest creation (i.e. the first parsing phase) in Fig. 13.4, adds a near-negligible extra cost to the total time required for both phases. Moreover, Fig. 13.5 shows that with selective unpacking, as n is increased, unpacking time grows roughly linearly for all levels of grandparenting (albeit always with an initial delay in unpacking the first result).

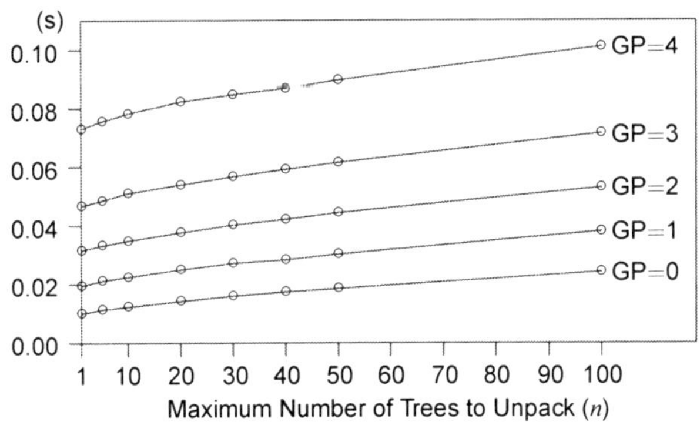

Fig. 13.5 Mean times for selective unpacking of all test items for n-best parsing with the ERG, for varying n and grandparenting (GP) levels

Table 13.3 Contrasting the efficiency of various (un-)packing settings in use with ERG on short (top) and medium-length (bottom) inputs; in each configuration, up to ten trees are extracted. *Unification* and *Copies* is the count of top-level FS operations, where only successful unifications require a subsequent copy (when creating a new edge). *Unpack* and *Total* are unpacking and total parse time, respectively

	Configuration	GP	Unifications (#)	Copies (#)	Space (kb)	Unpack (s)	Total (s)
≤ 15 words	Greedy best-first	0	1,845	527	2,328	–	0.12
	Exhaustive unpacking	0	2,287	795	8,907	0.01	0.12
		0	1,912	589	8,109	0.00	0.12
		1	1,913	589	8,109	0.01	0.12
	Selective unpacking	2	1,914	589	8,109	0.01	0.12
		3	1,914	589	8,110	0.01	0.12
		4	1,914	589	8,110	0.02	0.13
> 15 words	Greedy best-first	0	25,233	5,602	24,646	–	1.66
	Exhaustive unpacking	0	39,095	15,685	80,832	0.85	1.95
		0	17,489	4,422	33,326	0.03	1.17
		1	17,493	4,421	33,318	0.05	1.21
	Selective unpacking	2	17,493	4,421	33,318	0.09	1.25
		3	17,495	4,422	33,321	0.13	1.27
		4	17,495	4,422	33,320	0.21	1.34

Table 13.3 summarizes a number of internal parser measurements using the ERG with different packing/unpacking settings. Besides the difference in processing time, we also see a significant difference in *space* between exhaustive and selective unpacking. Also, the difference in *unifications* and *copies* indicates that with our selective unpacking algorithm, these expensive operations on typed feature structures are significantly reduced.

In return for increased processing time (and marginal loss in coverage) when using grandparenting features, Table 13.4 shows some large improvements in parse selection accuracy (although the picture is less clear-cut at higher-order levels of grandparenting[6]). A balance point between efficiency and accuracy can be made according to application needs.

Finally, we compare the processing time of the selective unpacking algorithm with and without instantiation failure caching and propagation (as described in Section 13.4 above). The empirical results for GG are summarized in Table 13.5, showing clearly that the technique reduced unnecessary hypotheses and instantiation

[6] The models were trained using the open-source TADM package (Malouf, 2002), using default hyper-parameters for all configurations, viz. a convergence threshold of 10^{-8}, variance of the prior of 10^{-4}, and frequency cut-off of 5. It is likely that further optimization of hyper-parameters for individual configurations would moderately improve model performance, especially for higher-order grandparenting levels with large numbers of features.

Table 13.4 Parse selection accuracy for various levels of grandparenting. The *exact match* column shows the percentage of cases in which the correct tree, according to the treebank, was ranked highest by the model; conversely, the *top ten* column indicates how often the correct tree was among the ten top-ranking results

Configuration	Exact match	Top ten
Random choice	11.34	43.06
No grandparenting	52.52	68.38
Greedy best-first	51.79	69.48
Grandparenting[1]	56.83	85.33
Grandparenting[2]	56.55	84.14
Grandparenting[3]	56.37	84.14
Grandparenting[4]	56.28	84.51

Table 13.5 Efficiency effects of the instantiation failure caching and propagation with GG, without grandparenting. All statistics are averages over the 1,941 items that complete within the resource bounds in all three configurations. *Unification*, *Copies*, *Unpack*, and *Total* have the same interpretation as in Table 13.3, and *Hypotheses* is the average count of hypothesized sub-trees

Configuration	Unifications (#)	Copies (#)	Hypotheses (#)	Space (kb)	Unpack (ms)	Total (ms)
Greedy best-first	5,980	1,447	–	9,202	–	400
Selective, no caching	5,535	1,523	1,245	27,188	70	410
Selective, with cache	4,915	1,522	382	27,176	10	350

failures. The design philosophy of the ERG and GG differ. During the first, forest creation phase, GG suppresses a number of features (in the HPSG sense, not the ME sense) that can actually constrain the combinatorics of edges. This move makes the packed forest more compact, but it implies that unification failures will be more frequent during unpacking. In a sense, GG thus moves part of the search for globally consistent derivations into the second phase, and it is possible for the forest to contain "result" trees that ultimately turn out to be incoherent. Dynamic programming of instantiation failures makes this approach tractable, while retaining the general breadth-first characteristic of the selective unpacking regime.

13.8 Discussion

The approach to n-best parsing described in this chapter takes as its point of departure recent work of Carroll and Oepen (2005), which describes an efficient algorithm for unpacking n-best trees from a forest produced by a chart-based sentence generator and containing local ME properties with associated weights. In an almost contemporaneous study, but in the context of parsing with treebank grammars, Huang and Chiang (2005) develop a series of increasingly efficient algorithms for unpacking n-best results from a weighted hypergraph representing a parse forest. The algorithm of Carroll and Oepen (2005) and the final one of Huang and Chiang (2005) are essentially equivalent, and turn out to be reformulations of an approach originally described by Jiménez and Marzal (2000) (although expressed there only for grammars in Chomsky Normal Form).

In this chapter we have considered ME properties that extend beyond immediate dominance relations, extending up to 4 levels of grandparenting. Previous work has often assumed properties that are restricted to the minimal parse fragments (i.e. sub-trees of depth one) that make up the packed representation (Geman and Johnson, 2002), suggesting that in unification-based frameworks it will always be possible to percolate additional information in the feature structure universe, i.e. making the grammar localize properties relevant to parse selection, even where such information may not be strictly required during the initial construction of the parse forest. To our best knowledge, this technique is applied in the parsers of Clark and Curran (2007) and Miyao and Tsujii (2008).

Probably the work closest in spirit to our approach is that of Malouf and van Noord (2004), who use an HPSG grammar comparable to the ERG and GG, non-local ME features, and a two-phase parse forest creation and unpacking approach. However, their unpacking phase uses a beam search to find a good (single) candidate for the best parse; in contrast—for ME models containing the types of non-local features that are most important for accurate parse selection—we avoid an approximative search and *efficiently* identify *exactly* the n-best parses. In a similar vein, Huang (2008) proposed an approach towards non-local features, combining exact decoding for local features with an approximative beam search for non-local features. Unlike our selective unpacking algorithm, the procedure of Huang (2008) works bottom-up with an extra sort step at each node, and n-best competitor sub-trees are kept based on the approximate score evaluated with local and non-local features so far. The beam-search makes the algorithm efficient, though like Malouf and van Noord (2004) it can no longer guarantee exact n-best enumeration in globally correct rank order.

Another influential line of investigation on handling non-local ranking properties is described by Miyao and Tsujii (2008), where a *feature!forest* is introduced to represent equivalence classes of parse fragments, with regards to ME features. Conceptually, this approach allows a feature forest to *not* be isomorphic to the parse forest, i.e. ME features that would be non-local to nodes of the parse forest can be projected onto an "embedding" feature forest, so as to be localized there. This technique may require some amount of cross-multiplication of local combinatorics and thus, in the abstract, is related to our use of contextualized decompositions in Section 13.5 above. However, Miyao and Tsujii (2008) only use the feature forest during the training of the statistical model: n-best decoding from a packed parse forest is not discussed in detail. Furthermore, they assume that parse trees are packed according to equivalence relations rather than subsumption, and (in a footnote) they suggest that the feature forest is not applicable to forests packed under subsumption. Conceptually, the algorithm described in this chapter can be viewed as a natural complement to the feature forest approach for parse selection, i.e. the decoding phase. It creates on the fly a mapping from the parse forest to an implicit feature forest. By exploring the (n-)best reading(s) first, however, the algorithm avoids "exploding" the total size of the feature forest by expanding out only a limited amount of local combinatorics, viz. only those sub-hypotheses that compete for participation in the n-best results.

When parsing with context free grammars, a (single) parse can be retrieved from a parse forest in time linear in the length of the input string (Billot and Lang, 1989). However, as discussed in Section 13.2, when parsing with a unification-based grammar and packing under feature structure subsumption, the cross-product of some local ambiguities may not be globally consistent. This means that additional unifications are required at unpacking time. In principle, when parsing with a pathological grammar with a high rate of failure, extracting a single consistent parse from the forest could take exponential time (see Lang (1994) for a discussion of this issue with respect to Indexed Grammars). In the case of GG, a high rate of unification failure in unpacking is dramatically reduced by our instantiation failure caching and propagation mechanism.

13.9 Conclusions and Future Work

We have described and evaluated an algorithm for efficiently computing the n-best analyses from a parse forest produced by a unification grammar, with respect to a Maximum Entropy (ME) model containing two classes of non-local features. The algorithm is efficient in that it empirically exhibits a linear relationship between processing time and the number of analyses unpacked, at all degrees of ME feature non-locality. It improves over previous work in providing the only exact procedure for retrieving n-best analyses from a packed forest that can deal with features with extended domains of locality and with forests created under subsumption. Our algorithm applies dynamic programming to intermediate results and local failures in unpacking alike.

The experiments compared the new algorithm with baseline systems representing other possible approaches to parsing with ME models: (a) a single phase of agenda-driven parsing with on-line pruning based on intermediate ME scores, and (b) two-phase parsing with exhaustive unpacking and post-hoc ranking of complete trees. The new approach showed better speed, coverage, and accuracy than the baselines.

Although we have dealt with the non-local ME features that in previous work have been found to be the most important for parse selection (i.e. grandparenting and n-grams), this does not exhaust the full range of features that could possibly be useful. For example, it may be the case that accurately resolving some kinds of ambiguities can only be done with reference to particular parts—or combinations of parts—of the HPSG feature structures representing the analysis of a complete constituent. To deal with such cases we are currently designing an extension to the algorithms described here which would add a "controlled" beam search, in which the size of the beam was limited by the interval of score adjustments for ME features that could only be evaluated once the full linguistic structure became available. This approach would involve a constrained amount of extra search, but would still produce the exact n-best trees.

References

Abney, S.P. (1997). Stochastic attribute-value grammars. *Computational Linguistics 23*, 597–618.

Billot, S. and B. Lang (1989). The structure of shared forests in ambiguous parsing. In *Proceedings of the 27th Meeting of the Association for Computational Linguistics*, Vancouver, BC, pp. 143–151.

Callmeier, U. (2002). Preprocessing and encoding techniques in PET. In S. Oepen, D. Flickinger, J. Tsujii, and H. Uszkoreit (Eds.), *Collaborative Language Engineering. A Case Study in Efficient Grammar-based Processing*. Stanford, CA: CSLI Publications.

Caraballo, S.A. and E. Charniak (1998). New figures of merit for best-first probabilistic chart parsing. *Computational Linguistics 24*(2), 275–298.

Carroll, J. and S. Oepen (2005). High-efficiency realization for a wide-coverage unification grammar. In R. Dale and K.F. Wong (Eds.), *Proceedings of the 2nd International Joint Conference on Natural Language Processing*, Lecture Notes in Artificial Intelligence, vol. 3651. Jeju, Korea: Springer, pp. 165–176.

Clark, S. and J.R. Curran (2004). Parsing the WSJ using CCG and log-linear models. In *Proceedings of the 42nd Meeting of the Association for Computational Linguistics*, Barcelona, pp. 104–111.

Clark, S. and J.R. Curran (2007). Wide-coverage efficient statistical parsing with CCG and log-linear models. *Computational Linguistics 33*(4), 493–552.

Copestake, A. (2002). *Implementing Typed Feature Structure Grammars*. Stanford, CA: CSLI Publications.

Crysmann, B. (2005). Relative clause extraposition in German. An efficient and portable implementation. *Research on Language and Computation 3*(1), 61–82.

Erbach, G. (1991). A flexible parser for a linguistic development environment. In O. Herzog and C.R. Rollinger (Eds.), *Text Understanding in LILOG*. Berlin: Springer, pp. 74–87.

Flickinger, D. (2000). On building a more efficient grammar by exploiting types. *Natural Language Engineering 6*(1), 15–28.

Geman, S. and M. Johnson (2002). Dynamic programming for parsing and estimation of stochastic unification-based grammars. In *Proceedings of the 40th Meeting of the Association for Computational Linguistics*, Philadelphia, PA.

Huang, L. (2008). Forest reranking: discriminative parsing with non-local features. In *Proceedings of the ACL-08: HLT*, Columbus, OH.

Huang, L. and D. Chiang (2005). Better k-best parsing. In *Proceedings of the 9th International Workshop on Parsing Technologies*, Vancouver, BC, pp. 53–64.

Jiménez, V.M. and A. Marzal (2000). Computation of the n best parse trees for weighted and stochastic context-free grammars. In *Proceedings of the Joint International Workshops on Advances in Pattern Recognition*. London: Springer, pp. 183–192.

Johnson, M., S. Geman, S. Canon, Z. Chi, and S. Riezler (1999). Estimators for stochastic 'unificationbased' grammars. In *Proceedings of the 37th Meeting of the Association for Computational Linguistics*, College Park, MD, pp. 535–541.

Kasami, T. (1965). An efficient recognition and syntax algorithm for context-free languages. Technical Report 65-758, Air Force Cambrige Research Laboratory, Bedford, MA.

Klein, D. and C.D. Manning (2001). Parsing and hypergraphs. In *Proceedings of the 7th International Workshop on Parsing Technologies*, Beijing, pp. 123–134.

Klein, D. and C.D. Manning (2003). A* parsing. Fast exact Viterbi parse selection. In *Proceedings of the 4th Conference of the North American Chapter of the ACL*, Edmonton.

Lang, B. (1994). Recognition can be harder than parsing. *Computational Intelligence 10*(4), 486–494.

Langkilde, I. (2000). Forest-based statistical sentence generation. In *Proceedings of the 1st Conference of the North American Chapter of the ACL*, Seattle, WA.

Malouf, R. (2002). A comparison of algorithms for maximum entropy parameter estimation. In *Proceedings of the 6th Conference on Natural Language Learning*, Taipei.

Malouf, R. and G. van Noord (2004). Wide coverage parsing with stochastic attribute value grammars. In *Proceedings of the IJCNLP Workshop Beyond Shallow Analysis*, Hainan.

Miyao, Y., T. Ninomiya, and J. Tsujii (2005). Corpus-oriented grammar development for acquiring a Head-Driven Phrase Structure Grammar from the Penn Treebank. In K.Y. Su, J. Tsujii, J.H. Lee, and O.Y. Kwong (Eds.), *Natural Language Processing*, Hainan Island, Lecture Notes in Artificial Intelligence, vol. 3248. Berlin: Springer, pp. 684–693.

Miyao, Y. and J. Tsujii (2008). Feature forest models for probabilistic HPSG parsing. *Computational Linguistics 34*(1), 35–88.

Moore, R.C. and H. Alshawi (1992). Syntactic and semantic processing. In H. Alshawi (Ed.), *The Core Language Engine*. Cambridge, MA: MIT Press, pp. 129–148.

Müller, S. and W. Kasper (2000). HPSG analysis of German. In W. Wahlster (Ed.), *Verbmobil. Foundations of Speech-to-Speech Translation* (Artificial Intelligence ed.). Berlin: Springer, pp. 238–253.

Oepen, S. and J. Carroll (2002). Efficient parsing for unification-based grammars. In S. Oepen, D. Flickinger, J. Tsujii, and H. Uszkoreit (Eds.), *Collaborative Language Engineering. A Case Study in Efficient Grammar-based Processing*. Stanford, CA: CSLI Publications, pp. 195–225.

Oepen, S., D. Flickinger, K. Toutanova, and C.D. Manning (2004). LinGO Redwoods. A rich and dynamic treebank for HPSG. *Journal of Research on Language and Computation 2*(4), 575–596.

Riezler, S., T.H. King, R.M. Kaplan, R. Crouch, J.T. Maxwell III, and M. Johnson (2002). Parsing the Wall Street Journal using a Lexical-Functional Grammar and discriminative estimation techniques. In *Proceedings of the 40th Meeting of the Association for Computational Linguistics*, Philadelphia, PA.

Toutanova, K., C.D. Manning, D. Flickinger, and S. Oepen (2005). Stochastic HPSG parse selection using the Redwoods corpus. *Journal of Research on Language and Computation 3*(1), 83–105.

Chapter 14
HPSG Parsing with a Supertagger

Takashi Ninomiya, Takuya Matsuzaki, Yusuke Miyao, Yoshimasa Tsuruoka, and Jun-ichi Tsujii

14.1 Introduction

For the last decade, fast, accurate and wide-coverage parsing for real-world text has been pursued in sophisticated grammar formalisms, such as head-driven phrase structure grammar (HPSG; Pollard and Sag, 1994), combinatory categorial grammar (CCG; Steedman, 2000) and lexical function grammar (LFG; Bresnan, 1982). They are preferred because they give precise and in-depth analyses explaining linguistic phenomena, such as passivization, control verbs and relative clauses. The main difficulty of developing parsers in these formalisms was how to model a well-defined probabilistic model for graph structures such as feature structures. This was overcome by a probabilistic model which provides probabilities of discriminating a correct parse tree among candidate parse trees in a *log-linear model* or *maximum entropy model* (Berger et al., 1996) with many features for parse trees (Abney, 1997; Johnson et al., 1999; Riezler et al., 2000; Malouf and van Noord, 2004; Kaplan et al., 2004; Miyao and Tsujii, 2005). Following this discriminative approach, techniques for efficiency were investigated for estimation (Geman and Johnson, 2002; Miyao and Tsujii, 2002; Malouf and van Noord, 2004) and parsing (Clark and Curran, 2004a, b; Ninomiya et al., 2005).

An interesting approach to the problem of parsing efficiency is using supertagging (Clark and Curran, 2004a, b; Wang, 2003; Wang and Harper, 2004; Nasr and Rambow, 2004; Ninomiya et al., 2006, 2007; Foth, 2006; Foth and Menzel, 2006), which was originally developed in (LTAG; Bangalore and Joshi, 1999) for lexicalized tree adjoining grammars. Supertagging is a process where words in an input sentence are tagged with "supertags," which are lexical entries in lexicalized grammars, e.g., elementary trees in LTAG, lexical categories in CCG, and lexical entries in HPSG. Bangalore and Joshi claim that if words can be assigned correct supertags, syntactic parsing is almost trivial (Bangalore and Joshi, 1999). What this means is that if supertags are correctly assigned, syntactic structures are

T. Ninomiya (✉)
Graduate School of Science and Engineering, Ehime University, 3 Bunkyo-cho, Matsuyama, Ehime, Japan
e-mail: ninomiya@cs.ehime-u.ac.jp

H. Bunt et al. (eds.), *Trends in Parsing Technology*, Text, Speech and Language Technology 43, DOI 10.1007/978-90-481-9352-3_14,

almost determined because supertags include rich syntactic information such as subcategorization frames. Nasr and Rambow showed that the accuracy of LTAG parsing reached about 97%, assuming that the correct supertags were given (Nasr and Rambow, 2004). The concept of supertagging is simple and interesting. The effects of this were recently demonstrated in the case of a CCG parser (Clark and Curran, 2004a) with the result of a drastic improvement in the parsing speed. Supertagging in their CCG parser was a technique to reduce the cost of parsing; ambiguity in assigning lexical entries to words is reduced by the light-weight process of supertagging before the heavy process of parsing. Wang and Harper also demonstrated the effects of supertagging with a statistical constraint dependency grammar (CDG) parser (Wang and Harper, 2004), and Foth et al. reported that accuracy was significantly improved by incorporating the supertagging probabilities into manually tuned Weighted CDG parsing (Foth et al., 2006; Foth and Menzel, 2006). They achieved an accuracy as high as the state-of-the-art parsers. However, a supertagger itself was used as an external tagger that enumerates candidates of lexical entries or filters out unlikely lexical entries just to help parsing, and the best parse trees were selected mainly according to the probabilistic model for phrase structures or dependencies with/without the probabilistic model for supertagging. In the case of supertagging of Weighted CDG (Foth et al., 2006), parameters for Weighted CDG are manually tuned, i.e., their model is not a well-defined probabilistic model.

We propose three probabilistic HPSG models with supertagging. First, we investigate an extreme case of HPSG parsing in which the probabilistic model is defined with only the probabilities of the supertagger; i.e., the model is defined with only the probabilities of lexical entry selection, and is never sensitive to characteristics of phrase structures. In most of the state-of-the-art parsers, probabilistic events are defined over phrase structures because phrase structures are supposed to dominate syntactic configurations of sentences. For example, probabilities were defined over grammar rules in probabilistic CFG (Collins, 1999; Klein and Manning, 2003; Charniak and Johnson, 2005) or over complex phrase structures of HPSG or CCG (Clark and Curran, 2004b; Malouf and van Noord, 2004; Miyao and Tsujii, 2005). Our model is simply defined as the product of the probabilities of lexical entry selection, which are provided by the discriminative method with machine learning features of word trigrams and part-of-speech (POS) 5-grams as defined in CCG supertagging (Clark and Curran, 2004a). The model is implemented in an HPSG parser instead of the phrase-structure-based probabilistic model; i.e., the parser returns the parse tree assigned the highest probability of supertagging among the parse trees licensed by an HPSG. Though the model uses only the probabilities of lexical entry selection, the experiments revealed that it achieved comparable accuracy as the previous phrase-structure-based model. Interestingly, this means that accurate parsing is possible using rather simple mechanisms.

We also investigate a hybrid model of the supertagger and the previous phrase-structure-based probabilistic model. In this hybrid model, the supertagger and the previous model are trained independently, and the probabilities of the previous model are multiplied by the supertagging probabilities. The model can be regarded as a variant of the statistical CDG parser (Wang, 2003; Wang and Harper, 2004), in which the parse tree probabilities are defined as the product of the supertagging probabilities and the dependency probabilities. In the experiments, we observed that the model improved parsing speed by around three times speed-ups, and accuracy by around 2.61 points in F-score, over the previous model. This implies that finer probabilistic models of lexical entry selection can improve the phrase-structure-based model.

Lastly, we propose a probabilistic model which properly incorporates the supertagger. In this model, the supertagger is trained first. The log-linear model for probabilistic HPSG is then trained so as to maximize its likelihood, given the supertagger probabilities as a reference distribution. This is the first model which properly incorporates the supertagging probabilities into a probabilistic parse tree model. We compared our models with the previous probabilistic model for phrase structures (Miyao and Tsujii, 2005). The previous model uses word and POS unigrams for its reference distribution, i.e., the probabilities of supertagging with word and POS unigrams. Our model can be regarded as an extension of a unigram reference distribution to an n-gram reference distribution with features that are used in supertagging.indexsupertagging.

Section 14.2 explains HPSG and the previous probabilistic models. Our models are presented in Section 14.3. Section 14.4 discusses our experiments, and Section 14.5 concludes the chapter.

14.2 HPSG and Probabilistic Models

HPSG (Pollard and Sag, 1994) is a syntactic theory based on lexicalized grammar. In HPSG, a small number of schemata describe general construction rules, and a large number of lexical entries express word-specific characteristics. The structures of sentences are explained using combinations of schemata and lexical entries. Both schemata and lexical entries are represented by typed feature structures, and constraints represented by feature structures are checked with unification.

An example of HPSG parsing of the sentence "*Spring has come*" is shown in Fig. 14.1. First, each of the lexical entries for "*has*" and "*come*" is unified with a

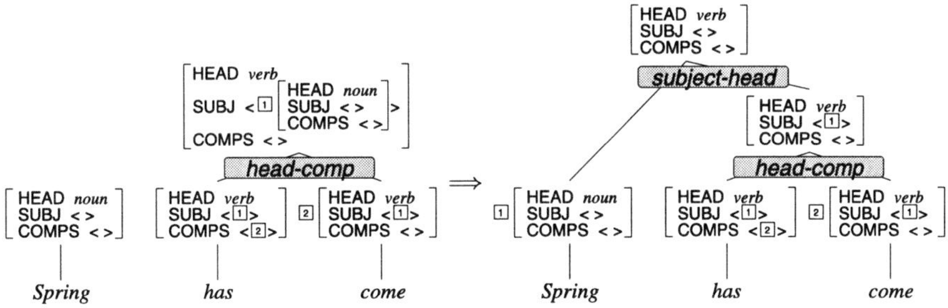

Fig. 14.1 HPSG parsing

daughter feature structure of the Head-Complement Schema. Unification provides the phrasal sign of the mother. The sign of the larger constituent is obtained by repeatedly applying schemata to lexical/phrasal signs. Finally, the parse result is output as a phrasal sign that dominates the sentence.

Given a set $\mathcal{W}$ of words and a set $\mathcal{F}$ of feature structures, an HPSG is formulated as a tuple, $G = \langle L, R \rangle$, where

$$L = \{l = \langle w, F \rangle | w \in \mathcal{W}, F \in \mathcal{F}\} \text{ is a set of lexical entries, and}$$
$$R \text{ is a set of schemata; i.e., } r \in R \text{ is a partial function: } \mathcal{F} \times \mathcal{F} \to \mathcal{F}$$

Given a sentence, an HPSG parser computes a set of phrasal signs, i.e., feature structures, as a result of parsing. Note that HPSG is one of the lexicalized grammar formalisms, in which lexical entries determine the dominant syntactic structures.

Previous studies (Abney, 1997; Johnson et al., 1999; Riezler et al., 2000; Malouf and van Noord, 2004; Kaplan et al., 2004; Miyao and Tsujii, 2005) defined a probabilistic model of unification-based grammars including HPSG as a *log-linear model* or *maximum entropy model* (Berger et al., 1996). The probability that a parse result T is assigned to a given sentence $\mathbf{w} = \langle w_1, \ldots, w_n \rangle$ is

(Probabilistic HPSG)

$$p_{hpsg}(T|\mathbf{w}) = \frac{1}{Z_{\mathbf{w}}} \exp\left(\sum_u \lambda_u f_u(T)\right)$$
$$Z_{\mathbf{w}} = \sum_{T'} \exp\left(\sum_u \lambda_u f_u(T')\right)$$

where λ_u is a model parameter, f_u is a feature function that represents a characteristic of parse tree T, and $Z_{\mathbf{w}}$ is the sum over the set of all possible parse trees for the sentence. Intuitively, the probability is defined as the normalized product of the weights $\exp(\lambda_u)$ when a characteristic corresponding to f_u appears in parse result T. The model parameters, λ_u, are estimated using numerical optimization methods (Malouf, 2002) to maximize the log-likelihood of the training data.

However, the above model cannot be easily estimated because the estimation requires the computation of $p(T|\mathbf{w})$ for all parse candidates assigned to sentence $\mathbf{w}$. Because the number of parse candidates is exponentially related to the length of the sentence, the estimation is intractable for long sentences. To make the model estimation tractable, Geman and Johnson (2002) and Miyao and Tsujii (2002) proposed a dynamic programming algorithm for estimating $p(T|\mathbf{w})$. Miyao and Tsujii (2005) also introduced a *preliminary probabilistic model* $p_0(T|\mathbf{w})$ whose estimation does not require the parsing of a treebank. This model is introduced as a *reference distribution* (Jelinek, 1998; Johnson and Riezler, 2000) of the probabilistic HPSG model; i.e., the computation of parse trees given low probabilities by the model is omitted in the estimation stage (Miyao and Tsujii, 2005), or a probabilistic model can be augmented by several distributions estimated from a larger and simpler corpus

(Johnson and Riezler, 2000). In (Miyao and Tsujii, 2005), $p_0(T|\mathbf{w})$ is defined as the product of probabilities of selecting lexical entries with word and POS unigram features:

(Miyao's model (Miyao and Tsujii, 2005))

$$p_{uniref}(T|\mathbf{w}) = p_0(T|\mathbf{w})\frac{1}{Z_\mathbf{w}} \exp\left(\sum_u \lambda_u f_u(T)\right)$$

$$Z_\mathbf{w} = \sum_{T'} p_0(T'|\mathbf{w}) \exp\left(\sum_u \lambda_u f_u(T')\right)$$

$$p_0(T|\mathbf{w}) = \prod_{i=1}^{n} p(l_i|w_i)$$

where l_i is a lexical entry assigned to word w_i in T and $p(l_i|w_i)$ is the probability of selecting lexical entry l_i for w_i. This reference distribution can be regarded as a supertagger with word and POS unigram features, but we call it *unigram reference distribution* to avoid confusion with the supertagger with word and POS n-gram features.

14.3 Probabilistic HPSG with a Supertagger

In the experiments, we tested parsing with Miyao's model explained in Section 14.2 and three other types of probabilistic models defined with the supertagger. The first one is the simplest probabilistic model, which is defined with only the supertagger's probabilities. It is defined simply as the product of the probabilities of selecting all lexical entries in the sentence; i.e., the model does not use the probabilities of phrase structures like the previous models.

Given a set of lexical entries, L, a sentence, $\mathbf{w} = \langle w_1, \ldots, w_n \rangle$, and the probabilistic model of lexical entry selection, $p(l_i \in L|w_i, \mathbf{w})$, the first model is formally defined as follows:

(Model 1)

$$p_{model1}(T|\mathbf{w}) = \prod_{i=1}^{n} p(l_i|w_i, \mathbf{w})$$

where l_i is a lexical entry assigned to word w_i in T and $p(l_i|w_i, \mathbf{w})$ is the probability of selecting lexical entry l_i for w_i.

The probabilities of lexical entry selection, $p(l_i|w_i, \mathbf{w})$, are defined as follows:

(Probabilistic Model of Lexical Entry Selection)

Table 14.1 Features for the supertagger

$f_{sptag} = \langle w_{i-1}, w_i, w_{i+1}, p_{i-2}, p_{i-1}, p_i, p_{i+1}, p_{i+2} \rangle$	
w_i	i-th word
p_i	part-of-speech for w_i
l_i	lexical entry for w_i
Combinations of feature templates	
$\langle w_{i-1} \rangle, \langle w_i \rangle, \langle w_{i+1} \rangle, \langle p_{i-2} \rangle, \langle p_{i-1} \rangle, \langle p_i \rangle, \langle p_{i+1} \rangle, \langle p_{i+2} \rangle, \langle p_{i+3} \rangle,$	
$\langle w_{i-1}, w_i \rangle, \langle w_i, w_{i+1} \rangle, \langle p_{i-1}, w_i \rangle, \langle p_i, w_i \rangle, \langle p_{i+1}, w_i \rangle, \langle p_i, p_{i+1}, p_{i+2}, p_{i+3} \rangle, \langle p_{i-2}, p_{i-1}, p_i \rangle,$	
$\langle p_{i-1}, p_i, p_{i+1} \rangle, \langle p_i, p_{i+1}, p_{i+2} \rangle, \langle p_{i-2}, p_{i-1} \rangle, \langle p_{i-1}, p_i \rangle, \langle p_i, p_{i+1} \rangle, \langle p_{i+1}, p_{i+2} \rangle$	

$$p(l_i|w_i, \mathbf{w}) = \frac{1}{Z_{w_i}} \exp\left(\sum_u \lambda_u f_u(l_i, w_i, \mathbf{w})\right)$$

$$Z_{w_i} = \sum_{l'} \exp\left(\sum_u \lambda_u f_u(l', w_i, \mathbf{w})\right)$$

where Z_{w_i} is the sum over all possible lexical entries for the word w_i. The feature templates used in our model are listed in Table 14.1 and are word trigrams and POS 5-grams.

The second model (model 3)[1] is a hybrid model of supertagging and the probabilistic HPSG. The probabilities are given as the product of model 1 and Miyao's model.

(Model 3)

$$p_{model3}(T|\mathbf{w}) = \frac{p_{model1}(T|\mathbf{w})}{p_0(T|\mathbf{w})} p_{uniref}(T|\mathbf{w})$$

where p_0 is the unigram reference distribution of p_{uniref}. In this model, the supertagger and the probabilistic HPSG model are independently trained, and the unigram reference distribution is replaced by the supertagger's probabilities. This model can be considered as a simple model in which the probabilities of the probabilistic HPSG is simply multiplied by the supertagger's probabilities. This model is supposed to be used in the case that we already have a probabilistic parser trained independently of the supertagger.

Finally, we propose a probabilistic model in which the supertagger is used as a reference distribution. This is an extension of Miyao's model (Miyao and Tsujii,

[1] We name our models model 1, model 3 and model 4 to keep consistency with our previous papers (Ninomiya et al., 2006, 2007).

2005) by replacing the unigram reference distribution with the supertagger. Our model is formally defined as follows:

(Model 4)

$$p_{model4}(T|\mathbf{w}) = \frac{1}{Z_{model4}} p_{model1}(T|\mathbf{w}) \exp\left(\sum_u \lambda_u f_u(T)\right)$$

$$Z_{model4} = \sum_{T'} p_{model1}(T'|\mathbf{w}) \exp\left(\sum_u \lambda_u f_u(T')\right)$$

In model 4, model 1 is used as a reference distribution. The only difference between model 3 and model 4 is the way in which model parameters are trained for phrase structures. In both models, the parameters for the supertagger (= the parameters of $p_{model1}(T|\mathbf{w})$) are first estimated from the word and POS sequences independently of the parameters for phrase structures. That is, the estimated parameters for lexical entries are the same in both models, and hence the probabilities of $p_{model1}(T|\mathbf{w})$ of both models are the same. Note that the parameters for lexical entries will never be updated after this estimation stage; i.e., the parameters for lexical entries are not estimated at the same time with the parameters for phrase structures. The difference of model 3 and model 4 is the estimation of parameters for phrase structures. In model 4, given the probabilities for lexical entries, the parameters for phrase structures are estimated so as to maximize the entire probabilistic model (= the product of the probabilities for lexical entries and the probabilities for phrase structures) in the training corpus.

Miyao's model also uses a reference distribution, but with word and POS unigram features, as is explained in the previous section. The only difference between model 4 and Miyao's model is that model 4 uses word and POS n-gram features.

14.4 Experiments

14.4.1 Implementation

We implemented the iterative parsing algorithm (Ninomiya et al., 2005) for the probabilistic HPSG models. It first starts parsing with a narrow beam. If the parsing fails, then the beam is widened, and parsing continues until the parser outputs results or the beam width reaches some limit. Though the probabilities of lexical entry selection are introduced, the algorithm for the presented probabilistic models is almost the same as the original iterative parsing algorithm.

The pseudo-code of the algorithm is shown in Fig. 14.2. In the figure, $\pi[i, j]$ represents the set of partial parse results that cover words $w_{i+1}, \ldots, w_j$, and $\rho[i, j, F]$

```
procedure Parsing(⟨w_1,...,w_n⟩, ⟨L,R⟩, α, β, κ, δ, θ)
  for i = 1 to n
    foreach F' ∈ {F|⟨w_i,F⟩ ∈ L}
      p = Σ_u λ_u f_u(F')
      π[i−1,i] ← π[i−1,i] ∪ {F'}
      if (p > ρ[i−1,i,F']) then
        ρ[i−1,i,F'] ← p
    LocalThresholding(i−1, i,α, β)
  for d = 1 to n
    for i = 0 to n−d
      j = i+d
      for k = i+1 to j−1
        foreach F_s ∈ φ[i,k], F_t ∈ φ[k,j], r ∈ R
          if F = r(F_s,F_t) has succeeded
            p = ρ[i,k,F_s] + ρ[k,j,F_t] + Σ_u λ_u f_u(F)
            π[i,j] ← π[i,j] ∪ {F}
            if (p > ρ[i,j,F]) then
              ρ[i,j,F] ← p
      LocalThresholding(i, j,κ, δ)
    GlobalThresholding(i, n, θ)
```

```
procedure IterativeParsing(w, G, α_0, β_0, κ_0, δ_0, θ_0, Δα, Δβ, Δκ, Δδ,
Δθ, α_last, β_last, κ_last, δ_last, θ_last)
  α ← α_0; β ← β_0; κ ← κ_0; δ ← δ_0; θ ← θ_0;
  loop while α ≤ α_last and β ≤ β_last and κ ≤ κ_last and δ ≤ δ_last and
θ ≤ θ_last
    call Parsing(w, G, α, β, κ, δ, θ)
    if π[1,n] ≠ ∅ then exit
    α ← α + Δα; β ← β + Δβ;
    κ ← κ + Δκ; δ ← δ + Δδ; θ ← θ + Δθ;
```

Fig. 14.2 Pseudo-code of iterative parsing for HPSG

stores the maximum figure-of-merit (FOM) of partial parse result F at cell (i, j). The probability of lexical entry F is computed as $\sum_u \lambda_u f_u(F)$ for the previous model, as shown in the figure. The probability of a lexical entry for models 1, 3 and 4 is computed as the probability of lexical entry selection, $p(F|w_i, \mathbf{w})$. The FOM of a newly created partial parse, F, is computed by summing the values of ρ of the daughters and an additional FOM of F if the model is Miyao's model, model 3 or model 4. The FOM for model 1 is computed by only summing the values of ρ of the daughters; i.e., weights $\exp(\lambda_u)$ in the figure are assigned zero. The terms κ and δ are the thresholds of the number of phrasal signs in the chart cell and the beam width for signs in the chart cell. The terms α and β are the thresholds of the number and the beam width for lexical entries, and θ is the beam width for global thresholding (Goodman, 1997).

14.4.2 Evaluation

We evaluated the speed and accuracy of parsing by using Enju 2.3β, the HPSG grammar for English (Miyao et al., 2005; Miyao and Tsujii, 2005). The lexicon of the grammar was extracted from Sections 02–21 of the Penn Treebank (Marcus et al., 1994) (39,832 sentences). The grammar consisted of 2,302 lexical entries for 11,187 words.[2] The probabilistic models were trained using the same portion of the treebank. We used beam thresholding, global thresholding (Goodman, 1997), preserved iterative parsing (Ninomiya et al., 2005) and quick check (Malouf et al., 2000).

We measured the accuracy of the predicate-argument relation output of the parser. A predicate-argument relation is defined as a tuple $\langle \sigma, w_h, a, w_a \rangle$, where σ is the predicate type (e.g., adjective, intransitive verb), w_h is the head word of the predicate, a is the argument label (MODARG, ARG1, ..., ARG4), and w_a is the head word of the argument. Labeled precision (LP)/labeled recall (LR) is the ratio of tuples correctly identified by the parser. Unlabeled precision (UP)/unlabeled recall (UR) is the ratio of tuples without the predicate type and the argument label. This evaluation scheme was the same as used in previous evaluations of lexicalized grammars (Hockenmaier, 2003; Clark and Curran, 2004b; Miyao and Tsujii, 2005). The experiments were conducted on an Intel Xeon 5160 server with a 3.0-GHz CPU. Section 22 of the Treebank was used as the development set, and the performance was evaluated using sentences of $\leq$ 100 words in Section 23. The performance of each model was analyzed using the sentences in Section 24 of $\leq$ 100 words. The total numbers of tested sentences in Sections 23 and 24 were 2,288 and 1,230 respectively.

The parsing performance for Section 23 is shown in Tables 14.2 and 14.3. Table 14.2 shows the performance using the correct POSs in the Penn Treebank, and Table 14.3 shows the performance using the POSs given by a POS tagger (Tsuruoka and Tsujii, 2005). LF and UF in the figure are labeled F-score and

Table 14.2 Experimental results for Section 23 (Gold POSs)

Models	LP (%)	LR (%)	LF (%)	UP (%)	UR (%)	UF (%)	Avg. time (ms)
Miyao's model	88.31	87.96	88.14	91.56	91.20	91.38	788
Model 1	87.36	87.26	87.31	89.91	89.81	89.86	247
Model 3	90.82	90.67	90.75	93.30	93.14	93.22	277
Model 4	91.11	90.90	91.01	93.45	93.24	93.35	280

Table 14.3 Experimental results for Section 23 (POS tagger)

Models	LP (%)	LR (%)	LF (%)	UP (%)	UR (%)	UF (%)	Avg. time (ms)
Miyao's model	86.40	86.25	86.32	90.53	90.37	90.45	834
Model 1	84.95	85.21	85.08	88.42	88.69	88.56	298
Model 3	88.70	88.75	88.73	92.14	92.19	92.17	351
Model 4	88.85	88.79	88.82	92.22	92.16	92.19	341

[2] An HPSG treebank is automatically generated from the Penn Treebank. Those lexical entries were generated by applying lexical rules to observed lexical entries in the HPSG treebank (Nakanishi et al., 2004). The lexicon, however, included many lexical entries that do not appear in the HPSG treebank. The HPSG treebank is used for training the probabilistic model for lexical entry selection, and hence, those lexical entries that do not appear in the treebank are rarely selected by the probabilistic model. The "effective" tag set size, therefore, is around 1,211, the number of lexical entries without those never-seen lexical entries.

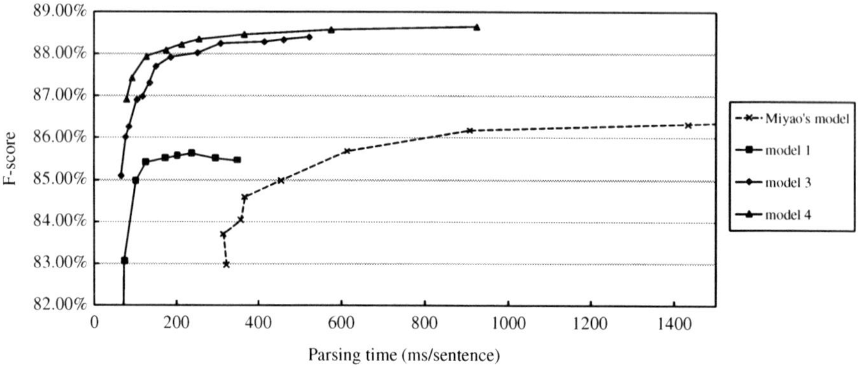

Fig. 14.3 F-score versus average parsing time for sentences in Section 24 of $\leq$ 100 words

unlabeled F-score. F-score is the harmonic mean of precision and recall. The parameters for beam searching were determined manually by trial and error using Section 22.[3] Our models significantly increased not only parsing speed but also parsing accuracy. Models 3 and 4 were around 2.8 times faster and had around 2.5 points higher precision and recall than Miyao's model. Surprisingly, model 1, which used only lexical information, was very fast and LF was lower than Miyao's model only by 0.8 points. When the automatic POS tagger was introduced, both precision and recall dropped by around 2 points, but the tendency towards improved speed and accuracy was again observed.

The average parsing time and labeled F-score curves of each probabilistic model for the sentences in Section 24 of $\leq$ 100 words are graphed in Fig. 14.3. The superiority of our models is clearly observed in the figure. Models 3 and 4 performed significantly better than Miyao's model, and model 4 performed the best among all the models. Model 1 was significantly faster, and its accuracy was comparable with Miyao's model.

14.4.3 Discussion

The best performer in terms of speed and accuracy was model 4. The increased speed was, of course, possible for the same reasons as the speeds of model 1. An unexpected but very impressive result was the significant improvement of accuracy

[3] The beam thresholding parameters for "Miyao's model" were $\alpha_0 = \kappa_0 = 18$, $\Delta\alpha = \Delta\kappa = 6$, $\alpha_{\text{last}} = \kappa_{\text{last}} = 36$, $\beta_0 = \delta_0 = 9.0$, $\Delta\beta = \Delta\delta = 3.0$, $\beta_{\text{last}} = \delta_{\text{last}} = 18.1$, $\theta_0 = 14.0$, $\Delta\theta = 4.0$, and $\theta_{\text{last}} = 26.1$. The beam thresholding parameters for "model 1" were $\alpha_0 = \kappa_0 = 9$, $\Delta\alpha = \Delta\kappa = 9$, $\alpha_{\text{last}} = \kappa_{\text{last}} = 45$, $\beta_0 = \delta_0 = 3.5$, $\Delta\beta = \Delta\delta = 5.0$, $\beta_{\text{last}} = \delta_{\text{last}} = 23.6$, $\theta_0 = 18.0$, $\Delta\theta = 5.5$, and $\theta_{\text{last}} = 40.1$. The beam thresholding parameters for "model 3" were $\alpha_0 = 11$, $\Delta\alpha = 11$, $\alpha_{\text{last}} = 55$, $\beta_0 = 4.5$, $\Delta\beta = 6.0$, $\beta_{\text{last}} = 28.5$, $\kappa_0 = 26$, $\Delta\kappa = 4$, $\kappa_{\text{last}} = 42$, $\delta_0 = 3.0$, $\Delta\delta = 2.25$, $\delta_{\text{last}} = 22.1$, $\theta_0 = 22.0$, $\Delta\theta = 3.0$, and $\theta_{\text{last}} = 34.1$. The beam thresholding parameters for "model 4" were $\alpha_0 = \kappa_0 = 12$, $\Delta\alpha = \Delta\kappa = 6$, $\alpha_{\text{last}} = \kappa_{\text{last}} = 30$, $\beta_0 = \delta_0 = 6.0$, $\Delta\beta = \Delta\delta = 3.0$, and $\beta_{\text{last}} = \delta_{\text{last}} = 15.1$. In "model 4", the global thresholding was not used.

Table 14.4 Comparison with recent studies. Experimental results for Section 23 (POS tagger)

Models	LP (%)	LR (%)	LF (%)	Avg. time (ms)
Model 4	88.85	88.79	88.82	341
Matsuzaki et al. (2007)	86.93	86.47	86.70	30
Sagae et al. (2007)	88.50	88.00	88.20	–

by 2.87 points in F-score, which is hard to attain by tweaking parameters or hacking features. This may be because the phrase structure information and lexical information complementarily improved the model. The lexical information includes more specific information about the syntactic alternation, and the phrase structure information includes information about the syntactic structures, such as the distances of head words or the sizes of phrases.

Nasr and Rambow (2004) showed that the accuracy of LTAG parsing reached about 97%, assuming that the correct supertags were given. We exemplified the dominance of lexical information in real syntactic parsing, i.e., syntactic parsing without gold-supertags, by showing that the probabilities of lexical entry selection dominantly contributed to syntactic parsing.

The CCG supertagging demonstrated fast and accurate parsing for the probabilistic CCG (Clark and Curran, 2004a). They used the supertagger for eliminating candidates of lexical entries, and the probabilities of parse trees were calculated using the phrase-structure-based model without the probabilities of lexical entry selection. Our study is essentially different from theirs in that the probabilities of lexical entry selection have been demonstrated to dominantly contribute to the disambiguation of phrase structures.

Table 14.4 shows comparison with other recent studies of HPSG parsing. The last two lines are the published results cited from (Matsuzaki et al., 2007) and (Sagae et al., 2007). Matsuzaki et al. proposed a technique for efficient HPSG parsing with supertagging and CFG filtering. They achieved drastic improvement in efficiency. Their parser ran around ten times faster than model 4. Instead, our models achieved better accuracy. Their efficiency is mainly due to elimination of ungrammatical lexical entries by the CFG filtering. They first parse a sentence with a CFG grammar compiled from an HPSG grammar, and then eliminate lexical entries that are not in the parsed CFG trees. Obviously, this technique can also be applied to the HPSG parsing of our models. We think that efficiency of HPSG parsing with our models will be drastically improved by applying this technique.

14.4.4 Evaluation of Supertaggers

We evaluated the performance of our probabilistic model as a supertagger.[4] The accuracy of the resulting supertagger on our development set (Section 22) is given

[4] In this experiments, we used an HPSG supertagger developed by using Enju 2.1. The grammar consisted of 3,797 lexical entries for 10,536 words. The "effective" tag set size was around 1,361, the number of lexical entries without those never-seen lexical entries.

Table 14.5 Accuracy of single-tag supertaggers. The numbers under "test data" are the PTB section numbers of the test data

	Test data	Accuracy (%)
HPSG supertagger (our supertagger)	22	87.51
CCG supertagger (Curran and Clark, 2003)	00/23	91.70/91.45
LTAG supertagger (Shen and Joshi, 2003)	22/23	86.01/86.27

Table 14.6 Accuracy of multi-supertagging

γ	Tags/word	Word acc. (%)	Sentence acc. (%)
1e-1	1.30	92.64	34.98
1e-2	2.11	95.08	46.11
1e-3	4.66	96.22	51.95
1e-4	10.72	96.83	55.66
1e-5	19.93	96.95	56.20

in Tables 14.5 and 14.6. The test sentences were automatically POS-tagged. Results of other supertaggers for automatically extracted lexicalized grammars are listed in Table 14.5. Table 14.6 gives the average number of supertags assigned to a word, the per-word accuracy, and the sentence accuracy for several values of γ, which is a parameter to determine how many lexical entries are assigned.

When compared with other supertag sets of automatically extracted lexicalized grammars, the (effective) size of our supertag set, 1,361 lexical entries, is between the CCG supertag set (398 categories) used by Curran and Clark (2003) and the LTAG supertag set (2920 elementary trees) used by Shen and Joshi (2003). The relative order based on the sizes of the tag sets exactly matches the order based on the accuracies of corresponding supertaggers.

14.5 Conclusion

We proposed three probabilistic models in which supertagging is integrated into the probabilistic model for HPSG. The first model is very simple. The probabilities of parse trees are defined with only the probabilities of the supertagger. Experiments revealed that the model achieved comparable accuracy with the previous model for probabilistic HPSG and that the implemented parser ran around three times faster. This indicates that accurate and fast parsing is possible using rather simple mechanisms. Second, we provided another probabilistic model, in which the probabilities for the leaf nodes in a parse tree are given by the probabilities of supertagging, and the probabilities for the intermediate nodes are given by the previous phrase-structure-based model. The experiments demonstrated not only speeds significantly increased by around three times but also impressive improvement in parsing accuracy by 2.61 points in F-score. Finally, we proposed a probabilistic model for HPSG parsing in which the reference distribution of the probabilistic HPSG is defined as the supertagger's probabilities. This model achieved the best performance in terms of accuracy and speed.

References

Abney, S.P. (1997). Stochastic attribute-value grammars. *Computational Linguistics 23*(4), 597–618.

Bangalore, S. and A. Joshi (1999). Supertagging: an approach to almost parsing. *Computational Linguistics 25*(2), 237–265.

Berger, A., S.D. Pietra, and V.D. Pietra (1996). A maximum entropy approach to natural language processing. *Computational Linguistics 22*(1), 39–71.

Bresnan, J. (1982). *The Mental Representation of Grammatical Relations*. Cambridge, MA: MIT Press.

Charniak, E. and M. Johnson (2005). Coarse-to-fine n-best parsing and maxent discriminative reranking. In *Proceedings of ACL'05*, Ann Arbor, Michigan, pp. 173–180.

Clark, S. and J.R. Curran (2004a). The importance of supertagging for wide-coverage CCG parsing. In *Proceedings of COLING-04*, Geneva, Switzerland, pp. 282–288.

Clark, S. and J.R. Curran (2004b). Parsing the WSJ using CCG and log-linear models. In *Proceedings of ACL'04*, Barcelona, Spain, pp. 104–111.

Collins, M. (1999). Head-driven statistical models for natural language parsing. Ph. D. thesis, University of Pennsylvania.

Curran, J.R. and S. Clark (2003). Investigating GIS and smoothing for maximum entropy taggers. In *Proceedings of EACL'03*, Budapest, Hungary, pp. 91–98.

Foth, K., T. By, and W. Menzel (2006). Guiding a constraint dependency parser with supertags. In *Proceedings of COLING-ACL-06*, Sydney, Australia, pp. 289–296.

Foth, K. and W. Menzel (2006). Hybrid parsing: using probabilistic models as predictors for a symbolic parser. In *Proceedings of COLING-ACL-06*, Sydney, Australia, pp. 321–328.

Geman, S. and M. Johnson (2002). Dynamic programming for parsing and estimation of stochastic unification-based grammars. In *Proceedings of ACL'02*, Philadelphia, Pennsylvania, pp. 279–286.

Goodman, J. (1997). Global thresholding and multiple pass parsing. In *Proceedings of EMNLP-97*, Providence, Rhode Island, pp. 11–25.

Hockenmaier, J. (2003). Parsing with generative models of predicate-argument structure. In *Proceedings of ACL'03*, Sapporo, Japan, pp. 359–366.

Jelinek, F. (1998). *Statistical Methods for Speech Recognition*. Cambridge, MA: The MIT Press.

Johnson, M., S. Geman, S. Canon, Z. Chi, and S. Riezler (1999). Estimators for stochastic "unification-based" grammars. In *Proceedings of ACL'99*, College Park, Maryland, pp. 535–541.

Johnson, M. and S. Riezler (2000). Exploiting auxiliary distributions in stochastic unificationbased grammars. In *Proceedings of NAACL-00*, Seattle, Washington, pp. 154–161.

Kaplan, R.M., S. Riezler, T.H. King, J.T. Maxwell III, and A. Vasserman (2004). Speed and accuracy in shallow and deep stochastic parsing. In *Proceedings of HLT/NAACL'04*, Boston, Massachusetts, pp. 97–104.

Klein, D. and C.D. Manning (2003). Accurate unlexicalized parsing. In *Proceedings of ACL'03*, Sapporo, Japan, pp. 423–430.

Malouf, R. (2002). A comparison of algorithms for maximum entropy parameter estimation. In *Proceedings of CoNLL-02*, Taipei, Taiwan, pp. 49–55.

Malouf, R., J. Carroll, and A. Copestake (2000). Efficient feature structure operations without compilation. *Journal of Natural Language Engineering 6*(1), 29–46.

Malouf, R. and G. van Noord (2004). Wide coverage parsing with stochastic attribute value grammars. In *Proceedings of IJCNLP-04 Workshop "Beyond Shallow Analyses"*, Sanya City, Hainan Island, China.

Marcus, M.P., B. Santorini, and M.A. Marcinkiewicz (1994). Building a large annotated corpus of English: the Penn Treebank. *Computational Linguistics 19*(2), 313–330.

Matsuzaki, T., Y. Miyao, and J. Tsujii (2007). Efficient HPSG parsing with supertagging and CFG-filtering. In *Proceedings of IJCAI'07*, Hyderabad, India, pp. 1671–1676.

Miyao, Y., T. Ninomiya, and J. Tsujii (2005). Corpusoriented grammar development for acquiring a head-driven phrase structure grammar from the Penn Treebank. In Keh-Yih Su, Jun'ichi Tsujii, Jong-Hyeok Lee, and Oi Yee Kwong (Eds.), *Natural Language Processing – IJCNLP 2004*, Lecture Notes in Artificial Intelligence, vol. 3248, pp. 684–693. Heidelberg: Springer.

Miyao, Y. and J. Tsujii (2002). Maximum entropy estimation for feature forests. In *Proceedings of HLT'02*, San Diego, California, pp. 292–297.

Miyao, Y. and J. Tsujii (2005). Probabilistic disambiguation models for wide-coverage HPSG parsing. In *Proceedings of ACL'05*, Ann Arbor, Michigan, pp. 83–90.

Nakanishi, H., Y. Miyao, and J. Tsujii (2004). An empirical investigation of the effect of lexical rules on parsing with a treebank grammar. In *Proceedings of TLT'04*, Tübingen, Germany, pp. 103–114.

Nasr, A. and O. Rambow (2004). Supertagging and full parsing. In *Proceedings of the 7th International Workshop on Tree Adjoining Grammar and Related Formalisms (TAG+7)*, Vancouver, British Columbia, Canada, pp. 56–63.

Ninomiya, T., T. Matsuzaki, Y. Miyao, and J. Tsujii (2007). A log-linear model with an n-gram reference distribution for accurate HPSG parsing. In *Proceedings of IWPT'07*, Prague, Czech Republic, pp. 60–68.

Ninomiya, T., T. Matsuzaki, Y. Tsuruoka, Y. Miyao, and J. Tsujii (2006). Extremely lexicalized models for accurate and fast HPSG parsing. In *Proceedings of EMNLP'06*, Sydney, Australia, pp. 155–163.

Ninomiya, T., Y. Tsuruoka, Y. Miyao, and J. Tsujii (2005). Efficacy of beam thresholding, unification filtering and hybrid parsing in probabilistic HPSG parsing. In *Proceedings of the IWPT'05*, Vancouver, British Columbia, Canada, pp. 103–114.

Pollard, C. and I.A. Sag (1994). *Head-Driven Phrase Structure Grammar*. Chicago, IL: University of Chicago Press.

Riezler, S., D. Prescher, J. Kuhn, and M. Johnson (2000). Lexicalized stochastic modeling of constraint-based grammars using log-linear measures and EM training. In *Proceedings of ACL'00*, Hong Kong, China, pp. 480–487.

Sagae, K., Y. Miyao, and J. Tsujii (2007). HPSG parsing with shallow dependency constraints. In *Proceedings of ACL'07*, Prague, Czech Republic, pp. 624–631.

Shen, L. and A.K. Joshi (2003). A SNoW based supertagger with application to NP chunking. In *Proceedings of ACL'03*, Sapporo, Japan, pp. 505–512.

Steedman, M. (2000). *The Syntactic Process*. Cambridge, MA: The MIT Press.

Tsuruoka, Y. and J. Tsujii (2005). Bidirectional inference with the easiest-first strategy for tagging sequence data. In *Proceedings of HLT/EMNLP'05*, Vancouver, British Columbia, Canada, pp. 467–474.

Wang, W. (2003). Statistical parsing and language modeling based on constraint dependency grammar. Ph. D. thesis, Purdue University.

Wang, W. and M.P. Harper (2004). A statistical constraint dependency grammar (CDG) parser. In *Proceedings of ACL'04 Incremental Parsing Workshop: Bringing Engineering and Cognition Together*, Barcelona, Spain, pp. 42–49.

Chapter 15
Evaluating the Impact of Re-training a Lexical Disambiguation Model on Domain Adaptation of an HPSG Parser

Tadayoshi Hara, Yusuke Miyao, and Jun-ichi Tsujii

15.1 Introduction

Domain portability is an important aspect of the applicability of NLP tools to practical tasks. Therefore, domain adaptation methods have recently been proposed in several NLP areas, e.g., word sense disambiguation (Chan and Ng, 2006), statistical parsing (Lease and Charniak, 2005; McClosky et al., 2006; Titov and Henderson, 2006), and lexicalized-grammar parsing (Johnson and Riezler, 2000; Hara et al., 2005). Their aim was to re-train a probabilistic model for a new domain at low cost. The success of these attempts in improving the accuracy for the domain was variable.

In this chapter, we propose a method for adapting an HPSG parser (Miyao and Tsujii, 2002; Ninomiya et al., 2006; Takashi Ninomiya et al., Chapter 14, this volume) trained on the WSJ section of the Penn Treebank (Marcus et al., 1994) to a biomedical domain. Our method re-trains a probabilistic model of lexical entry assignments to words in a target domain, and incorporates it into the original parser. The model of lexical entry assignments is a log-linear model re-trained only with machine learning features of word n-grams. Hence, the cost for the re-training is much lower than the cost of training the entire disambiguation model from scratch.

In the following experiments, we used an HPSG parser originally trained with the Penn Treebank, and evaluated a disambiguation model re-trained with the GENIA treebank (Kim et al., 2003), which consists of abstracts of biomedical papers. We varied the size of a training corpus, and measured the transition of the parsing accuracy and the cost required for parameter estimation. For comparison, we also examined other possible approaches to adapting the same parser. In addition, we applied our approach to the Brown corpus in order to examine the portability of our approach (Kučera and Francis, 1967).

T. Hara (✉)
Department of Computer Science, Faculty of Information Science and Technology,
University of Tokyo, Tokyo 113-0033, Japan
e-mail: harasan@is.s.u-tokyo.ac.jp

H. Bunt et al. (eds.), *Trends in Parsing Technology*, Text, Speech and Language Technology 43, DOI 10.1007/978-90-481-9352-3_15,

The experimental results revealed that, by simply re-training the probabilistic model of lexical entry assignments, we achieve higher parsing accuracy than with a previously proposed adaptation method. In addition, combined with the existing adaptation method, our approach achieves accuracy as high as that obtained by re-training the original parser from scratch, but with much lower training cost. In this chapter, we report these experimental results in detail, and discuss how disambiguation models of lexical entry assignments contribute to domain adaptation.

In recent years, lexical information has been shown to play a very important role for high accuracy of lexicalized grammar parsing. Bangalore and Joshi (1999) indicated that correct disambiguation with supertagging, i.e., assignment of lexical entries before parsing, enabled effective LTAG (Lexicalized Tree-Adjoining Grammar) parsing. Clark and Curran (2004a) showed that supertagging reduced cost for training and execution of a CCG (Combinatory Categorial Grammar) parser while keeping accuracy. Clark and Curran (2006) showed that a CCG parser trained on data derived from lexical category sequences alone was only slightly less accurate than one trained on complete dependency structures. Ninomiya et al. (2006) also succeeded in significantly improving speed and accuracy of HPSG parsing by using supertagging probabilities. These results indicate that the probability of lexical entry assignments is essential for parse disambiguation.

Such usefulness of lexical information has also been shown for domain adaptation methods. Lease and Charniak (2005) showed how existing domain-specific lexical resources on a target domain may be leveraged to augment PTB-training: part-of-speech tags, dictionary collocations, and named-entities. Our findings basically follow the above results. The contribution of this chapter is to provide empirical results of the relationships among domain variation, probability of lexical entry assignments, training data size, and training cost. In particular, this chapter empirically shows how much in-domain corpus is required for satisfactory performance.

In Section 15.2, we introduce an HPSG parser and describe an existing method for domain adaptation. In Section 15.3, we show our methods of re-training a lexical disambiguation model and incorporating it into the original model. In Section 15.4, we examine our method through experiments on the GENIA treebank. In Section 15.5, we examine the portability of our method through experiments on the Brown corpus. In Section 15.6, we discuss several recent pieces of research related to domain adaptation.

15.2 An HPSG Parser

HPSG (Pollard and Sag, 1994) is a syntactic theory based on a lexicalized grammar formalism. In HPSG, a small number of grammar rules describe general construction rules, and a large number of lexical entries express word-specific characteristics. The structures of sentences are explained using combinations of grammar rules and lexical entries.

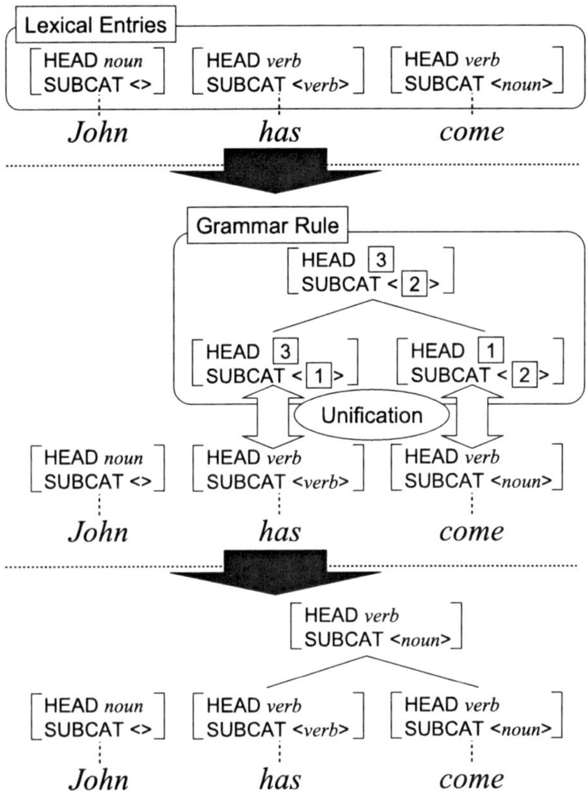

Fig. 15.1 Parsing a sentence "*John has come*"

Figure 15.1 shows an example of HPSG parsing of the sentence "*John has come.*" First, as shown at the top of the figure, an HPSG parser assigns a lexical entry to each word in this sentence. Next, a grammar rule is assigned and applied to lexical entries. In the middle of this figure, the grammar rule is applied to the lexical entries for "*has*" and "*come*." We then obtain the structure represented at the bottom of the figure. After that, the application of grammar rules is performed iteratively, and then we can finally obtain the parse tree as is shown in Fig. 15.2. In practice, since two or more parse candidates can be given for one sentence, a disambiguation model gives probabilities to these candidates, and a candidate given the highest probability is then chosen as a correct parse.

The HPSG parser used in this study is Ninomiya et al. (2006), which is based on *Enju* (Miyao and Tsujii, 2005). Lexical entries of Enju were extracted from the Penn Treebank (Marcus et al., 1994), which consists of sentences collected from The Wall Street Journal (Miyao et al., 2004). The disambiguation model of Enju was trained on the same treebank. The disambiguation model of Enju is based on a feature forest model (Miyao and Tsujii, 2002), which is a log-linear model (Berger

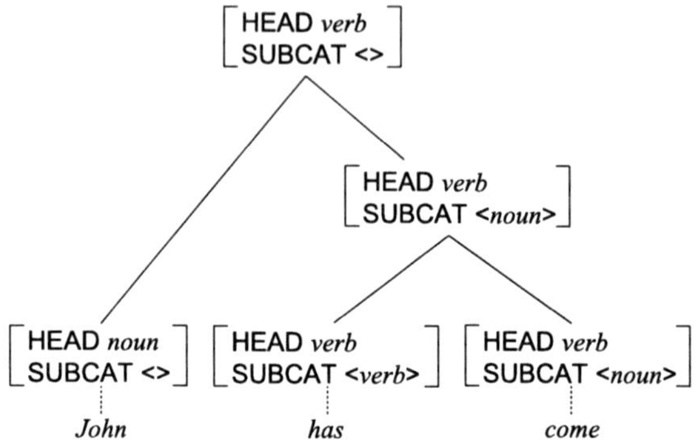

Fig. 15.2 An HPSG parse tree for a sentence "*John has come*"

et al., 1996) on packed forest structure. The probability, $p_E(t|\mathbf{w})$, of producing the parse result t for a given sentence $\mathbf{w} = \langle w_1, ..., w_u \rangle$ is defined as

$$p_E(t|\mathbf{w}) = \frac{1}{Z_s} \prod_i p_{lex}(l_i|\mathbf{w}, i) \cdot q_{syn}(t|\mathbf{l}),$$
$$Z_s = \sum_{t \in T(\mathbf{w})} \prod_i p_{lex}(l_i|\mathbf{w}, i) \cdot q_{syn}(t|\mathbf{l})$$

where $\mathbf{l} = \langle l_1, \ldots, l_u \rangle$ is a list of lexical entries assigned to $\mathbf{w}$, $p_{lex}(l_i|\mathbf{w}, i)$ is a probabilistic model giving the probability that lexical entry l_i is assigned to word w_i, $q_{syn}(t|\mathbf{l})$ is an unnormalized log-linear model of tree construction and gives the possibility that parse candidate t is produced from lexical entries $\mathbf{l}$, and $T(\mathbf{w})$ is a set of parse candidates assigned to $\mathbf{w}$. With a treebank of a target domain as training data, model parameters of p_{lex} and q_{syn} are estimated so as to maximize the log-likelihood of the training data.

Probabilistic model p_{lex} is defined as a log-linear model as follows.

$$p_{lex}(l_i|\mathbf{w}, i) = \frac{1}{Z_{w_i}} \exp\left(\sum_j \lambda_j f_j(l_i, \mathbf{w}, i)\right),$$
$$Z_{w_i} = \sum_{l_i \in L(w_i)} \exp\left(\sum_j \lambda_j f_j(l_i, \mathbf{w}, i)\right),$$

where $L(w_i)$ is a set of lexical entries which can be assigned to word w_i. Before training this model, $L(w_i)$ for all w_i are extracted from the training treebank. The feature function $f_j(l_i, \mathbf{w}, i)$ represents the characteristics of l_i, $\mathbf{w}$ and w_i, while corresponding λ_j is its weight. For the feature functions, instead of using unigram features adopted in Miyao and Tsujii (2005), Ninomiya et al. (2006) used "word trigram" and "POS 5-gram" features which are listed in Table 15.1. With the revised

Table 15.1 Features for the probabilities of lexical entry selection

Surrounding words	$w_{-1}w_0w_1$ (word trigram)
Surrounding POS tags	$p_{-2}p_{-1}p_0p_1p_2$ (POS 5-gram)
Combinations	$w_{-1}w_0$, w_0w_1, $p_{-1}w_0$, p_0w_0, p_1w_0, $p_0p_1p_2p_3$, $p_{-2}p_{-1}p_0$, $p_{-1}p_0p_1$, $p_0p_1p_2$, $p_{-2}p_{-1}$, $p_{-1}p_0$, p_0p_1, p_1p_2

Enju model, they achieved parsing accuracy as high as Miyao and Tsujii (2005), with around four times faster parsing speed.

Johnson and Riezler (2000) suggested a method for adapting a stochastic unification-based grammar including HPSG to another domain. They incorporated auxiliary distributions as additional features for an original log-linear model, and then attempted to assign proper weights to the new features. With this approach, they could incorporate various in-domain distributional information which was obtained with relative ease and succeeded in improving parsing accuracy of their LFG parser for a target domain.

Our previous work proposed a method for adapting an HPSG parser trained on the Penn Treebank to a biomedical domain (Hara et al., 2005). We re-trained a disambiguation model of tree construction, i.e., q_{syn}, for the target domain. In this approach, q_{syn} of the original parser was used as a *reference distribution* (Jelinek, 1998) of another log-linear model, and the new model was trained using a target treebank. Since re-training used only a small treebank of the target domain, the cost was small and parsing accuracy was successfully improved.

15.3 Re-training of a Disambiguation Model of Lexical Entry Assignments

Our idea of domain adaptation is to train a disambiguation model of lexical entry assignments for the target domain and then incorporate it into the original parser. Since Enju includes the disambiguation model of lexical entry assignments as p_{lex}, we can implement our method in Enju by training another disambiguation model $p'_{lex}(l_i|\mathbf{w}, i)$ of lexical entry assignments for the biomedical domain, and then replacing the original p_{lex} with the newly trained p'_{lex}.

In this chapter, for p'_{lex}, we train a disambiguation model $p_{lex-mix}(l_i|\mathbf{w}, i)$ of lexical entry assignments. $p_{lex-mix}$ is a maximum entropy model and the feature functions for it is the same as p_{lex} as given in Table 15.1. With these feature functions, we train $p_{lex-mix}$ on the treebanks both of the original and biomedical domains.

In the experiments, we examine the contribution of our method to parsing accuracy. In addition, we implement several other possible methods for comparison of the performances:

- baseline: use the original model of Enju
- GENIA only: execute the same method of training the disambiguation model of Enju, using only the GENIA treebank

- Mixture: execute the same method of training the disambiguation model of Enju, using both of the Penn Treebank and the GENIA treebank (a kind of smoothing method)
- HMT05: execute the method proposed in our previous work (Hara et al., 2005)
- Our method: replace p_{lex} in the original model with $p_{lex-mix}$, while leaving q_{syn} as it is
- Our method (GENIA): replace p_{lex} in the original model with $p_{lex-genia}$, which is a probabilistic model of lexical entry assignments trained only with the GENIA treebank, while leaving q_{syn} as it is
- Our method + GENIA: replace p_{lex} in the original model with $p_{lex-mix}$ and q_{syn} with $q_{syn-genia}$, which is a disambiguation model of tree construction trained with the GENIA treebank
- Our method + HMT05: replace p_{lex} in the original model with $p_{lex-mix}$ and q_{syn} with the model re-trained with our previous method (Hara et al., 2005) (the combination of our method and the "HMT05" method)
- baseline (lex): use only p_{lex} as a disambiguation model
- GENIA only (lex): use only $p_{lex-genia}$ as a disambiguation model, which is a probabilistic model of lexical entry assignments trained only with the GENIA treebank
- Mixture (lex): use only $p_{lex-mix}$ as a disambiguation model

The baseline method does no adaptation to the biomedical domain, and therefore gives lower parsing accuracy for this domain than for the original domain. This method is regarded as the baseline of the experiments. The GENIA only method relies solely on the treebank for the biomedical domain, and therefore it cannot work well with the small treebank. The Mixture method is a kind of smoothing method using all available training data at the same time, and therefore the method can give the highest accuracy of the three, which would be regarded as the ideal accuracy with the naive methods. However, training this model is expected to be very costly.

The baseline (lex), GENIA only (lex), and Mixture (lex) approaches rely solely on models of lexical entry assignments, and show lower accuracy than those that contain both of models of lexical entry assignments and tree constructions. These approaches can be utilized as indicators of the importance of combining the two types of models.

Our previous work (Hara et al., 2005) showed that the model trained with the HMT05 method can give higher accuracy than the baseline method, even with the small amount of the treebanks in the biomedical domain. The model is also much less costly to train than the Mixture method. However, the method was found not to give as high accuracy as the Mixture method.

15.4 Experiments with the GENIA Corpus

We implemented the models shown in Section 15.3, and then evaluated the performance of them. We compared the performances of the models from variousangles, by focusing mainly on the accuracy compared to training cost. Through the observations, the impact of re-training the lexical entry assignment models would be clarified.

15.4.1 Experimental Settings

The original parser, Enju, was developed on Section 02–21 of the Penn Treebank (39,832 sentences) (Miyao and Tsujii, 2005; Ninomiya et al., 2006). For training those models, we used the GENIA treebank (Kim et al., 2003), which consisted of 1,200 abstracts (10,848 sentences) extracted from MEDLINE. We divided it into three sets of 900, 150, and 150 abstracts (8,127, 1,361, and 1,360 sentences), and these sets were used respectively as training, development, and final evaluation data. The method of Gaussian MAP estimation (Chen and Rosenfeld, 1999) was used for smoothing. The meta parameter σ of the Gaussian distribution was determined so as to maximize the accuracy on the development set.

In the following experiments, we measured the accuracy of predicate-argument dependencies on the evaluation set. The measure is labeled precision/recall (LP/LR), which is the same measure as previous work (Clark and Curran, 2004b; Miyao and Tsujii, 2005) that evaluated the accuracy of lexicalized grammars on the Penn Treebank.

The features for the examined approaches were all the same as the original disambiguation model. In our previous work, the features for HMT05 were tuned to some extent. We evened out the features in order to compare various approaches under the same condition. The lexical entries for training each model were extracted from the treebank used for training the model of lexical entry assignments.

We compared the performances of the given models from various angles, by focusing mainly on the accuracy against the cost. For each of the models, we measured the accuracy transition according to the size of the GENIA treebank for training and according to the training time. We changed the size of the GENIA treebank for training: 100, 200, 300, 400, 500, 600, 700, 800, and 900 abstracts. Figures 15.3 and 15.4 show the F-score transition according to the size of the training set and the training time among the given models respectively. Tables 15.2 and 15.3 show the parsing performance and the training cost obtained when using 900 abstracts of the GENIA treebank. Note that Fig. 15.4 does not include the results of the Mixture method because this method took too much training cost as shown in Table 15.3. It should also be noted that training time in Fig. 15.4 includes time required for both training and development tests. Differences in accuracies from the baseline in Table 15.2 are statistically significant, according to a stratified shuffling test (Cohen, 1995) (p-value < 0.05).

In the rest of this section we analyze these experimental results by focusing mainly on the contribution of re-training the lexical entry assignment models. We first observe the results with the naive or existing approaches. On the basis of these results, we evaluate the impact of our method. We then explore the combination of our method with other methods, and analyze the errors to gain insight for future research.

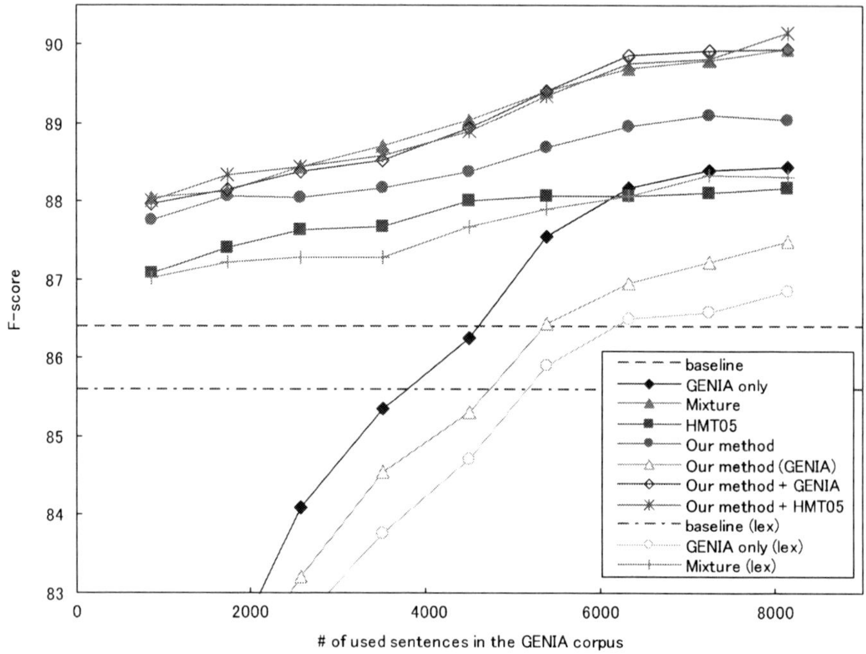

Fig. 15.3 Corpus size vs. accuracy for various methods

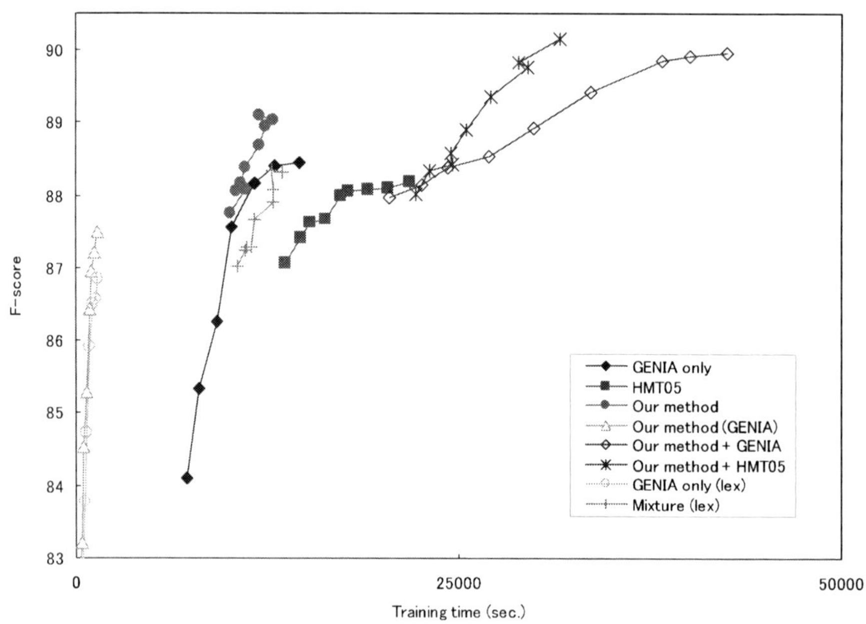

Fig. 15.4 Training time vs. accuracy for various methods

Table 15.2 Parsing accuracy and time for various methods

	GENIA Corpus				Penn Treebank			
	LP	LR	F-score	Time (s)	LP	LR	F-score	Time (s)
baseline	86.71	86.08	86.39	476	89.99	89.63	89.81	675
GENIA only	88.99	87.91	88.45	242	72.07	45.78	55.99	2,441
Mixture	90.01	89.87	89.94	355	89.93	89.60	89.77	767
HMT05	88.47	87.89	88.18	510	88.92	88.61	88.76	778
Our method	89.11	88.97	89.04	327	89.96	89.63	89.79	713
Our method (GENIA)	86.06	85.15	85.60	542	70.18	44.88	54.75	3,290
Our method + GENIA	90.02	89.88	89.95	320	88.11	87.77	87.94	718
Our method + HMT05	90.23	90.08	90.15	377	89.31	88.98	89.14	859
baseline (lex)	85.93	85.27	85.60	377	87.52	87.13	87.33	553
GENIA only (lex)	87.42	86.28	86.85	197	71.49	45.41	55.54	1,928
Mixture (lex)	88.43	88.18	88.31	258	87.49	87.12	87.30	585

Table 15.3 Training cost of various methods

	Training time (s)	Memory used (GB)
baseline	0	0.00
GENIA only	14,695	1.10
Mixture	238,576	5.05
HMT05	21,833	1.10
Our method	12,957	4.27
Our method (GENIA)	1,419	0.94
Our method + GENIA	42,475	4.27
Our method + HMT05	31,637	4.27
baseline (lex)	0	0.00
GENIA only (lex)	1,434	1.10
Mixture (lex)	13,595	4.27

15.4.2 Exploring Naive or Existing Approaches

Without adaptation, Enju reached a parsing accuracy of 86.4% in F-score, which was 3.4% point lower than the accuracy for the original domain, the Penn Treebank. This is the baseline of the experiments.

Figure 15.3 shows that, for less than about 4,500 training sentences, the GENIA only method could not obtain as high parsing accuracy as the baseline method. This result indicates that the training data is not sufficient to re-train the whole disambiguation model from scratch. However, if we prepared more than 4,500 sentences, the method could give higher accuracy than baseline with low training cost (see Fig. 15.4). On the other hand, the Mixture method could obtain the highest level of the parsing accuracy for any size of the GENIA treebank. However, Table 15.3 shows that this method required too much training cost. This would be a major barrier for further challenges for improvement with various additional parameters.

Advantages of the HMT05 method are that it could give higher accuracy than the baseline method for any size of the training sentences although the accuracy was lower than the Mixture method. The method could also be carried out in much smaller training time and lower cost than the Mixture method. On the other hand, when we compared the HMT05 method with the GENIA only method, for the larger size of the training corpus, the HMT05 method performed less well than the GENIA only method in parsing accuracy and training cost.

15.4.3 Impact of Re-training a Lexical Disambiguation Model

If we consider our method, it consistently gives higher accuracy than the baseline and the HMT05 methods. These results indicate that, for an individual method, re-training a model of lexical entry assignments might be more critical to domain adaptation than re-training the model of tree construction. In addition, for the small treebanks, our method could give as high accuracy as the Mixture method with much lower training cost. Our method could be a very satisfactory approach when applied to a small treebank. It should be noted that the re-trained lexical model could not give the accuracy as high as our method alone (see Mixture (lex) in Fig. 15.3). The combination of a re-trained lexical model and a tree construction model would have given such a high performance.

When we compare the training time for our method with the one for the HMT05 method, we observe that our method requires less time than the HMT05 method. This would be because our method requires only the re-training of the very simple model, that is, a probabilistic model of lexical entry assignments.

It should be noted that our method would not work only with in-domain treebanks. The Our method (GENIA) and the GENIA only (lex) methods could hardly give as high parsing accuracy as the baseline method. Although for the larger size of the GENIA treebank the methods could obtain a little higher accuracy than the baseline method, the benefit was very little. These results would indicate that using only the treebank in the target domain would be insufficient for adaptation. Table 15.4 shows the coverage of each training corpus for each treebank, and Fig. 15.5 focuses on the coverage transition for the GENIA corpus according to the size of the GENIA training set which would also support the above observation. They show that the GENIA treebank alone could not cover as many sentences in the GENIA corpus as the combination of the Penn Treebank and the GENIA treebank.

Table 15.4 Coverage of each training set

	Percentage of covered sentences	
Training set	For GENIA	For PTB
GENIA treebank	77.54	25.66
PTB treebank	70.45	84.12
GENIA treebank + PTB treebank	82.74	84.86

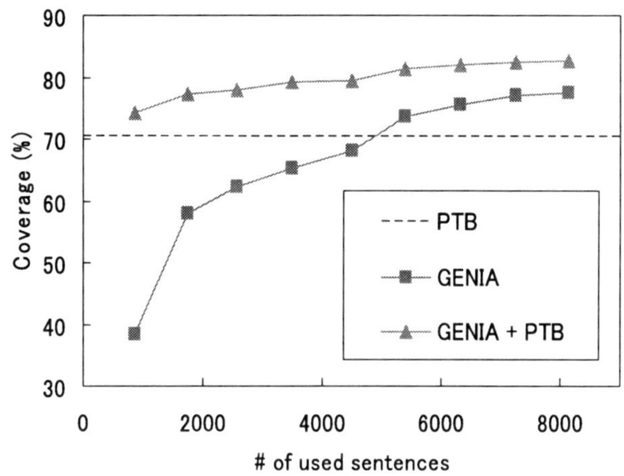

Fig. 15.5 Corpus size vs. coverage of each training set for the GENIA corpus

15.4.4 Effectiveness of Combining Lexical and Syntactic Disambiguation Models

When we compared Our method + HMT05 and Our method + GENIA with the Mixture method, we found that the former two models could yield as high parsing accuracies as the latter one for any size of the training corpus. In particular, for the maximum size, the Our method + HMT05 models could give a little higher parsing accuracy than the Mixture method. This difference was shown to be significant according to a stratified shuffling test (p-value < 0.10). This suggests that the Our method + HMT05 method has a beneficial impact. In addition, Fig. 15.4 and Table 15.3 show that training the Our method + HMT05 or Our method + GENIA model required much less time and PC memory than training the Mixture model. According to the above observation, we are able to say that the Our method + HMT05 method is the most preferable method.

Our method + HMT05 can obtain high parsing accuracy with less training time than the Our method + GENIA method. This difference in performance comes from the fact that the latter method trained $q_{syn-genia}$ only with lexical entries in the GENIA treebank, while the former trained q_{syn} with rich lexical entries borrowed from $q_{lex-mix}$. Rich lexical entries reduce the number of unknown lexical entries, and therefore improve the effectiveness of the feature forest model. On the other hand, the difference in lexical entries does not seem to affect the contribution of the tree construction model much, and consequently the parsing accuracy. In our experiments, the parameters for a tree construction model such as feature functions were not adjusted thoroughly, which might possibly decrease the benefits of the rich lexical entries.

15.4.5 Error Analysis

Table 15.5 shows the comparison of the number of errors for various models with the errors for the original model in parsing the GENIA corpus. For each of the

Table 15.5 Errors in various methods

	Total errors	=	Errors in common with baseline	+	Specific errors
GENIA only	2,889	=	1,906 (65.97%)	+	983 (34.03%)
Mixture	2,653	=	2,177 (82.06%)	+	476 (17.94%)
HMT05	3,063	=	2,470 (80.64%)	+	593 (19.36%)
Our method	2,891	=	2,405 (83.19%)	+	486 (16.81%)
Our method (GENIA)	3,153	=	2,070 (65.65%)	+	1,083 (34.35%)
Our method + GENIA	2,650	=	2,056 (77.58%)	+	594 (22.42%)
Our method + HMT05	2,597	=	1,943 (74.82%)	+	654 (25.18%)
baseline	3,542				
	Total errors	=	Common errors with baseline (lex)	+	Specific errors
GENIA only (lex)	3,320	=	2,509 (75.57%)	+	811 (24.43%)
Mixture (lex)	3,100	=	2,769 (89.32%)	+	331 (10.68%)
baseline (lex)	3,757				

methods, the table gives the numbers of common errors with the original Enju model and the errors specific to that method. If possible, we would like our methods to decrease the errors in the original Enju model while not adding new errors. The table shows that our method gave the smallest percentage of newly added errors among the approaches, except for the methods using only lexical entry assignments models. On the other hand, Our method + HMT05 approach gave over 25% of newly added errors, although we saw above that the approach gave the best overall performance.

In order to explore this phenomenon, we analyzed the errors for the Our method + HMT05 and the baseline models, and then classified them into several types. Table 15.6 shows a manual classification of possible causes of errors for the two models in a sample of 50 sentences. In the classification, one error often propagated and resulted in multiple errors of predicate-argument dependencies. The numbers in the table include such double counting. It would be desirable that the errors in the rightmost column were fewer than those in the middle column, which means that Our method + HMT05 approach did not produce more errors specific to the approach than the baseline.

With the Our method + HMT05 approach, errors for attachment ambiguity decreased as a whole. Errors for punctuation (comma) and lexical ambiguities of prepositions and modifiers and participles and adjectives also decreased. For these attributes, this approach could learn lexical properties of continuous words with the lexical entry assignment model, and could learn syntactic relations of words with the tree construction model. On the other hand, the errors for *to*-infinitives and verb subcategorization frame ambiguity considerably increased. These two types of errors have close relation to each other, because the failure to recognize verb subcategorization frames tends to cause the failure to recognize the syntactic role of the *to*-infinitives. These are errors that will be researched further in our future work.

When we focused on noun phrase identification, most of the errors did not differ between the two models. In the biomedical domain, there are many technical terms

Table 15.6 Types of disambiguation errors

	Number of errors		
Error cause	Common	Only baseline	Only adapted
Attachment ambiguity			
Prepositional phrase	12	12	6
Relative clause	0	1	0
Adjective	4	2	2
Adverb	1	3	1
Verb phrase	10	3	1
Subordinate clause	0	2	0
Argument/modifier distinction			
To-infinitive	0	0	7
Lexical ambiguity			
Preposition/modifier	0	3	0
Verb subcategorization frame	5	0	6
Participle/adjective	0	2	0
Test set errors			
Errors of treebank	2	0	0
Other types of error causes			
Comma	10	8	4
Noun phrase identification	21	5	8
Coordination/insertion	6	3	5
Zero-pronoun resolution	8	1	0
Others	1	1	2

which could not be correctly identified only with the disambiguation model. This could possibly explain why so many errors remain uncorrected. In order to properly cope with these terms, we might have to introduce some kind of dictionaries or named entity recognition methods.

15.5 Experiments with the Brown Corpus

The experimental results in Section 15.4 showed the impact of re-training a lexical entry assignment model in a biomedical domain. We next examined the portability of our approach for other domains through the experiments with the Brown corpus (Kuĉera and Francis, 1967). As in the previous experiments, we trained models given in Section 15.3 with the corpus, and then explored their performance variations among the applied models and among the target domains.

15.5.1 Brown Corpus

The Brown corpus consists of 15 domains, and the Penn Treebank gives bracketed version of the corpus for eight of the domains containing 19,395 sentences (Table 15.7). For the goal of adaptation, we used the domain containing all of these eight domains as a total fiction domain (labelled All) as well as the individual ones.

Table 15.7 Domains in the Brown corpus

Label	Domain	Number of sentences
CF	Popular lore	2,420
CG	Belles lettres	2,546
CK	General fiction	3,172
CL	Mystery and detective fiction	2,745
CM	Science fiction	615
CN	Adventure and western fiction	3,521
CP	Romance and love story	3,089
CR	Humor	812
All	Total of all the above domains	19,395

Table 15.8 Parsing accuracy for the Brown corpus

	F-score								
	ALL	CF	CG	CK	CL	CM	CN	CP	CR
baseline	83.1	85.8	85.4	81.1	77.5	85.3	82.8	85.2	76.6
Brown only	84.8	77.7	78.9	75.7	70.6	50.0	78.4	79.1	50.3
Mixture	**86.5**	86.6	**85.9**	82.5	**78.7**	84.8	84.3	**86.9**	76.5
HMT05	83.8	85.8	85.0	81.5	76.9	85.3	83.5	85.7	77.2
Our method	86.1	86.7	85.7	82.8	78.0	85.4	84.2	**86.9**	76.7
Our method (GENIA)	84.7	78.5	79.6	75.4	70.9	50.2	78.5	79.7	51.8
Our method + GENIA	86.0	86.1	85.4	**83.2**	77.1	83.4	84.2	85.8	76.9
Our method + HMT05	86.4	**86.8**	**85.9**	82.9	77.7	**85.6**	**84.4**	**86.9**	77.5
baseline (lex)	82.2	84.7	83.9	80.3	76.3	83.4	81.3	84.1	77.3
Brown only (lex)	83.9	77.1	77.8	75.1	70.4	50.0	77.1	78.8	50.6
Mixture (lex)	85.3	85.5	84.2	81.9	77.2	84.0	82.7	85.7	**77.6**

As in the experiments with the GENIA treebank, we divided sentences for each domain into three parts, 80% for training, 10% for development test, and 10% for final test. For the All domain, we merged all training sets, all development test sets, and all final test sets for the eight domains respectively.

Tables 15.8 and 15.9 show the parsing accuracy and training time for each domain with the various methods shown in Section 15.3. The methods are fundamentally the same as in the experiments with the GENIA corpus, except that the target corpus is replaced with the Brown corpus. In order to avoid confusion, we replaced GENIA in the names of the methods with Brown. Each of the bold numbers in Table 15.8 means that it was the best accuracy given for the target domain. It should be noted that the CM and CR domain contains very few sentences, and therefore we must consider that the results with these domains is not reliable.

15.5.2 Evaluation of Portability of Our Method

When we focus on the ALL domain, the approaches other than the baseline succeeded to give higher parsing accuracy than the baseline. This result shows that

Table 15.9 Consumed time for various methods for the Brown corpus

	Consumed time for training (×10 s)								
	ALL	CF	CG	CK	CL	CM	CN	CP	CR
baseline	0	0	0	0	0	0	0	0	0
Brown only	4,261	412	376	248	216	93	236	270	123
Mixture	38,356	19,045	15,949	15,630	21,036	13,134	17,011	22,405	18,425
HMT05	3,093	600	483	419	501	168	441	507	159
Our method	1,591	1,105	1,099	1,115	1,078	1,016	1,108	1,059	1,028
Our method (Brown)	327	31	37	31	25	5	32	32	9
Our method + Brown	13,043	2,463	2,185	2,017	1,918	1,200	1,916	2,092	1,346
Our method + HMT05	5,436	1,772	1,663	1,523	1,491	1,223	1,576	1,618	1,172
baseline (lex)	0	0	0	0	0	0	0	0	0
Brown only (lex)	300	32	37	31	25	5	32	32	9
Mixture (lex)	2,115	1,113	1,125	1,109	1,073	1,047	1,115	1,090	1,054

these approaches are effective not only for the GENIA corpus, but also for the Brown corpus. The Mixture method gives the highest accuracy which is 3.4 percent points higher than the baseline. The Our method + HMT05 approach also gives an accuracy as high as the Mixture method. In addition, as was the case with the GENIA corpus, this approach can be trained faster than the Mixture method. These results hold in general, the experimental results for the All domain show a tendency similar to that of the GENIA corpus as a whole, except for the smaller improvement with the HMT05 method.

When we focus on the individual domains, our method successfully obtains higher parsing accuracy than the baseline for all the domains. Moreover, for the CP domain, our method obtains the highest parsing accuracy among the methods. These results support the portability of re-training the model for lexical entry assignment. The Our method + HMT05 approach, which gave the highest performance for the GENIA corpus, also gives an accuracy improvement for the all domains, while it does not improve for the CL domain. The Mixture approach, which utilized the same lexical entry assignment model, could obtain 1.0 percent point higher parsing accuracy than the Our method + HMT05 approach. Table 15.10, which shows the lexical coverage with each domains, does not seem to indicate any noteworthy difference in lexical entry coverage between the CL and the other domains. As mentioned in the error analysis in Section 15.4, the model of tree construction might affect the performance in some way. In our future work, we must

Table 15.10 Coverage of each training set for the Brown corpus

	Percentage of covered sentences for the target corpus								
Training set	ALL	CF	CG	CK	CL	CM	CN	CP	CR
Target treebank	75.0	49.1	50.0	48.0	49.1	29.7	53.5	64.0	8.6
PTB treebank	70.0	72.1	68.9	66.4	68.9	78.6	70.0	77.6	47.1
Target + PTB	79.8	74.7	71.5	71.6	70.5	80.0	72.7	80.4	52.9

clarify the underlying causes of these results and would like to further improve the performance.

15.6 Related Work

In recent years, domain adaptation has been studied extensively. This section explores how our research is relevant to the previous works.

Our previous work (Hara et al., 2005) and the current research described in this chapter mainly focus on how to draw as much benefit from as small an amount of in-domain annotated data as possible. Titov and Henderson (2006) also took this type of approach. They first trained a probabilistic model on original and target treebanks and used it to define a kernel over parse trees. This kernel was used in a large-margin classifier trained on a small set of data only from the target domain, and the classifier was then used for reranking the top parses on the target domain. With this method, they achieved higher parsing accuracies for the Brown corpus than their original parser. In addition, they showed the significance of lexical distributional information for domain adaptation through the experiments where lexical and structural parameters were separately examined. Our research also succeeded in showing such significance through the experiments with the different framework while their reranking method could be incorporated into our framework, which might lead to further parsing accuracy improvement.

On the other hand, several studies have explored how to draw useful information from unlabelled in-domain data. Roark and Bacchiani (2003) adapted a lexicalized PCFG by using maximum a posteriori (MAP) estimation for handling unlabelled adaptation data. In the field of classifications, Blitzer et al. (2006) utilized unlabelled corpora to extract features of structural correspondences, and then adapted a POS-tagger to a biomedical domain. Steedman et al. (2003) utilized a co-training parser for adaptation and showed that co-training is effective even across domains. McClosky et al. (2006) adapted a re-ranking parser to a target domain by self-training the parser with unlabelled data in the target domain. Clegg and Shepherd (2005) combined several existing parsers with voting schemes or parse selection, and then succeeded in gaining an improvement of performance for a biomedical domain. Although unsupervised methods can exploit large in-domain data, the above studies could not obtain as high accuracy as that for an original domain, even with a sufficient size of the unlabelled corpus. On the other hand, we showed that our approach could achieve this goal with about 6,500 labelled sentences. However, when 6,500 labelled sentences cannot be prepared, it might be worth-while to explore a combination of the above unsupervised and our supervised methods.

As far as the biomedical domain is concerned, there have also been various works which dealt with domain adaptation. Biomedical sentences contain many technical terms which cannot be easily recognized without expert knowledge, and this damages performances of NLP tools directly. In order to solve this problem, two types of approaches have been suggested. The first approach is to use existing domain-specific lexical resources. Lease and Charniak (2005) utilized POS tags, dictionary collocations, and named entities for parser adaptation, and then succeeded in achieving accuracy improvement. The second approach is to expand lexical entries for a target domain. Szolovits (2003) extended a lexical dictionary for a target domain by predicting lexical information for words. They transplanted lexical *indiscernibility* of words in an original domain into a target domain. Pyysalo et al. (2004) showed experimentally that this approach improved the performance of a parser for Link Grammar. Since our re-trained model of lexical entry assignments was shown to be unable to cope with this problem properly (shown in Section 15.4), the combination of the above approaches with our approach would be expected to bring further improvement.

15.7 Conclusions

This chapter presented an effective approach to adapting an HPSG parser trained on the Penn Treebank to a biomedical domain. We trained a probabilistic model of lexical entry assignments in a target domain and then incorporated it into the original parser. The experimental results showed that this approach obtains higher parsing accuracy than the existing approach of adapting the structural model alone. Moreover, the results showed that the combination of our method and the existing approach could achieve parsing accuracy that is as high as that obtained by re-training an HPSG parser for the target domain from scratch, but with much lower training cost. With this model, the parsing accuracy for the target domain improved by 3.84% F-score, using a domain-specific treebank of 8,127 sentences. Experiments showed that 6,500 sentences are sufficient to achieve as high parsing accuracy as the baseline for the original domain. In addition, we applied our method to the Brown corpus in order to evaluate the portability of our method. Experimental results showed that the parsing accuracy for the target domain improved by 3.3 f-score points. On the other hand, when we focused on some individual domains, that combination approach could not give the desirable results. In future work, we would like to explore further performance improvements of our approach. For the first step, domain-specific features such as named entities could be much help for solving unsuccessful recognition of technical terms.

Acknowledgements This research was partially supported by Grant-in-Aid for Specially Promoted Research 18002007.

References

Bangalore, S. and A.K. Joshi (1999). Supertagging: an approach to almost parsing. *Computational Linguistics 25*, 237–265.

Berger, A.L., S.A.D. Pietra, and V.J.D. Pietra (1996). A maximum entropy approach to natural language processing. *Computational Linguistics 22*, 39–71.

Blitzer, J., R. McDonald, and F. Pereira (2006). Domain adaptation with structural correspondence learning. In *Proceedings of the 2006 Conference on Empirical Methods in Natural Language Processing*, Sydney, pp. 120–128.

Chan, Y.S. and H.T. Ng (2006). Estimating class priors in domain adaptation for word sense disambiguation. In *Proceedings of the 21st International Conference on Computational Linguistics and 44th Annual Meeting of the Association for Computational Linguistics*, Sydney, pp. 89–96.

Chen, S.F. and R. Rosenfeld (1999). A Gaussian prior for smoothing maximum entropy models. Technical Report, School of Computer Science, Carnegie Mellon University.

Clark, S. and J.R. Curran (2004a) The importance of supertagging for wide-coverage CCG parsing. In *Proceedings of the 20th International Conference on Computational Linguistics*, Geneva, pp. 282–288.

Clark, S. and J.R. Curran (2004b) Parsing the WSJ using CCG and log-linear models. In *Proceedings of the 42nd Annual Meeting on Association for Computational Linguistics*, Barcelona, pp. 104–111.

Clark, S. and J.R. Curran (2006). Partial training for a lexicalized-grammar parser. In *Proceedings of the Human Language Technology Conference and the Annual Meeting of the North American Chapter of the Association for Computational Linguistics*, New York, NY, pp 144–151.

Clegg, A.B., Shepherd A (2005). Evaluating and integrating treebank parsers on a biomedical corpus. In *Proceedings of the ACL 2005 Workshop on Software*, Ann Arbor, Michigan.

Cohen, P.R. (1995). *Empirical Methods for Artificial Intelligence*. Cambridge, MA: MIT Press.

Hara, T., Y. Miyao, and J. Tsujii (2005). Adapting a probabilistic disambiguation model of an HPSG parser to a new domain. In *Proceedings of the 2nd International Joint Conference on Natural Language Processing*, Jeju Island, pp. 199–210.

Jelinek, F. (1998). *Statistical Methods for Speech Recognition*. Cambridge, MA: The MIT Press.

Johnson, M. and Riezler, S. (2000). Exploiting auxiliary distributions in stochastic unification-based grammars. In *Proceedings of the First conference on North American Chapter of the Association for Computational Linguistics*, Seattle, WA, pp. 154–161.

Kim, J.D., T. Ohta, Y. Teteisi, and J. Tsujii (2003). GENIA corpus – a semantically annotated corpus for bio-textmining. *Bioinformatics 19*(suppl. 1), i180–i182.

Kučera, H. and W.N. Francis (1967). *Computational Analysis of Present-Day American English*. Providence, RI: Brown University Press.

Lease, M. and E. Charniak (2005). Parsing biomedical literature. In *Proceedings of the 2nd International Joint Conference on Natural Language Processing*, Jeju Island, pp. 58–69.

Marcus, M., G. Kim, M.A. Marcinkiewicz, R. Macintyre, A. Bies, M. Ferguson, K. Katz, and B. Schasberger (1994). The Penn Treebank: annotating predicate argument structure. In *Proceedings of ARPA Human Language Technology Workshop*, Plainsboro, NJ.

McClosky, D., E. Charniak, and M. Johnson (2006). Reranking and self-training for parser adaptation. In *Proceedings of the 21st International Conference on Computational Linguistics and the 44th Annual Meeting of the Association for Computational Linguistics*, Sydney, Australia, pp. 337–344.

Miyao, Y., T. Ninomiya, and J. Tsujii (2004). Corpus-oriented grammar development for acquiring a Head-driven Phrase Structure Grammar from the Penn Treebank. In *Proceedings of the First International Joint Conference on Natural Language Processing*, Hainan Island, China, pp. 684–693.

Miyao, Y. and J. Tsujii (2002). Maximum entropy estimation for feature forests. In *Proceedings of the Second International Conference on Human Language Technology Research*, San Diego, CA, pp. 292–297.

Miyao, Y. and J. Tsujii (2005). Probabilistic disambiguation models for wide-coverage HPSG parsing. In *Proceedings of the 43rd Annual Meeting on Association for Computational Linguistics*, Ann Arbor, MI, pp. 83–90.

Ninomiya, T., T. Matsuzaki, Y. Tsuruoka, Y. Miyao, and J. Tsujii (2006). Extremely lexicalized models for accurate and fast HPSG parsing. In *Proceedings of the 2006 Conference on Empirical Methods in Natural Language Processing*, Sydney, pp. 155–163.

Pollard, C. and I.A. Sag (1994). *Head-Driven Phrase Structure Grammar*. Chicago, IL: University of Chicago Press.

Pyysalo, S., F. Ginter, T. Pahikkala, J. Boberg, J. Jarvinen, T. Salakoski, and J. Koivula (2004). Analysis of link grammar on biomedical dependency corpus targeted at protein-protein interactions. In *Proceedings of the International Workshop on Natural Language Processing in Biomedicine and its Applications*, Geneva, pp. 15–21.

Roark, B. and M. Bacchiani (2003). Supervised and unsupervised PCFG adaptation to novel domains. In *Proceedings of the 2003 Conference of the North American Chapter of the Association for Computational Linguistics on Human Language Technology*, Edmonton, pp. 126–133.

Steedman, M., M. Osborne, A. Sarkar, S. Clark, R. Hwa, J. Hockenmaier, P. Ruhlen, S. Baker, and J. Crim (2003). Bootstrapping statistical parsers from small datasets. In *Proceedings of the Tenth Conference of the European Chapter of the Association for Computational Linguistics*, Budapest, pp. 331–338.

Szolovits, P. (2003). Adding a medical lexicon to an English parser. In *Proceedings of 2003 AMIA Annual Symposium*, Washington, DC, pp. 639–643.

Titov, I. and J. Henderson (2006). Porting statistical parsers with data-defined kernels. In *Proceedings of the Tenth Conference on Computational Natural Language Learning*, New York, NY, pp. 6–13.

Chapter 16
Semi-supervised Training of a Statistical Parser from Unlabeled Partially-Bracketed Data

Rebecca Watson, Ted Briscoe, and John Carroll

16.1 Introduction

Extant statistical parsers require extensive and detailed treebanks, as many of their lexical and structural parameters are estimated in a fully-supervised fashion from treebank derivations. Collins (1999) is a detailed exposition of one such ongoing line of research which utilizes the Wall Street Journal (WSJ) sections of the Penn Treebank (PTB). However, there are disadvantages to this approach. Firstly, treebanks are expensive to create manually. Secondly, the richer the annotation required, the harder it is to adapt the treebank to train parsers which make different assumptions about the structure of syntactic analyses. For example, Hockenmaier (2003) trains a statistical parser based on Combinatory Categorial Grammar (CCG) on the WSJ PTB, but first maps the treebank to CCG derivations semi-automatically. Thirdly, many (lexical) parameter estimates do not generalize well between domains. For instance, Gildea (2001) reports that WSJ-derived bilexical parameters in Collins' (1999) Model 1 parser contribute about 1% to parse selection accuracy when test data is in the same domain, but yield no improvement for test data selected from the Brown Corpus. Tadayoshi et al. (2005) adapt a statistical parser trained on the WSJ PTB to the biomedical domain by retraining on the Genia Corpus, augmented with manually corrected derivations in the same format. To make statistical parsing more viable for a range of applications, we need to make more effective and flexible use of extant training data and minimize the cost of annotation for new data created to tune a system to a new domain.

Unsupervised methods for training parsers have been relatively unsuccessful to date, including expectation maximization (EM) such as the inside-outside algorithm (IOA) over PCFGs (Baker, 1979; Prescher, 2001). However, Pereira and Schabes (1992) adapted the IOA to apply over semi-supervised data (unlabeled bracketings) extracted from the PTB. They constrain the training data (parses) considered within the IOA to those consistent with the constituent boundaries defined by the bracketing. One advantage of this approach is that, although less information

---

R. Watson (✉)
Computer Laboratory, University of Cambridge, Cambridge, UK
e-mail: Rebecca.Watson@cl.cam.ac.uk

H. Bunt et al. (eds.), *Trends in Parsing Technology*, Text, Speech and Language Technology 43, DOI 10.1007/978-90-481-9352-3_16,

is derived from the treebank, it generalizes better to parsers which make different representational assumptions, and it is easier, as Pereira and Schabes did, to map unlabeled bracketings to a format more consistent with the target grammar. Another is that the cost of annotation with unlabeled brackets should be lower than that of developing a representationally richer treebank. More recently, both Riezler et al. (2002) and Clark and Curran (2004) have successfully trained maximum entropy parsing models utilizing all derivations in the model consistent with the annotation of the WSJ PTB, weighting counts by the normalized probability of the associated derivation. In this paper, we extend this line of investigation by utilizing only unlabeled and partial bracketing.

We compare the performance of a statistical parsing model trained from a detailed treebank with that of the same model trained with semi-supervised techniques that require only unlabeled partially-bracketed data. We contrast an IOA-based EM method for training a PGLR parser (Inui et al., 1997), similar to the method applied by Pereira and Schabes to PCFGs, to a range of *confidence-based* semi-supervised methods described below. The IOA is a generalization of the Baum-Welch or Forward-Backward algorithm, another instance of EM, which can be used to train Hidden Markov Models (HMMs). Elworthy (1994) and Merialdo (1994) demonstrated that Baum-Welch does not necessarily improve the performance of an HMM part-of-speech tagger when deployed in an unsupervised or semi-supervised setting. These somewhat negative results, in contrast to those of Pereira and Schabes (1992), suggest that EM techniques require fairly determinate training data to yield useful models. Another motivation to explore alternative non-iterative methods is that the derivation space over partially-bracketed data can remain large (>1K) while the *confidence-based* methods we explore have a total processing overhead equivalent to one iteration of an IOA-based EM algorithm.

As we utilize an initial model to annotate additional training data, our methods are closely related to self-training methods described in the literature (e.g. McClosky et al., 2006; Bacchiani et al., 2006). However these methods have been applied to fully-annotated training data to create the initial model, which is then used to annotate further training data derived from unannotated text. Instead, we train entirely from partially-bracketed data, starting from the small proportion of "unambiguous" data whereby a single parse is consistent with the annotation. Therefore, our methods are better described as semi-supervised and the main focus of this work is the flexible re-use of existing treebanks to train a wider variety of statistical parsing models. While many statistical parsers extract a context-free grammar in parallel with a statistical parse selection model, we demonstrate that existing treebanks can be utilized to train parsers that deploy grammars that make other representational assumptions. As a result, our methods can be applied by a range of parsers to minimize the manual effort required to train a parser or adapt to a new domain.

Section 16.2 gives details of the parsing system that are relevant to this work. Sections 16.3 and 16.4 describe our data and evaluation schemes, respectively. Section 16.5 describes our semi-supervised training methods. Section 16.6 explores the problem of tuning a parser to a new domain. Finally, Section 16.7 gives conclusions and future work.

16.2 The Parsing System

Sentences are automatically preprocessed in a series of modular pipelined steps, including tokenization, part of speech (POS) tagging, and morphological analysis, before being passed to the statistical parser. The parser utilizes a manually written feature-based unification grammar over POS tag sequences.

16.2.1 The Parse Selection Model

A context-free "backbone" is automatically derived from the unification grammar[1] and a generalized or non-deterministic LALR(1) table is constructed from this backbone (Tomita, 1987). The residue of features not incorporated into the backbone are unified on each reduce action and if unification fails the associated derivation paths also fail. The parser creates a packed parse forest represented as a graph-structured stack.[2] The parse selection model ranks complete derivations in the parse forest by computing the product of the probabilities of the (shift/reduce) parse actions (given LR state and lookahead item) which created each derivation (Inui et al., 1997).

Estimating action probabilities, consists of (a) recording an action history for the correct derivation in the parse forest (for each sentence in a treebank), (b) computing the frequency of each action over all action histories and (c) normalizing these frequencies to determine probability distributions over conflicting (i.e. shift/reduce or reduce/reduce) actions.

Inui et al. (1997) describe the probability model utilized in the system where a transition is represented by the probability of moving from one stack state, σ_{i-1}, (an instance of the graph structured stack) to another, σ_i. They estimate this probability using the stack-top state s_{i-1}, next input symbol l_i and next action a_i. This probability is conditioned on the type of state s_{i-1}. S_s and S_r are mutually exclusive sets of states which represent those states reached after shift or reduce actions, respectively. The probability of an action is estimated as:

$$P(l_i, a_i, \sigma_i|\sigma_{i-1}) \approx \left\{ \begin{array}{ll} P(l_i, a_i|s_{i-1}) & s_{i-1} \in S_s \\ P(a_i|s_{i-1}, l_i) & s_{i-1} \in S_r \end{array} \right\} \quad (1)$$

Therefore, normalization is performed over all lookaheads for a state or over each lookahead for the state depending on whether the state is a member of S_s or S_r,

---

[1] This backbone is determined by compiling out the values of prespecified attributes. For example, if we compile out the attribute PLURAL which has 2 possible values (plural or not) we will create 2 CFG rules for each rule with categories that contain PLURAL. Therefore, no information is lost during this process.

[2] The parse forest is an instance of a *feature forest* as defined by Miyao and Tsujii (2002). We will use the term "node" herein to refer to an element in a derivation tree or in the parse forest that corresponds to a (sub-)analysis whose label is the mother's label in the corresponding CF "backbone" rule.

respectively (hereafter the I function). In addition, Laplace estimation can be used to ensure that all actions in the table are assigned a non-zero probability (the I_L function).

16.3 Training Data

The treebanks we use in this work are in one of two possible formats. In either case, a treebank T consists of a set of sentences. Each sentence t is a pair (s, M), where s is the automatically preprocessed set of POS tagged tokens (see Section 16.2) and M is either a fully annotated derivation, A, or an unlabeled bracketing U. This bracketing may be partial in the sense that it may be compatible with more than one derivation produced by a given parser. Although occasionally the bracketing is itself complete but alternative non-terminal labeling causes indeterminacy, most often the "flatter" bracketing available from extant treebanks is compatible with several alternative "deeper" mostly binary-branching derivations output by a parser.

16.3.1 Derivation Consistency

Given $t = (s, A)$, there will exist a single derivation in the parse forest that is compatible (correct). In this case, equality between the derivation tree and the treebank annotation A identifies the correct derivation. Following Pereira and Schabes (1992) given $t = (s, U)$, a node's span in the parse forest is *valid* if it does not overlap with any span outlined in U, and hence, a derivation is correct if the span of every node in the derivation is valid in U. That is, if no crossing brackets are present in the derivation. Thus, given $t = (s, U)$, there will often be more than one derivation compatible with the partial bracketing.

Given the correct nodes in the parse forest or in derivations, we can then extract the corresponding action histories and estimate action probabilities as described in Section 16.2.1. In this way, partial bracketing is used to constrain the set of derivations considered in training to those that are compatible with this bracketing.

16.3.2 The Susanne Treebank and Baseline Training Data

The Susanne Treebank (Sampson, 1995) is utilized to create fully annotated training data. This treebank contains detailed syntactic derivations represented as trees, but the node labeling is incompatible with the system grammar. We extracted sentences from Susanne and automatically preprocessed them. A few multiwords are retokenized, and the sentences are retagged using the POS tagger, and the bracketing deterministically modified to more closely match that of the grammar, resulting in a bracketed corpus of 6,674 sentences. We will refer to this bracketed treebank as S, henceforth.

A fully-annotated and system compatible treebank of 3,543 sentences from S was also created. We will refer to this annotated treebank, used for fully supervised training, as B. The system parser was applied to construct a parse forest of analyses which are compatible with the bracketing. For 1,258 sentences, the grammar writer interactively selected correct (sub)analyses within this set until a single analysis remained. The remaining 2,285 sentences were automatically parsed and all consistent derivations were returned. Since B contains more than one possible derivation for roughly two thirds of the data the 1,258 sentences (paired with a single tree) were repeated twice so that counts from these trees were weighted more highly. The level of reweighting was determined experimentally using some held out data from S. The baseline supervised model against which we compare in this work is defined by the function $I_L(B)$ as described in Section 16.2.1. The costs of deriving the fully-annotated treebank are high as interactive manual disambiguation takes an average of ten minutes per sentence, even given the partial bracketing derived from Susanne.

16.3.3 The WSJ PTB Training Data

The Wall Street Journal (WSJ) sections of the Penn Treebank (PTB) are employed as both training and test data by many researchers in the field of statistical parsing. The annotated corpus implicitly defines a grammar by providing a labeled bracketing over words annotated with POS tags. We extracted the unlabeled bracketing from the de facto standard training Sections (2–21 inclusive).[3] We will refer to the resulting corpus as W and the combination (concatenation) of the partially-bracketed corpora S and W as SW.

16.3.4 The DepBank Test Data

King et al. (2003) describe the development of the PARC 700 Dependency Bank, a gold-standard set of relational dependencies for 700 sentences (from the PTB) drawn at random from Section 23 of the WSJ (the de facto standard test set for statistical parsing). In all the evaluations reported in this paper we test our parser over a gold-standard set of relational dependencies compatible with our parser output derived (Briscoe and Carroll, 2006) from the PARC 700 Dependency Bank (DepBank, henceforth).

The Susanne Corpus is a (balanced) subset of the Brown Corpus which consists of 15 broad categories of American English texts. All but one category (reportage

[3] The pipeline is the same as that used for creating S though we do not automatically map the bracketing to be more consistent with the system grammar, instead, we simply removed unary brackets.

text) is drawn from different domains than the WSJ. We therefore, following Gildea (2001) and others, consider S, and also the baseline training data, B, as out-of-domain training data.

16.4 The Evaluation Scheme

The parser's output is evaluated using a relational dependency evaluation scheme (Carroll et al., 1998; Lin, 1998) with standard measures: precision, recall and F_1. Relations are organized into a hierarchy with the root node specifying an unlabeled dependency. Relations take the following form: (*relation subtype head dependent initial*) where *relation* specifies the type of relationship between the *head* and *dependent*. The remaining *subtype* and *initial* slots encode additional specifications of the relation type for some relations and the initial or underlying logical relation of the grammatical subject in constructions such as passive. There are 16 relations which form a hierarchy, shown in Fig. 16.1.

We determine for each sentence: the relations in the test set which are correct at each level of the relational hierarchy. A relation is correct if the head and dependent slots are equal and if the other slots are equal (if specified).[4]

The microaveraged precision, recall and F_1 scores are calculated from the counts for all relations in the hierarchy which subsume the parser output. The microaveraged F_1 score for the baseline system using this evaluation scheme is 75.61%,

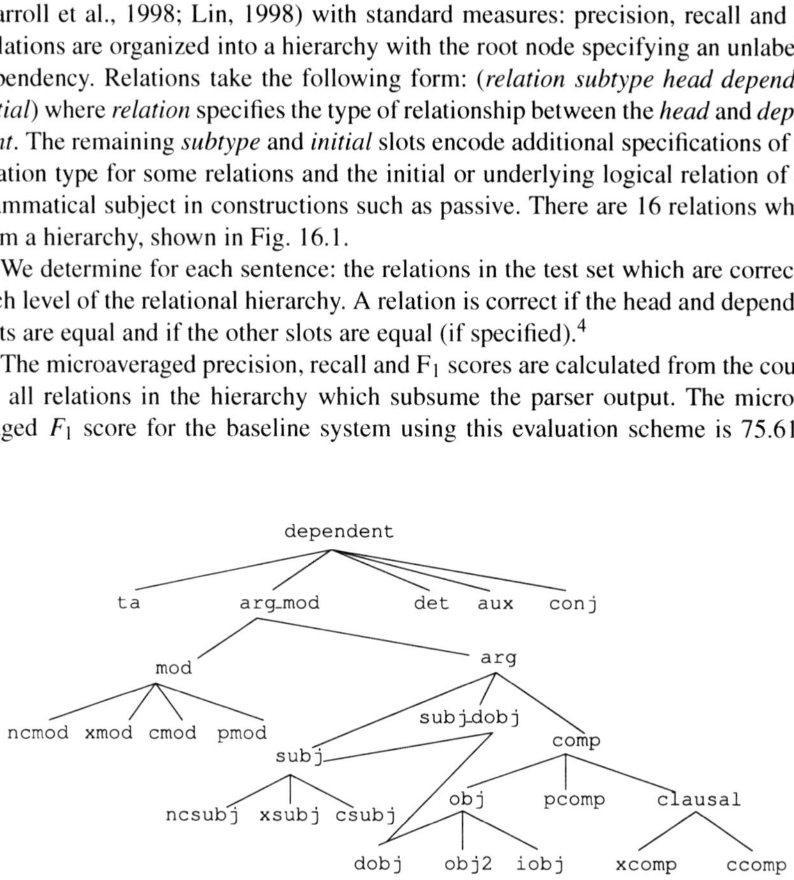

Fig. 16.1 The relational subsumption hierarchy

[4] If a relation is incorrect at a given level in the hierarchy it may still match for a subsuming relation (if the remaining slots all match); for example, if a *ncmod* relation is mislabeled with *xmod*, it will be correct for all relations which subsume both *ncmod* and *xmod*, e.g. *mod*. Similarly, the GR will be considered incorrect for *xmod* and all relations that subsume *xmod* but not *ncmod*. Thus, the evaluation scheme calculates unlabeled dependency accuracy at the *dependency* (most general) level in the hierarchy.

which—over similar sets of relational dependencies—is broadly comparable to recent evaluation results published by King and collaborators with their state-of-the-art parsing system (Briscoe et al., 2006).

16.4.1 Wilcoxon Signed Ranks Test

The Wilcoxon Signed Ranks (Wilcoxon, henceforth) test is a *non-parametric* test for statistical significance that is appropriate when there is one data sample and several measures. For example, to compare the accuracy of two parsers over the same data set. As the number of samples (sentences) is large we use the normal approximation for z. Siegel and Castellan (1988) describe and motivate this test. We use a 0.05 level of significance, and provide z-value probabilities for significant results reported below. These results are computed over microaveraged F_1 scores for each sentence in DepBank.

16.5 Training from Unlabeled Bracketings

We parsed all the bracketed training data using the baseline model to obtain up to 1K top-ranked derivations and found that a significant proportion of the sentences of the potential set available for training had only a single derivation compatible with their unlabeled bracketing. We refer to these sets as the *unambiguous training data* (γ) and will refer to the remaining sentences (for which more than one derivation was compatible with their unlabeled bracketing) as the *ambiguous training data*training data!ambiguous (α). The availability of significant quantities of unambiguous training data that can be found automatically suggests that we may be able to dispense with the costly reannotation step required to generate the fully supervised training corpus, B.

Table 16.1 illustrates the split of the corpora into mutually exclusive sets γ, α, "no match" and "timeout". The latter two sets are not utilized during training and refer to sentences for which all parses were inconsistent with the bracketing and those for which no parses were found due to time and memory limitations (self-imposed) on the system.[5] As our grammar is different from that implicit in the WSJ PTB there is a high proportion of sentences where no parses were consistent with the unmodified PTB bracketing. However, a preliminary investigation of no matches didn't yield any clear patterns of inconsistency that we could quickly ameliorate by simple modifications of the PTB bracketing. We leave for the future a more extensive investigation of these cases which, in principle, would allow us to make more use of this training data. An alternative approach that we have also

---

[5] As there are time and memory restrictions during parsing, the SW results are not equal to the sum of those from S and W analysis.

Table 16.1 Corpus split for S, W and SW

Corpus	$\mid \gamma \mid$	$\mid \alpha \mid$	No match	Timeout
S	1, 097	4, 138	1, 322	191
W	6, 334	15, 152	15, 749	1, 094
SW	7, 409	19, 248	16, 946	1, 475

explored is to utilize a similar bootstrapping approach with data partially-annotated for grammatical relations (Watson and Briscoe, 2007).

16.5.1 Confidence-Based Approaches

We use γ to build an initial model. We then utilize this initial model to derive derivations (compatible with the unlabeled partial bracketing) for α from which we select additional training data. We employ two types of selection methods. First, we select the top-ranked derivation only and weight actions which resulted in this derivation equally with those of the initial model (C_1). This method is similar to "Viterbi training" of HMMs though we do not weight the corresponding actions using the top parse's probability. Secondly, we select more than one derivation, placing an appropriate weight on the corresponding action histories based on the initial model's confidence in the derivation. We consider three such models, in which we weight transitions corresponding to each derivation ranked r with probability p in the set of size n either using $1/n$, $1/r$ or p itself to weight counts.[6] For example, given a treebank T with sentences $t = (s, U)$, function P to return the set of parses consistent with U given t and function A that returns the set of actions given a parse p, then the frequency count of action a_k in C_r is determined as follows:

$$\mid a_k \mid = \sum_{i=1}^{|T|} \sum_{j=1, a_k \in A(p_{ij})}^{|P(t_i)|} \frac{1}{j} \tag{2}$$

These methods all perform normalization over the resulting action histories using the training function I_L and will be referred to as C_n, C_r and C_p, respectively. C_n is a "uniform" model which weights counts only by degree of ambiguity and makes no use of ranking information. C_r weights counts by derivation rank, and C_p is simpler than and different to one iteration of EM as outside probabilities are not utilized. All of the semi-supervised functions described here take two arguments: an initial model and the data to train over, respectively.

Models derived from unambiguous training data, γ, alone are relatively accurate, achieving indistinguishable performance to that of the baseline system given either

[6] In Section 16.2.1 we calculate action probabilities based on frequency counts where we perform a weighted sum over action histories and each history has a weight of 1. We extend this scheme to include weights that differ between action histories corresponding to each derivation.

Table 16.2 Performance of all models on DepBank; $P(z)$ represents the statistical significance of the system against the baseline model

Model	Precision	Recall	F_1	$P(z)$
Baseline	77.05	74.22	75.61	–
$I_L(\gamma(S))$	76.02	73.40	*74.69*	0.0294
$C_1(I_L(\gamma(S)), \alpha(S))$	77.05	74.22	75.61	0.4960
$C_n(I_L(\gamma(S)), \alpha(S))$	77.51	74.80	76.13	0.0655
$C_r(I_L(\gamma(S)), \alpha(S))$	77.73	74.98	**76.33**	0.0154
$C_p(I_L(\gamma(S)), \alpha(S))$	76.45	73.91	75.16	0.2090
$I_L(\gamma(W))$	77.01	74.31	75.64	0.1038
$C_1(I_L(\gamma(W)), \alpha(W))$	76.90	74.23	75.55	0.2546
$C_n(I_L(\gamma(W)), \alpha(W))$	77.85	75.07	**76.43**	0.0017
$C_r(I_L(\gamma(W)), \alpha(W))$	77.88	75.04	**76.43**	0.0011
$C_p(I_L(\gamma(W)), \alpha(W))$	77.40	74.75	76.05	0.1335
$I_L(\gamma(SW))$	77.09	74.35	75.70	0.1003
$C_1(I_L(\gamma(SW)), \alpha(SW))$	76.86	74.21	75.51	0.2483
$C_n(I_L(\gamma(SW)), \alpha(SW))$	77.88	75.05	**76.44**	0.0048
$C_r(I_L(\gamma(SW)), \alpha(SW))$	78.01	75.13	**76.54**	0.0007
$C_p(I_L(\gamma(SW)), \alpha(SW))$	77.54	74.95	76.23	0.0618

W or SW as training data. We utilize these models as initial models and train over different corpora with each of the confidence-based models. Table 16.2 gives results for all models. Results statistically significant compared to the baseline system are shown in bold print (better) or italic print (worse). These methods show promise, often yielding systems whose performance is significantly better than the baseline system. Method C_r achieved the best performance in this experiment and remained consistently better in those reported below. Throughout the different approaches a domain effect can be seen, models utilizing just S are worse, although the best performing models benefit from the use of both S and W as training data (i.e. SW).

16.5.2 EM

Our EM model differs from that of Pereira and Schabes as a PGLR parser adds *context* over a PCFG so that a single rule can be applied in several different states containing reduce actions. Therefore, the summation and normalization performed for a CFG rule within IOA is instead applied within such contexts. We can apply I (our PGLR normalization function without Laplace smoothing) to perform the required steps if we output the action history with the corresponding normalized inside-outside weight for each node (Watson et al., 2005).

We perform EM starting from two initial models; either a uniform probability model, $I_L()$, or from models derived from unambiguous training data, γ. Figure 16.2 shows the cross entropy decreasing monotonically from iteration 2 (as guaranteed by the EM method) for different corpora and initial models. Some models show an initial increase in cross-entropy from iteration 1 to iteration 2, because

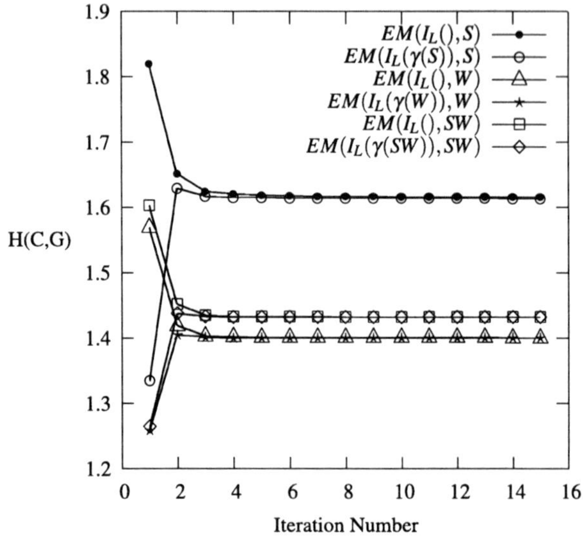

Fig. 16.2 Cross entropy convergence for various training data and models, with EM

the models are initialized from a subset of the data which is used to perform maximization. Cross-entropy increases, by definition, as we incorporate ambiguous data with more than one consistent derivation.

Performance over DepBank can be seen in Figs. 16.3, 16.4, and 16.5 for each dataset S, W and SW, respectively. Comparing the C_r and EM lines in each of Figs. 16.3, 16.4, and 16.5, it is evident that C_r outperforms EM across all datasets, regardless of the initial model applied. In most cases, these results are significant, even when we manually select the best model (iteration) for EM.

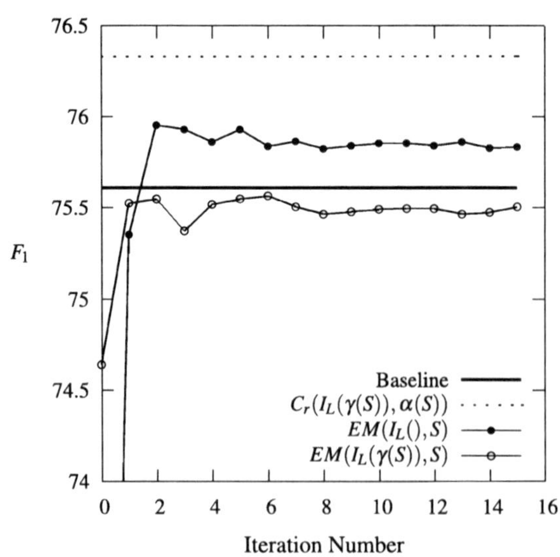

Fig. 16.3 Performance over S for C_r and EM

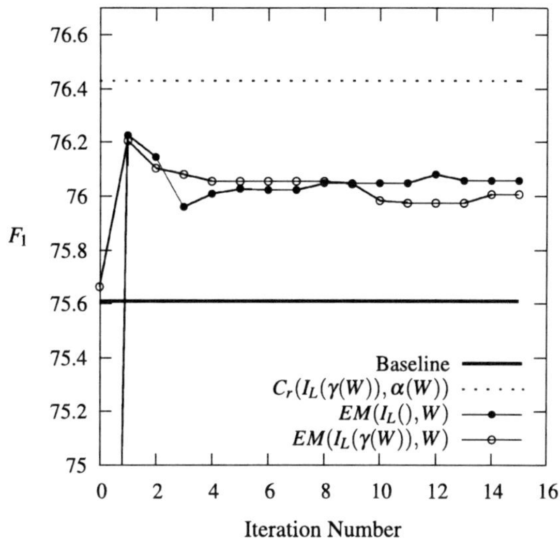

Fig. 16.4 Performance over W for C_r and EM

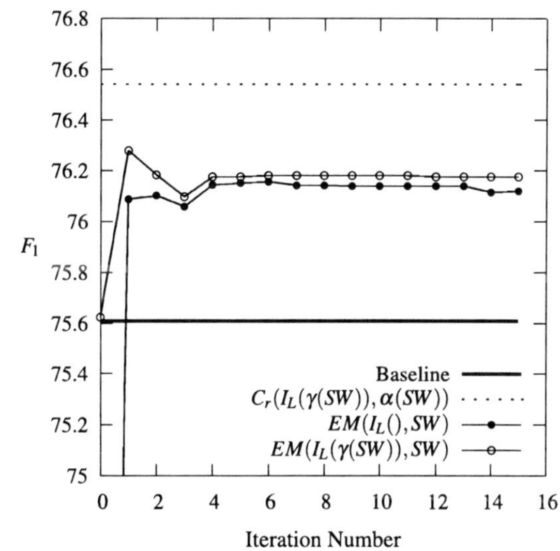

Fig. 16.5 Performance over SW for C_r and EM

The graphs of EM performance from iteration 1 illustrate the same "classical" and "initial" patterns observed by Elworthy (1994). When EM is initialized from a relatively poor model, such as that built from S (Fig. 16.3), a "classical" pattern emerges with relatively steady improvement from iteration 1 until performance asymptotes. However, when the starting point is better (Figs. 16.4 and 16.5), the "initial" pattern emerges in which the best performance is reached after a single iteration.

16.6 Tuning to a New Domain

When building NLP applications we would want to be able to tune a parser to a new domain with minimal manual effort. To obtain training data in a new domain, annotating a corpus with partial-bracketing information is much cheaper than full annotation. To investigate whether such data would be of value, we considered W to be the corpus over which we were tuning and applied the best performing model trained over S, $C_r(I_L(\gamma(S)), \alpha(S))$, as our initial model. Figure 16.6 illustrates the performance of C_r compared to EM.

Tuning using C_r was not significantly different from the model built directly from the entire data set with C_r, achieving 76.57% as opposed to 76.54% F_1 (see Table 16.2). By contrast, EM performs better given all the data from the beginning rather than tuning to the new domain. C_r generally outperforms EM, though it is worth noting the behavior of EM given only the tuning data (W) rather than the data from both domains (SW). In this case, the graph illustrates a combination of Elworthy's "initial" and "classical" patterns. The steep drop in performance (down to 69.93% F_1) after the first iteration is probably due to loss of information from S. However, this run also eventually converges to similar performance, suggesting that the information in S is effectively disregarded as it forms only a small portion of SW, and that these runs effectively converge to a local maximum over W.

Bacchiani et al. (2006), working in a similar framework, explore weighting the contribution (frequency counts) of the in-domain and out-of-domaintraining data!out-of-domain training datasets and demonstrate that this can have beneficial effects. Furthermore, they also tried unsupervised tuning to the in-domain corpus by weighting parses for it by their normalized probability. This method is similar

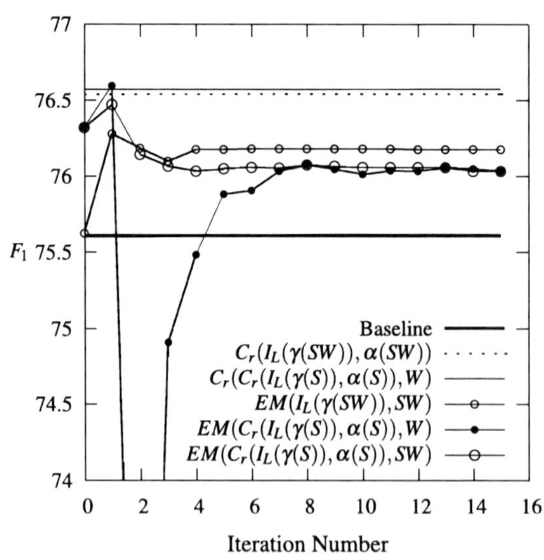

Fig. 16.6 Tuning over the WSJ PTB (W) from Susanne Corpus (S)

to our C_p method. However, when we tried unsupervised tuning using the WSJ and an initial model built from S in conjunction with our confidence-based methods, performance degraded significantly.

16.7 Conclusions

We have presented several semi-supervised *confidence-based* training methods which have significantly improved performance over an extant (more supervised) method, while also reducing the manual effort required to create training or tuning data. We have shown that given a medium-sized unlabeled partially bracketed corpus, the confidence-based models achieve superior results to those achieved with EM applied to the same PGLR parse selection model. Indeed, a bracketed corpus provides flexibility as existing treebanks can be utilized despite the incompatibility between the system grammar and the underlying grammar of the treebank. Mapping an incompatible annotated treebank to a compatible partially-bracketed corpus is relatively easy compared to mapping to a compatible fully-annotated corpus.

An immediate benefit of this work is that (re)training parsers with incrementally-modified grammars based on different linguistic frameworks should be much more straightforward—see, for example Oepen et al. (2002) for a good discussion of the problem. Furthermore, it suggests that it may be possible to usefully tune a parser to a new domain with less annotation effort.

Our findings support those of Elworthy (1994) and Merialdo (1994) for POS tagging and suggest that EM is not always the most suitable semi-supervised training method (especially when some in-domain training data is available). The confidence-based methods were successful because the level of noise introduced did not outweigh the benefit of incorporating all derivations compatible with the bracketing in which the derivations contained a high proportion of correct constituents. These findings may not hold if the level of bracketing available does not adequately constrain the parses considered—see Hwa (1999) for a related investigation with EM.

In future work we intend to further investigate the problem of tuning to a new domain, given that minimal manual effort is a major priority. We hope to develop methods which required no manual annotation, for example, high precision automatic partial bracketing using phrase chunking and/or named entity recognition techniques might yield enough information to support the training methods developed here.

Finally, further experiments on weighting the contribution of each dataset might be beneficial. For instance, Bacchiani et al. (2006) demonstrate improvements in parsing accuracy with unsupervised adaptation from unannotated data and explore the effect of different weighting of counts derived from the supervised and unsupervised data.

Acknowledgements The first author was funded by the Overseas Research Students Awards Scheme, and the Poynton Scholarship awarded by the Cambridge Australia Trust in collaboration with the Cambridge Commonwealth Trust. Development of the RASP system was supported by the EPSRC (grants GR/N36462, GR/N36493 and GR/T19919).

References

Bacchiani, M., M. Riley, B. Roark, and R. Sproat (2006). MAP adaptation of stochastic grammars. *Computer Speech and Language 20*(1), 41–68.

Baker, J.K. (1979). Trainable grammars for speech recognition. In D. Klatt and J. Wolf (Eds.), *Speech Communications Papers for the 97th Meeting of the Acoustical Society of America*. Cambridge, MA: MIT Press, pp. 557–550.

Briscoe, E.J. and J. Carroll (2006). Evaluating the accuracy of an unlexicalized statistical parser on the PARC DepBank. In *Proceedings of the 45th Annual Meeting of the Association for Computational Linguistics*, Sydney, Australia, pp. 41–48.

Briscoe, E.J., J. Carroll, and R. Watson (2006). The second release of the RASP system. In *Proceedings of COLING/ACL 2006 Interactive Presentation Sessions*, Sydney.

Carroll, J., E. Briscoe, and A. Sanfilippo (1998). Parser evaluation: a survey and a new proposal. In *Proceedings of 1st International Conference on Language Resources and Evaluation*, Granada, pp. 447–454.

Clark, S. and J. Curran (2004). Parsing the WSJ using CCG and log-linear models. In *Proceedings of 42nd Meeting of the Association for Computational Linguistics*, Barcelona, pp. 103–110.

Collins, M. (1999). Head-driven statistical models for natural language parsing. PhD dissertation, Computer and Information Science, University of Pennsylvania.

Elworthy, D. (1994). Does Baum-Welch re-estimation help taggers? In *Proceedings of 4th Conference on Applied Natural Language Processing*, Stuttgart, pp. 53–58.

Gildea, D. (2001). Corpus variation and parser performance. In *Proceedings of 2001 Conference on Empirical Methods in Natural Language Processing*, Pittsburgh, PA, pp. 167–172.

Hockenmaier, J. (2003). Data and models for statistical parsing with Combinatory Categorial Grammar. PhD dissertation, School of Informatics, The University of Edinburgh.

Hwa, R. (1999). Supervised grammar induction using training data with limited constituent information. In *Proceedings of 37th Annual Meeting of the Association for Computational Linguistics*, College Park, MI, pp. 73–79.

Inui, K., V. Sornlertlamvanich, H. Tanaka, and T. Tokunaga (1997). A new formalization of probabilistic GLR parsing. In *Proceedings of 5th International Workshop on Parsing Technologies*, Cambridge, MA, pp. 123–134.

King, T.H., R. Crouch, S. Riezler, M. Dalrymple, and R. Kaplan (2003). The PARC700 Dependency Bank. In *Proceedings of 4th International Workshop on Linguistically Interpreted Corpora*, Budapest, Hungary, pp. 1–8.

Lin, D. (1998). Dependency-based evaluation of MINIPAR. In *Proceedings of Workshop at LREC'98 on The Evaluation of Parsing Systems*, Granada.

McClosky, D., E. Charniak, and M. Johnson (2006). Effective self-training for parsing. In *Proceedings of Human Language Technology Conference and the 6th Annual Meeting of the North American Chapter of the Association for Computational Linguistics*, New York, NY, pp. 152–159.

Merialdo, B. (1994). Tagging English text with a probabilistic model. *Computational Linguistics 20*(2), 155–171.

Miyao, Y. and J. Tsujii (2002). Maximum entropy estimation for feature forests. In *Proceedings of Second International Conference on Human Language Technology Research*, San Diego, CA, pp. 292–297.

Oepen, S., K. Toutanova, S. Shieber, C. Manning, D. Flickinger, and T. Brants (2002). The LinGO Redwoods Treebank: motivation and preliminary applications. In *Proceedings of 19th International Conference on Computational Linguistics*, Taipei, pp. 1–5.

Pereira, F. and Y. Schabes (1992). Inside–Outside reestimation from partially bracketed corpora. In *Proceedings of 30th Annual Meeting of the Association for Computational Linguistics*, Newark, Delaware, pp. 128–135.

Prescher, D. (2001). Inside–outside estimation meets dynamic EM. In *Proceedings of 7th International Workshop on Parsing Technologies*, Beijing, pp. 241–244.

Riezler, S., T. King, R. Kaplan, R. Crouch, J. Maxwell III, and M. Johnson (2002). Parsing the Wall Street Journal using a Lexical-Functional grammar and discriminative estimation techniques. In *Proceedings of 40th Annual Meeting of the Association for Computational Linguistics*, Philadelphia, PL, pp. 271–278.

Sampson, G. (1995). *English for the Computer*. Oxford: Oxford University Press.

Siegel S. and N.J. Castellan (1988). Nonparametric statistics for the behavioral sciences (2nd ed.). New York, NY: McGraw-Hill.

Tadayoshi, H., Y. Miyao, and J. Tsujii (2005). Adapting a probabilistic disambiguation model of an HPSG parser to a new domain. In *Proceedings of the 2nd International Joint Conference on Natural Language Processing*, Jeju Island, pp. 199–210.

Tomita, M. (1987). An efficient augmented context-free parsing algorithm. *Computational Linguistics 13*(1–2), 31–46.

Watson, R. and E. Briscoe (2007). Adapting the RASP system for the CoNLL07 domainadaptation task. In *Proceedings of CoNNL Shared Task Session of EMNLP-CoNLL'07*, Prague, pp. 1170–1174.

Watson, R., J. Carroll, and E. Briscoe (2005). Efficient extraction of grammatical relations. In *Proceedings of 9th International Workshop on Parsing Technologies*, Vancouver, BC, pp. 160–170.

Index

H. Bunt et al. (eds.), *Trends in Parsing Technology*, Text, Speech and Language Technology 43, DOI 10.1007/978-90-481-9352-3,

Breinigsville, PA USA
13 October 2010
247310BV00006B/18/P

9 789048 193516